Papua New Guinea

a travel survival kit

Tony Wheeler

Papua New Guinea - a travel survival kit
4th edition

Published by
Lonely Planet Publications
Head Office: PO Box 88, South Yarra, Victoria 3141, Australia
US Office: PO Box 2001A, Berkeley, CA 94702, USA

Printed by
Singapore National Printers

Photographs by
Air Niugini
Tony Wheeler (TW)
Mark Lightbody (ML)
Richard Everist (RE)
Isabelle Tree (IT)
Front cover: Courtesy of Air Niugini
Back cover: Southern Highlands (RE)
            Trobriand Islands (RE)

Illustrations by
Peter Campbell

First Published
April 1979

This Edition
October 1988

National Library of Australia Cataloguing in Publication Data

Wheeler, Tony.
Papua New Guinea, a travel survival kit.

4th ed.
Includes index.
ISBN 0 86442 048 X.

1. Papua New Guinea - Description and travel - Guide- books.I. Title.

919.5'304
© Copyright Tony Wheeler 1988

Tony Wheeler

Born in England, Tony spent most of his younger days overseas due to his father's airline occupation. Those years included a lengthy spell in Pakistan, a shorter period in the West Indies and all his high school years in the USA. He returned to England to do a university degree in engineering, worked for a short time as an automotive design engineer, returned to university again and did an MBA, then dropped out on the Asia overland trail with his wife Maureen. They set up Lonely Planet in the mid-70s and have been travelling, writing and publishing ever since. Travel for Tony and Maureen is now considerably enlivened by their daughter Tashi and son Kieran.

Richard Everist

Richard grew up in Geelong, Australia. His chequered career includes such highlights as painting ships (not an artistic endeavour) in Geelong, a brief run-in with the law (as a student of) in Melbourne, marble polishing (not the little round ones) in London, and working as a tripping counsellor (not that kind) in Connecticut. In between travelling and spending as much time as possible around the Otway Ranges he has been involved with the print media as a cleaner, freelance writer, copy-writer, sub-editor and editor. He started work with Lonely Planet in 1985.

Lonely Planet Credits

Editor	Adrienne Ralph
Maps	Graham Imeson
	Todd Pierce
Cover design	Todd Pierce
Design	Vicki Beale
Illustrations	Peter Campbell
Typesetting	Ann Jeffree

Thanks to Sue Mitra for editoral support and Jon Murray for proofreading, Vicki Beale and Joanne Ryan for additional illustrations, and Chris Lee-Ack for additional map corrections.

This Book

Tony Wheeler researched and wrote the first two editions of *Papua New Guinea – a travel survival kit*. Mark Lightbody, the author of Lonely Planet's *Canada – a travel survival kit* researched the third edition and Richard Everist updated this, the fourth, edition.

It's not easy to produce a guidebook for Papua New Guinea - the expenses are high and the market is small – so we're particularly grateful to Air Niugini who sponsored flights to and from PNG and extensively around the country. Talair also sponsored several flights. Generous help was given by Pacific Expeditions; Trans Niugini Tours, Davara Hotels, Melanesian Tours and the Masurina Lodge.

Many individuals also gave freely of their time, expertise, information and hospitality. Warm thanks to Liz Ables; Peter Bai; Pauline Baker; Peter Barter; John, Bob & Pam Bates; Barry Byrne; Annette Caesar; Jack Cashman; David Choulei; Desak Drorit; Stewart Forsaythe; Patrick Gleeson; Peter & Chris Green; Moeka & Raka Helai, Helai Morea and Morea Grau; Kepeni Hohom; Ann Holdsworth; John Hunter; Judy Kapaith; Joseph Mokuma; Lez & Sandra Pereira; Julian Poye; John & Michelle Rayner; Bill Rudd; Tabah Silau; Ralf Stuttgen; David Tennenbaum; Keith & Catherine Thomas; Jennifer Varssilli; Cameron Venables; Peter Waliawi; James Yesinduma; and especially Margaret Milner who was an inspiration in many ways.

Peter Campbell's drawings from earlier editions of have been used, once again, in this edition. The section on PNG's parks was written by Murray D Bruce and Constance S Leap Bruce.

We greatly appreciate the contributions of the many people who put so much effort into writing and telling us (and future travellers) of their weird and wonderful experiences. One thing that came shining through in so many of those letters is that although PNG is not the easiest or cheapest country to travel around the effort is amply repaid. Thank you:

Ran Allouch (Isr); Carlo Andreis (I); Andre Aptroot (Nl); Stephen Armstrong; RE Bates; Stephen Bedding; Robert Binner (WG); Bev Blackley; Martin Borkent; Estelle Carlson (USA); Paul & Leslie Carr (UK); Peter Chaffey (UK); Michael & Margaret Clark (Aus); Tim Crotty (Aus); Don Daniels; Rolan Eberhard (Aus); Torun Elsrud (Sw); Debbie Ensenbacher (USA); David Eveleigh; Geraldine Flanagan (USA); Michael Frej (Sw); Patrick Frew (NZ); Don Gilder (USA); Noga Ginsburg (Isr); Cindy Goldstein (USA); David Greason (Aus); Berit Gustafsson (Sw); David Hayano (USA); Neil Hickson (PNG); VS Hill (UK); Robert Hogan (Aus); Brendon Hyde (Aus); Brent Ingram (USA); Annette Jeddin; Terry Kelly (Aus); Robert Kennington (NZ); Michael Kerrisk (NZ); Bob Kibble (Aus); T & A Kucharski (UK); Gabriel Lafitte (Aus); SE Lambeth (UK); Anita Lees (USA); Brendan Lynch (Aus); Jimmy Maik (PNG); Ruth March (USA); Andrew Martin (PNG); Phil Mellers; John Mills (UK); Ruda Milovenic (Aus); Rikie Mineba (PNG); Milan Momirov (USA); Joan Mosley; Marguerite Muzzey (USA); Wayne Nichols (HK); Kennedy Orereba; James Prest (Aus); Allouett Ran (Isr); Jim Ross (NZ); Heidi P Sanchez (USA); David Shoolvays (Isr); Ken Smith; Bill Snooks (Aus); Soren Sorenson (Den); Liz Steven (PNG); BN Swire (PNG); Penny Syddall; Isabella Tree (UK); Kenneth Truedson (Sw); Frans-Peter Verheijen (Nl); Michael Wayte (UK); Liz Wright; Keith Zahnle (USA): Oded D Zamir (Isr).

Aus – Australia, Den – Denmark, HK – Hong Kong, Isr – Israel, I – Italy, Nl – Netherlands, NZ – New Zealand, Sw – Sweden, WG – West Germany.

And the Next Edition

Things change – prices go up, good places go bad, bad ones go bankrupt and nothing stays the same. So if you find things better, worse, cheaper, more expensive, recently opened closed, please write and tell us. We really appreciate letters from travellers out on the road and, as usual, we try to show our appreciation for the best letters with a free copy of the next edition, or another LP guide if you prefer. Useful letters are also published in LP's *Update* a quarterly paperback that is available from bookstores and on subscription. See page 344 for further information.

Contents

Introduction

Papua New Guinea is truly the 'last unknown' – it was virtually the last inhabited place on earth to be explored by Europeans and even today some parts of the country have only made the vaguest contact with the west. It's also a last unknown for travellers and tourists. Yet it can be a fascinating and rewarding experience and not at all difficult to visit, although it takes a little ingenuity to avoid some of Papua New Guinea's steep prices. But where else in the world can you riverboat down a waterway famed for its dynamic art and its equally dynamic crocodiles? Climb a smoking volcano and in the same afternoon dive on what a keen scuba diver told me was the best reef he'd seen anywhere in the world? A Highland sing-sing can be a sight you'll never forget, a flight into one of PNG's precarious 'third level' airstrips is likely to be a fright you'll never forget. It's an amazing country and one that, as yet, is barely touched by the modern tourist trade.

A Visit to Papua New Guinea

You're visiting a country with a tourist trade in its infancy so you'll have to put up with a few associated expenses and problems along the way. To get the most out of PNG I think you have to approach it in one of two ways – which I call 'tight' and 'loose'.

By 'tight' I mean having everything arranged and sorted out beforehand. PNG is not a country where you can simply arrive and expect it all to happen – and waiting around can be frustrating and very expensive. So a package deal, which whisks you from place to place with the minimum of fuss and with everything packed in as tightly as possible, can save a lot of time and frustration.

On the other hand it is possible to do PNG 'loose' – if you're the sort of experienced shoestringer who can find places to stay in villages, doesn't mind hanging around in a port waiting for that elusive boat to come by, and can sit patiently waiting for things to happen. But make sure you're willing to put up with the discomforts of cheap travel PNG-style.

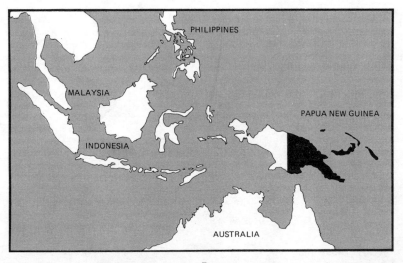

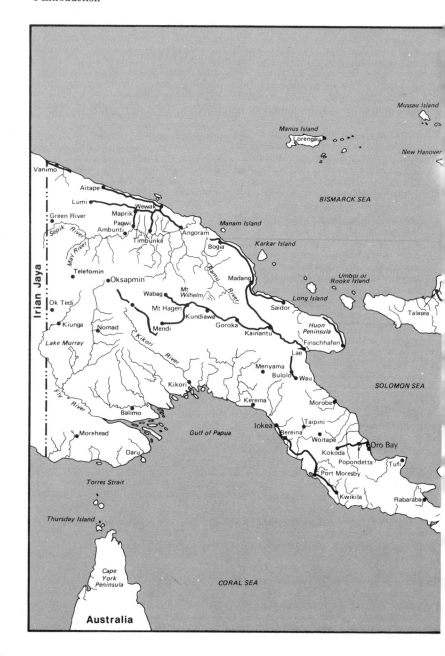

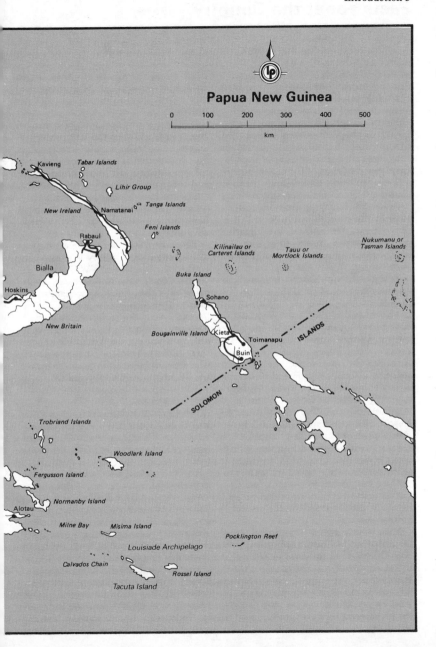

Papua New Guinea

Facts about the Country

WHAT'S IN A NAME?

Few countries have such a long and confusing name as Papua New Guinea. When the first Portuguese explorers came along they named it Ilhas dos Papuas – Island of the Fuzzy-Hairs – from the Malay word *papuwah*. Later Dutch explorers called it New Guinea, because they were reminded of Guinea in Africa.

Then, towards the end of the last century, the country was divided up between the Dutch, the Germans and the British. The western half became Dutch New Guinea, the north-eastern quarter became German New Guinea and the south-eastern quarter became British New Guinea. When Australia took over from the British in 1905 they renamed the south-eastern quarter the Territory of Papua.

At the start of WW I the Australians captured the German section and after the war this was assigned to Australia as a League of Nations Trust Territory. Australia had to run the two parts as separate colonies or, more correctly, a colony and a Mandated Trust Territory. After WW II the two were combined and administered as the Territory of Papua & New Guinea, sometimes written as Papua-New Guinea or Papua/New Guinea.

Finally, with independence, the country became simply Papua New Guinea. A search for a less cumbersome name for the country has produced Niugini, but this has not gained much favour and, so far, has only been applied to the national airline.

Meanwhile, across the border, the Dutch half of the island went on as Dutch New Guinea right up into the '60s when Indonesia started its push to take it over. In a last ditch attempt to keep it out of Indonesian hands, the Dutch renamed it West Papua, but it was too late. In 1962 the Indonesians took over and renamed it Irian Barat (West Irian) then later changed it to Irian Jaya (New Irian).

HISTORY

The history of PNG prior to the arrival of European colonists in the 19th century is only starting to be pieced together. The task is daunting. The highly fragmented indigenous cultures left no written records and the marks they made on the landscape have almost been completely erased; their houses, fields and artefacts have been swallowed by the tropical environment.

The incredible capacity the vegetation has for swallowing history is clear when you look for the scars of WW II. Although you still don't have to search far, whole bases have been completely engulfed by jungle. If you don't know precisely where to look, you can walk straight past bunkers, railways and bomb craters that are less than 50 years old. Little wonder there are few relics of the hunter/gatherers who are now believed to have settled on the island at least 50,000 years ago.

The First Arrivals

It is believed that humans reached PNG and then Australia by island hopping across the Indonesian archipelago from Asia, perhaps more than 50,000 years ago.

The migration was probably made easier by a fall in the sea level caused by an ice age. At no time was PNG completely joined to island South-East Asia but it was joined to Australia, probably until about 6000 years ago. As a result PNG shares many species of plants and animals (including marsupials) with Australia, but not with Indonesia. The Wallace Line, named after a 19th century naturalist, marks the deep water between Bali and Lombok, and Kalimantan and Sulawesi (in Indonesia) that formed a natural barrier to animals and humans. In order to reach PNG people had to cross open water on canoes or rafts.

There have been several waves of people from Asia, and this may be reflected in the distribution of Austronesian and non-Austronesian languages. The Austronesian languages are scattered along the coast and are spoken throughout Polynesia and Micronesia. The majority of Papua New Guineans speak non-Austronesian languages and, it is believed, arrived before the Austronesian language speakers.

As the world's climate warmed, the sea level rose isolating PNG and submerging the original coastal settlements. Parts of Huon Peninsula have subsequently risen due to volcanic activity. Evidence of early coastal settlements has been exposed – 40,000 year old stone axes have been found.

Most of the Highland valleys were settled by 10,000 years ago and the presence of shells amongst archaeological deposits show that by this time people were also trading with the coast. Some sites that have been excavated, however, date to much earlier.

Kuk Swamp in the Wahgi Valley (Western Highlands Province) has evidence of human habitation going back 20,000 years, but even more significantly there is evidence of gardening beginning 9000 years ago. This makes Papua New Guineans among the first farmers in the world. The main foods farmed at this stage are likely to have been sago, coconuts, breadfruit, local bananas and yams, sugar cane, nuts and edible leaves.

It is still uncertain when the pig and more productive starch crops (Asian yams, taros and bananas) were introduced but it is known that this occurred more than 5000 years ago, maybe as much as 10,000. Domesticated pigs – which continue to be incredibly important, ritually and economically, in contemporary society – and these new crops were probably brought to PNG by a later group of colonists from Asia.

The prehistory of the islands is shorter than that of the mainland. New Britain was settled more than 10,000 years ago, New Ireland by 6000 and Manus by 3500 years ago, followed by the remaining islands of Melanesia, Micronesia and Polynesia. Surprisingly, the South Papuan coast seems to have been mainly settled in the last 2000 years, and the more far-flung islands of Polynesia perhaps as little as 1000 years ago. Because of this relatively recent colonisation the linguistic and cultural links are closer – for instance, the word for two in Motu (spoken in the Port Moresby area), Fijian and Maori is *rua*.

Melanesian Society

Many observations about the past have some relevance to the present, although it is difficult to generalise because of the original cultural diversity and the uneven impact of modernisation. PNG is changing fast, but the vast majority of people remain dependent on subsistence agriculture and live in small villages. Many aspects of life are still carried out traditionally, and the social structure and an individual's responsibilities and privileges remain significantly unchanged.

Despite sophisticated agriculture and, in some areas, extraordinary maritime skills, the main tools and artefacts were made of wood, bone, pottery or stone. There was no metal working, no domestic animal power and the wheel was unknown. Extensive trading networks existed, especially along the southern coast and among the eastern islands, but also along the navigable rivers and between the coast and the Highlands. Shells were highly valued and in some places were used as a kind of currency, but other trade items included pottery, stone tools, obsidian, dyes, salt and sago.

The responsibility for the day-to-day work of gardening and caring for animals lay, most usually, with women, who were also responsible for the household. Men were concerned with the initial clearing of the bush, hunting, trade and warfare.

Young men and bachelors also worked for older men.

The social units were generally small, based on family, clan and tribe, the most important being the extended family. Some observers have described these communities as democratic Edens, where ownership was communal and everyone's basic needs were met. In reality, there was no universal franchise for voters, and village elders, or a 'big man' could hold virtually dictatorial powers. In some places, for instance Bougainville and the Trobriand Islands, hereditary chiefs and clear-cut classes developed.

In traditional PNG societies individual ownership did not exist in the same way as it does in western societies, but the accumulation of wealth and its display was often a vital prerequisite for prestige and power. Ownership was vested in the household, which was controlled by a male elder. Within and between the households of the village there were complicated networks of responsibility, which did provide a kind of social security.

Fundamental to the society were notions of reciprocity and family obligations: help, whether it be labour, land, food or pigs, was often given out of duty, or in the expectation of some kind of return (perhaps loyalty in time of war, assistance in organising some future feast). Surplus wealth was not traditionally accumulated for its own sake, but so it could be given away, creating prestige for the giver and placing obligations on the receiver.

In most cases a big man did not create a dynasty. Although a big man's son had a head start in life he still had to demonstrate qualities of his own: hardwork, bravery, leadership, trading skill, magical knowledge. Different societies sought different characteristics in their leaders but economic ability was common to all. Wealth was necessary in order for a man to develop dependents and supporters.

The creation of wealth required hard work, and since women were largely responsible for agricultural production it was essential for a man with any ambition to get married. And it was the big men who monopolised the supply of female labour. Big men decided whether a young man would remain a bachelor and would sometimes 'give' assistance to young men to help them meet the bride price. Polygamy was often a feature of leadership.

In many areas warfare and ritual cannibalism were commonplace and 'payback' killings perpetuated an endless cycle of feuding. Each small group was virtually an independent nation – so any dealings with the next door tribe were international relations. Although alliances were common, they tended to be shifting and expedient, rarely developing into large, long term federations.

The world for most Papua New Guineans was closely proscribed: beyond their own clan they were surrounded by hostile or suspicious neighbours who often spoke a completely different language. Although no quarter was ever given in war, and women and children were not in any way exempt from attack, fighting usually occurred in highly ritualised battles – and only after negotiations had failed. Bows and arrows and spears were the weaponry, and there were generally few casualties.

Potatoes & Axes

The first European impact on PNG was indirect but far reaching. The sweet potato was taken to South-East Asia from South America by the Portuguese and Spaniards in the 16th century and it is believed Malay traders then brought it to Irian Jaya, from where it was traded to the Highlands. The introduction of the sweet potato must have brought radical change to life in the Highlands – it is still the staple crop. Its high yield and tolerance for poor and cold soils allowed the colonisation of higher altitudes, the domestication of many more pigs, and a major increase in population.

The next development preceding the

permanent arrival of Europeans was the arrival of steel axes which were also traded from the coast up into the Highlands. The introduction of these more efficient axes reduced the workload of men (making axes, garden clearing, canoe making, etc), increased bride price payments and, because of the increased leisure time, encouraged war – all of which boosted the status and importance of big men.

European Contact

PNG's history of real European contact goes back little more than a century, although the island of New Guinea was known to the European colonial powers long before they came to stay.

The first definite European sighting of the island took place in 1512 when two Portuguese explorers sailed by. The first landing was also Portuguese: Jorge de Meneses landed on the Vogelkop Peninsula, the 'dragon's head' at the north-west corner of the island. He named it 'Ilhas dos Papuas' and got his name in the history books as the European discoverer of New Guinea. In the following centuries various Europeans sailed past the main island and its smaller associated islands, but the spreading tentacles of European colonialism had far richer prizes to grapple with. New Guinea was a big, daunting place, it had no visible wealth to exploit, but it most definitely did have some rather unfriendly inhabitants. It was left pretty much alone.

Only the Dutch made any move to assert European authority over the island and that was mainly to keep other countries from getting a toehold on the eastern end of their fabulously profitable Dutch East Indies empire (Indonesia today). They put their claim in by a round about method. Indonesian and Malay traders had for some time carried on a limited trade with coastal tribes for valuable items like bird of paradise feathers. So the Dutch simply announced that they recognised the Sultan of Tidor's sovereignty over New Guinea. Since in

turn, they held power over the island of Tidor, New Guinea was therefore indirectly theirs – without expending any personal effort. That neat little ploy, first put into action in 1660, was sufficient for over 100 years, but during the last century firmer action became necessary.

The British East India Company had a look at parts of western New Guinea back in 1793 and even made a tentative claim on the island, but in 1824 Britain and the Netherlands agreed that Holland's claim to the western half should stand. In 1828 the Dutch made an official statement of their claim to sovereignty and backed it up by establishing a token settlement on the Vogelkop. Nothing much happened for 50 or so years after that, although the coastline was gradually charted and Australia, now evolving from a penal colony towards independence, started to make noises about those foreigners claiming bits of land which were rightfully theirs.

A whole series of British 'claims' followed; every time some British ship sailed by somebody would hop ashore, run the flag up the nearest tree and claim the whole place on behalf of good Queen Vic. The good queen's government would then repudiate the claim and the next captain to sail by would go through the whole stunt again. In 1883 the Queensland premier sent the Thursday Island police magistrate up to lay yet another unsuccessful claim, but the next year Britain finally got around to doing something about their unwanted would-be possession. At the time the British population consisted of a handful of missionaries and a solitary trader.

There was still very little happening over on the Dutch side of the island, but on the north coast of the eastern half a third colonial power – Germany – was taking a definite interest. When Britain announced, in September 1884, that they intended to lay claim to a chunk of New Guinea, the Germans quickly raised the flag on the north coast. A highly arbitrary line was then drawn between German and British New Guinea. At that time no European had ventured inland from the coast and it was nearly 50 years later, when the Germans had long departed, that it was discovered that the line went straight through the most densely populated part of the island.

New Guinea was now divided into three sections – a Dutch half to keep everybody else away from the Dutch East Indies, a British quarter to keep the Germans (and anybody else) away from Australia, and a German quarter because it looked like it could be a damn good investment. The Germans were soon proved wrong; for the next 15 years the mosquitoes were the only things to profit from the German New Guinea Kompagnie's presence on the north coast. In 1899 the Germans threw in the towel, shifted to the happier climes of the Bismarck Archipelago and quickly started to make those fat profits they'd wanted all along.

Over in the Dutch half nothing was happening at all and the British were trying to bring law and order to their bit. In 1888 Sir William MacGregor became the administrator of British New Guinea and set out to explore his possession and set up a native police force to spread the benefits of British government. He instituted the policy of 'government by patrol' which continued right through the Australian period. In 1906 British New Guinea became Papua and administration was taken over by newly independent Australia. From 1907 Papua was the personal baby of Sir Hubert Murray who administered it until his death in 1940.

Exploration
Exploration was one of the most interesting phases of the early European development of PNG. This was almost the last place to be discovered by Europeans and the explorers were only too happy to put their daring deeds down on paper. Gavin Souter's book *The Last Unknown* is one of the best descriptions of these travels.

At first, exploration consisted of short trips in from the coast, often by parties of early mission workers. Later the major rivers were used to travel further into the forbidding inland region. The next phase was trips upriver on one side, over the central mountains and down a suitable river to the other coast – crossing the tangled central mountains often proved to be the killer in these attempts.

It is interesting to note that more than one early explorer commented on how the curiosity and even awe with which they were met on a first trip turned to outright antagonism on a second. It's more than likely that a lot of this was due to the extreme trigger-happiness of some visitors. The final death count from the exploration of New Guinea undoubtedly showed that the head-hunters had more to fear of the white explorers than vice versa.

From the time of the Australian takeover of British New Guinea, government-by-patrol was the key to both exploration and control. Patrol officers were not only the first Europeans into previously 'uncontacted' areas but were also responsible for making the government's presence felt on a more or less regular basis. The last great phase of exploration took place in the '30s and was notable for the first organised use of support aircraft. This last period included the discovery of the important Highlands region. By '39 even the final unknown area, towards the Dutch New Guinea border, had been at least cursorily explored. Since the war there have been more exploratory patrols and the country is now completely mapped.

World War I & II
Almost as soon as WW I broke out in Europe, New Guinea went through a major upheaval. Australian troops quickly overran the German headquarters at Rabaul in New Britain and for the next seven years German New Guinea was run by the Australian military. In 1920 the League of Nations officially handed it over to Australia as a mandated territory.

It stayed that way right up until WW II and this split government caused more than a little confusion for the Australians. In the south they had Papua, a place where they had to put money in to keep it operating and where the major purpose was to act as a buffer to an unfriendly state which was no longer there. In the north they had New Guinea, run by Germany as a nice little money spinner and continued in much the same way under the Australians. The discovery of gold at Wau and Bulolo, in the New Guinea half, only compounded the difficulties since the northern half became even more economically powerful in comparison to the south.

Then WW II arrived and all the northern islands and most of the north coast quickly fell to the Japanese. The Japanese steam-rollered their way south and soon Australia only held Port Moresby. The Japanese advance was fast but short-lived and by September 1942, with the Pacific War less than a year old and Port Moresby within sight, they had run out of steam and started their long, slow retreat. It took until 1945 to regain all the mainland from the Japanese, and the islands – New Ireland, New Britain, Bougainville – were not recovered until the final surrender, after the atom bombing of Hiroshima and Nagasaki.

The End of Colonialism

There was no intention to go back to the pre-war situation of separate administrations and in any case Port Moresby was the only major town still intact after the war, so the colony now became the Territory of Papua & New Guinea. The territory entered a new period of major economic development with a large influx of expatriates, mainly Australians. When it peaked in 1971 the expatriate population had expanded from the 1940 total of about 6000 to over 50,000. Since then it has fallen to closer to 25,000 and is still, gradually, declining.

The postwar world had an entirely different attitude towards colonialism and Australia was soon pressured to prepare Papua & New Guinea for independence. A visiting UN mission in 1962 stressed that if the people weren't pushing for independence themselves then it was Australia's responsibility to do the pushing. The previous Australian policy of gradually spreading literacy and education was supplemented by a concentrated effort to produce a small, educated elite to take over the reins of government.

Meanwhile, things were not going nearly so smoothly in the Dutch half of the island. Indonesian resistance to Dutch rule had been simmering, or occasionally

flaring up, almost from the moment the Dutch arrived. During WW II the Japanese released the political prisoners held by the Dutch and used them to form the nucleus of a puppet government. When the war ended, Sukarno, leader of the pre-war resistance to Dutch rule, immediately declared Indonesia independent and the British forces who arrived in Indonesia to round up the Japanese troops met with stiff Indonesian resistance. Britain quickly got out of that sticky mess, but the Dutch were not so sensible. For the next few years the Dutch East Indies was racked by everything from minor guerilla warfare to all out battles. Eventually Dutch military superiority got the upper hand, but politically the Indonesians out-maneouvred them and in 1949 the Republic of Indonesia came into existence.

Dutch New Guinea was the final stumbling block to a Dutch-Indonesian agreement. It was part of the Dutch East Indies therefore it should be part of Indonesia went the Indonesian argument. The Dutch were determined to hold on to it as a small face-saving gesture, so right through the '50s it continued as a Dutch colony, while the Dutch searched desperately for something to do with it. Obviously a political union with PNG would have been the most sensible thing. At that time, however, the Australians were not considering the prospect of an independent PNG and the problem of confronting Indonesia would have become an Australian problem, not a Dutch one, if the colonies were amalgamated.

The Dutch decided on a quick push to independence; in the late '50s they embarked on a crash programme to develop an educated elite and an economic base – a policy that pre-dated by some years similar moves by Australia. The Dutch started to pour money into their colony, an expensive scheme that soon had to be followed by Australia.

Unfortunately for the Dutch, things were not going too well in Indonesia. The economy there was falling apart, Sukarno's

government was proving to be notoriously unstable and his answer to these serious internal problems was simple – look for an outside enemy to distract attention. Holland proved an ideal target and the effort to 'regain' Dutch New Guinea became a national cause. As Sukarno started to flirt with Russia, the Americans became more and more worried and eventually opted for their long running policy of bolstering up corruption and inefficiency wherever it looks like falling on its face (or into the hands of Communists). The Dutch were politically out-maneouvred at the UN once again and in 1963 the Indonesians, with support from the US, took over.

Indonesia's economic collapse was rapidly accelerating by this time and it was in no shape to continue the massive investment projects the Dutch had initiated. By the time Sukarno fell from power in 1965, Irian Barat (west hot land), as it was renamed, had suffered an asset stripping operation with shiploads of Dutch equipment being exported and local businesses and plantations collapsing right and left. Relations with Australia were none too good; perhaps Sukarno's habit of referring to PNG as Irian Timor (East Irian) and Australia as Irian Selatan (South Irian) didn't help.

After Sukarno's departure relations rapidly improved, the Indonesian half of the island was renamed Irian Jaya (New Irian) and Australians and Indonesians cooperated on accurately mapping the border between the two halves. Part of the Dutch hand-over agreement was that the people should, after a time, have the right to vote on staying with Indonesia or opting for independence. In 1969 this 'Act of Free Choice' took place. The 'choice' was somewhat restricted by Indonesia's new President Suharto stating that: 'There will be an act of self-determination, of free choice, in West Irian but if they vote against Indonesia or betray or harm the Indonesian people, this would be treason.' When the 1000 'representative' voters made the act of free choice there was not a treasonable voice to be heard.

Independence

In PNG the progress towards independence was fairly rapid through the '60s. In 1964 a House of Assembly with 64 members was formed; 44 were elected in open competition, 10 were appointed and 10 were elected Australians. Internal self-government came into effect in '73, followed in late '75 by full independence. At this time, PNG still had a very low rate of literacy and there were parts of the country only just emerging from the stone age, where contact with government officials was still infrequent and bewildering. It is quite probable that the first time many people knew of a central government was when they were told to vote for their parliamentary representative!

A country divided by a huge number of mutually incomprehensible languages, where inter-tribal antipathy is common and where the educated elite accounts for such a small percentage of the total population would hardly seem to provide a firm base for democracy. Yet somehow everything has held together and PNG works fairly well, especially by new-nation standards. Papua New Guineans have generally dealt with the problems of nationhood with a great deal of success.

The Free Papua Movement

After Independence, PNG's most immediate problem appeared to be relations with its powerful neighbour Indonesia. Following Indonesia's takeover of Irian Jaya, the indigenous Papuans, who had been sold out so badly by the rest of the world, began to organise a guerrilla resistance movement – the Free Papua Movement, which is widely known as the OPM (Organisasi Papua Merdeka). Since its inception, it has fought with varying degrees of success against tremendous odds.

Each time violence has flared PNG has found itself squeezed between a practical need for good relations with Indonesia and

an obvious sympathy for the racially-related Papuan rebels. In balance, practicality has prevailed and PNG has done nothing to assist the rebels – even, on several occasions, handing alleged rebels back to the Indonesian authorities.

Indonesia has maintained tight control over news coming from Irian Jaya and since the late '70s the OPM has been dogged by factionalism, so it is difficult to separate fact from fiction in the fragmented accounts of the struggle that reach the press.

On a number of occasions the OPM has been declared a spent force, only to reappear, seemingly undaunted. The OPM has attracted scant overseas support, but armed with traditional weapons and small numbers of out-dated guns and captured rifles the rebels continue to operate.

The border itself is one of those arbitrary straight lines European bureaucrats were so fond of drawing, which have since caused so much misery. Poorly patrolled, until recently badly surveyed, and crossing some of the most isolated and rugged country on the island, it is not likely to hinder the rebels movements. The Indonesians have claimed they come and go with impunity.

Over the years the OPM has announced it has killed hundreds of Indonesian soldiers and that many 1000's of Papuans have been killed in indiscriminant retaliatory attacks. The Indonesian figures are much lower. There were major clashes in 1978, 1981 and 1983 – a number provoked by Indonesia's ambitious transmigration scheme. Irian Jaya has a total population of around 800,000 Papuans and 220,000 Indonesians and the Indonesian Government has plans to move in another 700,000 settlers!

In 1984 over 100 Melanesian soldiers in the Indonesian Armed Forces deserted to the OPM sparking a major Indonesian operation which in turn drove over 10,000 Papuans into PNG. Years later these refugees, and those that have come both before and since, remain a political football. Few have shown any interest in returning to Irian Jaya so the PNG government has belatedly decided to resettle them permanently. In the meantime they live in extremely basic conditions in camps close to the border: Blackwater, near Vanimo, and Green River, near the Sepik River, are two of the largest.

Since 1985 the flow of refugees has virtually stopped, indicating a quieter level of activity on the part of both the Indonesians and the OPM, and the relations between Indonesia and PNG have improved. It seems unlikely the real grievances of the Papuan people in Irian Jaya have been met, however, so the problems of the past are likely to recur.

Law & Order

The most publicised problem that faces PNG today is one that can go under the general heading of 'Law & Order'. The worst affected areas are the larger cities (Port Moresby, Lae, Madang, Rabaul, and Mt Hagen) and parts of the Highlands. The problem encompasses everything from traditional tribal wars and modern corruption, to personal violence. When you hear talk of *rascals* and the *rascal problem* this is what is being referred to – not schoolboy pranks.

As you travel around PNG and especially when you speak to white expats you will be hard put to keep this problem in perspective. Extreme paranoia is contagious and crime is a favourite topic of conversation. What you must continue to ask yourself is: How does it compare with home (think of the Sunday newspapers in your home city) and how does it relate to the friendliness and hospitality I meet everywhere I go?

Although the statistics are unreliable they do not suggest that the law and order situation in PNG is worse than in many other developing or, indeed, some western countries. See the Safety section in the Facts for the Visitor chapter for more information.

The law and order label has a tendency to obscure a complex question that involves a variety of related issues. The kneejerk response is 'more police and tougher sentencing' but this is unlikely to be a full answer – the problem would not have proved to be so intractable if it was. The real issues that must be looked at are some of the traditional attitudes, the impact of westernisation, the success or failure of economic development and education, and questions of economic justice, as well as the efficiency and relevance of the political system, police force and judicial system.

It is useful to remember that it is very easy to apply inappropriate western criteria, and what appears to be uncontrolled anarchy is often nothing of the sort. For instance, tribal war is not necessarily regarded by the Highlanders as a breakdown of law and order but as the process by which law and order is re-established. A case that appears to be straightforward assault may well be a community sanctioned punishment. Looting a store may be in lieu of the traditional division of a big man's estate.

Perhaps the greatest problem is that PNG is not yet a cohesive state, so rules of behaviour that will be strictly upheld within a community will not necessarily be upheld outside it. A man who would never dream of cheating someone in his village might be proud of robbing someone from a rival tribe and feel similarly free from constraints in a strange city.

Clan loyalties also make police work extremely difficult. A village will not necessarily cooperate in the arrest of one of its members – if the rascal's actions have not affected the village negatively, they will often not be seen as *wrong*. To avoid police becoming involved in their own clan's disputes they are tranferred to other areas where they don't know the terrain or the intricacies of local politics. Police and their families are also vulnerable to the threat of payback attacks – which, of course, are *justified* if the policeman has arrested an *innocent* relative.

In the rush for independence, Australia was forced to concentrate on developing an elite who was capable of running the country, and perhaps inappropriately, the model that was used as the basis for development was Australia. Big men were encouraged to develop cash crops, often permanently (mis)appropriating their follower's lands when they did so. The educated few took well-paid positions in a centralised bureaucratic structure that had been transplanted from Canberra.

This had a number of unfortunate side effects. The big men who were encouraged and protected by the Australian administration are now very wealthy and powerful, far outstripping the general populace. Although by Asian standards the problem is not acute, in the Highlands there is a genuine shortage of land, especially of land that is suitable for the development of coffee. The Moresby bureaucracy has continued to grow, creating a prosperous middle class and a city that draws the hopeful, the curious and the ambitious – only to surround them with unattainable goodies and dump them in shanty towns without work.

Although people rarely starve in PNG and the village or clan can nearly always meet most simple needs, there is a growing cash economy. People need money to pay tax; to buy second-hand clothes, beer, tobacco, rice and tinned fish; and to send their kids to school. This demand for cash and the limited opportunity most people have to make money obviously creates pressures. There is also a growing number of people who are alienated from their traditional villages (for instance, a family may be driven away because a member has broken a traditional taboo) and these people are completely dependent on the limited opportunities in the cities.

The education system has also come in for criticism – it has even been called an unemployment-producing machine. Although PNG definitely has an unemployment problem, this is, to a certain extent, caused by the unreal expectations of the educated. Nearly everyone in PNG has access to land so, discounting the difficulty of earning cash for day-to-day needs, 'unemployment' is often partly voluntary.

Young men, even those with minimal educational standards, aspire to the status and material wealth that was achieved by the small elite the Australians developed. These ambitious young men, usually unmarried and between about 18 and 30 years old, are drawn to the cities. Once there they take advantage of relatives (*wantoks*) who, under Melanesian tradition, are responsible for feeding and housing them. Unfortunately sufficient jobs just do not exist, so these bored young 'have-nots' wander the town, play cards and pool, drink beer and . . . .

Whatever the reasons, it's hard to pretend you're governing things well if people insist on impaling their neighbours with spears, the well-off middle class (including both local people and expats) are forced to live in barbed wire fortresses, economic development is threatened by corruption and disorder, schools are closed because the safety of teachers cannot be guaranteed, and people (especially women) cannot walk the streets at night.

On several occasions the army has been called in, a state of emergency has been declared and strict controls have been placed on beer sales. The positive effects of these crackdowns have been short term at best. The rascals melt into the bush, or relocate to terrorize some other community, and are back as soon as the heat is off. The longer term solutions are much more difficult, requiring shifts in public attitudes, and long term restructuring of the economy, the educational and political systems, the police and judiciary.

The changes required present a serious challenge to the country. The government's own INA/IASER 'Report on Law & Order in Papua New Guinea' (the 1984 Clifford Report) observed:

With 62 per cent of of the population under 24 (85 per cent in the towns), and with enormous numbers of them being half-educated, unemployed, under-employed, without any social role and very much frustrated, the danger of forceful (maybe violent) political change is near.

Cargo Cults

The recurrent outbreaks of 'cargo cultism' in New Guinea are a magnetic attraction for assorted academics.

The arrival of the first Europeans in New Guinea must have had much the same impact that a flying saucer landing would have on us. Like something from the film *Close Encounters of the Third Kind*, local history is divided up into the days of 'pre-contact' and 'post-contact'.

To many people the strange ways and mysterious powers of the Europeans could only be described by supernatural means. In religious systems where it is necessary to invoke the help of spirits to ensure, say, a good yam harvest, it is logical that the same principles be applied if you want manufactured goods. Some of the cult leaders can be regarded as early nationalists and in several cases the cults developed into important political movements.

Cult leaders theorised that the Europeans had acquired their machines and wealth from some spirit world and that there was no reason they too could not acquire similar 'cargo'. Some went further and insisted that the Europeans had intercepted cargo that was really intended for the New Guineans, sent to them by their ancestors in the spirit world. One cultist even suggested that the whites had torn the first page out of all their bibles – the page that revealed that God was actually a Papuan.

If the right rituals were followed, said the cult leaders, the goods would be redirected to their rightful owners. Accordingly, docks were prepared, or even crude 'airstrips' were laid out, for when the cargo arrived. Other leaders felt that if they mimicked European ways they would soon have European goods – 'offices' were established in which people passed bits of paper back and forth. But when people started to kill their pigs and destroy their gardens (as a prerequisite for the better days to come) or to demand political rights, the colonial government took a firm stand. Some leaders were imprisoned. However arresting cult leaders simply confirmed the belief that an attempt was being made to keep goods rightfully belonging to the New Guineans, so some cultists were taken to Australia to see with their own eyes that goods do not arrive from the spirit world.

The first recorded cargo cult outbreak was noted in British New Guinea in 1893. A similar occurrence in Dutch New Guinea dates back to 1867. Cargo cult outbreaks have occurred sporadically ever since. One of the largest took place in the Gulf area just after WW I, it was known as the 'Vailala Madness' and was considerably spurred on by the arrival of the first airplane in the region – as predicted by one of the cult leaders. The cults took another upswing after WW II when the people witnessed even more stunning examples of western wealth. Seeing black American troops with access to the goods had a particularly strong impact. A more recent example was the Lyndon Johnson affair on the island of New Hanover (see the section on New Ireland). No doubt there will be new events to keep academics happy for some time yet.

GEOGRAPHY

PNG lies barely south of the equator, to the north of Australia. It is the last of the string of islands spilling down from South-East Asia into the Pacific and really forms a transition zone between the two areas. After PNG you're into the Pacific proper – expanses of ocean dotted by tiny islands. PNG occupies the eastern end of the island of New Guinea.

Additionally, there are a collection of smaller islands around the main land mass. To the north, Manus, New Ireland and New Britain are all provinces of PNG, as are the eastern islands in Milne Bay and the North Solomons group. To the south, the Torres Straits Islands are part of the Australian state of Queensland. Some of these tiny islands are a mere stone's throw from the PNG coast.

PNG's remote and wild character is very closely tied to its dramatic geography. The place is a mass of superlatives – the mountains tower, the rivers rush, the ravines plunge – name a geographical cliche and PNG has it. These spectacular features have much to do with the country's diverse people and its current state of development. When a mighty mountain range or a wide river separates you from your neighbouring tribe you're unlikely to get to know them very well.

The central spine of PNG is a high range of mountains with peaks over 4000 metres high. It's unlikely that a permanent road across this daunting natural barrier will be completed until the end of this century although temporary tracks were attempted during WW II. Meanwhile, travel between the south and north coasts of PNG still means flying, unless you care to walk that is.

Great rivers flow from the mountains down to the sea. The Fly and the Sepik Rivers are the two largest: the Sepik flowing into the sea in the north, the Fly in the south. Both are navigable for long distances and both are among the world's mightiest rivers in terms of annual water flow.

In places the central mountains descend right to the sea in a series of diminishing foothills, while in other regions broad expanses of mangrove swamps fringe the coast – gradually extending as more and more material is carried down to the coast by the muddy rivers. In the western region there is an endless expanse of flat grassland, sparsely populated, annually flooded and teeming with wildlife.

PNG is in the Pacific volcano belt but, apart from a few exceptions along the north coast such as Mt Lamington, near Popondetta, which erupted unexpectedly and disastrously in 1951, the live volcanoes are not on the main land mass. There are a number of volcanic islands scattered off the north coast and in Milne Bay plus, of course, the active region on the north coast of New Britain.

One of the most interesting features of the geography of PNG is the central Highland valleys. As the early explorers pushed inland the general conclusion was that the central spine of mountains was a tangled, virtually uninhabited wilderness. In the '30s, however, the Highland valleys were accidentally discovered and the wilderness turned out to be the most fertile and heavily populated region of the country. The best known valleys are around Goroka and Mt Hagen, but there are other more remote places right across into Irian Jaya.

PNG is endowed with striking coral reefs making it a paradise for scuba divers. There are reefs around much of the mainland coast and, more particularly, amongst the islands of the Bismarck Sea and Milne Bay areas.

The major offshore islands – New Ireland, New Britain and Bougainville – are almost as mountainous as the mainland with many peaks rising to over 2000 metres.

CLIMATE

The climate is generally hot and wet year round, but there are some exceptions. Officially there's a wet and a dry season, but in practice, in most places, the wet just means it is more likely to rain, the dry that it's less likely. The exception is Port Moresby where the dry is definitely dry – the configuration of the mountains around Moresby account for this two season characteristic. The wetter time of the year is from December to March, the drier time May to October. During the two transition months (April and November) it can't make up its mind which way to go and tends to be unpleasantly still and sticky.

Two places in PNG further confuse the pattern by being drier in the 'wet' and wetter in the 'dry'. They are Lae and Wewak and again the cause is the peculiar configuration of the mountains surrounding them.

Rainfall, which is generally heavy, nonetheless varies enormously. In dry, often dusty Port Moresby the annual rainfall is about 1000 mm (40 inches) and, like places in northern Australia, it is short and sharp and is then followed by long dry months. Other places can vary from a little over 2000 mm (80 inches) in Rabaul or Goroka, to over 4500 mm (175 inches) in Lae. In extreme rainfall areas, such as West New Britain or the northern areas of the the Gulf and Western Provinces, the annual rainfall can average 6000 mm or more per year – a drenching 20 feet.

Temperatures on the coast are reasonably stable year round – hovering around 25°C to 30°C, but the humidity and winds can vary widely, changing the way each day feels. As you move inland and up, the temperatures drop fairly dramatically. In the Highlands the daytime temperatures often climb to the high 20°Cs but at night it can get quite cold. During the dry season, when there is little cloud cover to contain the heat, Highland mornings can be very chilly. If you keep moving up into the mountains you'll find it colder still. Although snow is rare it can occur on the tops of the highest summits and ice will often form on cold nights.

Port Moresby Dry, dusty and windy from May to October.

Lae & Morobe In Lae it's hot and humid from November to February, wetter but cooler from May to October with the heaviest rain in June, July and August. In Wau and Bulolo it is the exact opposite.

Highlands In most of the Highlands the rain comes from November to April but is generally not unpleasant. May to October is cooler and drier. In the southern Highlands the wet lasts a bit longer at both ends and it is more likely to rain at any time year round.

Madang Rainy, often thunderstorms, from November to May.

Sepik July to November is the dry season and the wettest time is between December and April.

Gulf & Western The Gulf region is very wet year round – heaviest between May and October. Inland in Western can also be very wet.

Northern The wet season is from October to May with the heaviest rain at the beginning and end of the season.

Manus November to April wet season.

New Ireland November to April wet season in most of the country, inverted on a small part of the south coast.

New Britain November to April on the north side is the wet season (including Rabaul), while on the south side of the island the rain comes May to October and comes much heavier.

North Solomons January to April is wet but cooler, November and December are pretty hot.

Milne Bay Unpredictable year round – two possible wet seasons and periods of high wind. February to March and September to October are likely to be the best months.

FAUNA & FLORA
The major mountainous region forming part of the backbone of New Guinea and its rugged terrain of high peaks and deep valleys is home to the many and varied highland communities which have come to be the best known attraction for visitors. Here, too, once can find the greatest wealth of PNG's animals and plants.

Of about 9000 species of plants, over 200 are tree-size, mostly found in the lowlands rainforest, but extending to an upper limit of 3500 metres, where pines and antarctic beech thrive (more reminiscent of Tasmania or New Zealand), and above this on the higher mountains are alpine lakes and meadows. Most of PNG is forested, with shifting cultivation widespread, even in areas where it is very steep. Commercial logging is generally localised, but expanding, often with clear felling methods used. After extracting the commercial timber, the remainder may often be burned for farming purposes. In the south are extensive savannas similar to those of northern Australia.

PNG's wealth of wildlife does not contain large and spectacular animals, like elephants and tigers, but is interesting in many other ways. There are about 250 species of mammals, mostly bats and rats, including about 60 marsupials and notably tree kangaroos. There are also two kinds of egg-laying echidnas (spiny anteaters).

It is for its 700 or so bird species that PNG's wildlife is most renowned. New Guinea is the home of 38 of the world's 43 spectacular and gaudy species of bird of paradise, with their bizarre displays and mating rituals. Also numerous in species in PNG, the closely related bower birds may lack incredible feathering in their males, but more than make up for it in their skill in building not only bowers but elaborate maypoles and gardens, complete with a well-kept lawn and flower arrangements.

Among more familiar birds, PNG can boast more kinds of parrot, pigeon and kingfisher species than anywhere else in the world. All sizes and colours can be found, from the world's largest, such as the crowned pigeons, to the world's smallest, such as the pygmy parrots, which scurry along small branches and feed on lichens.

Many other groups are represented, with a general similarity to Australian bird life, but often more colourful. Perhaps the most notable of all are the giant cassowaries. Related to the Australian emu, they are stockier birds adapted to forest areas and with a large, horny casque

Bird of Paradise

for crashing through the undergrowth. Like the bird of paradise, cassowaries are of great ceremonial significance to many of PNG's tribal groups.

Also represented in PNG are about 200 species of reptiles, including two crocodiles and 13 turtles, as well as about 100 snakes, which are much feared by the local people and often a cause for the repeated burning of some grassland areas, especially in the Highlands.

PNG is a paradise for insects and contains many thousands of species, notably a beautiful variety of birdwing butterflies, including the world's largest butterfly, Queen Alexandra's Birdwing. Some insects, such as the brilliant green scarab beetles, are used as body ornaments although the most famous ornaments, of course, are the bird of paradise plumes, seen at their best at the Highland shows. They are very valuable not only for singssings, but as bride prices, and are carefully stored for use over many years.

Conserving the diversity of PNG's natural resources is complicated by the ancient customs of traditional land holdings and the government reluctance to alienate the people concerned. Totally protected areas are few. Prior to independence only two national parks were established, and only one since, but others have been proposed. A compromise concept is Benchmark Reserves protecting small parts of exploited areas.

The National Parks Board also recognises Provincial Parks and Local Parks, better known as Wildlife Management Areas. The latter are intended as multi-purpose areas, especially for the management of specific types of wildlife used for food or other functions. They are popular in aiding local communities to prevent over-exploitation, such as of the the eggs of scrub turkeys (megapode) mounds, or certain kinds of bird of paradise, and are the responsibility of the local groups using the areas. An advantage with this arrangement is that for any commercial exploitation in a particular area, the rights of the people living in the affected area are given priority and the guidelines are clearly established in local Land Use Management Plans.

Also important is the concept of Protected Species, in which all wildlife belongs to the traditional land owners, but the same restrictions apply as in Wildlife Management Areas. The list originally began in the 1920s to protect the bird of paradise and egret from extensive commercial exploitation for their valuable plumes. Added later were most of the birdwing butterflies, the long-nosed echidnas and others. Since independence many more have been added as part of PNG's cooperation with international conservation objectives.

While overall there appears to be no real concern for forest and wildlife, there is much concern for the lower montane forests and their wildlife in the Highland areas where the land is more densely populated and casual subsistence cutting and commercial firewood harvesting (for the tea and coffee industries) is widely practised. Most of the spectacular birds of paradise are only found in this zone, where hunting pressures lead to widespread local extinctions of populations scattered through the many valleys. A significant number are already confined to remoter areas.

The major threat is caused by the uncontrolled casual cutting of forests, as all other exploitation is now under some form of control, and the major danger of this casual cutting is that there is no real understanding of the effects it has on wildlife and plant populations.

In coping with PNG's conservation needs, the future will see a greater use of the Wildlife Management Areas. The government finds Totally Protected Areas an unsuitable prospect, except in more remote areas and some of the islands, due to the land ownership situation. Thus national parks as we know them in other countries are unlikely to number more than a few.

Fortunately, as Wildlife Management Areas are often invoked by local requests, arranging management to suit the local needs is much easier. Even whole provinces can be so declared, with the major restriction being the prohibition of modern firearms for obtaining wildlife.

Through the National Parks Boards and other organisations, PNG has now developed many successful wildlife management and conservation projects, with much attention focused on public education and awareness. A prime theme in these ongoing developments remains that of conservation through utilisation.

Large scale commercial exploitation is unlikely to be as disastrous in PNG as in neighbouring countries to the west. This is not only because of the recognition of traditional land ownership, but also because of the serious social, economic and environmental problems which are resulting right next door. Indonesian Irian Jaya is now coming under serious exploitation pressures. To the east the same pressures are found in the Solomon Islands. The long term future in PNG remains uncertain, but the current developments in conservation awareness are very encouraging.

If you want to see some of the wildlife of PNG the two main national parks offer some variety: one is close to Port Moresby, the other near Wau. Some facilities are available for visitors and for the latest information you can write to the PNG National Parks Board, PO Box 5749, Boroko. For information on Wildlife Management Areas contact the Division of Wildlife, Department of Lands & Environment, PO Box 2585, Konedobu. In Wau you can arrange to stay at the Wau Ecology Institute, PO Box 77, Wau. If you are particularly interested in birds contact the PNG Bird Society, PO Box 1598, Boroko. They can organise field trips. These arrangements can, of course, be made well in advance, or on arrival in PNG.

Apart from these two main parks there is a third on Mt Wilhelm in the Simbu Province, which protects the summit areas above the tree line. It is thus not as accessible or organised for visitors, yet.

No Wildlife Management Areas are listed here, but there are now a fair number scattered through the country and it is best to find out the details for any particular province through the Wildlife Division. In the Highlands near Mt Hagen, there is the Wildlife and Bird of Paradise Sanctuary at Baiyer River, mentioned in the Mt Hagen section of this book.

Kingfisher

Variarata National Park

This 1063 hectare park is 42 km by road from Port Moresby and protects the western escarpment of the Sogeri Plateau, extending to the Astrolabe Mountains. There are upland rainforests and savanna areas here, with several walking trails. There is a good variety of birds and other wildlife here, and it offers an excellent opportunity to see birds of paradise. The reddish plumed Raggiana Bird of Paradise is common here, but the resplendent adult males may be hard to find although its characteristic 'wah-wah' call is a feature of the forests. At over 600 metres elevation the cooler plateau is a popular escape from Port Moresby. A trip to the park can be combined with other activities, such as visiting the the junction of the Kokoda Trail.

McAdam National Park

This 2076 hectare park is between Wau and Bulolo with one of its boundaries along the Bulolo River. The stream dissected areas centred on the Bulolo River Gorge are found here. The park includes lowland rainforest to about 1000 metres, then submontane oak-dominated forests to about 1800 metres and above this are beech-dominated forests with dense bamboo to about 2000 metres. The wildlife includes a large variety of mid-montane species. Echidnas, cuscuses, cassowaries and birds of paradise are some of the highlights.

If you stay at the Wau Ecology Institute, you will hear about other places worth visiting as a result of the extensive surveys they have conducted over many years. The most accessible of these areas is Mt Kaindi (2362 metres). There is a road to the summit, with accommodation and facilities at the top. While the lower slopes have been cut over, an exploration from the summit offers the opportunity to explore the forests and see some of the wildlife of the upper vegetation zones. To make it even easier the Institute has published a guidebook to the mountain,

which is also intended to be an introduction to general New Guinea montane ecology.

The best way to see PNG and its wildlife is to do a little exploration of your own.

- **Murray D Bruce**
- **Constance S Leap Bruce**

GOVERNMENT

PNG has a three-tiered system of democratic government (national, provincial and local) based on the Australian and Westminster models. There is a ceremonial head of state, the Governor General, who is elected by parliament and an independent judiciary and public service.

The most important political forum is the National Parliament and all citizens have voting rights in elections that are held every four years. The parliament elects the Prime Minister, who in turn appoints ministers from members of his party and/or coalition. The National Parliament has ultimate control over the lower levels of government, including the administration of the national budget and the right to veto laws proclaimed by lower levels of government that it feels are not in the national interest.

The decentralised provincial government was introduced in 1976 in an attempt to move government closer to the people. Nineteen provinces and a separate National Capital District were formed, each with an elected Provincial Assembly, an executive council and Premier. The National Parliament retains ultimate control and a number of provincial governments have been suspended for mismanagement. Each of these governments has wide powers over education, health and the economy, and the right to levy certain taxes and fees. Finally, there are over 150 local councils.

National Politics

National politics is a world of shifting alliances. No single party has ever governed in its own right – each successive government has been dependent on shaky, unreliable coalitions. Party discipline is also loose and party members are prone to act independently, changing allegiances overnight and voting as it suits them and, sometimes, their bank balances.

The national parliament is elected on a first past the post system, where the candidate with the highest number of votes is successful and there is no limit to the possible number of candidates. In practice this means that members of parliament are frequently elected with less than 10% of the total vote. This not only leads to considerable disenchantment on the part of the majority but also, it is sometimes argued, corruption and tribalism. For instance, it is possible for a candidate to split the electorate's vote along tribal lines by encouraging representatives of each tribe in a constituency to stand. Our theoretical candidate would then concentrate on ensuring the loyalty of his own tribe, and perhaps picking up a few votes here and there by spreading a little bit of financial goodwill. The total number of votes that it is necessary to attract can then be very small.

Such unstable arrangements also mean that very few members of parliament survive more than one electoral term, leaving the parliament short of experience and continuity. There has been considerable criticism of this situation, but as yet no sitting parliament has had the political courage to challenge the status quo.

The political parties themselves are not distinguished so much by ideology as by the personality of their leaders and their regional bases. Generally, there appears to be a remarkable degree of consensus about the kind of society that should be created. All parties basically favour a mixed economy, with governments overseeing and, sometimes, operating alongside private enterprise. Only the details and emphases differ: To what extent should government be decentralised? What controls should be placed on multinationals and expatriates? What emphasis should be placed on rural development?

The country's first prime minister, Michael Somare ('The Chief'), proved to be a remarkably astute politician with the ability to forge working compromises between diverse groups of people. In 1980, however, Somare's government finally fell to a no confidence vote and Sir Julius Chan, an equally astute politician from the island of New Ireland, became prime minister. Earlier, when Chan's People's Progress Party (PPP) was in coalition with Somare's Pangu Party, Chan had been deputy prime minister to Somare.

After his fall from power Somare proved to be just as adept in his role as leader of the opposition and when elections were held in 1982 he and the Pangu Party were returned to power, ahead of an opposition led by Sir Iambakey Okuk's National Party. This government shattered in 1984 when Paius Wingti, Somare's deputy, defected to the opposition, led a no confidence motion and became the new prime minister. Wingti formed a coalition which was led by his new People's Democratic Movement (PDM), made up largely of Pangu defectors, and his deputy was . . . Sir Julius Chan. Somare formed an opposition coalition with Father John Momis' Melanesian Alliance (MA).

Although the ability of the parliament to bring down governments with a no confidence vote is largely recognised as destructive, the parliament has resisted arguments that this power should in any way be circumscribed.

The elections that were held in 1987 were a close-run affair. The largest single group of successful candidates were independents with no overt party allegiance, which left Wingti and Somare scrabbling for support amongst the independents' ranks. Finally, some two months after the first vote was cast, the new parliament met and voted Mr Wingti prime minister for a second term, with a very slim margin over Somare. It would take a brave person to predict that Wingti will hold his diverse and unruly coalition together and see out his theoretical four year term.

David Greason, writing for the Melbourne *Age*, put 10 years of turbulent politics in a nutshell:

Back in 1977 there was Somare and Chan against Okuk. Then it was Chan and Okuk against Somare. Then it was Somare and Wingti against Okuk and Momis. Then it was Somare and Momis against Wingti, Chan and Okuk.

ECONOMY

Until recently the economy was said to rest on copper, coffee, cocoa and copra. This ignored the fact that most people lived within a successful subsistence economy (growing a small part of the total coffee, cocoa and copra crops) and the contribution made by Australian grants. Since the mid 1980s copper has been overtaken by gold as the single largest item on the export account, the value of copra exports and the Australian grant have declined markedly, but at least 85% of the population are basically still subsistence farmers.

PNG is in the enviable position of having a booming and increasingly diversified mineral sector and largely untapped forestry and fishing resources. Further reserves of gold, copper, silver, nickel, oil and gas are being discovered, virtually daily. In most regions there is sufficient arable land to both produce agricultural surpluses and ensure that people do not starve. The relative size of the population and this natural wealth means that PNG has tremendous economic potential and in terms of the Pacific's island states it is a giant.

There is very little squalor in PNG, and beggars are effectively nonexistent. There are nutritional problems in some parts of the country (a shortage of protein is an age-old difficulty) but virtually everybody is fed and clothed, even if they are unemployed in the city. This is due in large part to the *wantok* system, a unique Melanesian system of clan responsibility. Wantok, literally means 'one talk', or common language, signifying a shared

origin. Under the system, members of a clan look after one another and share the clan's wealth. This system continues to be tremendously influential and has worked well in situations where only one family member earns a wage – a single wage will often be distributed among dozens of people.

All is not perfect however, and these very advantages can be seen as a two-edged sword. As many other countries have discovered, overseas controlled capital-intensive primary industries, can seriously distort development, aside from the risks of depending on unstable commodity prices. The geographical features which are in some ways so bountiful also mean that there are tremendous transport and communication difficulties.

Even the wantok system has its negative side. It encourages unemployed youths to venture to cities, and some argue that it can sap individual initiative and put a considerable strain on individuals who have to reconcile traditional responsibilities with the demands of a modern economy.

There is also an increasing gap between the expectations of those with an education and available jobs, and between the growing need for cash and the opportunity to make it. As yet, discontent has not manifested itself as a significant political force but it does show itself in the urban shanty towns with their associated crime problems, and disputes over land ownership, especially in the Highlands.

The most significant characteristic of the economy, however, is that the vast majority of the population is still entirely dependent on semi-traditional agriculture. The remaining minority are almost all involved in either government services (on the Australian model), mining (basically controlled by multi-national companies), large-scale plantations (often owned by local capitalists), or the service industries. The cliched juxtaposition of a traditionally-dressed tribesman standing beside a jet aircraft accurately reflects the startling schism between the two groups.

There is virtually no manufacturing industry, because of a shortage of skilled labour, high wages and the small size of the market. PNG imports include almost all manufactured goods and many basic foodstuffs, not a few of which could be produced locally (fish and rice in particular).

Perhaps the most critical problem is that there is insufficient local capital to establish import replacement industries, despite the fact that there is a powerful and wealthy group of local businessmen. The Australian administration fostered an elite based on the existing 'big men' or clan leaders and educated administrators, but the total numbers are still small. In addition, Australia was not averse to the idea of a captive export market.

Mining

The drop in Australian aid has in large part been offset by the income derived from mining. In the early 1970s the giant Panguna copper mine on Bougainville generated nearly a third of the national income, but this mine has now been joined by the equally massive mine at Ok Tedi which is now chewing through a copper mountain with a gold cap! Mining now contributes close to 60% of PNG's export income, and, through taxes and government-owned shares, around 40% of internal revenue.

Bougainville is now nearing the end of its life, but this loss should be more than compensated for by Ok Tedi and numerous new mines. Ok Tedi, in the remote Star Mountains of Western Province, is currently the largest gold mine outside South Africa, but even it will be eclipsed by new mines. Gold production at Porgera in Enga Province is projected to reach 650,000 ounces a year and Lihir Island in New Ireland Province has a production target of one million ounces a year – at current prices Lihir alone will be worth approximately US$300 million a year. To complete the picture, add oil in the Gulf of

Papua and the Highlands, more gold mines, particularly on the islands, and the fact that exploration is far from complete.

The cost of developing mines in the difficult climate and geography of the country is enormously high and remains the province of multi-national companies. The PNG Government has bargained shrewdly with these companies, however, to ensure both government and local share-holdings, and significant compensation for displaced traditional landowners. The Wingti Government plans to invest the profits from this mineral bonanza in agricultural development.

Agriculture

Agricultural exports are dominated by coffee which accounts for around 20% of total exports. Its importance is greater than this because it is one of the most important sources of cash income for the most populous area of the country – the Highlands. It is largely controlled by local capitalists who own the large plantations, but a significant proportion of the total crop comes from small clan holdings. The population density of the Highlands and the unequal distribution of suitable coffee-producing land is arguably the source of considerable friction.

Unfortunately, like most other crops, coffee is subject to major fluctuations in price and to disease. Coffee rust, a largely preventable disease, is currently threatening the industry, particularly the small growers who are not aware of the techniques that limit its damage.

Copra (dried coconut kernels which are processed into vegetable oils and other coconut products) was the backbone of the economy for many years but has now slipped far behind coffee and cocoa. Production was something of a political football as the copra plantations were looked upon as a colonial relic that did not fit with PNG's independent status, but the main problem was, and is, very low prices on the world commodity markets. Since independence there has been a dramatic drop in output and a major fall in plantation employment – the work is simply too unrewarding.

Oil palms are partly responsible for the decline in the copra price as they are a considerably more efficient source for vegetable oils. Major oil palm plantations are being developed in Oro Bay, Milne Bay and West New Britain Provinces.

Cocoa's big problem has been local diseases but, like coffee, it has been aided by good prices and the development of highly productive hybrid varieties. Tea has not been the great success once expected although Highland tea is quite pleasant. Rubber production has grown slowly but steadily.

The huge, inaccessible timber resources have only begun to be exploited, but the industry has already suffered from corruption and environmental abuse. The enormous potential of fishing around the coast is also beginning to be appreciated – the implementation of the 200-mile fishing zone has prompted Asian countries to involve themselves in fishing projects with PNG. Unfortunately, tinned fish remains a major import – even on islands surrounded by fish.

Australian Grant

In the first year after WW II the annual Australian grant was only about half a million kina, but it grew steadily and rapidly through the '50s and '60s and reached around A$200 million a year in the late '70s. The Australian Government now intends to gradually cut the annual grant back, although in 1987/88 it amounted to more than A$300 million. As a percentage of the national budget this represents a decline from around 50% at the time of independence to 19%. The PNG Government intends that this should be reduced to less than 5% by the mid 1990s.

This large figure can be put into a new perspective when you consider that a tremendous proportion of the money will be swallowed by the expensive Australian-developed public service (administered by both the national government and the 20 provincial governments) that some people regard as quite inappropriate. Kenneth Good in his book *Papua New Guinea – A False Economy* (Anti-Slavery Society, 1986) claims that in 1981 the national government consumed 40% of the country's gross domestic product, and that in 1980 Australia exported goods to PNG worth over A$400 million importing only A$74 million in return.

POPULATION & PEOPLE

The population is estimated at around three and a half million. Over a third of the population is concentrated in the Highland provinces. Some authorities divide the people into Papuans, predominantly descended from the original arrivals and Melanesians, who are more closely related to the peoples of the Pacific. Additionally, some people, particularly in outlying islands, are closer to being pure Polynesian or Micronesian. The dividing line between these definitions is a very hazy one. Politically, four regional groupings, reflecting cultural and historical links, have developed: Papuans (from the south), Highlanders, New Guineans (from the north) and Islanders.

There is a wide range of physical types, from the dark Buka people of the North Solomons, who are said to have the blackest skins in the world, to the lighter, more Polynesian people of the south Papuan coast. After a spell in PNG you'll soon learn to recognise the shorter, often bearded, Highland men and many other distinct groups of people. Diversity of languages goes along with this diversity of racial characteristics. The same rugged terrain that kept their physical features from mixing also kept their languages and cultures separate. It has been estimated that there are over 700 languages spoken in New Guinea.

Expatriates

There is still a considerable expatriate population, although it has fallen considerably from its 1971 peak of around 50,000 to a current figure closer to 25,000. The expatriate population today is made up of a wide variety of nationalities. Although Australians are still in the majority, there are Germans, English, Americans, Chinese and Philipinos, amongst many others.

At independence many long term Australian and Chinese residents were eligible for PNG citizenship, but only on the condition that they renounced their original citizenship. Many did so and some now hold positions of considerable political and economic importance. There are even a number of white members of parliament.

The expatriates are a diverse group with an amazingly varied outlook on life in general, and their position in PNG in particular. Someone once said if you come to PNG you've got to be a missionary, a mercenary (one after money, not a shoot and kill type) or a misfit. Sometimes you seem to be talking to all three types at once. The Bible thumpers seem to thump Bibles harder than anywhere else, the 'in it for what it's worth' brigade seem to be in it deeper than anywhere else, and the 'my world is falling apart' gang can be seen propping up the bar and taking solace in the bottle.

Although some mission workers have been criticised for their blinkered attitudes and destructive impact on traditional culture others have done extremely valuable work setting up schools, farms, airports, hospitals, shipping companies, and working amongst the hapless people lured by the 'big city' aura of towns like Port Moresby. They continue to have a very strong influence on the country. There's also a large and diverse volunteer contingent including Peace Corps, Cuso and VSO workers amongst others. Most work for low wages and have jobs teaching, nursing, researching or helping with development projects.

Expatriate workers are usually in the country on short-term, lucrative contracts with international companies. Often they lead lives that are totally divorced from reality, commuting between air-conditioned offices, their company-provided houses (invariably surrounded by barbed wire) and some sort of club. Partly as a consequence of this isolation their attitudes to, and perceptions of, the country are sometimes quite inaccurate.

What's in a Name (Part 2)

Western residents are almost always known as expats and the indigenous people are frequently referred to as nationals – never ever natives. The term nationals is itself increasingly out of favour; many Papua New Guineans prefer, where a label is necessary at all, to be described by their tribal or regional name or as Papua New Guineans. In more remote areas westerners will still occasionally find themselves referred to as *masta* or *missus*, but most people, especially in the cities, now find this offensively colonial. The colonial era is still sometimes referred to as the *taim bilong masta*.

HOLIDAYS & FESTIVALS

Each of the twenty provinces of PNG has its own provincial government day and these are usually a good opportunity to enjoy local *sing-sings* (ceremonies and dances in traditional dress). Generally, however, sing-sings are local affairs with no fixed yearly schedule, so you'll have to depend on word of mouth to find out about them. Shows and festivals have a tendency to change dates between years, although usually only by a few days.

1 January
  New Years Day

Late January/early February
  Chinese New Year in places like Lae or Rabaul with a Chinese community.

22 February
  New Ireland Provincial Government Day

26 February
Simbu Provincial Government Day

Easter
Traditional church services.

20 April
Oro Provincial Government Day

June-August
Yam Harvest Festival (Trobriand Islands)

6 June
Madang Provincial Government Day
Maborasa Festival (Madang) – with dancing, choirs and bamboo bands

Mid June
Port Moresby Show – traditional and modern events
Central Provincial Government Day

25 June
Morobe Provincial Government Day
Frangipani Festival – commemorating the first flowers to blossom after the 1937 eruption of Matupit

7 July
Milne Bay Provincial Government Day

Late July
Mt Hagen Show – a massive gathering of clans with traditional dances and dress; this used to alternate with the Goroka Show, but became an annual event in 1988

Mid August
Goroka Show – this used to occur on even numbered years, but may become annual

16 August
Southern Highlands Provincial Government Day

25 August
Manus Provincial Government Day

1 September
North Solomons Provincial Government Day
North Solomons Festival of Arts

16 September
Independence Day – a great time to be in PNG with many festivals and sing-sings, all around the country
Malangan Festival (Kavieng or Namatanai, in New Ireland) – the two week festival includes the famous tree-dancers
East Sepik Provincial Government Day

17 September
West New Britain Provincial Government Day

20 September
Western Provincial Government Day

13-26 November
Tolai Warwagira (Rabaul) – a two week festival of sing-sings and other events

4 October
Enga Provincial Government Day

1 December
Gulf Provincial Government Day

6 December
Western Provincial Government Day

25 December
Christmas

PIDGIN - *TOK PISIN*

A recent survey calculated that there were 717 languages in PNG, 45% of all the languages in the world. With this amazing basis for mutual incomprehension it's not surprising that there has long been a search for a common linking language.

During the early days of British New Guinea and then Australian Papua, the local language of the Moresby coastal area, Motu, was slightly modified to become 'Police Motu', and spread through Papua by the native constabulary. It is still quite widely spoken in the southern Papuan part of PNG, and you can easily pick up a Motu phrasebook in Port Moresby.

In the northern German half of the country the German planters were faced exactly the same communication difficulties as the British. Their solution was Pisin, a local word that was corrupted into Pidgin – a term used today to define any trade language, a sort of mid-way meeting point between two languages. The PNG version of Pidgin is now sometimes known as Neo-Melanesian, but more frequently just as Papua New Guinean Pidgin or *Pisin*. It is very close to the Pidgin spoken in Vanuatu and the Solomons.

Pisin has taken words from many languages, including German, but it is primarily derived from English. Since it first came into use around Rabaul during the German days the Melanesian words used in Pisin are mainly from the languages of East New Britain. There are, however, a number of words indicating other foreign influences. Milk, for example, is *susu* as in Indonesia, although in Pisin *susu* can also mean breasts.

Pisin has at times been damned and condemned by everybody from the UN down. It's been called 'baby talk', 'broken English', 'demeaning' and much worse. There were a number of attempts to discourage its use, but the language has proven to be vigorous and effective, supplanting Motu even in Port Moresby.

In some ways, particularly because of its limited vocabulary, Pisin is not an ideal language. There are only about 1300 words in Pisin and they have to cover the same territory covered by 6000 English words. This frequently results in very roundabout and wordy descriptions. An absurd example of this is the word for cow. There is no separate word for bull or cow, they're described collectively as a *bulmakau* (bull-and-a-cow). *Meri* is the word for woman or female so a cow is described as a female-bull-and-a-cow or a *bulmakau meri*. Despite this disadvantage the language is easily learnt and is often very evocative.

Learning Pidgin can be a hell of a lot of fun. Many words or phrases make perfect sense if you just read them out slowly and thoughtfully, although spoken rapidly they're not easy to follow. I saw a sign outside a cinema in Madang announcing that the film showing was a *piksa bilong bigpela man/meri tasol*. That is, it was a 'picture for big-fellow men and women only', in other words it was for adults only. Who was that uniformed Englishman at the independence day celebrations? None other than the *nambawan pikinini bilong misis kwin*, that is to say the 'eldest child of the Queen' – er Prince Charles! A public library? That's a *haus buk bilong ol man/meri*.

There are quite a few Pidgin words and phrases that have crept into everyday English in PNG. You can always recognise somebody who has spent some time in PNG by the way they say *tru* instead of 'really', 'that's right' or 'you don't say'. Nobody leaves PNG when their work is completed, they *go pinis*. It's never dinner time, always *kai* (food) time, which is followed not by dessert but by *sweet kai*. You'll also be told *maski* which means 'don't bother'. If something is totally unimportant or doesn't matter at all, then it's *samting nating* (something-nothing) And a private problem, your own affair, is *samting bilong yu*. Nobody gets fired in PNG, they're *raused* from *rausim* or 'thrown out' – that one dates right back to German days.

If your Pidgin is less than perfect, it is wise to append *yu save?* or *nogat?* (meaning you understand or not?) to just about any sentence. *Save* is pronounced 'savvy'. Note that p and f are virtually interchangeable in Pidgin.

Greetings

hello	*gude*
good morning	*moning*
good afternoon	*apinun*
see you later	*lukim yu bihain*
how are you?	*yu stap gut?*
I'm fine	*mi stap gut*

Commands & Questions

May I take a photo?
  inap my kisim poto?
Put it there.
  putim long hap
Show me.
  soim me

Stop here!
stap! *
Is it far?
em i longwe?
near, close by
klostu
a very long way
longwe tumas
I would like to buy ....
mi laik baim ....
Where is the ....?
we stap wanpela ....?
How much does that cost?
em i hamas? **
I want something to eat.
mi laikim sampela kaikai
That is mine.
em bilong mi
Be careful!
lukautim gut!
Go away!
yu go! ***
Don't touch! (or) Put it down!
lusim!

* The word *stap* has many functions including to stay or to be present or to indicate the progressive form – *em i kaikai i stap* (he is eating).
** Many townspeople add *kostim* (*em i kostim hamas?*) but it is better Pidgin not to.
*** It is very impolite to say *raus*, it means 'leave (the house ....)' more than simply 'go away'.

Small Talk
What is your name?
wanem nem bilong yu? *
Where are you from?
ples bilong yu we?
I don't understand.
mi no klia gut
I don't know.
mi no save
Speak slowly.
tok isi

* Although this is correct Pidgin it would be very much against the custom to ask

somebody their name, although things are changing in the big towns. Even people that know each other's names will not use them and at meetings they will go on for hours without the chairman calling one person's name. They might call somebody *kona* – the one in the corner, or *hagen* – somebody from around Hagen, or *mausgras* – the one with the beard, or even *grinpela kolsiot* – the one with the green sweater. Anything to avoid using their real name.

Some Useful Words

yes	*yes*
no	*nogat*
thank you	*tenkyu*
a little	*liklik*
plenty	*planti*
big	*bikpela*
aircraft	*balus*
airport	*ples balus*
bathroom	*rum waswas*
bedroom	*rum slip*
toilet	*liklik haus*
child	*pikinini*
decorations or uniform	*bilas*
forbidden	*tambu*
man/woman	*man/meri*
hospital	*haus sick*
police station	*haus polis*
letter, book, ticket	*pas**
luggage	*kago*
newspaper	*niuspepa*
photo	*poto*
towel	*taul** *
countryman or friend	*wantok*** *

* Anything with writing on it.
** A towel used to be a *laplap bilong waswas* but that is now rather old fashioned.
*** Literally means 'one-talk', somebody who speaks the same language – the *ples tok*, language of the place.

Food
food	*kaikai**
restaurant	*haus kaikai*

menu	*pas bilong kaikai*
tea	*ti*
coffee	*kopi*
eggs	*kiau*
sugar	*suga*
meat	*abus*
unripe coconut	*kulau*
water	*wara*
drink	*dring*
breakfast	*kaikai bilong moning*
lunch	*kaikai bilong belo*
dinner	*kaikai bilong apinun*

* Shortening it to simply *kai* is really Australian Pidgin.

Pronouns

I	*mi*
you	*yu*
he/she/it	*em* *
they	*ol*
we (including the person spoken to)	*yumi*
we (excluding the person spoken to)	*mipela*
you (plural)	*yupela*
everybody	*olgeta* **

* Note that *em* is followed by *i* to introduce the verb as in *em i kaikai i stap* or *em i no*

sing-sing. Similarly after they *ol i wokabout i go*.

** Note that *ol* indicates the plural as in *ol haus* (houses) while *olegeta haus* means 'all the houses' – each of them.

Verbs & Tenses

Tenses are all the same except you append *pinis* (finish) to make it past tense: *mi kaikai pinis* means 'I have eaten'. Two common verbs:

| bring, give or take | *kisim* |
| fasten, shut or lock | *fasim* |

Finally, some Pidgin confusion. My brother is my *brata* and my sister is my *susa* but Maureen's brother is her *susa* and her sister is her *brata*. In other words your *brata* is always the same sex, your *susa* always the opposite. Today *sista* is also in common use, however, and that has the same meaning as in English. Note that *kilim* just means to hit (but hard), to kill somebody (or something) you have to *kilim i dai*.

Careful of the sexual phrases – *pasim* means to copulate with, not to push! And while you can *ple tenis* (play tennis), *ple* is also a euphemism for intercourse. A man's trunk or suitcase may be a *bokis*, but a women's *bokis* is her vagina. And a

---

INSTRUCTIONS FOR THE OPERATION OF THE EMERGENCY LOCATOR BEACON.
Remove Rubber Plug, Insert Finger & Push The Rubber Toggle Switch Downwards.

SAPOS BALUS I BUGARAP, YU MAS WORKIM DISPELA OL SAMTING,
Rausim Lik Lik Gumi, Putim Finga Bilong Yu Long Hole Na Suim Switch Oli Karamapim Long Gumi Igo Daun.

Workim Ol Dispela Samting Taim Balus I Bugarap.

What to do if your *balus* (plane) should *bugarup*. It's been pointed out to me that the Pidgin in the above sign is none too good though! Another traveller wrote that he saw a balus safety instruction leaflet on Solair informing you that when *balus go bugarup yu mas rausim fols tits* – which actually means you should remove your false teeth!

blak bokis is not a black suitcase but a flying fox or bat! You'll love the standard reply to 'how far is it?' – *longwe liklik*. It doesn't actually mean a long way and not a long way, it translates more like 'not too near, not too far'.

Books

Like any language it takes a lot of study to understand Pisin fully, but you can be communicating on at least a basic level with remarkable speed. Lonely Planet publishes a pocket-sized *Language Survival Kit* called *Papua New Guinea phrasebook* that includes grammatical notes, many useful phrases and a vocabulary. There are a number of alternative phrasebooks and dictionaries that are easily available. The best places to look are the Christian Bookshops in PNG; there is usually one in every town and they have all sorts of literature in Pidgin, including, needless to say, a Pidgin Bible.

There is no substitute for actually hearing the language and if you want to get a head start before you get to PNG there is an excellent language course that includes two tapes and an exercise book. It was prepared under the auspices of the Summer Institute of Linguistics, a missionary group, and is called *A Programmed Course in New Guinea Pidgin* by Robert Litteral (The Jacaranda Press – now Jacaranda Wiley – Brisbane).

If you'd like to learn a little Motu, which is still quite commonly used in the Papuan part of PNG, then look for *Say it in Motu* (Pacific Publications, Sydney) by Percy Chatterton.

Facts for the Visitor

VISAS

The story on visas has made a number of abrupt about faces over the years, so it is wise to check the regulations with a PNG consular office before you depart. In countries where there is no PNG consular office apply to the nearest Australian office.

If you are a bona fide tourist with an outward ticket, sufficient funds, about K300 per month and plan to stay no more than 30 days, you can get a visa on arrival at Port Moresby airport for K5.

This 'easy visa' system applies only to people who fly into Port Moresby and only to citizens of certain countries, including Australia, Canada, New Zealand, USA, United Kingdom, most of PNG's near Pacific and Asian neighbours and a number of western European countries, including West Germany. It does not apply to people visiting for business purposes and it cannot be extended. There can also be long queues for on-the-spot visas so, all in all, it's preferable to get your visa before you leave home.

A normal visa requires one photo, costs the equivalent of K5 for a business or tourist visa and permits a stay of up to two months. Since they seem to give you what you ask for, ask for the maximum time rather than have to face the problem of extending. The Migration Office in Waigani, Port Moresby is the only place in the country where you can extend visas and the procedure is slow and frustrating – worth avoiding if you can. Travellers who have tried extending their visas by mail from other parts of the country have generally found it impossible, and have had to trek back to Port Moresby to retrieve their passports. If you do intend to do this, use a courier rather than mail.

Officially you may be asked to show your inward and outward ticketing, that you have sufficient funds and that you have made some sort of accommodation arrangements when applying for your visa. In practice that is unlikely to happen, although you may have to show your outward ticket on arrival. If you're coming in by yacht, you're up for K10 for a yacht permit.

In Australia there is a PNG High Commission in Canberra and a Consulate-General in Sydney. The general consensus is that the Sydney office is the best place to apply for your visas. Allow at least a week for the process. Although many travellers fly from Cairns in northern Australia, the nearest PNG Consulate is in Brisbane.

Jayapura in Irian Jaya is another relatively common exit point to PNG (it's only a few minutes flying time from the border) but PNG has no consular representation there either and you will not be given a visa on arrival at Vanimo or Wewak. It's long way back to Jakarta and the PNG Embassy.

You *must* already have a visa if you wish to enter PNG through any port other than Port Moresby. Make sure your visa will still be valid when you arrive. PNG offices abroad are:

Australia
> PNG High Commission, Foster Crescent, Yarralumla. PO Box 572, Manuka, ACT 2603 (tel 73 3322)
> PNG Consulate-General, Somare Haus, 100 Clarence St, Sydney. GPO Box 4201, Sydney, 2001 (tel 29 5151)
> PNG Consulate, United Dominion House, 127 Creek St, Brisbane. PO Box 220, Brisbane, 4001 (tel 221 7915)

Belgium
> PNG Embassy, Avenue Louise 327, Box 20/21, 1050 Brussels (tel 640-34-95)

Fiji
> PNG High Commission, 6th floor, Ratu Sukuna House, Suva. PO Box 2447, Government Buildings, Suva (tel 25-421)

Indonesia
  PNG Embassy, 6th floor, Panin Bank Centre, Jalan Jendral Sudirman 1, Jakarta 10270 (tel 71 1226)
Japan
  PNG Embassy, Mita Kokusai Building 3F 313, 4-2B Mita 1-Chome, Minato-Ku, Tokyo (tel 454 7801/4)
Malaysia
  PNG High Commission, 1 Lorong Ru Kedua, off Jalan Ru, Ampang, Kuala Lumpur (tel 47 4202)
New Zealand
  PNG High Commission, 11th floor, Princess Towers, 180 Molesworth St, Wellington. PO Box 9746, Courtenay Place, Wellington (tel 73 1560)
Philippines
  PNG Embassy, Dasmarinas Village, 2224 Paraiso St, Makati, Metro Manila (tel 88 0386)
UK
  PNG High Commission, 14 Waterloo Place, London SW1R 4AR (tel 930 0922)
USA
  PNG Embassy, 6th floor, 1140 19th Street NW, Washington DC 20036 (tel 659 0856)
  PNG Permanent Mission to the UN, Room 1005, 100 East 42nd Street, New York 10017 (tel 682 6447)
West Germany
  PNG Embassy, Gotenstrasse 163, 5300 Bonn 2, West Germany (tel 37 6855)

To/From Indonesia

The visa situation for people travelling to or from Indonesia is tricky. Regulations can change overnight, and the left hand rarely knows what the right hand is doing. We quite regularly receive tales of woe from travellers, so it pays to be flexible in your plans if you want to incorporate both Indonesia and PNG in your itinerary.

One recent letter described someone arriving in Ambon, after using a two-day transit visa to get through Jayapura, and spending two days struggling with the bureaucracy which hadn't heard they could give him a 60 day tourist pass. Finally a telex arrived from Jakarta and 'the threats of deportation disappeared, they gave me two months and everything was OK'.

Officially you can get two-month tourist passes for Indonesia on arrival at international ports, if you have an onward ticket and your passport is valid for a minimum of six months. The pass is actually distinct from a visa (visas are issued by Indonesian embassies) but it is still a stamp in your passport. These ports are Jakarta, Denpasar (Bali), various places in Sumatra, Manado (Sulawesi), Ambon (Maluku), Biak (Irian Jaya) and Kupang (Timor). Jayapura (just over the border from Vanimo, in Irian Jaya) is in a category of its own.

It is possible to get a one-month visa to Indonesia and a two-day transit pass to Jayapura at the Indonesian Embassy in Port Moresby, as well as other embassies and consulates around the world. Fifteen day extensions are allegedly possible, but you have to pay an expensive 'landing tax' and the process is likely to provide interesting insights into Indonesian bureaucracy. The visa and pass take four days to be issued. You need an onward ticket from Jayapura, a couple of photos and K2.20. You do not have to present your application in person, so you could use registered mail or a courier to ferry your passport to and from wherever you happen to be (sounds risky to me).

On at least one occasion the Indonesians have expressed their displeasure at PNG attitudes to the OPM rebels in Irian Jaya by halting the issue of visas from Port Moresby. Since it is impossible to predict when or if the OPM issue will once again flare up it may be wise to get your Indonesian visa at home.

Once you get to Jayapura, clutching your one-month visa and two-day transit pass, it *may* be possible to *convince* the authorities you need to go inland into Irian Jaya. To get into the mountains you need a police permit (a *surat jalan*) from the main police station in Jayapura which costs 1000 rp and requires four photographs. Certain parts of Irian Jaya are off limits, but the police will tell you where you can go.

Apparently there are no problems or time restrictions placed on you if you enter Irian Jaya from other parts of Indonesia using your tourist pass. The police permit for the interior is just a formality. It seems, however, if you plan to exit from Jayapura, it is much easier if you are travelling on a visa (it is theoretically essential).

If you fly into Biak on the flight from Los Angeles you can get your two-month Indonesian tourist pass and your two-day Jayapura transit visa at the airport. If you have firm plans to leave Jayapura for PNG, you would be wise to get a visa and the two-day Jayapura transit pass at home, spend your two days in Jayapura, and not attempt to disappear into the mountains.

Before you leave Jayapura you must get an exit stamp from the Jayapura police. An exit stamp is not required if you depart Jayapura for other parts of Indonesia.

Although it all sounds frighteningly complex, people using the Jayapura-Biak-Los Angeles flight have not had problems so long as they have a visa, and a transit pass to Jayapura which they have not overstayed. In addition, if they have left Jayapura for Vanimo, they have needed a Jayapura police exit stamp and, of course, a PNG visa.

If you enter PNG from Indonesia and plan to exit through Indonesia, do not forget to get a new Indonesian visa in PNG – once you have left Indonesia, the original visa or pass is finished whether or not the time has expired.

To/From Australia

All nationalities (except New Zealanders) require a visa for Australia which is issued free at consulates and is usually valid for six months. Extensions beyond the six month period seem to be somewhat arbitrary – sometimes they will and sometimes they won't. Visitors aged between 18 and 26 from Britain, Ireland, Canada, Holland and Japan can be eligible for a 'working holiday' visa.

In general the Australian High Commission in Port Moresby seems to be pretty cooperative and very quick in issuing visas. Some travellers seem to use PNG as a convenient way of extending their stay in Australia without having to face the hassles of a straightforward extension. They travel round Australia for their initial six months, spend some time in PNG, and come back to Australia for another six months.

PAPERWORK

The only essential document is your passport. You do not need an International Health Certificate in PNG, but you do for a number of Asian countries (Indonesia for one). There are no youth hostels. A valid overseas license is all you need to drive a car for up to three months from the day you arrive.

International Student Identity Cards are very useful – they can save you a fortune. All the airlines offer significant student discounts and so, believe it or not, do some Public Motor Vehicles (PMVs, PNG's privately run answer to public transport). Air Niugini sometimes requires an International Student Concession Form, which should be available from your school or institution.

CUSTOMS

Visitors are allowed to import 200 cigarettes (or equivalent amount of tobacco) and one litre of alcoholic drinks duty free. Personal effects that you have owned for a year (this might be difficult to judge!) are also duty free. You won't have any problem with your camera, film and walkperson. There is quite a thorough check made of your gear at Jackson's Airport, Port Moresby.

There are also controls on what you can take out of the country – some items of cultural and historical significance are prohibited exports. This includes anything made before 1960, traditional stone tools, some shell valuables from Milne Bay, and any item incorporating human remains or bird of paradise plumes. As a tourist you are unlikely to be sold anything of this nature, but if you are in doubt and you don't like the idea of robbing a country of its heritage, you can get your artefact checked at the National Museum in Moresby. Stone tools and artefacts should definitely be checked, because they are often of astonishing antiquity and may provide vital clues to PNG's past.

If you plan to buy artefacts, check your home country's import and quarantine regulations. Many artefacts incorporate animal skins or bones from protected animals, for instance, and these may be prohibited imports. If you are carrying the artefacts with you, you will also be subject to the regulations of countries you enter on your way home.

If you clear Customs you have entered a country even if you are 'transiting' in a couple of days. The fact that you are an American tourist staying in Cairns for two days will not be an adequate defence against Australian regulations. At the very least, you will spend an unhappy half hour unwrapping, then re-wrapping, your precious artworks after they have been inspected. Crocodile skin (it doesn't make any difference if it came from a farm), tortoise shell, some turtle shells, birds of paradise (and their plumes) are all prohibited imports to Australia because they are considered to be, or belong to, endangered species.

Australian quarantine regulations apply to all wooden articles (including all carvings), and all animal products (including bones and skins). If any of these things are judged to be possible quarantine risks you will have to pay to have them irradiated, a process that may take up to a week. This is problem if you are catching a plane to the US in two days, or if you are clearing Customs in Sydney and catching a connecting flight to Melbourne.

You can minimise the risk of this by checking potential purchases yourself. Bone will automatically be treated, signs of borer in wood will mean problems, and hair or untanned skin will also require treatment.

There are a number of ways around the problem if you simply must have that hairy mask with the boar's tusks. If you have a lot of artefacts consider sending them all directly home, either by surface mail or ship. If you are a genuine transit passenger (ie you will not clear Australian Customs) Australian regulations will not apply to you. If you do clear Customs you can have your goods kept in a quarantine bond store (controlled storage) for the duration of your stay, although this is not to be recommended for fragile or very expensive artefacts. You can also, at your considerable expense, have the artefacts shipped under quarantine bond to your port of departure (if you land in Cairns, say and depart from Sydney).

MONEY

The unit of currency is the kina (pronounced 'keenah') which is divided into 100 toea (pronounced 'toy-ah'). Both are the names of traditional shell money and this connection to traditional forms of wealth is emphasised on the notes too. It's not just chance that the K20 note, the largest denomination note, features an illustration of that most valuable of village animals, the pig.

Kina & Toea Coins

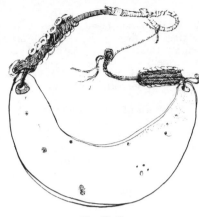

Kina Shell

A\$1 = K0.65
US\$1 = K0.83
UK£1 = K1.63
NZ\$1 = K0.59
HK\$1 = K0.11
S\$1 = K0.43
DM1 = K0.54

At the time of independence the kina was on a par with the Australian dollar and many expatriates took great pains to ensure that their future salaries should be set in dollars rather than kina. This was a major mistake since the kina zoomed steadily ahead for years after independence. A high value kina does wonders for keeping the inflation rate down but it does make the country uncomfortably expensive for outsiders.

Most international currency travellers' cheques are acceptable. Banks can be found in all the big towns, but off the beaten track you may have trouble finding a place to change money. Don't run short. If you plan to spend time in the villages, make sure you have smaller denomination notes and a supply of coins.

There is one easy way of carrying money around and that is to open a passbook savings account with a PNG bank. You can then withdraw money from your account at any branch around the country: it's faster than changing travellers' cheques and you get interest on your money. It's relatively simple and straightforward to have money transferred to a bank in PNG from overseas.

The Papua New Guinea Banking Corporation (PNGBC) will honour pass-

book savings accounts (with blacklight signatures) held by customers of the Australian Commonwealth Bank. Using your Commonwealth Bank passbook, you can withdraw up to A$300 a week at any PNGBC branch.

The PNGBC was once a part of the Commonwealth Bank and is widely represented, so is Westpac and, to a lesser extent, the Bank of South Pacific (a member of the National Australia Group) and the Australia & New Zealand Banking Group (ANZ). Banking hours are 9 am to 2 pm from Monday to Thursday and 9 am to 5 pm on Fridays.

Credit Cards

Plastic money is yet to take off significantly, although both American Express and Diners Club are accepted by the ritzier hotels and restaurants and by Air Niugini and Talair. Amex will give cash advances from their office in Port Moresby (the Coral Seas Travel Service, located in the PNGBC Building).

The ubiquitous Australian Bankcard is unknown and neither Mastercard nor Visa are accepted. Under special circumstances (extreme desperation!) the main Westpac branches will charge a customer the price of a call to Australia (to check credit worthiness) and issue cash advances against a Mastercard. The PNGBC will do the same with a Commonwealth Bank Keycard.

Bargaining & Tipping

Bargaining is not a natural part of most day to day transactions. It is never a game or an integral, enjoyable part of shopping as it is in Asia. Prices in the markets are set and fair (often they are clearly displayed) and prices on PMVs are also set.

The only time you will come across anything approximating bargaining (serious negotiation would be a more appropriate description) is when you are being charged for a photograph, buying artefacts or are hiring a guide or boatman. With artefacts you are inevitably offered an outrageous first price and you are expected to ask for the 'second price'. This is normally what the vendor believes his goods are worth, but there is, if the vendor is desperate for cash, sometimes a 'third price'.

Sometimes negotiations for things like a river trip will take days – don't forget about Melanesian time. Be low key, not aggressive. This is not an Asian game and you could easily offend someone.

Do not tip, it isn't expected.

Traditional Wealth

Although the country has shifted to a cash economy to a great extent, traditional forms of wealth are still very important, particularly in the Highlands and on the Milne Bay islands. A wad of banknotes can never have the same impact as kina shells, cassowaries or pigs. A large sow might be worth around K600, but most Papua New Guineans would rather have the pig. Unfortunately another sign of wealth that is now displayed at paybacks and at ceremonial exchanges in the Highlands is a good stack of beer.

Kina shells are large half-moons cut from the gold lip pearl shell – they are worn as personal embellishments, particularly for ceremonial occasions in the Highlands. The kina coin (there is no one kina note) has a large hole in the centre, probably with the idea that it too could be worn round the neck. They are the most tangible reminder of the centuries old trade links across the country.

In the Highlands, another traditional display of wealth is the *aumak*, a chain of tiny bamboo rods worn around the neck. Each rod indicates that the wearer has lent out 10 or so kina shells. A long row of these little lengths of bamboo is an indication of great wealth.

In Milne Bay, traditional money is still commonly used alongside the modern paper version. Shell money is worn like a necklace and is made of hundreds of small, finely ground, red shell disks. A necklace is worth about K2 an inch. Leaf money or *doba* is made out a bundle of etched and dried banana leaves (one bundle equals about 20 toea) and grass skirts are also negotiable currency (K3 to K5). *Bagi*, the elaborate shell jewellery that is ritually traded around the islands, is the most important mark of prestige and wealth.

COSTS

PNG is expensive and one of the primary reasons for this sad state of affairs is the spectacular geography. Because the country is so mountainous and rugged and includes so many offshore islands, air transport is often the only feasible method of moving goods and people – and this is expensive.

Another factor is historical: PNG has shot from the stone age to the plastic age in an incredibly short period of time, and in many places these two ages and related economies continue to operate side by side. The plastic-age, money-oriented economy is centred on the towns. This includes the hotels and restaurants that largely fill the needs of expats, public servants and others who have large incomes and expense accounts. It also includes the markets, trade stores and PMVs, which are relatively cheap and meet the needs of normal people. Unfortunately the top end of the town-based economy is expensive and the bottom end fails to deliver everything a budget traveller needs.

There is, for instance, no tradition of cheap hotels and restaurants (like there is in Asia) because when Papua New Guineans travel, they stay with their wantoks (relatives). No real urban culture has developed (cities are a very new idea), so street life and night life are virtually non-existent. Cheap, pleasant eating spots are extremely rare – there is no demand for them.

Another reason for high costs in the cash economy is that many commodities, including basic foodstuffs, are imported.

Australia did not encourage the development of industries that would compete with Australian producers and for many years regarded PNG as a captive export market. Because the PNG market is so small, import-replacement industries are only developing slowly.

Once you start walking and get out of the towns, however, you move into another, almost cashless, economy where you can live for virtually nothing – for there is virtually nothing to buy! The possibilities for shoestring travel are limitless and the rewards are terrific. You can walk through areas where roads don't exist, you can buy canoes and travel down rivers. All you have to do is get to the end of a secondary road and start putting one foot in front of the other. There's always a place to stay – in village guesthouses, kiap houses, missions, community schools or police stations.

Amongst the travellers who do this are a hardy breed who proudly boast of travelling for weeks virtually without spending a toea. This is certainly possible, but only if you abuse the hospitality of the villages and the missions, can survive for long periods on sago or sweet potato (we're talking breakfast, lunch and dinner) and enjoy walking and paddling. This kind of travel can be very demanding but, discounting the question of exploiting the locals, there is no better way to see the country or meet the people. And sago for a week is definitely bearable!

Despite the offers of local hospitality, paying your own way is very important. Two or three kina for a night's accommodation and a kina or some sort of trade store food in exchange for a meal is fair. Melanesian hospitality is based on an exchange system with the aim of cultivating a long term relationship. The tourist, passing through, has no role in this tradition of hospitality. When you do give or pay something in exchange for this hospitality, traditional responsibilities are fulfilled, the village is supported and, hopefully, the next visitor is welcomed.

The bottom line is that if you don't restrict your travel to a single, well-planned shoestring expedition, you will find yourself spending a lot of money. Beware of some entrepreneurs who try to make a virtue out of this by claiming they only want to attract 'quality' tourists – meaning big spending, wealthy tourists! I think it's one thing to try to attract 'quality' tourists by offering superior, albeit expensive, standards and quite another to ask these 'quality' tourists to pay expensively for the same old shoddy standards misrepresented as 'quality'.

Unfortunately shoddy is a word that is appropriate to quite a few places in PNG, and even those that are not shoddy can rarely be described as good value. The Melanesian outlook on life – an easygoing approach that is in refreshing contrast to the outlook most westerners have – can, in western terms, lead to things happening slowly and carelessly. In general, the country badly needs more reasonable prices.

From an entirely selfish point of view, all this may not be a bad thing. The cost and relative difficulty of travel means very few places in the country are affected by mass tourism. There does, however, appear to be a growing awareness on the part of the government that tourism could make a worthwhile contribution to the economy. Some attempts at setting up policies and dealing with industry problems are in the works, so the situation could begin to change. It seems inevitable that the numbers of visitors will increase – so get there as soon as you can!

TOURIST INFORMATION

There are few outlets for general tourist information in PNG and not many outside. One of the best sources is Air Niugini. They play a major role in promoting tourism and most offices are helpful and have some printed information to give away. If you're outside the country, don't forget the embassies (see the Visas section for addresses) and, if you want glossy pictures, contact tour operators (see the Activities section for addresses).

The PNG Tourist Office intends to establish an information office at the airport, just to the left of the exit to the international arrivals hall, but this has been planned for some time. They do, however, publish a visitors guide and an annual accommodation directory which is useful for up-to-date information on hotel prices.

A number of provincial governments have officials whose responsibilities include tourism, although they don't have a specific department. You would stand a good chance of reaching them if you addressed your query: Tourist Officer, Department of Commerce, (name of province). There are actually real live Tourist Offices in Madang and Rabaul – both are worth visiting – and a number of other provincial boards, bureaus and offices.

National
Air Niugini
  PO Box 7186, Boroko, PNG (tel 25 9000)
PNG Tourist Office
  PO Box 7144, Boroko, PNG (tel 25 1269)

Provincial
East New Britain Tourist Office
  PO Box 385, Rabaul, East New Britain, PNG (tel 92 1813)
East Sepik Tourist Board
  BMS Freemail Bag, Wewak, East Sepik Province, PNG (tel 86 2112)
Manus Division of Commerce, Culture & Tourism
  PO Box 111, Lorengau, Manus Province, PNG (tel 40 9088)
Milne Bay Visitors' Bureau
  PO Box 337, Alotau, Milne Bay Province, PNG (tel 61 1114)
North Solomons Tourism Office
  PO Box 123, Arawa, North Solomons Province, PNG (tel 95 1244)
West New Britain Tourist Office
  PO Box 425, Kimbe, West New Britain, PNG (tel 93 5057)

GENERAL INFORMATION
Post
There is no mail delivery service so if you're writing to people within PNG you must address your letters to post office boxes. Box numbers of hotels and useful companies are given throughout the book. Add the name of the relevant town and the province:

Niugini Guest House
PO Box 108
Wewak
East Sepik Province

There's a poste restante service at most post offices. Underline the surname and print it clearly if you want the letter to arrive safely. Even then you have to cross your fingers. On a recent trip to PNG, of five letters sent to me, I only got one. All of them had been mailed with plenty of time in hand.

The amount of time a letter takes to be delivered varies radically - it can take from three days to three weeks to travel between Australia and PNG. However, if you have a fixed address, mail usually seems to be quite reliable.

The overseas mail service from PNG is generally good. Wrap parcels carefully as surface mail can be very rough. Allow about three months for parcel post from PNG to North America. If they're packed in cardboard cartons, with paper packing, masks or other purchases should get back OK.

Postage Rates

letters within PNG	15t
aerogrammes	35t
airmail letters per 20 gm to:	
Australia, New Zealand	35t
Asia	45t
Europe, North America	45t

Telephones
The phone system in PNG, although limited to the main centres, is extremely good - another example of how the infrastructure seems totally out of line with the overall economy. You can direct

dial between all the main centres, and there are no area codes to worry about. Long distance calls within PNG are cheaper from 6 pm to 6 am. You can also direct dial Australia, even from public pay phones. Simply dial 3 then the Australian area code and number.

Pay phones are like the green Australian STD (Standard Trunk Dialling) phones. It costs 10t for local calls. Keep feeding coins in each time the light shines for long distance or overseas calls. Your money is refunded if the call fails or if you've inserted more coins than you have used. Unfortunately, pay phones can be hard to find, particularly in Port Moresby where there are not enough phones to start with and many are vandalised. Some big hotels may allow you to use their phones but the cost is likely to be higher.

Electricity
The electric current on the national grid is 240 volts, AC 50Hz (the same as in Australia). While all the towns have electrical supplies most of PNG does not have power, other than that provided by the occasional privately owned generator.

Time

The time throughout Papua New Guinea is the same as Australian Eastern Standard Time – nine or 10 hours ahead of GMT. PNG is so close to the equator, day and night are almost equal in duration and it gets dark quickly. The sun rises about 6 am and sets at about 6 pm.

Don't confuse PNG official time with the unofficial Melanesian time. Melanesian time can be very flexible; make sure you roll with it rather than fight against it! The west's clock-watching phobia has not yet infected much of the South Pacific, so you should not assume other people will regard punctuality as a primary virtue – there are other priorities. Although it's as well to remember that things will often be half an hour late, don't forget they can also be half an hour early!

Business Hours

Most offices are open from 7.45 or 8 am to 4 pm. Shops generally stay open later, especially on Friday nights and they're also open on Saturday mornings. Trade stores and snack bars usually have more liberal hours.

Banks are open 9 am to 2 pm, Monday to Thursday and until 5 pm on Friday. At Port Moresby airport there's a bank agency which opens for the arrival of all international flights – but not necessarily for departures.

Post offices are open 9 am to 5 pm and are also open on Saturday mornings. There's generally not much point in visiting government offices between 12.30 and 2 pm even though lunch officially starts at 1 pm and finishes at 1.30 pm.

Alcohol licensing regulations vary from province to province, so the hours publicans can sell beer vary.

Weights & Measures

Papua New Guinea uses the metric system. See the back pages of this book for conversion tables.

MEDIA
Newspapers

It's often said that one of the best ways to understand a small place is to read the papers – from cover to cover, classified ads and all. There are two dailies: the *Post Courier*, which is a part of Citizen Rupert Murdoch's empire, and the *Niugini News*, which was owned by the mainstream churches' Word Publishing Company, but was sold to Talair late in 1987. Both are tabloid size, but more serious than that format usually indicates.

Make sure you look for the *Grass Roots* comic strip in the *Post Courier* – it is hugely popular, very funny and, like all good cartoons, not afraid of attacking sacred cows, let alone pigs! Otherwise, the readers' letters provide the most local colour. There's always at least one letter complaining about or, praising the PMVs, the rudeness of some segment of the population or the rough deal some public figure is currently getting. Not quite as regular, but almost, are the scandalised letters from missionaries who appear to be in a state of constant anxiety that Sodom and Gomorrah will turn up in PNG. Other vexing questions include bride prices and the ever present rascal problem.

If you buy nothing else, it is worth buying the *Times of PNG* (which is still produced by the Word people), a good-quality weekly review that will give you excellent background on current issues and some interesting and provocative columns. The commentators have a wide range of perspectives and the paper is rarely 'churchy', apart, that is, from in the amazing Bishop David Hand's column. At the risk of quoting the good Bishop (and Censorship Board member) out of context, a recent column included the following:

It is said that Adolf Hitler, knowing how thoroughly pornography can weaken the will and character, flooded Holland and France with such material prior to invading them, and – despite much bravery – they fell like 'ninepins' in 1939/40.

Once a month the *Times* includes a free colour magazine, *Travellers' Times*, that you cannot afford to miss. It includes up-to-the-minute information on places to stay and things to do and does not concentrate exclusively on expensive resorts.

The Word people also publish a weekly magazine in Pidgin – *Wantok*. If you doubt the vitality and utility of the Pidgin language make sure you buy a copy.

In remote parts of the country a newspaper, no matter how old, is worth more than its newsstand price – the paper is used to make roll-your-own cigarettes. Imported newspapers are preferred for a 'quality smoke' with connoisseurs giving unanimous approval to the *Sydney Morning Herald*.

The Rise & Fall of the Phantom

This is a sad saga of the mighty Phantom – you know, the 'ghost who walks', the guy in the tight-fitting one-piece suit who lives in the Skull Cave of Bangalla and runs around righting wrongs and never marrying Diana. For a while the Phantom, hero of countless comic strips, was immensely popular in PNG and this popularity briefly put PNG newspapers into the world spotlight.

The Phantom's rise to national fame began when *Wantok* started operations in 1972 and published the comic strip translated into Pidgin. Soon his fame spread through the

country and copies of *Wantok* were zealously hoarded until someone able to read came by and provided a public reading. The government put the Phantom to work for them – promoting the virtues of toothbrushes or, as in the poster illustrated, the nutritional wonders of the peanut: 'If you eat plenty of peanuts you'll grow up strong, just like the Phantom'. Posters were no sooner pinned up in villages than they were swiped for home decorations.

But disaster lurked near to hand. The *Post Courier* also ran the Phantom and in fact held exclusive rights. In 1977 they decided that the Pidgin Phantom had to go. Their strip was in English, and ran well ahead of the *Wantok* version, but international copyright laws proved stronger than the hero of the Skull Cave. A flurry of protests were carried as far as the Australian Foreign Minister who decided it was not really important enough to justify taking action.

Sadly, you can no longer read such poetic lines as those that were written to the Phantom by his greatest admirer, 'Lewa bilong mi, longtaim tumas mi no bin lukim yu. Wataim bai me lukim yu gen? Mi krai long yu. Mi Diana.' You can't even read the considerably less poetic English version; the Phantom has retired to his cave.

Radio & Television

The National Broadcasting Commission operates an AM and FM radio station in Port Moresby, as well as a number of provincial services.

Television is a recent introduction. Although satellite TV and videos have been available for some time there were no local stations until midway through 1987 when two stations began transmitting to the Port Moresby area. Both stations are privately owned by Australian companies (Niugini Television Corporation by Kevin Parry and Media Niugini by Alan Bond) although there are moves afoot to force them to be 50% locally owned.

Videos are widespread and popular throughout the country – you'll see them in hotels, trade stores and kai shops. Unfortunately, the films they show are often low-quality and extremely violent.

Satellite dishes are also becoming more common. Depending on where you are it is possible to receive TV programmes from Australia (the ABC), Malaysia, or Guam (American).

There was a great deal of debate before local TV stations were allowed: Does the country need TV? What controls should there be? What effect will there be on the local culture? A quick glance through a newspaper TV guide will show the critics' fears are justified. It is difficult to imagine how the stations argue that shows like *My Three Sons*, *Minder* and *A Team* will make a positive contribution to PNG society – although they're certainly not as bad as video *Rambos*.

In late 1987 a bill was introduced to Parliament to force local ownership of the TV stations, but also to give powers of censorship over all the media to a tribunal, and the Minister for Communications. The reaction from the press and opposition politicians has been one of outrage.

HEALTH

No vaccinations are necessary unless you are coming from a country where yellow fever or cholera is a problem. An International Health Card is not required. With the exception of malaria, there are no serious health problems. It is, however, a rugged country where the environment demands respect and the medical services are often overstretched.

Each provincial capital has a hospital and the quality of the staff is apparently good – but they're short of equipment and crowded, so if you did get seriously sick you'd be wise to fly out to Australia, or home. There are private doctors (they're not cheap) in most main towns and dentists in Moresby, Lae and Rabaul.

As much protection as possible is always a wise idea when travelling, so in addition to the *essential* malaria tablets consider cholera, tetanus, typhoid and hepatitis vaccinations.

Simple cuts and scratches can very easily get infected in the tropics, so special care should be taken to keep them clean and dry. Mercurochrome will help and an antibiotic cream or powder is a very useful item to carry. On my first visit to PNG a simple little graze on my ankle took a dose of penicillin to heal it up when I eventually got home. An anti-histamine cream or tablets can also be handy to deal with insect bites or skin allergies and reactions.

Health Insurance

Get some! You may never need it but if you do it's worth a million. There are lots of travel insurance policies available and any travel agent will be able to recommend one. Get one which will pay for your flight home if you are really sick. Make sure it will cover the money you lose for forfeiting a booked flight, and that it will cover the cost of flying your travelling companion home with you. Get your teeth checked before you set out.

Medical Kit

Give some careful thought to your medical kit if you plan to get off the beaten track, although this is not necessary if you are staying in the towns. The further you get from the towns in general the further you will be from medical help. PNG has an impressive system where health workers live in the villages, but there is a shortage of trained people and even if you do find someone, the facilities and drugs they have are often very limited.

Take medical advice and research how to treat yourself if you are going to be isolated for any length of time. John Hatt's book *Tropical Traveller* is a very worthwhile investment. You should be in a position to treat malaria, dysentery, lacerations (it's not hard to hurt yourself with a machete), sprains (it's very rugged country), insect and snake bites (some are highly venomous) and respiratory diseases (colds and even pneumonia are common in the Highlands).

Malaria
The most serious health risk is malaria. It virtually wiped out the early German attempts at colonising the north coast and it's still a very serious problem. Although it is the isolated villagers who suffer the most, the disease kills quite indiscriminately and, sometimes, in spite of medical care. Fortunately, prevention is simply a matter of taking a regular dose of the anti-malarial drugs you are prescribed.

Malaria has shown a frightening capacity to mutate drug-resistant strains. PNG is now host to malarial strains that can cause cerebral malaria and are resistant to Chloroquine, the most popular anti-malarial drug. Tell your doctor where you are going and he will probably prescribe Maloprim, in addition to Chloroquine, unless there is a specific contraindication. You will have no problems getting the appropriate drugs in PNG but the course of medication must be started some weeks before you arrive and continued after you leave.

Many local health workers and nurses decry the use of Fansidar, which is also sometimes used as an adjunct to Chloroquine. Aside from being dangerous in its own right (it is actually banned as a preventive measure in some parts of the world due to its side effects) it is also used as a last-ditch cure. No one is happy about the prospect of a Fansidar-resistant strain developing, a prospect that becomes more likely the more indiscriminately it is used.

You can take further precautions to avoid malaria by preventing mosquitoes from biting with repellent, nets, or clothing which gives more body coverage. The most important time to keep covered is in the evenings and early night. Dengue fever, also carried by mosquitoes, is another PNG health danger.

Heat
Beware the tropical sun! Wear a hat that is broad enough to shade the back of your neck (especially if you're in a boat or a canoe) try to keep your skin covered and apply liberal quantities of an effective sunscreen. The sun can be deceptive. If it is lightly overcast you can still get burnt; if you are at any decent altitude in the Highlands, you have less atmospheric protection and the fact that you're not hot does not mean you're not cooking.

Make sure you drink plenty of liquid and, especially if you're very active, replace the salt you lose through sweating. If you're only passing a small quantity of very yellow urine, drink more water; if you're suffering unusual cramps, add more salt to your food.

Heat can also make you impatient and irritable. Make sure you're dressed appropriately in light, preferably cotton, clothes, and try to take things at a slower pace if you find it gets to you. You will discover an appropriate Melanesian pace sooner or later, but it's better if it's sooner!

You may be unlucky enough to suffer from prickly heat when you first arrive. This is a condition where sweat droplets are trapped under the skin (because your pores aren't able to cope with the volume of water) forming many tiny blisters. Anything that makes you sweat makes it worse. Calamine lotion or zinc-oxide based talcum powder will give some relief but, apart from that, all you can do is take it easy for a few days until you acclimatise.

Cold

Not only do you have to worry about getting too hot, but also about getting too cold! Admittedly this is only relevant if you plan to climb the mountains, but if you do, you must be prepared to cope with extreme weather conditions. Even snow is possible on Mt Wilhelm, although that might be preferable to the more likely fog and rain. Hypothermia (otherwise known as exposure) is a quick and effective killer and once again prevention is better than cure.

It's deceptively easy to fall victim to hypothermia through a combination of wind, wet clothing, fatigue and hunger, even if the air temperature is well above freezing. Hypothermia's symptoms include a loss of rationality so people can fail to recognise their own condition and the seriousness of their predicament.

Symptoms are exhaustion, numb skin (particularly toes and fingers), shivering, slurred speech, irrational or violent behaviour, lethargy, stumbling, dizzy spells, muscle cramps and violent bursts of energy. Anticipate the problem if you're cold and tired, and recognise the symptoms early. Immediate care is important since hypothermia can kill its victims in as little as two hours.

The first response should be to find shelter from wind and rain, remove wet clothing and replace with warm dry clothing. The patient should drink hot liquids (not alcohol) and eat some high calorie, easily digestible food. These measures will usually correct the problem if symptoms have been recognised early. In more severe cases it may be necessary to place the patient in a sleeping bag insulated from the ground, with another person if possible, while the he/she is fed warm food and hot drinks. Do *not* rub the patient, place him/her near a fire, try to give an unconscious patient food or drink, remove wet clothes in the wind, or give him/her alcohol.

Altitude – Mountain Sickness

Although you are more likely to be affected by altitude in the Himalaya or the Andes it is quite possible to be affected on a number of PNG's mountains.

Mountain Sickness, Soroche, Altitude Sickness, Acute Mountain Sickness (AMS) – whatever you call it – can in extreme cases be fatal. In all probability however, you will only be lightly affected.

AMS starts to become noticeable at around 3000 metres, becomes pronounced at 3700 metres, and then requires adjustments at each 500 metres of additional elevation after that. The summit of Mt Wilhelm is over 4500 metres high, so if you make a sudden ascent from Lae to Kegsugl, by PMV or plane, and then commence the climb without giving your body a couple of days to adjust to the new altitudes you are likely to make the expedition unnecesarily difficult, even dangerous. Your body has to undergo a physiological change to absorb more oxygen from the rarefied air and this takes time.

Mild symptoms to be expected over 3000 metres are headaches and weakness; loss of appetite; shortness of breath; insomnia, often accompanied by irregular breathing; mild nausea; a dry cough; slight loss of co-ordination; and a puffy face or hands in the morning. If you experience a few of these symptoms you probably have a mild case of altitude sickness which should pass. You should rest until the symptoms subside but if the symptoms become more severe or do not improve you may have to descend to a lower altitude. Monitor your condition carefully and realistically.

Severe altitude sickness brought on by a rapid ascent to high altitudes can result in pulmonary oedema (the lungs fill with fluids), or a cerebral oedema (fluid collects on the brain) which can be fatal.

Symptoms of severe altitude sickness include marked loss of co-ordination, dizziness, and walking as if intoxicated; severe headaches; serious shortness of breath with mild activity; severe nausea and vomiting; extreme lassitude, loss of interest in food, conversation, and self-preservation; abnormal speech and behavior, progressing to delirium and coma; reduced urine output; bubbly breath, or persistent coughing spasms that produce watery or coloured sputum.

The only cure for AMS is immediate descent to lower altitudes. When any combination of these severe symptoms occur, the afflicted person should descend 300 to 1000 metres *immediately*, the distance increasing with the severity of the symptoms. When trekking, such a descent may even have to take place at night (responding quickly is vital), and the disabled person should be accompanied by someone in good condition. There's no cure for AMS except descending to lower altitudes, but a pain-killer for headaches and an anti-emetic for vomiting will help relieve the symptoms.

Diarrhoea & Dysentery
Although this problem does not seem to be nearly as severe in PNG as in some of the neighbouring Asian countries it is likely you'll get some kind of diarrhoea when you first arrive. This is the normal lot of travellers whose bodies are adapting to strange food and water and you'll probably recover quickly.

Food, at least in the main cities, is generally problem free and town water is drinkable. If you do plan to rough it in the bush, consider taking some kind of vitamin and mineral tablets to supplement your diet of sago and sweet potato. Outside the towns you are wise to be wary of the water, unless you're sure you know its history! Until you are very high in the mountains, the crystal-clear stream that looks so inviting is likely to have gone through several backyards! Take water purification tablets, preferably iodine based, as the iodine is effective against cysts and other resilient nasties. It doesn't taste great, but that's a small price to pay.

Avoid rushing off to the pharmacy and filling yourself with antibiotics at the first signs of a problem. The best thing to do is eat nothing and rest, avoid travelling and drink plenty of liquid (black tea or sterile water). About 24 to 48 hours should do the trick. If you really can't cope with starving, keep to a diet of yoghurt, boiled vegetables, apples and apple juice. After a severe bout of diarrhoea or dysentery you will be dehydrated and this often causes painful cramps. Relieve these by drinking fruit juices or tea into which a small spoonful of salt has been dissolved; maintaining a correct balance of salt in your bloodstream is important.

If starving doesn't work or if you really have to move on and can't rest, there is a range of drugs available. *Lomotil* is probably one of the best, though it has come under fire recently in medical literature. The dosage is two tablets, three times a day for two days. If you can't find Lomotil, then try *Pesulin* or *Pesulin-O* (the latter includes tincture of opium). The dosage is two teaspoons, four times daily for five days.

Ordinary traveller's diarrhoea rarely lasts more than about three days. If it lasts for more than a week you must get treatment, move on to antibiotics, or see a doctor.

If you are unfortunate enough to contract dysentery there are two types: bacillary, the most common, acute and rarely persistent; and amoebic, persistent and more difficult to treat. Both are characterised by very liquid shit containing blood and/or excessive amounts of mucus.

Bacillary dysentery attacks suddenly and is accompanied by fever, nausea and painful muscular spasms. Often it responds well to antibiotics or other specific drugs. Amoebic dysentery builds up more slowly, but is more dangerous, so get it treated as soon as possible. See a doctor.

SAFETY

Unfortunately, on the rare occasions when PNG is featured in the outside world's news media, it is likely to be a sensationalist report about some kind of violence. As a result of these reports and the foggy, often inaccurate notions many people have of the past (featuring fierce, head-hunting warriors), PNG is often unjustifiably classified as a high-risk country.

You will get your first taste of these attitudes when you tell your friends your planned destination: 'You're going *where*?' You will get your second taste when you get to Moresby, where houses are barricaded like you've never seen them before, and start talking to expats. Everyone will have a favourite gruesome story they will want to tell you. Do not be deterred! If you take reasonable care and use a bit of common sense, you are most unlikely to experience anything other than tremendous friendliness and hospitality.

You will certainly not get an arrow in the back or have your head hunted. Even looked at historically, this should be seen in perspective. In the early days of colonisation the local people were fighting white invaders who were often very unsavoury characters. The Highlands were still being opened up in the '50s and until that time there was no indigenous concept of a large western-style nation; each tribe was, in effect, a sovereign state so its relations with its neighbours or the white invaders were 'foreign affairs'. And foreign affairs often became warfare, although never on a scale to match the conflicts most countries in Europe have witnessed.

Payback squabbles, land disputes and the like, can still develop into full-scale tribal wars, but they are confined to the direct participants. I heard a reliable story of fighting stopping so a tour group could cross a battlefield, and many expats will tell you of battles they have watched from close at hand. These are not exploits I would recommend unless you are very confident that you know what you are doing, but all reports suggest that as long as you don't put yourself in the firing line at the wrong time (and this will be quite obvious, one way or another) you will be left alone as a complete irrelevance!

Although a little caution is wise wherever you are, the places where people are most likely to have difficulties are in the larger towns, and parts of the Highlands. In common with many other countries, it is not always safe to wander around at night and this is doubly the case for women. It should be noted that crime is in no way race related and that relations between different nationalities are remarkably good.

Unfortunately the rascal (crime) problem has grown worse over the past few years. Some of the background to this is discussed at greater length in the Law & Order section of the Facts About the Country chapter. An increase in expectations among the young, unemployment in the towns, land shortages in the Highlands, unequal economic distribution, a police force that lacks effectiveness and even some traditional Melanesian attitudes, are all contributing factors.

Whatever the reasons, you have to be careful, but without becoming paranoid! Make friends with Papua New Guineans, don't close yourself off. Not only will this add to your enjoyment, but also to your security – you will be identified with a local and have access to first-hand advice and information. There are few places in the world where a smile and a greeting ('*Moning*', '*Apinun*') are so well received.

You cannot afford to be entirely naive about your popularity, however, because you may well be regarded as a potential source of status, or even wealth. How do you judge whether someone is sincere, or up to no good? There's no easy answer, but you do have to be sceptical and you do have to use your brains. Even if you do decide that someone is all right, don't put yourself in a vulnerable position until you have more than a first impression to go on.

Women should always dress conservatively, even when swimming. Outside the resorts, bikinis do not provide sufficient cover – a laplap (sarong) can come in handy as a wrap. Take your cue from the local women – sometimes you'll notice them washing *fully* clothed. Whether on a beach or in a city, lone women should restrict their movements to areas where there are other people around and never wander off by themselves.

In many ways Papua New Guinean women have a very hard time and this does effect the situation for visitors. Except in the cities, women are almost always subservient to men and physical abuse is common. In many parts of of the country a women never initiates a conversation with a man, never talks to a male outside her family, never eats at the same table as men, never even sleeps in the same house as any man, including her father or husband.

A lone, western woman traveller has no local parallels and, to a certain extent, a special case will be made of her. Virtually throughout the country, however, it will be difficult for women to have a normal conversation with a man without being misinterpreted as a flirt. Similarly, but in reverse, a western man who attempts to initiate a conversation with a Papua New Guinean woman can cause embarrassment and confusion.

Despite the obvious difficulties we have received a number of letters from women who have clearly enjoyed travelling around by themselves. And throughout the country you'll find women working as administrators, entrepreneurs, pilots, teachers, nurses, missionaries, adventure travel tour guides . . . so it definitely can be done!

I would recommend that women do not travel alone in PNG, especially if they haven't travelled before in a highly sexist society.

Port Moresby, Lae and Mt Hagen have a reputation for having the worst crime problems, followed by almost all the Highland towns, Rabaul, Kieta, Madang and Wewak. It's not worth considering walking around Moresby, Lae and Hagen at night. Even in a group, you are vulnerable and there's just no point. There is nothing to see or do on the streets. If you plan to go out to a restaurant or club, catch the last PMV, which normally runs sometime between 6 and 6.30 pm, and get a lift or a taxi home. It's worth being especially careful on the fortnightly Friday pay nights – things can get pretty wild.

If you're travelling in the Highlands, it's wise to stay off the roads after dark; the risks of hold-ups are far greater at night. The Baiyer River road is particularly dangerous – ask around in Mt Hagen before you head out that way, whatever transport you plan to use and whatever the time of day. Plan to catch PMVs early in the morning so you will reach your destination in daylight, with plenty of time to get your bearings and find somewhere to sleep before dark.

You are most unlikely to have any trouble on a PMV, but if you're by yourself, it probably pays to pick a clean, newish one with a reasonably mixed crowd of men and women on board. Not that you often see empty PMVs! It isn't particularly common, but there are pickpockets and bag snatchers, so be a little cautious in crowded places like PMVs, bus stops and markets. Don't ever leave valuables unattended in any public place.

Everything is saner and better away from the towns – the people are friendlier and there are considerably fewer problems. If you are staying in the villages and you have a choice, stay with a family rather than in an empty haus tambaran or haus kiap. It's safer and more fun. In most cases, you'll also be much better off with a guide who speaks the local *ples tok* (dialect). You won't be so likely to get lost, the guide will know when and who to ask for the various permissions you will need (to camp, to cross someone's land, etc) and you'll have automatic introductions to local people. If you are looking for a guide, start by asking around for someone reliable at missions, government offices, schools or trade stores. Whatever your plans, talk to as many people as you can and listen to their advice.

We have *never* had any problems anywhere in the country. As one traveller wrote:

Everywhere I went I met friendly people. I was always the only white person on board PMVs yet people would offer me food and go out of their way to be helpful. I was even invited to spend the night in someone's home in Goroka. Walking along the road to Baiyer River, I had a bloke run up to me and hand me a pineapple. Coming in to Lae after dark, the PMV drove me to the door of the friends with whom I was staying. Meeting people like that, even if I couldn't talk to many of them, really was the high point of my visit to PNG.

FILM & PHOTOGRAPHY
PNG is very photogenic and you can easily run through a lot of film, particularly if you happen on some event like a big Highland sing-sing. Bring more film than you'll need and then more again. Film is easily available in the major towns, but it is fairly expensive, even by Australian standards.

Protect your film and your camera from the dust, humidity and heat as much as you can. It is worth considering taking a small cleaning kit, and spare batteries. You're unlikely to have your luggage X-rayed before you get into a Sepik canoe, but a lead-lined film bag will help to keep your film cool.

Allow for the high intensity of the tropical sun when making your settings. Even on bright sunny days, however, it can be surprisingly dim in the jungle or a shady village so you'll also need long exposures, especially if you're taking photos of dark-skinned people. I found I used quite a lot of ASA (ISO) 400 film, and a flash can also be useful, particularly for shots inside the Sepik haus tambarans.

Never take a photograph in or of a haus tambaran (or any other 'spirit house') without asking permission. These are holy places and you could quickly find yourself in trouble if you do not respect the wishes and feelings of their guardians. It's best to ask several of the male elders first to make sure you do actually speak to someone who has the authority to grant your request.

You'll find the local people are generally very happy to be photographed, even going out of their way to pose for you, particularly at sing-sings. It is absolutely essential to ask permission before you snap. However, at the very least, remember the standards of privacy you would expect at home, although this is not fail-safe – you cannot assume your standards are appropriate until you ask. Don't, for instance, take a photo of someone washing in their bathroom, even if the bathroom is a jungle stream.

You'll rarely have to pay for photographing somebody, but some people, usually men dressed in traditional style, do request payment – about 50t is average but it can be a lot more. People are aware that western photographers can make money out of their exotic photos and see no reason why they shouldn't get some of the action. If you've gone ahead and taken a photo without getting permission and establishing a price, you may well find yourself facing an angry, heavily-armed Highlander who is demanding 10 kina in payment. It would take some nerve to argue.

ACCOMMODATION
The one unfortunate generalisation that you can make about accommodation is that it is too expensive. Overall the quality is pretty good, although often not worth the price, and in most towns your options are limited.

Booking ahead is a good idea, especially

for moderately priced hotels and guest-houses. Most are only small and don't take many people before they are full. Spend a few toea to make a booking over the excellent phone system and you could avoid arriving to find the one cheap place is full, and the only alternative is a luxury hotel room or a wet tent. Booking ahead is especially important if there is a festival of some kind. Transport between airports and towns is often non-existent or exorbitant in price, so most hosts will pick you up, if they know you're coming – another saving. If you're booking by mail remember there is no postal delivery and you must write to a post office box number.

Camping

There are virtually no real camping grounds in PNG, so unless you plan to camp in police station compounds or do some serious hiking, a tent is of little value.

There are a number of problems with camping. Firstly, every square inch of country has a traditional owner whose permission *must* be obtained before you set up occupation. It may look like deserted bush to you, but there will almost always be people coming and going around what are, in fact, their traditional properties. The owner may live just around the corner or miles away and when you find him you may well be offered room in a hut anyway. Secondly, there is a problem with security, and you're obviously particularly vulnerable out in the middle of the bush by yourself.

If you are planning to bushwalk, a tent is useful, although you may find it superfluous until you get into the mountains. At low altitudes you are most likely to be following a reasonably well-travelled route (the whole country is criss-crossed with a spider web of well-used walking tracks) and you will either come across villages or bush shelters at regular intervals. The shelters are built especially for weary travellers, like you, to use.

A tent fly can be very useful for helping to waterproof one of these structures and a well-ventilated tent inner can be used as a ground sheet, mosquito net, changing room and general insect barricade in huts wherever you are. The situation does change when you get to higher altitudes because the population density drops, and the weather is much more severe.

Places to Stay – bottom end

In most main centres and towns there are few, if any, inexpensive places to stay. There are no Youth Hostels and virtually no youth-hostel style places, although there are cheap church-run hostels in Lae and Rabaul.

The lifesavers in many towns are the mission-run guesthouses and hostels. The Lutheran guesthouses are particularly good. Although they're not cheap by Asian standards (K10 to K20, meals included), they are much cheaper than hotels and always immaculately kept. They usually offer generous servings of fairly plain food in their communal dining rooms, after a blessing. Although their first responsibility is to look after visiting missionaries and church people, they are usually happy to take travellers if they have room.

Do not expect to treat these places like a hotel; they're quiet and family oriented. Despite this, all sorts of people use them and they are good meeting places. The missionaries can also be helpful with local information and are often very interesting people in their own right. The churches play a very big role in PNG and staying in one of their hostels will give you the opportunity to get a first-hand view of how they operate.

In a few places (including Madang, Mt Hagen and Tufi) there are lodges offering a simple, basic room in a traditional-style house. These are cheap and interesting (K6 to K20) and, perhaps with some luck, may spread. Still, PNG remains off the main Asian route so with low numbers of visitors this sort of thing is not encouraged.

If you're willing to rough it a bit and get well off the track, your accommodation costs can be negligible. Most villages will have a spare hut, or at least spare floor space, where you can stay.

Remember to pay your way. Two to five kina for a night's accommodation, a kina or some trade store food in exchange for a meal is reasonable. Melanesian hospitality is usually given to foster a long term relationship and is based on the idea of exchange. As a transient tourist you don't fit into the traditional patterns, but if you do give something in exchange for hospitality, you will be meeting your traditional responsibility, helping the village, and hopefully ensuring a welcome for the next traveller who comes along.

In many parts of the country, particularly the Highlands, it's worth looking for a *haus kiap* – these are houses kept for the use of the patrol officers (*kiaps*). Since independence government-by-patrol has gone into decline and there are fewer houses around. Many are slowly falling apart – in any case they're often little more than a roof over your head.

You will often find either police, district officers, health workers, teachers, mission workers or expats willing to offer you a place to stay but *do not* expect this as a matter of course. Some people may be only too pleased to see you but, equally, there will be many who have no interest in you at all! It is immensely preferable to write or phone ahead, and set something up in advance, if you can. Remember that many of these people are very poorly paid so, again, make sure you pay your way.

The high schools are often quite isolated and they are all boarding schools, so you could get lucky and find a spare bed with them. It's likely you'll have to sing for your supper, or at the very least do a lot of talking! The school headmaster is certain to be a good source of local information. Last but not least, police stations around the country almost always allow you to camp on their grounds, or use a spare room in their barracks, for no charge.

Places to Stay - top end

Most of the top end hotels are relatively recent constructions, often in a motel style with a few carvings tacked on. Prices range from a little to a lot higher than similar places in Australia. Singles range from K50 to K80. The major centres all have at least one reasonably high standard place. Moresby has a Travelodge and several other five-star hotels but the prices are astronomically high: how does K105 for a single sound?

There are two exceptional luxury hotels, whose nearest equivalents are the famous African safari lodges, and they should not be missed if you have the necessary funds: the Karawari Lodge lies deep in the jungle on a tributary of the Sepik and, best of all, the Ambua Lodge perches at 2000 metres on a ridge in the Southern Highlands overlooking the extraordinary Tari valley.

Another option combines the virtues of comfort and mobility: the *Melanesian Explorer*, soon to be joined by the *Melanesian Explorer II*, is a small, well-appointed ship that cruises the Sepik and the north coast as far as the islands of Milne Bay.

Some of PNG's older hotels were delightfully Somerset Maughamish, right down to the ceiling fans lazily swirling the balmy tropical air, but there are not many left, and most of those that have survived are fading fast.

FOOD

While the food is generally uninspiring, you should manage to eat reasonably well, most of the time. Unless you get off the beaten track, however, you probably won't have much opportunity to try local food. To a western palate that is no great loss since the average diet is made up of bland, starchy foods with very little protein. Western-style PNG food tends to be unimaginative (the roast and three veg category), although if you're prepared to pay top prices, the food in hotels and restaurants can be good. Making up something yourself is an option worth considering. The markets are cheap and fair.

Local Food

In much of the low-lying swamp country the staple food is sago (*saksak*) – a tasteless, starchy extract that is washed from the pith of the sago palm. In the Highlands the staple is the sweet potato (*kaukau*), a native of South America that was brought to Asia by the Spanish and Portuguese around the end of the 15th century. Elsewhere, taros, yams and bananas form the starchy basis of subsistence communities' diets. The situation is sometimes a little more inspiring along the coast because there is excellent seafood and the cooking makes heavier use of spices and even, sometimes, spices like ginger.

The most recent staples to be added to the PNG diet are rice and tinned fish. Their importance is clear if you check a smaller trade store's shelves: they often stock nothing more than rice, tinned mackerel, tobacco and salt. Many people who live in the cities, or who don't have access to a garden, have no other affordable choice. In some parts of the country the tinned fish helps to alleviate a natural protein shortage.

Because of the country's limited animal life, protein deficiency has traditionally been a problem. In many regions potential game (reptiles, birds, rodents and small marsupials) is scarce, but hunting is still important. Apart from fresh fish, which are only available on the coast and some of the rivers, pigs are the main source of meat protein, although they are not generally eaten on a day-to-day basis, but saved for feasts. Chicken is now quite popular although, strangely, eggs are rarely eaten. New varieties of vegetables are also being introduced and developed for local consumption and as cash crops, particularly in the fertile soil of the Highlands valleys.

The most famous local cooking style is the *mumu*, which is an underground oven. A pit is dug, fire-heated stones are placed in the bottom, meat and vegetables are wrapped in herbs and leaves and placed on the stones, the pit is sealed with more branches and leaves, and the contents roast and steam. For feasts the pits may be hundreds of feet long, and filled with hundreds of whole pigs.

Town Food

In all the big towns you'll be able to eat comparatively well in hotels or restaurants. At these places you'll usually find reasonable quality Australian-style food, at prices that are, unfortunately, quite a lot higher than in Australia. Think in terms of K10 and up. Chinese restaurants are reasonably widespread but they are also expensive.

Many of the mission hostels supply meals to their guests and these tend to be very good value. In general, however, the shoestring traveller or backpacker will discover that attempting to find something cheap and wholesome is a frustrating experience.

One possibility that is always worth checking is *The Club*. Almost every town has a club – at one time they were havens for white colonialists, but today their memberships are completely open. The drop in the expat population has thrown many of them on hard times however, and they are generally only too happy to sign in 'out of town' visitors. In most, you'll find you can get excellent, economical *counter meals*. This is an Australian institution: you order your meal at the counter and eat in the bar. There will usually be a blackboard menu offering something like steak sandwiches or burgers with salad and french fries for about K5, sometimes less. Hotels also often have counter meals.

The fast food that is available from kai bars ranges from unthinkably awful to OK. It's usually fried – fish, chicken, lamb chops, rice and chips are the staples – and tends to be monotonous and greasy. You'll find kai bars in every town; bear in mind they usually close by 6.30 pm. Many towns now have sandwich bars or cafes and the large Steamships and Burns Philp chain stores always have a takeaway counter with decent sandwiches. That's about it for prepared food though – nothing exotic, no spices, nothing to write home about.

In addition, there are markets where food is very inexpensive and all the main towns have well-stocked supermarkets. There is no bargaining in the outdoor markets; prices are set and fair and are often clearly displayed. Apart from the starch crops you will find coconuts, pawpaws, sugar cane, corn and various green, leafy vegetables. Some of the cheaper hostels (Salvation Army, CWA) have cooking facilities, but even if you don't have a stove handy, it's easy to rustle up a breakfast or a lunch.

Anyway you cut it, you'll find the cost of eating is a lot lower in neighbouring Indonesia.

Vegetarian Food

You might expect a country where protein deficiency is a chronic problem to be a vegetarian's paradise. In this case you would be wrong. Some of the Chinese restaurants have vegetarian dishes, and you may find reasonable salads at some of the hotel smorgasbords, but in general the pickings are thin (and you will be too, if you are not careful).

The big hotels and restaurants can normally put something together, but in the mission hostels it's a bit more awkward. There's no menu; everyone eats whatever happens to have been cooked and that's that. Again it's possible to organise an exception – after a suitably tiresome explanation.

In the bush, I guarantee you'll find it tedious eating sago, yams or sweet potato for breakfast, lunch and dinner. Meat is sometimes produced and, since you're a visitor, a special effort will be made to procure some. It is very difficult to explain the concept of vegetarianism in Pidgin to someone who belongs to a society that revolves around the killing and eating of pigs! You also run the risk of offending a host who has killed something or other in your honour.

So, make sure you have got cooking equipment, bring vitamin and mineral tablets and, if you are a less than strict vegetarian, you may consider temporarily relaxing your preference!

Beer

The Australian beer culture has been accepted a little too wholeheartedly in PNG. Until 1963, Papua New Guineans were strictly forbidden to consume alcohol; it was for whites only. As the country moved towards self-government, it became obvious that there could not be two laws, one for the locals, one for the expats. Thus, despite some anguished cries that nobody would be safe on the streets, the pubs were opened to all. Twenty-five years later it is clear the effect of beer on PNG has not been a happy one, although you can still walk the streets.

Perhaps there is a connection between the feast-or-famine mentality associated with a pig kill and the consumption of beer: a clan hoards its pigs for months then kills a large number for a feast and embarks on a non-stop orgy of over-consumption. Whatever the reason, some

Papua New Guineans have a propensity to keep on drinking until they are either broke or flat on the floor. This is often conducted in depressing, open-air public bars where it's a simple matter of sink another and another and another until they're all gone.

Various means of fighting the drink problem have been tried – advertising is forbidden, there are heavy taxes and drinking hours are restricted – but none of these measures seem to have much of an effect.

It is worth keeping track of Friday pay nights. If there is going to be trouble, this is the night it is most likely to happen, be it fights, car accidents or robberies. If you're planning to sleep within shouting distance of a bar, forget it!

There are two beers, South Pacific (known as SP) and San Miguel (known as San Mig) both good and both brewed by the same company. A small bottle (known as a *stubby* to Australians) costs about K1 to K1.20. Wine and spirits are very costly, partly in an attempt to restrict their use.

Betel Nut
All through Asia people chew the nut of the Areca palm known as betel nut or, in Pidgin, *buai*. Although it's a (relatively) mild narcotic and digestive stimulant and is widely used in PNG, it's unlikely to attract many western drug fans.

The betel nut is too acidic and slow acting to chew by itself – in PNG, betel nut users generally chew it with lime and seed stalks from a pepper plant. The reaction between the lime and the nut produces the narcotic effect and the extraordinary red stains you'll see splattered along footpaths everywhere. One of the side effects is incredible salivation, which the unpractised find difficult to swallow. The resultant spit can appear to be a most impressive haemorrhage. Prolonged use leads to black teeth, a mouth that is stained a permanent red and, in some cases, mouth cancer.

You'll see the nuts, lime and mustard stalks for sale in every market; sometimes there'll be virtually nothing else. If you decide to try it, take lessons with a local expert. Nuts vary in potency, it is possible to burn yourself with the lime and nausea is a common side effect for the unpractised (remember that first cigarette!).

BOOKS & BOOKSHOPS
There are plenty of books about PNG – all

the wild country, the amazing tribes, the fantastic cultures and the glamour of the last frontier has attracted countless writers and photographers. It was one of the last great areas for European exploration and developed its own sub-category of literature: 'patrol officers' memoirs'. It had a dramatic role in WW II and the developments leading up to Independence were also intriguing. The books that follow are just a small selection of the many that have been written.

Bookshops
You won't find a great selection of books on the country except in Port Moresby, although Mt Hagen, Goroka, Madang and Lae also have shops with reasonable selections. Probably the best bookshop in the country is the University Bookshop in Port Moresby. The Post Newsagent in Moresby also has quite a good selection.

Every major town has a Christian book-shop, and although they stock plenty of books proving Darwin was wrong, and more of that ilk, they can also be very useful. They quite often have excellent stationery supplies (pens, notebooks, envelopes) and interesting general selections as well. They all stock various Pidgin dictionaries and grammar guides and a range of books written in Pidgin, which are useful if you are making a serious attempt to learn the language.

History & Exploration
It's difficult to find much information about the country before Europeans arrived. The simple truth is that not a great deal is known, although this glaring gap is now gradually being filled.

Gavin Souter's intriguing book on the exploration and development of New Guinea, *The Last Unknown* (Angus & Robertson, Sydney, 1963), is the book to read if you read nothing else on PNG. The descriptions of the early explorers, some of whom were more than a little strange, is positively enthralling. It barely touches on WW II and stops well before the '60s rush to independence, but it is a highly enjoyable read. You may have to search for a copy since it's out of print.

Papua New Guinea's Prehistory by Pamela Swadling (PNG National Museum & Art Gallery with Gordon & Gotch, Port Moresby, 1981) gives an excellent introduction to the early history of human settlement and the development of agriculture. It shows how painstaking archaeological research is beginning to piece together a picture of ancient PNG societies and is fascinating reading. The Museum Bookshop sells copies.

Parliament of a Thousand Tribes by Osmar White (Heinemann, Melbourne, 1965) was released in an updated Wren paperback in 1972, but is also now out of print. It covers WW II and the post-war years better than the *The Last Unknown*, although it also misses out on the rapid changes of the '70s.

Some of the early explorers' own accounts are highly colourful, but long out of print. Captain Moresby's *Discoveries and Surveys in New Guinea and the d'Entrecasteaux Islands: A Cruise of HMS Basilisk* was published way back in 1876.

The fiery and controversial Italian explorer Luigi D'Albertis had his book, *New Guinea: What I Did and What I Saw* published in 1880. A more recent reassessment of this interesting character is *Rape of the Fly* by John Goode (Nelson, Melbourne, 1977).

Probably the most interesting of all the early explorers' stories would have to be Captain J A Lawson's *Wanderings in the Interior of New Guinea* which was published in 1875. Not since his epic visit has Mt Hercules (over a thousand metres higher than Everest) been seen again – or the New Guinea tiger, the waterfalls larger than Niagara or even the giant daisies or huge scorpions.

The patrol officers' memoirs category came into its prime between the wars and some of the books written then, when patrol officers were not only explorers but also the force of government, are classics of their kind. *Across New Guinea from the Fly to the Sepik*, I F Champion (1932), covers Champion's agonisingly difficult traverse of central New Guinea. *The Land that Time Forgot*, Mick Leahy & Mick Crane (1937), tells of the discovery of the Highlands. Another to look for is *Papuan Wonderland*, Jack·Hides (1936).

Amazingly, Leahy carried a movie camera when he first explored the highlands and his astonishing film of those first meetings forms the core of a highly acclaimed film, *First Contact*. The old film is counterpointed with modern film of the people, on both sides, who took part in that first close encounter. If you get a chance to see the film, don't miss it.

There are also some much more recent reminiscences of those exciting days on patrol. J K McCarthy's *Patrol into Yesterday* (Cheshire, Melbourne, 1963) is another book I would highly recommended for exciting reading. 'My New Guinea Years', as he subtitled it, covered first contact with the erratic and violent Kamea people, the successful escape from Rabaul in WW II and other high adventure.

The late Colin Simpson, the well-known Australian travel writer, spent quite a lot of time in PNG during the '50s and wrote three books on the land, its people and the explorers, many of whom he met. Parts of all three books were combined into *Plumes and Arrows* (Angus & Robertson, Sydney, 1962) which was available in paperback.

If you're interested in the OPM's struggle in Irian Jaya and the attitudes of the Indonesia and PNG Governments, the best book to read is *Indonesia's Secret War – The Guerilla Struggle in Irian Jaya* by Robin Osborne (Allen & Unwin, Sydney, 1985). It gives a fascinating and sometimes depressing insight into modern imperialism and politics.

Papua New Guinea – A False Economy by Kenneth Good (Anti-Slavery Society, London, 1986) is a controversial and highly critical analysis of the damage caused by European colonialism and the heritage it has left behind. It may come as a bit of shock to Australians who believe their country brought nothing but sweetness and light. It argues that the western model of economic development is inappropriate to PNG, and along the way covers history and politics from pre-contact society to the present day.

Because the history of European contact is so recent it has been well documented in photographs. You'll find a lot of interesting pictures in *A Pictorial History of New Guinea* by Noel Gash and June Whittaker (Jacaranda, Brisbane, 1975). *Taim Bilong Masta* is the book companion to an Australian Broadcasting Commission 'verbal history' of the Australian period. It's extremely readable and full of interest, recommended.

World War II
For a very readable account of the decisive fighting on the Kokoda Trail, culminating in the bitter struggle to recapture Buna and Gona from the Japanese, look for *Bloody Buna* by Lida Mayo. Originally published by Doubleday, New York, in 1974, it is also available in a cheap paperback. Although the author is an American, it is not altogether complimentary to MacArthur or the US forces.

The amazing courage of the coast watchers, who relayed information from behind the Japanese lines, knowing that capture would mean a most unpleasant death, is also well documented. Look for Eric Feldt's *The Coast Watchers* (Oxford University Press, 1946 and Lloyd O'Neil, Melbourne, 1975). A more recent study is Walter Lord's *Lonely Vigil – The Coastwatchers of the Solomons* (Viking Press, New York, 1978). Peter Ryan's *Fear Drive My Feet* (Angus & Robertson, Sydney, 1959) recounts some nerve-racking adventures behind the Japanese lines around Lae.

Some people find poking around the rotting relics from the war an interesting

exercise – *Rust in Peace* by Bruce Adams (Antipodean Publishers, Sydney, 1975) tells you where to look, not only in PNG but also in other parts of the Pacific. *Battleground South Pacific*, photos Bruce Adams, text Robert Howlett (Reeds, Sydney, 1970), also has much interesting material on the war. *Pacific Aircraft Wrecks – & where to find them*, Charles Darby (Kookaburra, Melbourne, 1979), is mainly devoted to WW II wrecks in PNG and has many fascinating photographs of these aircraft.

People
If you visit Rabaul, you'll no doubt develop an interest in Queen Emma's highly colourful life which is described in *Queen Emma* by R W Robson (Pacific Publications, Sydney, 1965). A recent novel, based around her life, is *Queen Emma of the South Seas* by Geoffrey Dutton (Macmillan, Melbourne, 1976).

A more recent story, about an equally colourful character, covers Bobby Gibbes' role in post-war aviation and is described in *Sepik Pilot* by James Sinclair (Lansdowne, Melbourne, 1971). Flying in PNG in the '50s was clearly one hell of a business! James Sinclair is also the author of *Wings of Gold: How the Aeroplane Developed New Guinea*, retracing the development of aviation between the wars, when PNG was a pioneer in civil aviation.

Wildlife
PNG's exotic and colourful bird life has inspired many equally colourful books. The biggest and smartest of the lot would have to be *The Birds of Paradise & Bower Birds* by William Cooper and Joseph Forshaw (William Collins, Sydney, 1977) – at about $100 a copy it's definitely for the serious ornithologist only!

For the amateur bird-watcher, the best field manual (although it's a little bulky) is *Birds of New Guinea* by Beehler, Pratt & Zimmerman (Princeton University Press, 1986).

A little more down to earth, in price at least, are two books you can find in Port Moresby. *Birds in Papua New Guinea* by Brian Coates (Robert Brown & Associates, Port Moresby, 1977) and *Wildlife in Papua New Guinea* by Eric Lindgrom (Robert Brown & Associates, Port Moresby or Golden Press, Sydney, 1975) provide an interesting introduction with plenty of excellent photographs.

Anthropology

PNG has been a treasure house for anthropologists and from Malinowski to Margaret Mead, they've made their names here. They're still flocking in today. Malinowski's books are covered in the Trobriand Islands, Milne Bay Province section of this book - they're weighty, academic books yet very readable.

Margaret Mead's *Growing Up in New Guinea* was first published in 1942, but is still available in a paperback Penguin. She conducted her studies on Manus Island and returned there after the war to investigate the dramatic changes that had taken place as a result of the enormous impact a wartime American base. Her second Manus book was *New Lives for Old* (Morrow, New York, 1956). A good deal of controversy surrounds her observations, but the books are well written and very readable.

The High Valley by Kenneth H Read (George Allen & Unwin, London, 1966) is a very readable account of the time the author spent in a Highlands village in the early post-war years, when the impact of European culture was only just reaching the valley around present-day Goroka.

Gardens of War - Life & Death in the New Guinea Stone Age by Robert Gardner & Karl G Heider (Random House, New York, 1968 and also in a Penguin large format paperback) describes the ritual warfare of New Guinea tribes, dramatically illustrated with many photographs. Fierce inter-village fighting was still common in the remote parts of Irian Jaya which the authors visited in the '60s.

Cargo cults have also come in for a lot of study. They are a fascinating example of the collision between primitive beliefs and modern technology. The classic book on these cults is *Road Belong Cargo* by Peter Lawrence (Melbourne University Press, 1964) but there have been a number of earlier books such as F E Williams' 1934 study, *The Vailala Madness in Retrospect* (Kegan Paul, London) or P Worsley's 1957 book *The Trumpet Shall Sound: A Study of Cargo Cults in Melanesia* (Macgibbon & Kee, London).

Culture & Arts

Man as Art: New Guinea Body Decoration by M Kirk is a beautiful coffee table photographic book illustrating the extravagant body decoration of the Highlanders.

The Artefacts & Crafts of Papua New Guinea - a Guide for Buyers is a very useful little booklet produced for the Handcraft Industry of Papua New Guinea. It has over 250 pictures and short descriptions of a very wide variety of PNG artefacts. If you do intend to buy something (if you don't, this book will change your mind!) it will be invaluable. If you can't find it anywhere else, look for it at the University Bookshop.

General Description

The *Papua New Guinea Handbook - Business & Travel Guide* (Pacific Publications, Sydney) last came out in a new edition at the end of 1985 - lots of facts, figures, tables and fairly dry information. Ann Mallard's *A Traveller's Guide to New Guinea* (Jacaranda, Brisbane, 1969) is now long out of print and out of date, but was an excellent overall guide to the country - one to look for in libraries.

One of the most interesting of the 'wow, look at these pictures' books is *The World's Wide Places - New Guinea*, one of the glossy Time-Life series. This one is by Roy Mackay with photographs by Eric Lindgrom and covers the spectacular terrain and wildlife very well.

A more general visitor's view of the country can be found in *New Guinea* by Milton and Joan Mann (Kodansha International, Tokyo, 1972). One of the Japanese 'This Beautiful World' series – lots of interesting photographs and a readable description of a short visit to PNG.

Port Moresby – Yesterday & Today, by Ian Stuart (Pacific Publications, Sydney, 1970) is an interesting account of the history and development of the country's capital city. Yachties intending to visit should look for *Cruising Papua New Guinea* by Alan Lucas (Horowitz, Sydney, 1980).

Odds & Ends

A couple of residents raved about *The Hot Land*, by John Ryan (Macmillan, Melbourne, 1970) while I was in the country. It's a journalist's account and therefore a lot of the contemporary reporting is already out of date, but the material on discovering long lost aircraft wreckage, the bits of local history, the drawn out business of marking the border to Dutch (later Indonesian) New Guinea, and the story of the Buka baby farm are all quite fascinating.

The Crocodile, by Vincent Eri, was the first published novel by a Papuan (Jacaranda, Brisbane, 1970 – available in a Penguin paperback). It provides an interesting look at the contact between Europeans and locals from the rarely seen, other side of the fence.

The Visitants by Randolph Snow (Picador paperback, 1981) won the 1979 Patrick White Award. It's a novel set on a remote island in 1959 and deals with the meeting of two very different cultures – theirs and ours.

Ian Downs, an Australian businessman from the Highlands (where he was earlier a pioneering patrol officer) who was deeply involved in the early steps towards self-government, publicised his views in a novel titled *The Stolen Land* (Jacaranda, Brisbane, 1970 and in a Wren paperback).

Something in the Blood, by Trevor Shearston (University of Queensland Press) is a recent collection of short stories. *The Snail Race* and *The Talking Pig* are two recent children's books from Robert Brown & Associates.

The *Liklik Book* is PNG's own Whole Earth Catalog of self sufficiency and appropriate technology. For the full story of the Ok Tedi project and its environmental effects look for *Ok Tedi, Pot of Gold* by R Jackson (University of PNG).

Finally, *In Papua New Guinea*, by Christina Dodwell (Oxford Illustrated Press, Yeovil, England, 1983) is a delightful recent account of an enterprising young Englishwoman's adventures through Papua New Guinea on foot, by horse and a four month solo trip down the Sepik by dugout canoe. It also proves, once again, that the facility the English have for producing superbly eccentric travellers is far from dead!

MAPS

You can get good topographical maps from the Central Mapping Bureau in Waigani, Port Moresby. Some of the Provincial Lands and Survey Departments also sell these maps (there is a good range in Mt Hagen) but the office in Moresby is the most likely to have complete stocks.

The best, easily available general maps are the *Tourist Guide to Papua New Guinea* (which includes city maps) produced by Shell and the PNG Office of Tourism, and *Robinson's Papua New Guinea* produced by Runaway Publications. You won't have any trouble finding one or the other. Look for the excellent Sepik River map available in Wewak – see the Sepik section for details.

THINGS TO BUY

Papua New Guinea's arts and handicrafts have been recognised as the most vital in the Pacific. The art is amazingly varied for the same reason as there are so many languages – lack of contact between different villages and groups of people. Particularly on the Sepik, where art is so important and so energetic, you'll find villages only a few km apart with styles that are totally distinct. At the Chambri Lakes, for example, the people in Aibom express themselves purely through clay pots – which no other Sepik village makes. Only minutes away at Chambri, the people specialise in masks and spears of a very distinctive and easily recognised style.

The Sepik is easily the best known area for artefacts; in fact, there's a temptation to think of all PNG art in terms of the Sepik when actually there is far more to be found.

The strength of Sepik art is largely due to its spiritual significance. Every Sepik village has to have its haus tambaran, the men's spirit house. In this men-only club are stored the carvings that represent the various spirits. Since carvings have to be replaced fairly frequently or produced for special ceremonies, it is a living and continuous craft. Today much of the spiritual significance may be lost, although certain ancient pieces are still zealously protected, but the craft continues – for the benefit of collectors and tourists.

Elsewhere the pattern may not be so instantly recognisable as in the Sepik, but the crafts are there. You'll find pottery in many areas, ritual Hohoa boards in the Gulf region, island carvings and shell money, or more recently introduced crafts like the attractive, coarse weavings of the Highlands.

Like everything else in PNG, artefacts are not cheap – particularly if you compare them to the more detailed, but less dynamic, carvings in Indonesia or the Philippines. The price inflation of carvings is also rather astonishing – I've seen prices 600 to 800% higher in artefacts shops in PNG than at source, and there's another huge price jump if you buy them outside the country.

There are a couple of reasons for this (apart from plain, straightforward profit).

First of all the channels from the carver to the shops are lengthy and imperfect – long 'buying trips' have to be undertaken for artefact dealers to obtain their stock-in-trade. Secondly, many PNG artefacts are extremely unwieldy or very fragile – there's not a lot of thought given to meeting airline handling requirements and weight allowances, thank God! So transport can be difficult and many items are really only suitable for purchase by museums which can handle shipping problems. Transporting a Sepik garamut drum or orator's stool would just about require a crane.

Arts and handicrafts anywhere in the world, and in PNG in particular, face two great dangers – lack of interest or too much interest. When the religious or spiritual reasons for an art form have died out – through changes in culture or circumstances – the art can die too unless there is a new reason for it, such as demand from collectors. But it's a two-edged sword, for too much demand can prompt careless, sloppy or lazy work. So if you like a piece – buy it. You'll be doing something to keep the craft alive. But be discerning – better one, more expensive, carefully made item than half a dozen shoddy ones. You'll like it better in the long run too.

In the Sepik area in particular watch for hastily done carvings resembling traditional forms but lacking detail and finesse. Also some are artificially aged to make them appear more genuine and valuable. Watch for shoe polish used as a stain to disguise wood types and to simulate age. See the Customs section in this chapter for a discussion on the possible difficulties with Customs regulations.

The descriptions that follow are just a few of the enormous varieties of styles and types of artefacts you may see in PNG, there is far more than this actually available. There are good shops in Port Moresby, Lae and a number of other PNG towns – information on them is in the relevant sections of this book. In some places artefact sellers gather outside hotels; their prices tend to be considerably inflated over what you would pay elsewhere. If you want to get a preview of New Guinea art in Australia, I suggest you visit New Guinea Primitive Arts, 6th floor, 428 George St, Sydney.

Pottery

The village of Aibom, near the Chambri Lakes, is virtually the only place on the Sepik to specialise in pottery. Aibom pots are noted for their relief faces which are coloured with lime. They are made by the coil method and are very cheap on the Sepik, but rapidly become more expensive as you move further away because, like other PNG pottery, they are very fragile.

Other interesting pots can be found at Yabob and Bilbil villages near Madang, at Zumim near the Highlands Highway from Lae and from the Porebada people in the Central Province. The Amphlett Islanders in Milne Bay also make very fine and very fragile pottery. No pottery is glazed in PNG and it is also often poorly fired so it all suffers from extreme fragility.

Weapons

The Chambri Lake carvers produce decorative spears remarkably similar to their masks. Perhaps with tourists in mind, they can be dismantled and are relatively easy to transport. Bows and arrows are available from a number of places including the Highlands and Bougainville Island. Shields are also popular artefacts as they often have a decorative and spiritual role just as important as their function of protection for a warrior. In the Highlands the ceremonial Hagen Axes are similarly half-tool, half-ritual. Here you will also see the lethal cassowary-claw tipped Huli Picks or on the Sepik the equally nasty bone daggers.

Spirit Boards, Story Boards & Cult Hooks

In the Gulf Province the shield-like Hohao or Gope boards are said to contain the spirits of powerful heroes or to act as guardians of the village. Before hunting trips or war expeditions the spirits contained in the boards were called upon to advise and support the warriors.

At Kambot, on the Keram River, a tributary of the Sepik, story boards are a modern interpretation of the fragile bark carvings they used to make. The boards illustrate, in raised relief, incidents of village life and are one of my favourite examples of New Guinea art.

Cult hooks – small ones are Yipwons while larger ones are Kamanggabi – are carved as hunting charms and carried by their owners in a bag to ensure success on the hunt, the small ones anyway. Food hooks are used to hang bilums of food from the roof to keep it away from the rats, but also have a spiritual significance.

Bilums

Bilums are the colourful string bags and are made in many parts of the country. They are enormously strong and expand to amazing sizes – they are used for everything from transporting or storing food to carrying a baby. Good bilums can be rather expensive, particularly in the towns. They are time consuming to make since the entire length of string is fed through every loop. Most bilums are now made of plastic or nylon strings rather than natural fibres, which in some ways is a shame; on the other hand, you can hardly mourn the continuing development of such a vital handicraft, especially when the colour and beauty of the new designs is so striking.

Bowls

The Trobriand Islanders are prolific carvers of everything from stylised figures to decorated lime gourds, but my favourites are the beautifully carved bowls. They are generally carved from dark wood and laboriously polished with a pig's tusk. The rims are patterned, often to represent a fish or turtle.

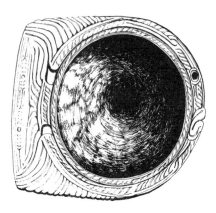

Trobriand Bowl

The Tami Islanders near Lae are also renowned for their carved bowls. Further offshore the Siassi Islanders carve deep, elliptical bowls which are stained black and patterned with incised designs coloured with lime. In Milne Bay, the Woodlark Islanders carve bowls somewhat similar to those from the neighbouring Trobriands.

Masks

Masks in Papua New Guinea are more often intended as decoration than as something to be worn. They are found particularly along the Sepik River, but also in other parts of the country. The Chambri masks from the villages on the Chambri Lakes are the most modernistic of the Sepik masks – instantly recognisable by their elongated design and glossy black finish with incised patterns in brown and white; colours which are unique to Chambri. They make nice gifts because they are smaller than the general run of Sepik masks, easily transportable since they are solid without projecting teeth, horns or other features, and they are very cheap. Small Chambri masks at the village or in Wewak are only one or two kina.

At Korogo, on the Sepik, the masks are made of wood then decorated with clay in

Chambri Mask

which shells, hair and pigs' teeth are embedded. Other distinctive Sepik mask styles are found at Kaminabit and Tambanum. Masks from the Murik Lakes have an almost African look about them. At Maprik the yam masks are woven from cane or rattan. Masks are also carved at Kiwai Island, near Daru on the southern, Papuan coast.

Musical Instruments

Drums are the main musical instruments in PNG. The predominant drums are the large garamut drums found on the Sepik and made by hollowing out a tree trunk and the smaller kundu drum, which is hour glass shaped and with a tympanum formed of lizard or snake skin. Trobriand drums are somewhat similar.

Other instruments include the sacred flutes which are always found in male-female pairs and are generally reserved for initiation rites; the bull roarers which are spun round on a length of cord, the pottery whistles of the Highlands and the small, but eerie sounding, Jews harps also found in the Highlands.

Other Odds & Ends

Buka baskets, from Bougainville in the North Solomons, are said to be the finest baskets in the Pacific. They are very expensive. Similar, but coarser, baskets are found in the Southern Highlands. Figures of various types are carved on the Murik Lakes, the Yuat River and in the Trobriand Islands. The Trobriand Islanders also carve very fine walking sticks and some delightful little stools and tables. The walking sticks are often carved from ebony, which is now very rare and found only on Woodlark Island. Tapa cloth, made from tree bark, is beaten and decorated in the Northern Province. Shell jewellery can be found at many coastal towns, particularly Madang and Rabaul.

WHAT TO BRING

The best advice, wherever you go, is to take too little rather than too much. Keep in mind that the domestic airlines have a baggage weight limit of 16 kg, although as a tourist you can usually slip by if your bags weigh around 20 kg. The generally warm climate makes things easy – even in the cool Highlands a sweater is all you'll ever need for the evenings. Naturally what you plan to do and how you plan to travel will shape what you need to take. For instance, the only time you'll need a coat is if you go mountain climbing: it snows on top of Mt Wilhelm.

General

Most of the time all you will require is lightweight clothing, T-shirts, sandals and swimming gear. Natural fibres, cotton in particular, will be most comfortable in the sticky, coastal humidity. Long-sleeved shirts are not necessary except on the most formal occasions, although they can be very useful as sun and mosquito protection. Coats and ties are virtually never required. Men will find Australian-style 'dress' shorts can be worn for almost

Kundu Drum

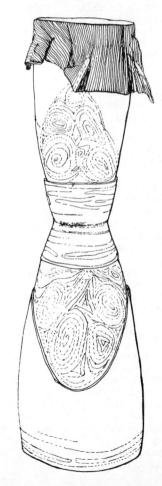

any occasion, but lightweight trousers are nice to have for restaurants and cool Highlands evenings. A hat, large enough to shade the back of your neck, and sunglasses will also be useful.

Women must take care to dress modestly; the often scanty styles of traditional dress should not be seen as a license to uncover. Mission influenced people can be very prudish and, especially from a security point of view, it's not a good idea to call attention to yourself with revealing clothes. A below-the-knee dress is the best solution, although where this is impractical trousers are OK, as long as they're not ridiculously tight. Shorts are definitely not a good idea. A bikini will also be inappropriate at all but the most westernised and protected locations.

Unlike Asian countries, PNG is not a good place to buy clothes; although you can buy all the essentials in the main towns, they aren't cheap. On the other hand, the day-to-day western commodities that can be difficult to find in Asia (toothpaste, toilet paper, tampons, etc) are easy to obtain. It is worth carrying a roll of toilet paper (handy if you're likely to be using bush toilets), band-aids and antiseptic, some drug to help you cope with diarrhoea, an effective sun cream and insect repellant.

The most flexible and useful items for carrying your baggage are travel backpacks. These are packs whose internal frames and adjustable harnesses can be zipped away into a compartment. You can use them as packs when you're bushwalking or looking for a hotel, and with the harness hidden they look smart and you don't run into problems with straps snagging on airport conveyer belts or bus seats. They do tend to be expensive unfortunately. A cheap alternative is a duffle bag with a shoulder strap. Unless you're on a tour or can afford taxis, you will have to do some walking, so make sure your baggage can be easily carried. Packing your things in separate plastic bags helps keep everything organised and dry.

A day pack is handy for carrying a camera (remember you have to take care of cameras because of the humidity and dust), a rain poncho, water bottle (essential if you're walking or can't survive on Coke) and your travel survival kit! If you don't need your daypack to be waterproof, buy a bilum when you arrive. A money belt or pouch is essential – some areas of the country are renowned for the skill of the local pickpockets. Because of the heat, a pouch or belt and its contents can soon become sodden with sweat, so make sure paper items are sealed in plastic.

A folding umbrella can be extremely useful. A mask and snorkel is definitely worth having, as hire shops are few and far between, prices are high, and virtually every beach is a snorkeller's delight. A sarong or *laplap* (the PNG version) can be used as a dressing gown, a beach towel, an addition to a skimpy bathing suit, a bed sheet and, of course, a sarong. Consider taking some cutlery, a bowl, plate and mug so you can make your own breakfast or lunch. A Swiss Army knife with a can opener, bottle opener and scissors will be invaluable. A small torch is handy for late night toilet expeditions (vital if you're in a village). Some light nylon cord, another all purpose item, is useful for shoelaces, a washing line, tying parcels . . . .

If you're not bushwalking, sleeping bags and tents are debatable propositions. If you anticipate spending some time in the Highlands, where the nights can get cold, it is worth considering a bag that is lightweight and compact. They're handy if someone offers you some floor space, and if you're concerned about visitors in the night (of the insect variety) or even if you just want a cushion. A mosquito net is essential if you're going to the Sepik, but you can get these in Moresby. See the Sepik section for details of other items you will need on the river.

Walking & Canoeing

It does not pay to underestimate your

potential isolation or the extreme conditions the environment can dish out – you must be properly equipped if you plan any serious walking or canoeing. Lonely Planet's *Bushwalking in Papua New Guinea* gives a detailed rundown of what you will need. There are no specialist bushwalking shops so you must bring major items with you. You can get bush knives (machetes), matches, tinned and dried food, torches and batteries and mosquito nets locally, but you'll look long and hard for a good tent or portable stove. A medical kit is also essential – see the Health section in this chapter.

Briefly, you need a tent (with a fly and ground sheet), sleeping bag, stove and cooking equipment (kerosene and gas are available, methylated spirits can be bought at chemists), firelighters, rope, decent boots, compass and maps, waterproof jacket or poncho, water canister, waterproof matches, a signalling mirror, torch and, possibly, a bush knife.

THINGS TO DO

Apart from the standard look-at-the-scenery-and-people occupations, there are a number of areas of special appeal. One is the prolific artistic activity (see the Artefacts section), and there are also activities like skin-diving and mountain climbing.

Bushwalking

For detailed information on walking and climbing see the Lonely Planet book *Bushwalking in Papua New Guinea*. Considering how similar much of the country is to Nepal – vast areas of rugged, mountainous terrain where the only way to get from village to village is to fly or walk – it is surprising that bushwalking has not caught on the same way trekking has in the Himalaya. I think it's an activity that should grow enormously.

Once you're out in the bush you'll find that your expenses plummet. Your major costs will be paying for guides and porters, where they are necessary. Expect to pay

them between K5 and K10 a day in addition to their food and possibly some equipment.

The best known walking track in PNG is definitely the Kokoda Trail (see the Port Moresby & Central chapter) but there are literally hundreds of other lesser known, but even more interesting walks. The whole country is criss-crossed with tracks, and in most parts of the country there is rarely more than a day's walk between villages. There really is no limit to the alternatives. Don't forget the possibility of coastal walks (especially in Milne Bay) and various mountain and volcano climbs (Mt Victoria, Mt Giluwe, Mt Lamington, Matupit).

You will find that in many parts of the country there will be two possible forms of transport: flying, which can be very expensive, and walking. If the latter does appeal (for whatever reason!) all you have to do is get to the end of the PMV route and start . . . . If you have the time, you will find this challenging, cheap and very rewarding.

Some of the most interesting walks include:

Kokoda Trail (5 – 7 days) This is a difficult walk over the mountainous spine between the north and south coasts. The trail follows the route that was taken by the Japanese after they landed on the north coast. After almost reaching Moresby, they were driven back by Australian and American troops in some of the most bitter fighting of the war. There are relatively few villages and it isn't a particularly interesting walk from a cultural point of view, but the country is superb and getting from one end to another is a feat to be proud of.

The trail provides an important alternative to flying, as there are no roads between Moresby and the north coast or the Highlands. There are other less well-known possibilities, but this is the route most travellers use if they don't want to, or can't afford to, · fly. Guides are not essential, but are recommended. See the Port Moresby and Central chapter.

Mt Wilhelm (3 – 4 days) Mt Wilhelm is the tallest mountain in PNG, and at 4509 metres, it's a serious mountain by any standards. It is a relatively easy walk (no technical climbing is required) and anyone with reasonable fitness should be able to make the summit, if the conditions allow. It can be very cold and even snow on top, and at the higher levels climbers are vulnerable to altitude sickness. The climb is highly recommended; not only do you see traditional Chimbu villages on your way to the mountain, but the views from the top are spectacular. Guides are not required as the track is clearly marked, but porters can be very helpful, depending on your fitness. See the Highlands chapter.

Nipa to Lake Kutubu (3 – 4 days) The lodge at Lake Kutubu is one of the most exciting new developments in PNG. It is run by local people and is simply not to be missed. Although you can fly most of the way (from Mendi to Pimaga), it is well worth considering the walk, which goes through a beautiful part of the Southern Highlands, at least one way. A guide is essential. See the Highlands chapter.

Lake Kopiago to Oksapmin (3 – 4 days) This is an extremely difficult, but nonetheless, particularly interesting walk. Starting at the very end of the Highlands Highway you cross the Strickland River's spectacular gorge. It is possible to continue on to Telefomin and this would take another six to eight days. From Telefomin you can catch planes to places in the Sepik River basin like April River. A guide is essential and it is worth considering a porter, particularly for the steep stretches into and out of the Strickland Gorge and especially if you plan to go as far as Telefomin. See the Highlands chapter.

Mt Wilhelm to Madang (3 days) This is a relatively easy way of getting between the Highlands and the north coast. The walk follows a four-wheel drive track which takes off the main Mt Wilhelm road just before Kegsugl and goes through Bundi and on to Brahman where, with a bit of luck, you'll find a PMV to Madang. A guide is not essential. See the Highlands chapter.

Wau to Salamaua (3 days) This is a very interesting possibility because both the starting and finishing points have excellent places to stay and it could be worked into an interesting alternative to the common air hop between Moresby and Lae. Wau is in the Eastern Highlands and is home to the Wau Ecology Institute and Salamaua is a beautiful, laid-back coastal resort south of Lae. You could fly from Moresby to Wau, spend some time around Wau, walk to Salamaua, spend some time diving, then catch a boat to Lae. It's a reasonably hard walk but the track is OK. A guide is recommended. See the Lae & Morobe chapter.

Woitape to Taipini (3 days) This is an interesting walk and there are airports at both places and a road now runs to Fane, near Woitape. A guide is recommended. See the Port Moresby & Central chapter.

A number of companies offer organised treks. They're not cheap, but they are worth considering if you have limited time. It's hard to guarantee itineraries at the best of times in PNG, but professional companies will probably have a better chance of sticking to them than you will. Some of them also go to places you would be hard pushed to reach yourself, even if you did find out they existed. The following list includes agents for other operators (for instance Sobek markets some of Pacific Expedition's tours), but they are included because the addresses may be handy. Most have a range of different tours in addition to bushwalking:

Melanesian Tourist Services
   PO Box 707, Madang, PNG (tel 82 2766)
   Suite 105, 850 Colorado Blvd, Los Angeles,
   CA 90041, USA (tel (213) 256 1991)
   Alt-Schwanheim 50, 6000 Frankfurt 50,
   West Germany (tel 35 6667)
Niugini Adventure
   PO Box 295, Kundiawa, Chimbu Province,
   PNG (tel 75 1304)
Niugini Tours
   PO Box 665, Mt Hagen, PNG
   2618 Newport Blvd, Newport Beach, CA
   92663, USA (tel (714) 675 2250)
   Lower Ground, 100 Clarence Street,
   Sydney, Australia (tel (008) 221757)
   353 Remuera Rd, Auckland 5, New Zealand
   (tel (09) 50 3334)
Pacific Expeditions
   PO Box 132, Port Moresby, PNG
   (tel 25 7803)
Sobek's International Explorer's Society
   Sobek, PO Box 1089, Angels Camp, CA
   95222, USA (tel (209) 736 4524)
Trans Niugini Tours
   PO Box 371, Mt Hagen, PNG
   (tel 52 1490)
   408 East Islay, Santa Barbara, CA 93101,
   USA (tel (805) 569 0558)
   Marketing Services, Suite 433, 52-54 High
   Holborn, London, UK, (tel (01) 242 3131)
   New Guinea Adventure Centre, PO Box
   1827, Cairns, Qld 4870, Australia
   (tel (070) 51 0622)
Tribal World
   PO Box 86, Mt Hagen, PNG (tel 52 1555)
Wokabaut Papua New Guinea
   Outdoor Travel Centre, 377 Little Burke St,
   Melbourne, Vic 3000, Australia
   (tel (03) 67 7252)
World Expeditions
   3rd Floor, 377 Sussex St, Sydney, NSW
   2000, Australia (tel (02) 264 3366)
   Suite 602, Wellesley House, 126 Wellington
   Pde, East Melbourne, Vic 3002, Australia
   (tel (03) 419 2920)
   Venturetreks, PO Box 37610, Auckland,
   New Zealand (tel 79 9855)

River Journeys

PNG has some of the world's largest, most spectacular rivers. The Sepik is often compared to the Amazon and the Congo Rivers, and the Sepik Basin is an artistic and cultural treasure house.

There are a number of rivers that local people use as 'highways'. These include the Sepik and some of its tributaries (including the April, May and Keram), the Ramu, the Fly and a number of other rivers that flow into the Gulf of Papua. Local people can travel by river between the Irian Jaya border and, virtually, Madang, using the Sepik, Keram and Ramu. On these rivers there is often an assortment of different craft, ranging from dugout canoes to tramp steamers.

If you do want to spend time on a river, there are a number of possibilities: you can buy your own canoe and paddle yourself; you can use PMV boats (unscheduled, inter-village, motorised, dugout canoes); you can charter a boatman and motorised canoe when you get to the river; you can sail with a small trading vessel; you can go on tours of varying degrees of comfort (ranging from rough to luxurious); you can run a number of rivers in inflatable rafts; and you can sail in a cruise ship with all mod-cons.

All the following options are discussed in some detail in the Sepik chapter:

Canoeing I did not come across any fibreglass canoes on my travels, but it is possible (not always easy) to buy dugout canoes to paddle yourself. The price varies widely from K10 to K60 a canoe, depending on where you are, the size and condition of the canoe, and so on. Paddling downstream is the only viable possibility. Accommodation and food are normally available in the villages – meaning floor space in a longhouse and sago and smoked fish in the stomach. In order to survive this happily you have to be prepared to rough it, and be reasonably fit, independent and well equipped. Once you're actually afloat you'll spend very little money, although it is important to pay your way.

This kind of travel is most popular on the Sepik (we're talking a few hundred people a year) because the reasonably dense population and the fascinating art and culture means there are interesting villages at regular intervals. The river and its flood plain is so large it is not particularly interesting paddling, however, so it is worth considering one of the tributaries.

Motorised Canoes Another alternative, if you are prepared to rough it and live in the villages, is using the inter-village PMV canoes. The problem with this is that although they are relatively cheap they only run according to demand – there are no schedules. Traffic builds up between Wednesday and Saturday because of people moving around for markets, but can be very quiet early in the week and non-existent on Sundays. Using this method you need plenty of time and patience.

If you are short of time, you can charter a motorboat and driver locally. This is, however, very expensive: probably somewhere between K10 and K20 per hour of running time (due to the high cost of operating two-stroke engines).

If you have limited time, a tour on the Sepik may be worth considering, although they are expensive. One option is the local freelance operators you can contact on the river at Ambunte, Pagwe and Angoram. Some of these people are reputable and some are definitely not, so it pays to be cautious. You're looking at around K80 a day for a canoe and boatman.

There are definite advantages to having a decent guide on the Sepik; you will inevitably miss places, people and things without someone to lead the way, introduce you and explain. The established operators on the Sepik either use dugout canoes or flat-bottomed boats and their tours vary considerably in the degree of luxury they offer. Some are luxuriously based at the Karawari Lodge (Trans Niugini Tours), while some are based in the villages (Pacific Expeditions).

Companies that handle canoe/boat tours on the Sepik are Niugini Tours, Pacific Expeditions, Sobek's International Explorer's Society, Trans Niugini Tours

and Tribal World. See the Bushwalking section for their addresses. There are also two local companies worth contacting: the Angoram Hotel (tel 88 3011), PO Box 35, East Sepik, PNG; and Santon Tours (tel 86 2248), PO Box 496, Wewak, PNG.

River Boats There are alternatives if you prefer to have something more substantial than a canoe beneath you. On the Sepik there is a small cargo boat which, every three weeks or so, runs from Madang up to Green River. It's cheap, slow and the living conditions are primitive. Contact Poromon Shipping (tel 82 2636), PO Box 486, Madang, PNG.

The Ok Tedi mine site near the Irian Jaya border is serviced by barges on the Fly that run from Daru. You may, if you're lucky, be able to get a ride.

Finally, Melanesian Tourist Services (address in Bushwalking section) runs a luxurious cruise boat, the *Melanesian Explorer*, from Madang to Green River, stopping off in the villages along the way.

River Rafting Shooting down PNG's turbulent mountain rivers in inflatable dinghies is a sport still in its infancy, but one that has tremendous potential. Not only is rafting great fun, but you also get to see some spectacular country from an unusual perspective. Regular trips, ranging in length from one to five days, are available on the Watut River, which runs from near Wau down to meet the Markham River, the Wahgi River, in the Highlands between Kundiawa and Mt Hagen (although this was closed *temporarily* because of rascal activity), and the Vanapa and Angabanga Rivers, near Port Moresby.

The two companies that run trips are Niugini Adventure (Watut and Wahgi Rivers) and Pacific Expeditions (Vanapa and Angabanga Rivers). Sobek represents both these outfits in America. See the Bushwalking section for the relevant addresses.

Caving

Caves in the limestone regions of the Southern Highlands may well be the deepest in the world, but to date they have only been very briefly explored. The Atea Kanada Cave extends for 30.5 km, making it one of the longest caves in the southern hemisphere and Asia.

Diving

Diving is one of the fastest growing attractions in PNG. If the experts can be believed, this is because PNG can be compared more than favourably with established diving meccas like the Red Sea, the Caribbean, and the Great Barrier Reef.

Going to PNG and not looking under the water would be like going to Nepal and not looking at the mountains! Snorkelling is the cheapest and easiest way, but there are also a number of dive operators who offer courses, equipment and tours.

There are plenty of excellent places to dive and there is lots to see. The coast is surrounded by coral reefs, and many are easily accessible to snorkellers. There is, in general, excellent visibility, an abundance of reef and pelagic fish, dramatic drop offs, shells, and soft and hard corals. Those who like diving on wrecks will find the reefs are liberally dotted with sunken ships – either as a result of the reefs or of WW II.

Dive equipment and boats are available in Madang, Rabaul (East New Britain), Port Moresby, Kimbe (West New Britain), Alotau (Milne Bay), Lorengau (Manus), Salamaua/Lae (Morobe), Kieta (Bougainville) and on Wuvulu Island (East Sepik). See the appropriate chapters for information on accommodation.

Madang This is probably the most popular location for divers, in probably the most tourist-oriented PNG city. Diving is good all year round. There are superb dives close to luxury hotels, and Hansa Bay, the resting place for at least 34 Japanese ships, is within striking distance up the coast. All the ships lie in shallow water (less than 25 metres) and are now covered in corals and fish. It's a beautiful site, especially when the active volcano at Manam Island lights the sky.

Diving Specialists of PNG (you'll find them in the grounds of the Madang Resort Hotel) have a bush-material lodge close to a Hansa Bay village, where groups can stay; Jais Aben is just outside Madang and is a combination research station and luxury hotel specially organised for divers.

Diving Specialists of PNG
    PO Box 337, Madang, PNG (tel 82 2655, ext 287)
Jais Aben Resort
    PO Box 105, Madang, PNG (tel 82 3311)

Rabaul Built around the massive, flooded caldera of an ancient volcano, Rabaul was a major Japanese base; there are no fewer than 104 diveable war wrecks in the harbour. Visibility is often a staggering 30 to 40 metres and diving is good all year. Rabaul still lives under the threat of volcanic eruptions, but the location is spectacular and the town itself is cosmopolitan and enjoyable.

Rabaul Dive & Tour Services
    PO Box 1128, Rabaul, East New Britain, PNG (tel 92 7145)

Port Moresby When people talk about the dry and dusty capital they usually omit to say that there is a magnificent deep-water harbour ringed with coral reefs and dotted with islands. The best diving is in April and May and between November and January. Bob and Dinah Halstead run courses and dive trips and they also take their dive boat down to Milne Bay:

Tropical Diving Adventures
    PO Box 1644, Boroko, PNG (tel 25 7429)

Kimbe Diving in East New Britain has many people raving about excellent visibility, volcanic caves draped in staghorn coral, dramatic drop-offs, sharks, turtles . . . . The only operator is based at the Walindi Plantation Resort which is on a huge oil palm plantation, fringed by volcanic mountain and a beautiful bay:

Walindi Dive
    PO Box 4, Kimbe, West New Britain, PNG
    (tel 93 5441)

Wuvulu Island This is acclaimed as one of the great dive sites of the world. Described by James Michener as 'the most perfect atoll', and a favourite place for Jacques Cousteau, Wuvulu rises straight up from an undersea plateau 2000 metres deep. There are no rivers or creeks so the water is unbelievably clean and there are sharks, turtles, manta rays and tuna. There is equipment and a lodge with room for 12 people:

Lus Development Corporation.
    PO Box 494, Wewak, East Sepik Province,
    PNG (tel 86 2548)

Alotau, Lorengau, Salamaua/Lae, Kieta All these places offer superb diving. Milne Bay Marine Charters has a purpose-built, 36-foot boat to give divers access to islands to the east. The Lorengau Dive Shop services Manus Island. Salamaua Haus Kibung is based in Lae, and operates a very reasonably-priced resort at the sleepy village of Salamaua. The diving around Bougainville has also had good reports. The contact addresses are:

Milne Bay Marine Charters
    PO Box 176, Alotau, Milne Bay, PNG
    (tel 61 1167)
Lorengau Dive Shop
    PO Box 108, Lorengau, Manus
    (tel 40 9159)
Salamaua Haus Kibung
    PO Box 3778, Lae, PNG (tel 42 4428)
Dive Bougainville
    PO Box 661, Arawa, North Solomons, PNG
    (tel 95 2595)

Cruising

If you don't own your own cruising yacht (and when you see PNG's islands and harbours you will wish you did), there are three alternatives left to you. The first is to use the coastal shipping; the second is to take a tour; the third is to crew a yacht. The coastal shipping situation is covered in greater detail in the Getting Around chapter.

Basically there are scheduled links between Moresby and the Gulf Province ports, between Oro Bay (near Popondetta) and Vanimo, and the main islands off the north coast. There are no passenger vessels linking the north and south coasts. In addition to these small ships there are local boats and canoes that go literally everywhere – but for these you have to be in the right place at the right time.

The big news is a new passenger-only vessel, the *Mamose Express*, run by Lutheran Shipping (tel 42 2813), PO Box 1459, Lae, PNG. It's clean and comfortable, runs between Oro Bay and Wewak stopping on the way, takes two and a half days and costs K72 in tourist class.

Melanesian Tourist Services will soon add the *Melanesian Explorer II* to their empire, which will free the *Melanesian Explorer* from its Sepik River duty for full time cruising around the coast, and the islands of Milne Bay. Pacific Expeditions sail *wagas* (traditional outrigger dug-outs about 10-metres long) around the untouched islands of the Louisiade Archipelago. See the Bushwalking section for the relevant addresses.

There are thriving yacht clubs in Port Moresby, Lae, Rabaul and Wewak and it is possible that you might be able to find a berth, if you have some experience.

Fishing

Sport fishing has enormous potential. Unless they have permission from traditional owners, however, fishermen could easily get themselves in trouble. You can't waltz up to a stream, or the edge of the ocean and just cast in a line – everything and every square inch of PNG is owned by someone, including streams and reefs. The fish are definitely there – including trout in the Highlands, reef and pelagic fish offshore – and if you do get permission from the traditional owners, you should have some excellent fishing.

Several tours are offered by Sea New Guinea (tel (02) 267 5563), 100 Clarence St, Sydney, Australia. One is based at the Walindi Plantation in West New Britain (black bass, tarpon, jungle perch), another is based at the Ambua Lodge in the Southern Highlands (trout). The most famous fishing destination in PNG, however, is the Bensbach Lodge on the Bensbach River near the Irian Jaya border, and the fish is barramundi. It's a beautiful area with superb wildlife, and 20 kg barramundi *are common*. See the Western & Gulf chapter.

It is possible to hire boats in several towns. The deep water fishing is, allegedly, incredible, with sharks, marlin and other game fish. Most of the dive operators have boats that can be chartered (see the Diving section for addresses), also:

Trans Melanesian Marina
    PO Box 477, Port Moresby, PNG
    (tel 21 2039)
Rookes Marine Repairs
    PO Box 427, Madang, PNG (tel 82 2325)

Surfing/Windsurfing
I only saw surfable waves on Bougainville just outside Kieta, although I was told that there is surf around Wewak in the correct season (September to January).

The problem is that most accessible PNG beaches are in the lee of reefs or islands and don't open onto the ocean. If you have access to a boat and can get out to the reefs themselves, there are bound to be waves, especially off the eastern coasts of New Ireland and Bougainville, and the unprotected East Sepik coast. Australian surfers working at the Bougainville copper mine told me of one popular reef break outside Kieta, endearingly known as Shark Alley! If you do go exploring, it would be best to avoid June, July and

August when the prevailing winds are south-easterly.

The very characteristics which make surfing problematical make windsurfing viable: sheltered harbours, strong winds between June and August and, if you're interested, waves outside lagoons. Windsurfing is quite popular, particularly in Moresby, Madang and Rabaul. Although you won't always find it easy to get hold of a board, most of the top-end hotels on the coast have one or two which they hire. The yacht clubs would also be good places to start your enquiries.

War Wreckage
At the end of WW II the country was littered from end to end with the wreckage of Allied and Japanese aircraft, ships and army equipment. Most of it has been shipped out by bands of scrap dealers, but there is still much to be seen.

There is a national register of aircraft wreckage and from time to time aircraft missing since WW II are still stumbled upon. In *The Hot Land*, John Ryan tells of some of these recently located aircraft and writes of some which are still being searched for. *Pacific Aircraft Wrecks* gives information about wreckage of aircraft all over Papua New Guinea. See the Diving section for some information about shipwrecks. East New Britain (near Rabaul) is littered with reminders of the war (tunnels, bunkers, landing craft and shipwrecks); there are also many relics at the southern end of Bougainville.

War-buffs can have a fine time poking around debris. Surprisingly, one consistent comment on Japanese aircraft wrecks is that they are generally in better condition than the Allied wrecks due to their superior corrosion protection! Deja vu?

Flora & Fauna
There is a huge variety of spectacular birds. A keen bird-watcher should try to include a visit to a swampy area like the Blackwater Lakes near the Sepik (for water birds) the Highlands (for birds of

paradise) and the islands (for sea birds). The entire country is a paradise for butterfly enthusiasts. There are many rare species and many others that, to a non-expert, are simply huge and beautiful (PNG has the world's largest butterfly). Finally there are orchids; again PNG has more than its fair share.

Getting There

Although there are some wild-and-wonderful ways of getting to PNG, almost everybody arrives by air. And the vast majority fly from Australian east coast cities to Port Moresby. An increasing number of people are using two relatively new routes that link the USA west coast with PNG: Continental flies to Port Moresby via Hawaii and Micronesia, and Garuda (Indonesia's national airline) flies to Biak in Irian Jaya (Indonesia) from where you can make connections to Jayapura (Irian Jaya) and Vanimo on the north coast of PNG. There are also regular flights from Singapore, Manila, Honiara and Munda in the Solomon Islands, and Port Vila in Vanuatu. Otherwise, there are a few visiting yachts, an occasional cruise ship, and a few intrepid travellers coming by local boats through the islands.

Since independence Air Niugini has been the national 'flag carrier' operating between Australia and Asia. Australian connections are also made by Qantas, Australia's international airline. Continental Airlines began operations across the Pacific to PNG in 1988, and it is quite likely there will be further flights and routings added to this destination. Unfortunately, Port Moresby remains beyond the reach of the popular Circle Pacific Fares, a variation on the round-the-world theme, but this may change.

With the exception of the relatively small number of people who come in through Vanimo virtually every other air traveller is chanelled through Port Moresby. Since most tourists are interested in the Highlands, the Sepik or the north coast, and there are no roads connecting Moresby to these places, visitors are forced to connect with expensive domestic flights to get to their final destination. In recent years there has been talk of opening another international airport on the north coast to overcome this problem and various local groups are lobbying for international airports on Manus Island, at Wewak, Madang and Lae (put your money on Madang).

PNG is a popular stopping point for cruising yachties, either heading through Asia or the Pacific. If you ask around it's often possible to get a berth on a yacht heading off somewhere interesting. Often yachties depend upon picking up crew to help them sail and to help cover some of the day to day costs. The best places in PNG to find a yacht are Port Moresby, Madang and Rabaul. These days cargo ships are expensive and very rarely take tourists.

Airport Departure Tax

There is a K10 airport departure tax for all international departures from PNG. In the past, the tax has been as low as K2 and as high as K20.

TO/FROM AUSTRALIA
Air

Air Niugini flies from Sydney, Brisbane and Cairns. They fly Sydney/Brisbane/Port Moresby twice a week, Cairns/Port Moresby three times a week, and there's also a weekly Sydney/Port Moresby flight. The quickest and cheapest is the weekly one hour and 20 minutes flight from Cairns; the direct flight from Sydney takes three hours 40 minutes; and the flight from Sydney via Brisbane takes over five hours.

Qantas fly to Port Moresby twice a week from Sydney via Brisbane once a week direct from Sydney.

Fares between Australia and Port Moresby start from:

from	one-way	APEX return
Sydney	A$501	A$613
Brisbane	A$409	A$501
Cairns	A$244	A$309

The APEX return fare is the cheapest return fare to PNG and – like many cheap fares – has strict conditions. Apex fares must be paid in full 21 days prior to departure. They are available on direct services (no stopovers) only and allow for a minimum stay of 12 days and a maximum stay of 30 days. The most important limitation to this fare is that amendments to travel dates or cancellations incur heavy penalties, from A$100 up. However many travellers will find the savings on this fare will outway the flexibility of a full economy fare.

The only international flight out of Australia cheaper than Cairns/Moresby is the Merpati flight between Darwin and Kupang (Timor) which is A$132. An interesting budget possibility, discussed in the following Indonesia section, would be to fly to Moresby from Cairns, fly to Jayapura (Irian Jaya) from Vanimo, travel through Indonesia, then fly Kupang/Darwin. Combining north Queensland and the Barrier Reef with Papua New Guinea is already a popular itinerary.

Note that Customs are very thorough with people coming into Australia from PNG, particularly at Cairns. You can expect to be very carefully searched.

Sea

Some hardy travellers have hopped across the Torres Strait Islands from Thursday Island (just off the tip of Cape York Peninsular, Queensland) to Daru (Western Province). The Torres Strait Islands are Australian territory and dot the waters of the narrow straits. There are plenty of fishing boats operating between them. It used to be quite easy to get a boat going to Daru, but this may now be more difficult. The Torres Strait Islanders recently began a campaign demanding greater autonomy and one of their grievances is the uncontrolled movement of PNG fishermen. This may have increased official interest and reduced the number of boats.

The Australian Government's new found interest in the islands may also mean you have passport problems. The snag is that you are given an Australian departure stamp when you leave Thursday Island. After that you've officially left Australia and are not allowed to visit the Torres Straits Islands. In the past, Thursday Island officials admitted this was impossible to police, but things may have changed. A first-hand report would be gratefully received.

You can get to Thursday Island by boat or fly from Cairns for around A$190 with Air Queensland. From Daru you can fly to Port Moresby for K98 with Air Niugini.

TO/FROM ASIA

Air Niugini have weekly flights to Singapore and Manila (Philippines) from where it is possible to make connections to virtually anywhere in the world. The fare to Singapore starts from K744/804 one-way/return, and to Manila starts from K605/786 one-way/return. Again the cheap return fares listed here have complex limitations and conditions and you should check out the rules attached to any fare with the airline or a travel agent.

TO/FROM INDONESIA

Although Indonesia and PNG share a lengthy land border it is not possible for travellers to make land crossings, and even hopping between the two countries by boat is impossible. You would be extremely unwise to attempt either of these methods. The only direct connection between the two countries is a short flight between Jayapura (Irian Jaya) and Vanimo on the north coast. Air Niugini has a flight from Wewak, a major hub for transport along the north coast and to the Sepik, to Vanimo (K72) every Wednesday, and this links with a Douglas Airways flight to Jayapura (K33). You can then hook up with the Indonesian domestic airlines and with a flight that leaves from Biak for the USA west coast.

Once you are on the Indonesian domestic network your possibilities are limitless. Garuda has an excellent-value airpass: US$300 gives you 20 days and five stopovers, US$400 gives you 40 days and 10 stopovers, and US$500 gives you unlimited travel for two months. The major hub accessible from Jayapura is Ujung Pandang (Sulawesi) which is US$248 one way, and from there you can connect to places like Jakarta for US$141, or Denpasar (Bali) for US$68. There are also regular inter-island ferries.

One interesting budget possibility would be to fly into PNG from Cairns (Queensland, Australia), travel around by land and sea, take the obligatory flight across the PNG-Indonesia border, travel around Indonesia using an airpass or the local ferries, then fly from Kupang (Timor) to Darwin (Northern Territory, Australia) with the Indonesian airline Merpati (A$132 one way). What you save on fares you will probably spend on food and board, but you will certainly spend many interesting weeks travelling.

There is no direct flight between Port Moresby and Jakarta but you can fly via Singapore using Air Niugini and Singapore Airlines for K699.

Travelling in Indonesia

The most important thing to remember on arriving in Jayapura is you are no longer in PNG. Be on your guard, be prepared to be ripped off. In particular the taxi drivers into town are a mercenary crowd. The official fare into the town is 750 rp per person, and there's a taxi counter in the aiport terminal where you can buy a ticket. If you charter a taxi the trip will cost 10,000 rp. Alternatively, just walk 10 minutes down the road directly in front of the terminal to the main road where you can pick up a ride for 750 rp.

The only place you can get Indonesian rupiah is Moresby. Don't bring too much, as you'll get a better price in Jayapura itself, but not at the airport. See the Facts for the Visitor chapter for important notes about Indonesian visas.

See *South-East Asia on a Shoestring* or *Indonesia – a travel survival kit*, and *Australia – a travel survival kit* for more details.

TO/FROM THE PACIFIC
Air

There are air links between PNG and Guam (Micronesia), Hawaii, Honiara and Munda (Solomon Islands), and Port Vila (Vanuatu). With careful planning, all sorts of itineraries around the Pacific and including PNG are possible.

Continental flies from Hawaii to Guam for US$325, then on Thursdays and Fridays Guam/Port Moresby for US$360 each way. Guam is the main hub for air travel in Micronesia and you can add on individual fares to ports in Micronesia or buy four coupons that entitle you to four flights for US$279. For more information on Micronesia see *Micronesia – a travel survival kit*.

Air Niugini flies from Port Moresby to Honiara via Kieta (Bougainville Island) and then on to Port Vila twice a week. From Moresby to Honiara is K228; from Kieta to Honiara is K111; from Port Moresby to Port Vila is K498. It is possible that this flight will be extended to Suva the capital of Fiji. Solomon Islands Airlines (the Solomons' national airline; book through Air Niugini) flies from Kieta to Munda on New Georgia Island three times a week for K53. Daily flights connect Munda and Honiara and the fare is S$87. For more information on the Solomon Islands see *Solomon Islands – a travel survival kit*.

The tiny (and very rich) island state of Nauru is the focal point for many interesting possibilities, including Honolulu / Guam / Nauru / Honiara / Port Moresby, or Honolulu / Nadi (Fiji) / Nauru / Honiara / Port Moresby.

Air fares on these Pacific routes are a bit of a puzzle since Guam/Honolulu and other routes between the USA and Micronesia are treated like US domestic routes with nice low fares.

Sea

There's a very interesting 'back door' route to PNG and the Solomon Islands, although it can be a little difficult due to immigration and official hassles. Basically it's an island-hopping route between Honiara (Solomon Islands) and Arawa (North Solomons, PNG). From Honiara you go to Gizo (Gizo Island), from Gizo to Korovou (Shortland Island), from Korovou to Buin (Bougainville Island), from Buin to Arawa.

It is likely to cost you as much as flying, but working your way island-to-island along 'the slot' of WW II fame is likely to

be a hell of a lot more interesting. The Solomon Islands Airline has flights that follow this island hopping route, including a flight between Shortland Island and Honiara.

At surface level, three boats ply between Honiara and Gizo Island every week: the *Iuminao*, the MV *Hiliboe* and the *Ulusaghe*. The fares are around S$28. There are several rest houses in Gizo Town for around S$10 per night. From Gizo there is a weekly council boat, the MV *Lanalau*, that makes the day-long trip to Koravou on Shortland Island. It costs S$19. Accommodation is scarce in Koravou, although there is sometimes room in an empty house beside the police station, or in the District Council Guest House.

There's no immigration office at Korovou, so you must get an exit stamp at Gizo, or a statement from the Korovou police saying you've cleared customs with them. You'll also need a valid PNG visa. There are motor canoes to Kangu Beach south of Buin on Bougainville and the best time to get a ride is Friday afternoon or very early Saturday morning when people are travelling to the Buin market. The journey takes 90 minutes and costs S$6 or K3. If you have to charter a canoe expect to pay at least S$25, although some people have been charged a lot more.

Buin is about 15 km inland from the coast. If you're lucky, there'll be a truck to the small town for around K1.50. There is no customs officer in Buin, but there is one in Arawa. Visit the District Manager in Buin who will notify the officials in Arawa you have arrived, then get your passport stamped in Arawa. The only place to stay is the Buin Guest House, which cost a whopping K50 per night including meals. You can change money at the Chinese trade stores. There's a good unsealed road to Arawa and there are PMVs that do the three-hour journey for around K5. Apparently there have been problems with overcharging on this route – you may have to stand up for your rights.

Top: Moresby Harbour from Paga Hill, Port Moresby (RE)
Bottom: PNG's parliament building in Port Moresby is built in the style of a
Maprik-area (East Sepik Province) haus tambaran (ML)

In Arawa you will need to show your exit stamp from the Solomons and your PNG visa to the Immigration Officer. This is also the place to get your exit stamp for PNG if you're heading to the Solomons. In the past there has been some reluctance to give exit stamps, but there have been no recent reports of problems. You'll have to pay a K10 departure tax and you'll be given a clearance letter for the police at Korovou. In Buin, ask around at the market for people going back to Korovou. When you get to Korovou see the police who will give you a letter to present to the immigration authorities in Gizo.

Every few years the governments of both countries threaten to close this border, or to impose stricter controls, so check the situation with the authorities in Honiara and Arawa. To the distress of the bureaucrats, the local people basically disregard the border – the trade route has existed for generations and there is a good deal of intermarriage. For more details on this route see David Harcombe's *Solomon Islands – a travel survival kit*.

TO/FROM NORTH AMERICA

There are four obvious alternatives: a flight to Australia plus a flight to Port Moresby from Sydney, Brisbane or Cairns; a Continental flight to Port Moresby via Honolulu and Guam; a Garuda flight via Honolulu to Biak, then to Jayapura, then to Vanimo on PNG's north coast; and a flight to an Asian port like Manila then a flight to Port Moresby. But many other variations including destinations in Asia and the Pacific are possible.

There is quite a deal of aggressive discounting across the Pacific, so it is important to get competent, up-to-date advice. Shop around, and check the Sunday travel sections of papers like the *Los Angeles Times*, *San Francisco Examiner* and *New York Times*. See the Indonesian, Asian, Pacific and Australian sections in this chapter for more details and ideas.

The most direct route to Port Moresby is Continental's flight. Flying from the west coast to Honolulu will cost around US$250 return, from Honolulu to Guam US$325 each way, from Guam to Port Moresby US$360 each way, a total of US$1620 return. This is fairly expensive compared with the Australian or Asian routes.

A return economy fare to Sydney can cost anywhere between US$850 and US$1500 plus around US$440 for an APEX return flight to Port Moresby. A return fare to Manila can be as low as US$600 plus around US$850 for a return flight to Port Moresby.

The cheapest method is Garuda's Los Angeles/Honolulu/Biak (Irian Jaya, Indonesia) flight. From Biak you fly to Jayapura, which is a short hop across the PNG-Irian Jaya border from Vanimo. This is especially worth considering if your travel plans only involve the Sepik and the north coast, because if they do, there is no pressing reason to go to Port Moresby. The only inconvenience is that the poor connections mean you have no alternative but to spend at least one night in Jayapura. There are three flights a week between Biak and Los Angeles (Wednesday, Friday and Sunday) for a bargain US$472 one way, US$800 return. From Biak you catch a domestic flight to Jayapura for US$58, then a weekly Douglas Airways flight (a subsidiary of Air Niugini) to Vanimo for US$36, where you can hook into PNG's domestic system.

Leaving PNG, the Douglas Airways flight on Wednesdays gets you to Jayapura too late to catch the Wednesday flight from Biak, so you have to fill in Wednesday and Thursday night in Jayapura or Biak. An air-con hotel room will cost around US$20 a night, although you could spend a lot less for a losmen (guesthouse). If you depart from the USA on Sunday, you arrive in Jayapura on Tuesday (remember the international dateline) which means you only have to wait one night for the PNG-bound flight on Wednesday. See important notes on visas in the Facts for the Visitor chapter. The flight-only component works out to US$988 return.

TO/FROM EUROPE

There are a million and one alternatives when you start talking about a trip to the other side of the world. This section only gives an indication of a few of the most obvious possibilities: via Indonesia, Singapore, the Philippines, America and the Pacific and/or Australia.

London remains the best place in Europe to buy cheap fares. Look for free magazines like *LAM – London's Australasian Magazine* and do the rounds of travel agents and 'bucket shops' for discount tickets. There are many options and discounts that come into play for long flights and complex itineraries, so make sure you shop around. Some of the alternatives discussed in the other sections of this chapter will be relevant if your destination is not exclusively PNG.

If you fly the most direct route to Port Moresby via Singapore you'll be looking at a total fare of around £900 return, depending on what sort of deal you get for Singapore (this figure assumes something like £400 for a Singapore return).

The cheapest method will, however, probably be to fly to Australia. If you buy a discount return ticket to Australia and tag on a Cairns/Moresby APEX return the trip will cost you around £775 (assuming the Australian ticket is around £650). If you fly to Australia, then Port Moresby, then Singapore and then home the cost will be more like £1400.

If you fly to Port Moresby via America and the Pacific the cost will be around £700 one way.

Adding the PNG-Australia sector to a round-the-world airfare is a great option if you have the time to take advantage of some of the stopovers available enroute to/from PNG.

Warning

This chapter is particularly vulnerable to change – prices for international travel are volatile, routes are introduced and cancelled, schedules change, rules are amended, special deals come and go, borders open and close. Airlines and governments seem to take a perverse pleasure in making price structures and regulations as complicated as possible and you should check directly with the airline or a travel agent to make sure you understand how a fare (and ticket you may buy) works. In addition, the travel industry is highly competive and there are many lurks and perks. The upshot of this is that you should get opinions, quotes and advice from as many airlines and travel agents as possible before you part with your hard-earned cash. The details given in this chapter should be regarded as pointers and are not a substitute for careful, up-to-date research.

Getting Around

AIR

Civil aviation was pioneered in PNG and there is no country that was more dependent on flying for its development. Even today, when a sketchy road network is beginning to creep across parts of the country, an enormous proportion of passengers and freight travel by air. Geographic realities continue to dictate this situation: the population is small and scattered, often isolated in mountain valleys and on tiny islands. Unfortunately, these factors also mean that flying is expensive. And, if you have limited time, it's virtually unavoidable.

There are four main carriers on domestic routes and numerous small charter operations. The four main outfits are: Air Niugini (the national carrier), Talair, Douglas Airways and MAF (Missionary Aviation Fellowship – known to some as the Missionaries' Air Force!).

You may well come across a distinction between first-level, second-level and third-level airlines for the first time when you visit PNG. First-level describes a carrier that operates internationally, second-level covers airlines that make the major domestic connections (Air Niugini and Talair) and third-level translates to mean an airline that operates between all the tiny towns and villages (Talair, Douglas Airways, MAF and all the rest).

Air Niugini operates half a dozen Fokker F28s (jets), and De Havilland Dash 7s (turbo-props) on its domestic routes. Talair is one of the largest commercial light-aircraft operators in the world, with a fleet that includes two Dash 8s, Bandeirantes, Twin Otters, Britten Norman Islanders, Cessnas and Beechcraft Barons. Douglas Airways is now a subsidiary of Air Niugini and along with MAF its fleet is dominated by small aircraft.

You should really try to make at least one flight in a small aircraft while you're in the country – preferably somewhere up in the hills where flying can be a real experience. There are more than 400 licensed airfields so there are plenty of opportunities – 18 could be described as second-level (large enough for F28s), while the rest are third-level (suitable for small aircraft only).

Air Niugini now has a number of low-fare packages. If you make an APEX (see the Getting There section) return booking outside PNG you are eligible for a 20% discount on domestic flights. Breaks are permitted (flights don't have to connect) but the problem is that you have to book at least 21 days in advance and the cancellation fees can equal 50% of the fare and more. If you are a full-time student under 25 years old you are eligible for a 25% reduction on domestic fares.

If you're making a booking outside PNG you need to have an International Student Concession Form. I didn't hear of anyone needing this when they bought discount tickets in PNG (a student card was sufficient) but you might be wise to get one just in case.

Nambawan Fares are worth considering, but they can only be booked in PNG and the conditions are fairly limiting. Basically, you can get a 40% discount on a return fare, if you stay away for a minimum of seven days and a maximum of 30. Weekend Excursion Fares are similar – again there is a 40% discount and severe restrictions. You have to make your outward journey on Friday or Saturday and return on Sunday or Monday. Both these fares only apply at certain times of the year so make sure you check whether they will be applicable.

Talair, Douglas Airways and MAF all offer student discounts of 25% (you must have current ID), but they don't really get into fancy discount structures. Talair does have Excursion Fares with a 20% discount for overseas travellers who fly to PNG on an Excursion Fare (these are priced mid way between APEX and full economy fares; you don't have to book them in advance, but a minimum stay overseas is usually obligatory). This discount is available for all flights, but is only available from Talair International Offices in Port Moresby.

Air Niugini, Talair and Douglas Airways all have computerised booking systems so bookings are usually quite efficient and can be made from anywhere in the world; they are linked to the Qantas system, so you can make bookings at any Qantas office. This level of sophistication does not apply to every PNG airport – some terminals can be more accurately described as sheds.

Book ahead, if possible, because the planes are small and fill up quickly. If you're told a flight is full, it's often worth trying again - they don't always seem to end up that way. Travel can be more difficult during the Australian school holidays. Many expats bring their children up from their boarding schools and flights are heavily booked around Christmas, early February, late June and late September.

Remember that you may have to fly in *light* aircraft. If you do, flying out with a two-metre garamut drum tucked under your arm might be difficult. Not only is your baggage weighed (16 kilos is the official limit, although 20 is usually accepted) – so are you.

Unpredictable weather combined with mechanical problems and complex schedules can frequently lead to delays. If one plane is late at one airport the whole schedule can be thrown out. Considering the terrain, the airstrips and the weather, reliability is fair and the safety record is very good. The pilots are extremely skilful – keep telling yourself this as you approach flat-topped ridges masquerading as airports! Many young pilots are intent on building up their command experience so they can move on to a first-level airline, but others stay on because 'PNG has the best flying in the world'.

For the addresses of Air Niugini's overseas offices see the Getting There chapter. Remember that prices and discount offers are prone to change. Other useful addresses include:

Air Niugini
    PO Box 7186, Boroko, Port Moresby
    (tel 27 3542)
Talair
    PO Box 108, Goroka, Eastern Highlands
    (tel 72 1355)

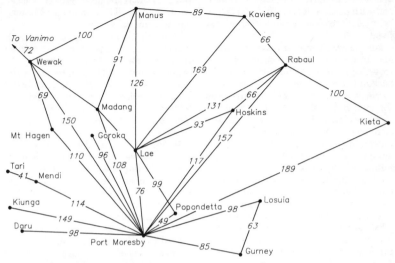

Major Domestic Routes

Fares in Kina

Douglas Airways
  PO Box 7186, Boroko, Port Moresby
  (tel 25 3499)
MAF
  PO Box 273, Mt Hagen, Western Highlands
  (tel 55 1434)

Aviation History
After a couple of false starts and some extravagant ideas of exploring the country by Zeppelin airships, aviation arrived in 1922 when a small seaplane made a flight from Port Moresby. A few other pioneering flights followed, but it was the development of the Wau and Bulolo gold fields that really launched aviation in New Guinea.

Cecil John Levien, one of the pioneers on these gold fields, soon realised that they would never be successfully exploited as long as getting men and supplies up from the coast involved a long hard slog across difficult terrain, peopled by unfriendly tribes. After a number of unsuccessful attempts to interest Australian operators, Levien pushed through a proposal that his own Guinea Gold company should set up an air service, which they named Guinea Airways.

Their pilot, 'Pard' Mustar, had to do far more than just fly their first DH-37 biplane. First he arranged for an airstrip to be constructed at Lae (the local jail provided prisoners to build it) then he walked from Salamua to Wau to supervise the airstrip construction there. Next he had to travel back to Rabaul where the DH-37 had arrived in pieces as sea cargo. Then he had to assemble it and fly to Lae – a 650 km journey, much of it over sea or unexplored jungle, in a single engined aircraft of less than total reliability.

In April 1927 Mustar took off on his first flight to Wau – and couldn't find it! He returned to Lae, took more directions and advice and tried again with an equal lack of success. Finally, on his third attempt and with an experienced guide on board, he made the first of many 50-minute flights.

For the next couple of years passengers and freight were shuttled back and forth. It cost £33 to fly up to Wau, only £10 to fly back, by comparison with K35 today. There were a number of other carriers on the run, but Guinea Airways were the most successful. Ray Parer was one who commenced operations with a DH-4 at much the same time, but lack of finance always held his Bulolo Gold Fields Aeroplane Service back.

Mustar quickly realised the need for more capacity and reliability and before the end of 1927 he went to Germany to buy a Junkers W-34 at the astronomical cost of £8000. It may have been expensive, but at the time it was the very latest thing in cargo aircraft and could lift over a ton. A second W-34 soon followed and with these aircraft Guinea Airways operated a service that proved the real possibilities of air transport just as convincingly as the much better publicised flights of Lindbergh or Kingsford-Smith. Wau became the busiest airfield in the world and more air freight was lifted annually in New Guinea than in the rest of the world put together!

Mustar left New Guinea, but in 1929 was called back to attempt a scheme that, to many people at the time, must have seemed like something in the realms of science fiction. He had to find a way of flying gold dredges weighing 3000 tons onto the gold fields! Mustar's answer was to dismantle the dredges and buy another Junkers, the G-31, a three-engined, all-metal monster which cost £30,000 and could lift three tons. In the early '30s a fleet of these aircraft carried not just gold equipment, but also workers and even the first horses ever to be transported by air.

Throughout the '30s more and more aircraft and operators came into New Guinea and the fierce competition dramatically forced down the air freight rates. In 1931 regular services started between the gold fields and Port Moresby on the south coast.

Holden's Air Transport Services developed but was later taken over by Guinea Airways. The air service started by the island traders W R Carpenter & Co was longer lasting. In 1937 they absorbed Pacific Aerial Transport (originally formed by gold fields pioneer Ray Parer) and became Mandated Airlines Ltd (MAL).

In 1938 they started the first airmail service between PNG and Australia. Guinea Airways also expanded south into Australia operating a successful service between Adelaide and Darwin via Alice Springs using the ultra-modern, twin-engined Lockheed Electra.

Also during the '30s, pioneer missionaries proved that the airplane could be put to spiritual as well as secular use; possibly the first ever aerial mapping was conducted (in 1935); and aircraft supplied the prospectors and explorers who were opening up the final hidden parts of the country. One of the most spectacular forays was made by the wealthy American Richard Archbold who used a Catalina amphibian and discovered the Grand Valley of the Baliem in Dutch New Guinea.

The arrival of the Japanese in 1942 abruptly ended civil aviation. Most PNG-based aircraft were caught on the ground by the first devastating raids on Lae, Salamua and Bulolo. The aircraft that survived made a final desperate series of flights to evacuate civilians away from the advancing Japanese.

When the war ended, aviation in PNG was a whole new story. In 1944 Qantas took over MAL's Australia-PNG connections and got their first toehold in the country. Guinea Airways were unable to obtain a licence to operate in PNG from the post-war Labor Government and Qantas became the dominant airline. Using DC3s and then DC4s Qantas started regular passenger services between Australia and PNG and during the '50s they built up a quite incredible fleet of aircraft for internal use. They operated everything from Beaver and Otter STOL aircraft, through DH-83 and DH-84 biplanes to Catalina, Short Solent and Sandringham flying boats. PNG was looked upon as a very useful training ground for pilots who would later fly on Qantas' international network.

In 1960 the Australian Government decided that Qantas should be a purely international airline and domestic services were handed over to Australia's domestic airlines, Ansett-ANA and Trans-Australia Airlines (TAA, now Australian Airlines) since PNG was considered to be part of Australia. MAL had been the main opposition to Qantas, swallowing smaller competitors such as Gibbes' Sepik Airways, but it was in turn engulfed by Ansett. TAA and Ansett-MAL operated turbo-prop Lockheed Electras and, later, Boeing 727s between Australia and PNG. Internally, they supplemented their DC3 workhorses with Fokker F27 Friendships in 1967.

Air Niugini was formed on 1 November 1973, almost immediately after the start of self government and took over Ansett's and TAA's PNG-based aircraft. Today Air Niugini, a very young airline with a very long pedigree, operates an Airbus 310 on international routes, and Fokker F28s and De Havilland Dash 7s on its domestic routes. Talair, now the major third-level carrier, began as Territory Airlines Ltd (TAL) in 1952 and now has scheduled operations into 130 airports.

SEA

For those that have the time, there is a wide variety of interesting sea transport. There are numerous small ships and private boats that carry passengers along the north coast and out to the many islands. If you are an easygoing, independent traveller who is prepared to rough it you'll find it relatively easy to get to ports,

villages and islands way off the beaten track. Although there are a number of other smaller operations the main shipping companies and their head offices are:

Coastal Shipping Company Pty Ltd
    PO Box 423, Rabaul, East New Britain
    (tel 92 1733)
Lutheran Shipping
    PO Box 789, Madang (tel 82 2577 or
    82 2146)
Burns Philp Shipping
    Musgrave St, Port Moresby (tel 22 9241)
    Pacific New Guinea Line
    PO Box 2192, Lae, Morobe Province
    (tel 42 1990)

The major coastal towns are connected by sparse but regular, scheduled services, while in more remote places it's just a matter of sitting back and waiting until something comes by.

Most of the coastal ships are small freighters with deck and cabin class accommodation. Conditions can be grim. It is essential, on any of these freighters, to take food of your own. Your fare will include meals but these will amount to rice and tinned fish and may or may not be edible. At the very least, take fruit and drinks with you.

If you're travelling deck class, a sleeping bag and a tent fly (for shade and shelter) will be handy. Make sure your luggage is waterproof and take a clothes' peg to put on your nose when you approach the toilet. Timetables often bear little relation to reality: there are delays caused by weather, cargo loading and unloading, extra stops . . . .

The most important exception is a new passenger-only vessel, the *Mamose Express*, run by Lutheran Shipping. It's clean and comfortable, runs between Oro Bay (near Popondetta) and Wewak stopping at Lae, Finschhafen and Madang on the way. There is a 50% student discount but even without this it is still very good value – a real lifesaver for budget travellers. See the fare tables following.

There are other scheduled links between Moresby and the Gulf Province ports; out to the islands, from Lae to Rabaul (New Britain); and between Rabaul, Lorengau (Manus), Kavieng (New Ireland) and Kieta (Bougainville). There are no passenger vessels linking the north and south coasts. Make sure you book ahead if you want to travel in December.

North Coast

Lutheran Shipping has a virtual monopoly on passenger shipping along the north coast and services Oro Bay, Lae, Finschhafen, Madang, Wewak, Aitape, Vanimo and intermediate ports. The most important possibility is the *Mamose Express*, although there are also a number of notorious freighters, if you're happy to cope with fairly primitive facilities.

The *Mamose Express'* tourist class consists of air-conditioned bucket seats and berths, and deck class has air-vented bucket seats and berths. Both classes have video 'entertainment' and there is a snack bar which serves soft drinks and pies, etc. Don't rely on the following schedule, it could change; remember students and children are 50% cheaper:

Eastbound

Port	Time	Tourist	Deck
Wewak	d 3 pm Tue	K27	K18
Madang	a 6 am Sun		
Madang	d 7 pm Sun	K18	K12
Finsch.	a 9 am Mon		
Finsch.	d 11 am Mon	K19	K12
Lae	a 5 pm Mon		
Lae	d 8 pm Mon	K27	K18
Oro Bay	a 12 pm Tue		

Westbound

Port	Time	Tourist	Deck
Oro Bay	d 2 pm Tue	K27	K18
Lae	a 6 am Wed		
Lae	d 9 am Wed	K14	K9
Finsch.	a 3 pm Wed		
Finsch.	d 5 pm Wed	K18	K12
Madang	a 6 am Thu		
Madang	d 7 pm Thu	K27	K18
Wewak	a 10 am Sat		

Through Rates

Ports	Tourist	Deck
Lae-Finsch.	K14	K9
Lae-Madang	K18	K12
Lae-Wewak	K45	K30
Wewak-Oro Bay	K72	K48

Islands

Coastal Shipping Enterprises runs vessels to the islands off the north coast, including Manus, New Britain, New Ireland and Bougainville. All their ships are small freighters so don't expect luxury. Most have at least one or two cabins, which are air-conditioned and contain four berths, but some only have deck space; you must book ahead for cabins and you may have to share, but reservations are not accepted for deck class. The food varies between deck and cabin class; if you travel deck class take your own and you're probably wise to do the same, even in cabin class. Safety regulations prohibit them carrying passengers and 'dangerous' cargo at the same time; cargo takes priority so you can lose your reservation at any time.

The MV *Cosmaris* has one cabin and goes from Rabaul to Lorengau (Manus Island) departing every second Tuesday; the cabin costs K80, deck class K40. There are two ships a week between Rabaul and Lae: the MV *Kimbe Express* has no cabins and departs on Fridays; the MV *Beaumaris* has two cabins for K80 and departs on Tuesdays; deck class on both vessels costs K44 and the journey takes three days. The MV *Atolls Enterprise* makes a monthly voyage to Bougainville (deck class only for K34) and also makes what would be a fascinating two-week swing through the islands east of Bougainville. Foreign students are not given a discount. The Pacific New Guinea Line's MV *Kris* also does the Lae-Rabaul run, leaving Lae on Fridays and costing K44.

Lutheran's MV *Makaya* does a fortnightly voyage to Lorengau from Lae for K33, deck class only. The MV *Tawi*, which is operated by the Manus Provincial Government (tel 40 9088), Shipping

Officer, MPG, PO Box 111, Lorengau, plies between Lorengau, the outer islands of Manus, Wuvulu Island, Wewak and Madang. Wewak or Madang to Lorengau takes from five to seven days and there is a return voyage every couple of weeks. There's no straightforward schedule and Madang-Manus is about K30. I heard of the *Joseph Wyett*, also operated by the Manus Government, which apparently goes between Wewak and Manus every three weeks.

There are no scheduled services around the islands in Milne Bay Province but small boats are coming and going all the time – the best place to find these is in Alotau and Samarai.

Local boats and canoes go literally everywhere, but you do have to be in the right place at the right time. The major companies list shipping in the Shipping Notes section of the *Post Courier*; for the rest, however, you'll only find out by going down to the docks or to the markets and asking. If you have a philosophical attitude to comfort and itineraries, persistence will get you everywhere.

South Coast

The main passenger operator on the south coast is Burns Philp Shipping based in Port Moresby, with vessels that go east to Milne Bay and west to ports in the Gulf Province. Their office is down by the docks. Either the MV *Purari* or the MV *Malalo* leaves for the Gulf every Tuesday or Wednesday. If you left on Tuesday, you'd get to Kerema on Wednesday morning for K34, to Ihu on Thursday for K40, and to Baimuru on Friday for K46. It is probably worth trying Steamships as well, but they weren't interested in passengers when I asked.

RIVER

There are a number of rivers that local people use as 'highways'. These include the Sepik and some of its tributaries (including the April, May and Keram), the Ramu, the Fly and a number of other rivers that flow into the Gulf of Papua. On these rivers there is often an assortment of different craft, ranging from dugout canoes to tramp steamers.

If you are prepared to rough it and live in the villages, it possible to use inter-village PMV canoes. The problem with this is that although they are relatively cheap they only run according to demand – there are no schedules. Traffic builds up from Wednesday through to Saturday because of people moving around for markets, but can be very quiet early in the week and non-existent on Sundays.

If you are short of time, you can charter a motorboat and driver locally. This is, however, very expensive: probably somewhere between K10 and K20 per hour of running time (this is due to the high cost of operating two-stroke engines).

ROAD

There is still a very limited network of roads around the country. The most important is the Highlands Highway, which is sealed from Lae to Mt Hagen, unsealed from Mt Hagen to Tari, and a four-wheel drive track between Tari and Lake Kopiago where it stops. There are some reasonable dirt roads east and west along the coast from Port Moresby, along the north coast east and west of Madang, into the Sepik basin from Wewak, and the Germans bequeathed good roads on New Britain and New Ireland. There is no road between Moresby and the Highlands or between Moresby and the north coast.

Wherever there are roads there is public transport – privately run Public Motor Vehicles (PMVs) – and on the major routes this is regular and cheap. Every major town has cars for hire, but they are expensive and, unless you get a four-wheel drive, not much more useful than the PMVs.

If you do drive, bear in mind the tourist office's recommendations if you are involved in an accident: Don't stop; keep driving and report the accident at the nearest police station. This applies regardless of who was at fault or how serious the accident is (whether you've run over a pig or hit a person). Tribal concepts of payback apply to car accidents. You may have insurance and you may be willing to pay, but the the local citizenry may well prefer to take more immediate and satisfying revenge. There have been a number of instances where drivers who have been involved in fatal accidents have been killed or injured by the accident victim's relatives. A serious accident can mean 'pack up and leave' for an expat.

Any valid overseas license is OK for the first three months you're in PNG. Cars drive on the left side of the road. The speed limit is 50 km per hour in towns and 100 km per hour in the country.

PMVs

Public Motor Vehicles are one of the secrets to cheap travel in PNG and a very successful example of local enterprise. Twenty-five years ago they didn't exist, now they seem indispensable and they go wherever there are roads. Most PMVs are comfortable Japanese mini-buses, but they can be trucks with wooden benches, or even small, bare pick-up trucks.

Rural PMVs pick up and drop off people at any point along a pre-established route. You can more or less assume that anything with lots of people in it is a rural PMV, although officially they have a blue number plate beginning with P. In the urban areas there are established PMV stops (often indicated by a yellow pole or a crowd of waiting people) and the number plates are orange. The destination will be indicated by a sign inside the windscreen or called out by the driver's assistant.

Stick your hand out and wave downwards and they will generally stop. PMVs have a crew of two: the driver, who usually maintains an aloof distance from the passengers; and the 'conductor', who takes fares and generally copes with the rabble. On most occasions the conductor sits up front next to the passenger-side

window, so when the PMV stops, he's the man to ask about the PMV's destination. If it's heading in the right direction and there's a centimetre or two of spare space, you're on. You don't pay – yet.

There are standard fares for PMVs. Ask your fellow passengers if you want to be certain what they are, but it is very unlikely you will be ripped off. If you are a student, try for a student discount; this won't always be forthcoming, but it can be generous when it is. In the towns you pay the conductor at the end of the trip after you've disembarked. If you tell the conductor where you want to go when you start, he'll let the driver know when to stop. If you make your mind up as you go, just yell 'Stup' (the Pidgin for 'stop' is correctly spelt *stap*).

In the country they quite frequently collect the fare either midway through the journey or 15 minutes or so before your final destination. It seems too many passengers were escaping into the bush without paying! Because of the general improvement in road standards and the fierce competition, fares have scarcely increased at all over the last few years.

Some expats you speak to may suggest that PMVs are unsafe. Ignore these comments. You'll find that the people who are most hysterical about the dangers of riding on PMVs are the people who've never set foot in one. If the vehicle looks in pretty good shape and the driver does too, you are most unlikely to have any problems. Most drivers are very careful. They simply cannot afford to hit a stray person or pig (think of the compensation and the paybacks) let alone injure one of their passengers. You are not immune to armed holdups when you travel on PMVs in the Highlands but if you travel during the day and avoid pay afternoons (every second Friday) you're safer in a PMV than in a private car.

Make sure you get to your destination before dark and if you don't, ask the driver to deliver you to wherever you plan to stay. If you're looking for long-distance

PMVs always start at the markets *early* in the morning and, if you're travelling alone, you're probably safest to pick one with a reasonable crowd of passengers of both sexes. PMVs leave town when they're full (and I mean full) so if you're the first on board you can spend a very frustrating hour or two circling around looking for more passengers. Market days (usually Friday and Saturday) are the best days for finding a ride. On secondary roads, traffic can be thin early in the week.

Not only is PMV travel cheap but it's also one of the best ways to meet the locals.

Hitching

It is possible to hitch-hike, although you'll often be expected to pay the equivalent of a PMV fare. In some places any passing vehicle is likely to offer you a ride. That is, *if* there is a passing vehicle. You're wisest to wave them down, however, otherwise it's possible they'll think you're a mad tourist walking for the fun of it. If your bag is light, it's also sometimes possible to hitch-hike flights from small airports.

Car Hire

It is possible to hire cars in most main centres but because of the limited road network (with the exception of the Highlands) you usually won't be able to get far. The major car rental organisations are Budget, Hertz and Avis-Nationwide. One or other of them will have cars in every major town, including on the islands of Manus, New Britain, New Ireland and Bougainville. There are also a few smaller, local firms that are sometimes cheaper than the internationals; they are mentioned in the appropriate chapters.

Costs are high, partly because the cars have such a hard life and spend so much time on unsealed roads. All rental rates with the big operators are made up of a daily or weekly charge plus a certain charge per km. In addition you should probably budget for insurance at around K12 a day. Typical costs and cars are:

	per day	per km
Suzuki Alto	K23	20t
Ford Laser	K34	26t
Mazda 626	K42	30t
Mazda 929	K46	32t
Nissan Four-wheel Drive	K46	32t

In addition, remote area surcharges of around K10 a day may apply. Make sure you won't be charged extra if you drop a car off somewhere other than your starting point. There are one-way rental rates between Lae and the various Highland towns, for example Lae to Mt Hagen would cost K120. The three main operators all have desks at Jackson's Airport, Port Moresby:

Avis-Nationwide
    PO Box 3533, Boroko (tel 25 8299)
Budget
    PO Box 503, Boroko (tel 25 4514)
Hertz
    PO Box 4126, Boroko (tel 25 4495)

WALKING & CANOEING

The best and cheapest way to come to grips with PNG is to walk. See some of the walks suggested in the Things To Do section of the Facts for the Visitor chapter. With a judicious mix of walks, canoes, PMVs, coastal ships and third-level planes PNG can change from a very expensive country to a relatively reasonable one.

Accommodation and food is normally available in the villages – meaning floor space, and sago or sweet potato – and once you're afloat or on foot you will spend very little money.

For detailed information on walking and climbing see the Lonely Planet book *Bushwalking in Papua New Guinea*. Your major costs will be paying for guides and porters, where they are necessary. Expect to pay them between K5 and K10 a day in addition to buying their food, providing sleeping gear and space and possibly some equipment. It is possible to buy dugout canoes for between K10 and K60 a canoe. Canoeing is most popular on the Sepik – see the Sepik chapter for a more detailed discussion of the options.

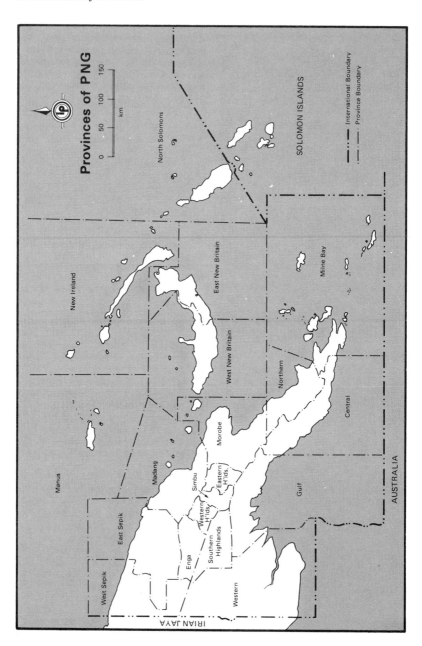

Provinces of PNG

km
0 50 100 150

North Solomons

SOLOMON ISLANDS

New Ireland

East New Britain

Mine Bay

Manus

West New Britain

Madang

Morobe

Northern

Central

East Sepik

Simbu

Eastern
H'lds

Gulf

West Sepik

Enga

Western
H'lds

Southern
Highlands

Western

IRIAN JAYA

AUSTRALIA

-··-··- International Boundary
-·-·-·- Province Boundary

Port Moresby & Central

Area 29,940 square km
Population 300,000
Port Moresby 160,000

The Central Province covers the narrow coastal strip along the south coast from the Gulf of Papua almost to the eastern end of the mainland, plus the southern half of the central mountain range. Port Moresby, the capital of PNG, is situated about half way along the coast on a superb natural harbour. A rain shadow affects the city area and it is much drier than the rest of the country. The dry, brown, northern-Australian look of Moresby fades into the usual lush green as you move away from the capital. In the dry season Port Moresby can suffer from extended droughts and restrictions on water use.

HISTORY

There were two groups of people living in the Port Moresby area when the first white men arrived. They were the Motu and the Koitabu. The Motu were a seagoing people with an Austronesian language that has close links with other Melanesian and Polynesian languages. It seems probable that they were relatively late arrivals from the coast (possibly migrating from island Melanesia less than 2000 years before the Europeans) and they lived in harmony with the Koitabu who speak an inland, non-Austronesian language.

The Motuan people were great sailors and their impressive boats, called *lakatois*, were up to 15 metres long, and capable of carrying a large cargo and crew. They were rigged with one or two masts and strange crab-claw shaped sails.

The high point of the Motuan year was the annual *hiri* trading voyage – each Motuan village had a counterpart village in the Gulf region with which it traded clay pots for sago. The Motuans were not great farmers, perhaps because of the dry climate and limited agricultural potential of the Moresby area, as well as their heritage, so they depended on Gulf sago for their survival.

Motu villages were built on stilts over the harbour. Hanuabada (meaning 'the great village') was the largest of their communities and still exists today, although in a considerably changed form.

The first European visit they received was in 1873 when Captain John Moresby, investigating the south coast of the mysterious island of New Guinea, sailed into the harbour. He spent several days trading with the villagers at Hanuabada and was very impressed with the people and their lives. In his diary he asked himself, 'What have these people to gain from civilisation?'

One year later the London Missionary Society established its first outpost and the missionaries were soon followed by traders, and 'blackbirders' who recruited indentured labourers and were little better than slavers. For a time the blackbirders' 'kanaka' labourers were as important an export as beche de mer and pearl shell.

The island's interior remained largely unexplored and 'unclaimed' by Europeans as Britain had sufficient colonial problems to attend to without the addition of New Guinea. Finally, in 1888, under pressure

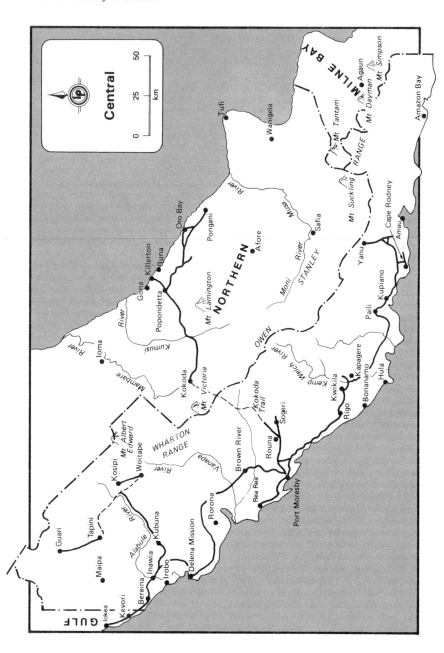

from colonists in Australia and because of trepidation about the intentions of the Germans who held the northern half of the island, British New Guinea was formally claimed and Port Moresby became its capital. The remarkable 10 year administration of Sir William MacGregor commenced. MacGregor established the government in Moresby, the national police force and personally explored large tracts of the rugged island.

In 1906 the colony was handed over to newly independent Australia. In 1907 Sir Hubert Murray took over administration of Papua, as it had been renamed and ran it until the day he died in 1940, at the age of 78, while out 'on patrol' at Samarai in Milne Bay Province.

Papua was overshadowed by New Guinea, north of the central mountains, for much of the period between the two wars. The discovery of gold at Wau and Bulolo plus the productive plantations on the offshore islands made New Guinea much more important economically. WW II shifted the spotlight back to Port Moresby because it became the staging post for the Allies fighting along the Kokoda Trail. Moresby remained in Allied hands throughout the war.

After the war Papua and New Guinea were administered as one territory. Since the northern New Guinea towns were little more than rubble, Port Moresby retained its position as the country's administrative headquarters – a position it continues to hold, although there has been occasional pressure to move the capital elsewhere. Lae, with its central location and excellent communications to the important Highlands, is the usual suggestion.

Port Moresby's isolation is its main drawback. It is the only major town in the southern half of the country and there are no road connections to any other important town. Nevertheless it is now firmly established as the capital and largest city in the country.

GEOGRAPHY

Central Province consists of a narrow coastal strip rising rapidly to the 4000-metre heights of the Owen Stanley Range. Port Moresby is in the centre of the driest area of the whole country and this dry region extends about 100 km along the coast on either side.

PEOPLE

Many of the coastal people of the Central Province seem more closely related to the Polynesians of the Pacific Islands than to the stockier inland people. The indigenous groups around Moresby were the Motu, a seagoing, trading people and the Koita, an inland people with hunting and gardening skills who coexisted with the Motu. Further into the mountains lived the feared Koiari people and to the northwest, the Mekeo.

During the early years of English and then Australian contact the Motu language was adopted by the administration and spread throughout the territory in the form of 'Police Motu'. Its position as lingua franca has now been usurped by the spread of Pidgin, although many Papuans still speak 'Police Motu'.

Port Moresby is a cosmopolitan city and apart from the largest foreign community in the country, expats make up about eight to 9% of the city's population, almost every tribal group in PNG is represented. Since the war, people have been drawn from around the country for education and jobs, especially from the Gulf and Western Provinces. People from the undeveloped west make up a high proportion of those who live in the shanty villages. You will also see people from many other parts of the country.

Port Moresby

Port Moresby was the capital of British New Guinea and, after the hand over to Australia, it became the capital of Papua.

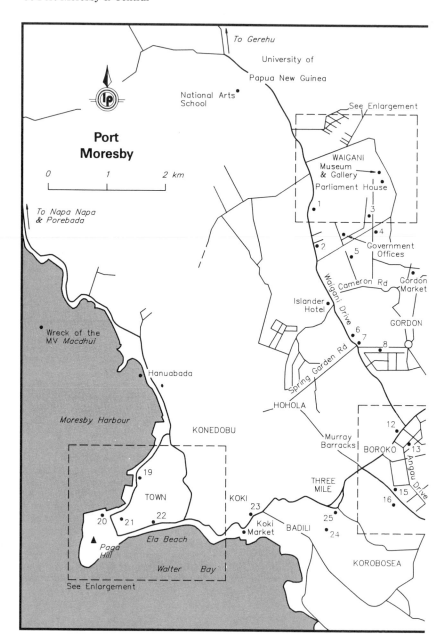

To Gerehu

University of
Papua New Guinea

National Arts
School

**Port
Moresby**

0   1   2 km

To Napa Napa
& Porebada

See Enlargement

WAIGANI

Museum
& Gallery

Parliament House

1

3

4

2

5

Government
Offices

Cameron Rd

Gordon
Market

Waigani Drive

Islander
Hotel

GORDON

Spring Garden Rd

6

7

8

Wreck of the
MV Macdhui

Hanuabada

HOHOLA

Murray
Barracks

12

Moresby Harbour

KONEDOBU

BOROKO

13

Angau Drive

THREE
MILE

15

16

19

TOWN

KOKI

23

25

24

20

21

22

Koki
Market

BADILI

Ela Beach

Paga
Hill

Walter Bay

KOROBOSEA

See Enlargement

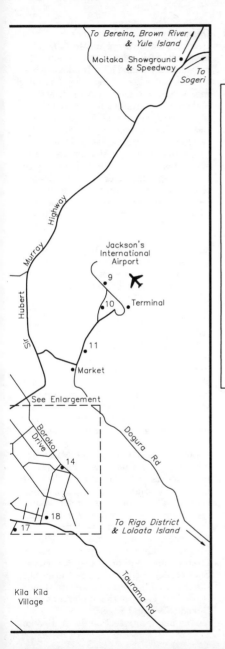

1 Germania Club
2 PMV Stop
3 Australian High Commission
4 Indonesian Embassy
5 Teachers College
6 PMV Stop
7 Hanuacraft
8 PNG Arts & Pacific Expeditions
9 Talair
10 Air Niugini Head Office
11 Granville Motel
12 PMV Stop
13 Boroko Post Office
14 Kwangtung Village Restaurant
15 Country Womens' Association
16 Hospital
17 Shanghai Gardens
    Restaurant/Niugini Arts
18 Spagetti House
19 Yacht Club
20 GPO
21 Travelodge
22 Davara Hotel
23 Salvation Army Hostel
24 Pacific View Apartments
    (Embassies)
25 YWCA

Between the wars PNG was administered in two parts, Papua, with Port Moresby as its capital, and Australian New Guinea (the ex-German territory), with its capital at Rabaul in New Britain. After WW II the country was governed as one entity with Port Moresby as its capital, a role that has become even more significant since independence in 1975.

Many people find 'Moresby', as it is known locally, a rather dismal place. It is dry, hot and dusty for much of the year and that's only the start of its problems. Expatriate residents, who almost without exception have cars, may not find it annoying, but one of Moresby's biggest drawbacks is its amazing sprawl. It is not so much a city as a collection of widely separated suburbs. Moresby also suffers from a 'big city' syndrome – it attracts people in search of fame and fortune. Naturally many fail to find either and a large number end up living in squalid, unserviced squatter settlements. They contribute to Moresby's high crime rate, particularly the house-breaking that leads to the expats' fanatical security precautions.

The gloom is not all-pervading – there are interesting things to see and do around the city. At present, almost every visitor to the country is forced to go through Moresby and it is worth spending a couple of days looking around and acclimatising. It is, after all, an important part of the country.

Throughout PNG, 'knowing' somebody can be enormously helpful, and this is especially the case in Moresby. If you do have an address, or you do know somebody, look them up! If you don't know anybody, try to meet people with similar work or leisure interests, or better still, contact them before you leave home.

If you still dislike Moresby, remember this important rule: never judge a country by its capital city.

Orientation

Getting your bearings in Moresby is no easy task as it spreads out around the coast and the inland hills. It takes a while to work out where things are. The hills mean that getting from A to B, a short distance in a straight line, may involve lengthy detours around the intervening terrain. Fortunately, PMVs run regular services between all areas of the city.

The town centre, if Moresby can claim such a feature, is on a spit of land which ends in Paga Hill – there are good views of the harbour and town from the summit lookout. The centre has the majority of Moresby's older buildings, the shipping docks and wharves, most of the major commercial office buildings, the conspicuous Travelodge and the large Steamships and Burns Philp shops.

If you follow the coast round to the north, past the docks, you'll come to the Sir Hubert Murray Stadium, then Konedobu (a government office centre), then Hanuabada (the original Motuan stilt village).

East from the town centre, the main road runs alongside popular Ela Beach until you reach Koki where there are shops, the Salvation Army, the colourful Koki Market and another, smaller stilt village. From Koki, the road divides into two one-way sections and climbs steeply up Three Mile Hill before dropping down to Boroko.

Boroko (also known as Four Mile – it is about four miles from 'town') has, in some departments, overtaken town as the most important commercial and shopping centre. There are numerous shops, restaurants, banks, airline agencies and there's a new, efficient post office.

If you continue along the Hubert Murray Highway you pass Jackson's International Airport (also known as Seven Mile). A few miles past the airport the road divides, heading west to Brown River and east to the mountains, the Kokoda Trail and Sogeri.

The main intersection is at Boroko

where there is a T-intersection between the Hubert Murray Highway and Waigani Drive which runs out to the north-west. Waigani Drive takes you between Hohola (residential) and Gordon (industrial, with an excellent market) to Waigani (the sprawling government centre about four km from Boroko).

A little beyond Waigani you reach the university campus. After the campus, one road turns west back to the coast (joining the coast road seven or eight km out from Hanuabada) and another continues to Gerehu, a fast growing residential suburb.

Information

There are plans to establish a tourist information desk at the airport to the left of the exit to the international arrivals' 'lounge'. You'll see a sign for one as you leave – but that may well be the extent of it.

There is a Papua New Guinea National Tourist Office (tel 25 1269), PO Box 7144, Boroko, in the Savings & Loan building at Waigani. It may be worth giving them a call, or writing before you arrive; they do produce a Visitors Guide, an annual Accommodation Directory and, in conjunction with Shell, a good map.

Don't be backward about asking the locals for advice – 99.99% of the time they'll be friendly and helpful, even in Moresby, the big smoke.

The best bet for 'official' help while you are at the airport (if the Tourist Information desk hasn't materialised yet), is the Air Niugini desk in Air Niugini's domestic section of the main terminal, next door to the international arrivals' section. Air Niugini offices around town will also provide information (see the Port Moresby Getting There section for addresses) and they are also agents for Philippine Airlines and Garuda.

If you're really stuck, you could call the Travelodge (tel 21 2266) – the people on the front desk are helpful and will try to answer your questions.

If you want help with your plans and itinerary, consider contacting Pacific Expeditions (tel 25 7803), PO Box 132, Port Moresby. They operate a number of adventure tours (day tours and rafting trips from Moresby, canoeing the Sepik, trekking the Highlands, etc) so they know a lot about the country. They also deal with a number of interesting village guesthouses. If you're not interested in tours, they're quite happy (for a moderate charge) to help you work out a personal itinerary.

Trans Niugini Tours (tel 21 7308), PO Box 1396, Port Moresby, are more up-market (they run the Bensbach, Karawari and Ambua Lodges and tours) and they also have an office in Moresby, at the Queensland Insurance Building in town, although their head office is in Mt Hagen.

Bank The impressive Papua New Guinea Banking Corporation (PNGBC) building in town is also home to the local American Express agency, the Coral Sea Travel Services (tel 21 4422), PO Box 813, Port Moresby. You can get a cash advance in your own currency that you can then change to kina.

The head offices for Niugini-Lloyds, Westpac and ANZ are in the same area, but branches are widely distributed around the city. The airport has a bank that opens for all incoming flights. Normal banks close at 2 pm Monday to Thursday, 5 pm on Friday. Air Niugini, Talair, the large hotels and better restaurants all accept American Express and Diners Club.

Post The poste restante desk at the main post office in town is efficient and reliable but, for many travellers, the new post office at Boroko will be equally efficient, and much more convenient.

Consider having your mail sent to Poste Restante, Boroko, especially if you plan to stay nearby. Both these main post offices have philatelic counters. The hours are from 8.30 am to 4.30 pm, Monday to Friday, and from 8.30 to 11.30 am on Saturdays.

Diplomatic Missions Port Moresby, more particularly Waigani, is the only place in the country where you can get visas for Indonesia and Australia, or renew a PNG visa. The Immigration Section for the Department of Foreign Affairs is on the ground floor of the Central Government Office at Waigani (tel 27 1170), PO Wards Strip, Waigani.

The following list of embassies and high commissions (for Commonwealth countries) is not exhaustive. It's worth making a phonecall if you plan to visit between 12 and 2 pm – some, including the Indonesian Embassy, close completely for two hours.

Australia
    Sir Maori Kiki Drive off Melanesian Way, Waigani, PO Box 739, Port Moresby (tel 25 9333)
United Kingdom
    3rd floor, United Church Bldg, Douglas St, Port Moresby, P0 Box 739, Port Moresby (tel 21 2500)
    – there are plans for a move to Waigani near the Indonesian Embassy
France
    9th floor, Pacific View Apartments, 1/84 Pruth St, Korobosea, PO Box 1155, Port Moresby (tel 25 2971)
Federal Republic of Germany
    2nd floor, Pacific View Apartments, 1/84 Pruth St, Korobosea, PO Box 73, Port Moresby (tel 25 2988)
Indonesia
    1 & 2/410 Sir John Guise Drive, Waigani, PO Box 7165, Boroko (tel 25 3116)
Japan
    4th & 5th floors, ANG House, Cuthbertson St, Port Moresby, PO Box 1040, Port Moresby (tel 21 1800)
New Zealand
    Magani Crescent, Waigani, PO Box 1144, Boroko (tel 25 9444)
The Philippines
    Islander Village, Wards Rd, Hohola, PO Box 5916, Boroko (tel 25 6577)

United States of America
    Armit St, Paga Hill, Port Moresby, PO Box 1492, Port Moresby (tel 21 1594)

Books & Maps Excellent, detailed maps are available at the National Mapping Bureau in Waigani (National Mapping Bureau, Department of Lands & Environment, PO Box 5665, Boroko), although they're not cheap. They have a full range of topographic maps of varying scales, as well as other specialised, national, single-sheet maps showing airfields, roads, etc. Don't even think of bushwalking without getting a set of relevant topographic maps. If you write to them, they'll send you a list of what they have in stock and you can order by mail.

The Shell *Tourist Guide to PNG* (a map) is good value and is available from Shell petrol stations and the PNG Office of Tourism.

There's a small Port Moresby public library on Ela Beach, the big National Library (an independence gift from Australia that houses a huge PNG collection) at Waigani, an excellent library at the university, and another interesting collection in the National Archives, also at Waigani. All these are open to the public.

There are several good places to buy books. The book section in the huge downtown Steamships department store has a varied selection, including guidebooks and Pidgin dictionaries. City News in the Morgoru Motu Building on the sea side of Steamships and the airport newsagent are both reasonably well stocked.

It's worth visiting the Institute of Papua New Guinea studies in Angau Drive, Boroko; they sell publications by local authors and films, videos and recordings of traditional culture and music.

Last, but probably best, the University Bookstore has many books on the country, as well as guides and a reasonable collection of fiction.

If you're planning to spend any length

of time in Moresby, make sure you get hold of a copy of *Port Moresby – a Guide to the Capital*. It's available from a few outlets, but if you can't find it anywhere else, it can be bought at the Australian High Commission (the Women's Group put it together). It covers all sorts of practical details a resident will find useful – from lists of pre-schools to motor mechanics.

Emergency The general phone number for emergencies (police, fire and ambulance) is 000. The Port Moresby General Hospital (tel 24 8100) is in Taurama Rd, Korobosea.

Warning Be careful. The crime rate is high, and the statistics for rape are particularly bad. As a general rule, do not walk around the streets at night as even in a group you can be vulnerable.

If you are planning to 'hit the town', catch a PMV to your chosen venue, and catch a taxi home. Be especially wary on pay Fridays. Women should dress modestly and should not stray too far from other people and central areas of activity, even during the day. You should never leave any possessions unattended and in crowded places you should be aware that there are, occasionally, pickpockets. Do not advertise your wealth.

Walking up Paga Hill is all right during the day, especially at lunch time, but you would be unwise to go alone. Be careful walking past the shanty settlement on Three Mile Hill above Koki and behind Waigani around the golf club. Stay out of the shanty towns and Hanuabada unless you have a local guide; if you don't know what you are doing and where you're going, you can very easily get into trouble.

There are no problems with using PMVs or wandering around the markets.

Lastly, don't overreact! If you are careful, you would have to be extremely unlucky to have any problems.

Port Moresby City

'Town' retains some sense of history, although there are few old buildings left and modern, characterless office blocks are now in the majority. ANG House and the Travelodge dominate the skyline.

At the other end of Douglas St from the Travelodge is the PNGBC building – it's the most interesting modern building in town, with some interesting, traditionally influenced decoration on the facade. Also check out the dugout canoe from the Gulf region which hangs from the ceiling. At about 25 metres long, it is said to be one of the largest canoes ever made. An inscription describes its ceremonial use. The PMV stop is on Musgrave St between the bank and the very pink Papua Hotel (there are plans for yet another five-star international hotel on this site).

The National Parliament and the National Museum used to share a building just behind ANG House but the museum moved out to Waigani in 1977 and the parliament followed in 1984.

Paga Point, where the old town is situated, ends in a high hill – it's worth getting up to the top for the fine views over the town, the harbour and the encircling reefs. It's quite a popular spot at lunch times, but if you walk up, you would be wise to go in a group.

The oldest building still standing in Moresby is the Ela Uniting Church in Douglas St between Steamships and the ANZ building. It was opened by the London Missionary Society in 1890 and is one of the city's last forlorn links with the past.

Hanuabada

Past the docks to the north lies Hanuabada, the original Motuan village. Although it is still built out over the sea on stilts, the original wood and thatch houses were destroyed by fire during the war. They were rebuilt in all-Australian building materials, corrugated iron and fibro-cement, and the surroundings are now littered in non-biodegradable rubbish.

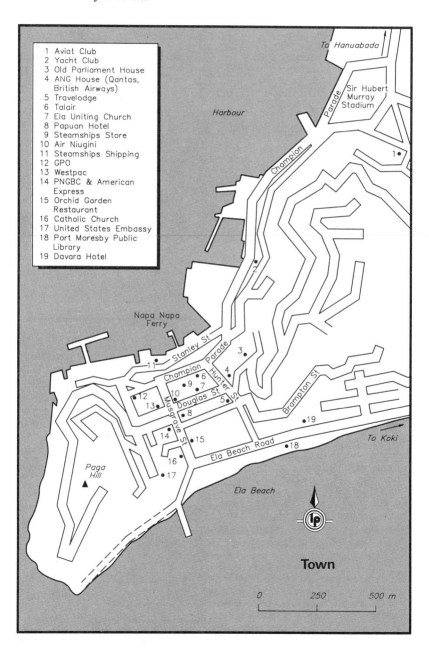

1 Aviat Club
2 Yacht Club
3 Old Parliament House
4 ANG House (Qantas, British Airways)
5 Travelodge
6 Talair
7 Ela Uniting Church
8 Papuan Hotel
9 Steamships Store
10 Air Niugini
11 Steamships Shipping
12 GPO
13 Westpac
14 PNGBC & American Express
15 Orchid Garden Restaurant
16 Catholic Church
17 United States Embassy
18 Port Moresby Public Library
19 Davara Hotel

To Hanuabada

Sir Hubert Murray Stadium

Harbour

Parade

Champion

Napa Napa Ferry

Stanley St

Parade

Champion

Hunter St

Douglas St

Musgrave St

Brampton St

Ela Beach Road

To Koki

Paga Hill

Ela Beach

Town

0   250   500 m

Hanuabada is no longer the beautiful village that Captain Moresby found in 1873, but it's still an interesting place and the people have retained many traditional Motuan customs.

The name Hanuabada is commonly used to describe six interlinked villages. In fact, Hanuabada correctly describes only one of the six villages that have grown together: collectively and officially they are known as the Poreporena Villages.

Unfortunately it is not acceptable to wander around the villages if you are not a guest, or don't have a local guide. In some senses individual houses are more like single rooms in one great house, so if you wander around the walkways without knowing what you are doing and where you are going, you are certain to seriously offend people by invading their privacy.

Metoreai

The site for the first white settlement in Papua lies beyond Hanuabada on the ridge. The building, which now belongs to the United Church, was once the headquarters of the London Missionary Society and their first missionary, Reverend N G Lawes, arrived here on 21 November 1874. There's a stone cairn and a plaque to mark this event and another monument commemorates the pastors from the South Sea islands.

Ela Beach

Heading south down Musgrave or Hunter Streets, you soon hit the long sandy stretch of Ela Beach. It's a popular spot for lazing on the sand and recent work on tree planting and pathways will make it more appealing. There are a couple of kai bars at the town end of the beach, close to the remains of Sea World.

The beach is not much good for swimming, particularly at low tide, because the water is very shallow and weedy. There are also many black sea urchins – careful where you step, the spines can be very painful. Windsurfing is popular.

St Mary's Catholic Cathedral is on Musgrave St, near Ela Beach, and has a Sepik haus tambaran style front.

Koki

Ela Beach runs up to the headland at Koki, where there is a cluster of shops, the Salvation Army hostel, the Koki Market and another stilt village.

The Koki Market may not be the best market in the country, but it is quite possibly the best known and it is a colourful, interesting spot. Saturday is the big market day although there's always plenty of activity. Koki Market is particularly strong for seafood: local fishermen pull their boats up nearby. There are PMV stops on both sides of the road at the market.

The Girl Guides' Handicraft Shop is close to the market and has a small collection of crafts from various places around the country. They also have an extensive postcard collection and books on the country, including guides and Pidgin dictionaries. The shop is closed on Sundays, but they also have branches in the Travelodge and Islander Hotels that are open seven days a week. Profits go to the Girl Guides movement. Pacific Arts is a few buildings away, towards Boroko, but their collection is not always very inspiring.

Boroko

Continuing up Three Mile Hill, past the YWCA, you come to Boroko (Four Mile). This is now the most important shopping centre, with a new post office, banks, airline agencies, a smallish market, several shopping plazas and a number of Chinese-owned general stores. However, nothing matches the Steamships shop in town. There are also a number of restaurants and kai bars, some of which are quite cheap, and a couple of places to stay. There are even some human touches, like a square, a pedestrian mall and even a pedestrian overpass.

Boroko's success is due, in part, to its

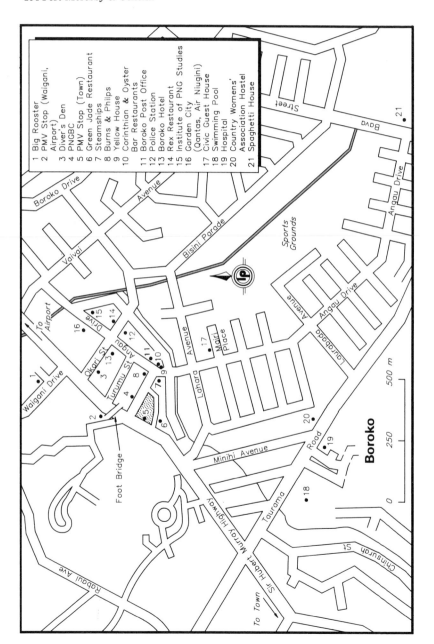

1 Big Rooster
2 PMV Stop (Waigani, Airport)
3 Diver's Den
4 PNGBC
5 PMV Stop (Town)
6 Green Jade Restaurant
7 Steamships
8 Burns & Philps
9 Yellow House
10 Corinthian & Oyster Bar Restaurants
11 Boroko Post Office
12 Police Station
13 Boroko Hotel
14 Rex Restaurant
15 Institute of PNG Studies
16 Garden City (Qantas, Air Niugini)
17 Civic Guest House
18 Swimming Pool
19 Hospital
20 Country Womens' Association Hostel
21 Spaghetti House

Boroko

central position at the intersection of Waigani Drive and the Hubert Murray Highway. Because of this it also has the largest PMV station which is well worth avoiding at peak hours. PMVs leave from both sides of the Hubert Murray Highway (linked by the overpass).

The Institute for PNG Studies at the northern end of Angau Drive has some particularly interesting tapes of traditional music for sale.

Gordon

If you turn left into dusty Waigani Drive, instead of continuing out on the Highway towards Six Mile and the airport, you come to the main drag heading out to the government centre, the university and Gerehu. Gordon is on the right a couple of km from Boroko.

This is not an attractive part of Moresby, unless you like breweries and factories, but it is the home for PNG Arts (Pacific Expeditions) and Hanuacraft. These two shops are well worth a visit; both are open seven days a week (from 9 am to 5 pm Monday to Friday, 11 am to 4 pm weekends); and both will pack and ship your purchases overseas. There is a PMV stop on the corner of Spring Garden Rd; if you're coming from Boroko, Spring Garden Rd is before the roundabout.

There's also an attractive market that some people claim is the best in the country, a couple of km off Waigani Drive and accessible by PMV. The Gordon Market is the best place to catch PMVs for Bomana, Sogeri, etc.

Waigani

Along Waigani Drive, past the Islander Hotel on the left (a Travelodge clone) and about half a km to the right, is the government centre. Most PMVs will let you off on the main road before continuing towards Gerehu, although at peak hours there will be a number marked 'W'gani' or 'Office' that will travel direct to the Central Government Office. No PMVs service the museum or the parliament.

Waigani has been dubbed 'Canberra in the Tropics' and there's more than a little truth in that description. There's a handful of flashy, modern buildings with a lot of empty space between them and the only way you can get around is by private car or on foot.

There are five main government buildings grouped together. The 'Pineapple' Building (Marea Haus) is the distinctively ugly high rise on the corner of John Guise Drive and Kumul Avenue. On the opposite corner, the first building you come to, Haus Tomakala, is a rather more innocuous high rise that has a Talair agency and a snack bar with reasonable prices on the ground floor. The large, three-story Central Government Office, on the corner of Kumul and Melanesian Way across from the 'Pineapple', is home to the Immigration Section, a post office and an Air Niugini office – be prepared for frustration if you want to extend your visa. The National Mapping Bureau is behind the Central Government Office on Melanesian.

Parliament Building The new parliament building had its first session in May 1984 and, with Prince Charles on hand, was officially opened in August. It's an impressive building, as it should be at a cost of K22 million. Built in a Maprik haus tambaran style, it sits on a hill fronted by fountains, a full two km from the PMV stop on Waigani Drive. A taxi from Boroko will cost about K8.

The proceedings inside are interesting as they require simultaneous translations into English, Pidgin and Motu, the three main languages of PNG. It's open from 9 am to 12 noon and from 1 to 3 pm. There's a cafeteria with standard offerings under the front forecourt.

National Museum & Art Gallery The museum is not far from the parliament building. The displays justify the effort spent on reaching them and, as a further reward, the building is air-conditioned.

There's a shady courtyard area in front, with wooden tables and seats, which is serviced by a most uninspiring snack bar. If you packed your lunch it would be a pleasant place to eat.

You'll need at least an hour or two to see the excellent displays covering the geography, animal life, culture and history of PNG. There are superb examples of masks, shields and totems, a magnificent Milne Bay outrigger canoe decorated in cowry shells, as well as exhibits on local foods and shells. A small courtyard has some (live) birds, lizards and a tree kangaroo.

The museum is open Monday to Friday from 8.30 am to 3.30 pm and on Sunday from 1 to 5 pm. Admission is free. There is an interesting bookshop at the entrance. Although the selection of books is limited, there are a number of publications about prehistory and culture that are hard to find anywhere else. The bookshop closes between 1 and 2 pm.

University of Papua New Guinea

After Waigani, you first come to the Administrative College, then to the attractive and spacious university. It's close to the main road and plenty of 'Gerehu' PMVs run by. The university has a good bookshop (to the right when you come in the main entrance) and a fairly extensive library. There is also a Coffee Shop (to the left of the entrance and the mural) with decent, good-value meals.

A bit further past the university are the Botanical Gardens, with a very fine orchid collection. Orchid cultivation is a big deal in Port Moresby and PNG as a whole. I managed to get myself invited to an orchid-fanciers' barbecue, but despite not knowing an orchid from a sunflower (well almost) I did not feel alone!

National Arts Schools

A little beyond the university entrance and on the opposite side of Waigani Drive, a normal suburban road leads to the National Arts School, PO Box 5098, Boroko. It's less than half a km from the main road, easy walking distance from the university.

There are often people selling *buai* (betel) on the side of the road – for artistic inspiration perhaps? There are music, art and drama schools, and the students and staff are friendly and interesting. If you have a strong interest in any of these areas it would be worth getting in touch and checking it out.

The National Art School (tel 25 5477) has an art gallery that sells original paintings and prints. Some fascinating, vibrant fusions of modern and traditional art are produced and sold. The art gallery is next to the main car park.

Ask someone in the adjoining office to show you the prints they have for sale in addition to the works on display. Excellent quality colour prints by well-known painters like Kauage, John Mann and Akis are sold for between K8 and K35; black and white prints are cheaper.

The National Music School (tel 25 5477) has some outstanding students – don't miss an opportunity to see them perform. There are several groups and some play music around town. It's worth phoning on the off chance that something is happening.

The National Theatre School (tel 25 2524) is on the opposite side of town. A new theatre, made from green treated timber, should be in operation in 1988. Regular performances are planned. Phone for information and while you're at it ask if anything is happening at the University Open Theatre.

Islands, Beaches & Reefs

In Moresby Harbour, off Hanuabada, the wreck of the Burns Philp cargo ship *MacDhui* can be seen just breaking the surface. It was sunk by Japanese aircraft in the early days of the Pacific War. Its mast now stands in front of the Royal Papua Yacht Club. Manubada Island is used for weekend beach trips but beware –

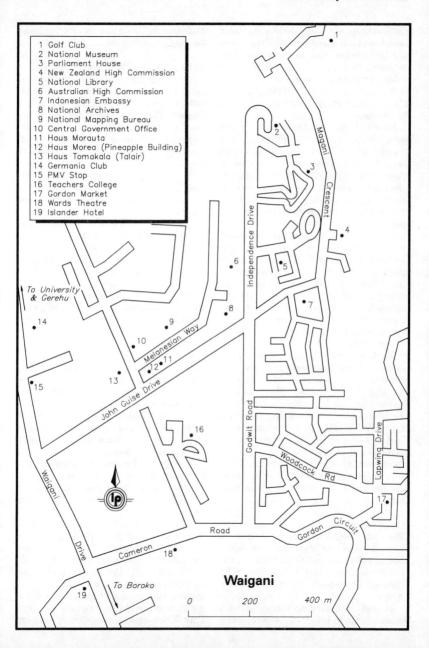

1 Golf Club
2 National Museum
3 Parliament House
4 New Zealand High Commission
5 National Library
6 Australian High Commission
7 Indonesian Embassy
8 National Archives
9 National Mapping Bureau
10 Central Government Office
11 Haus Morauta
12 Haus Morea (Pineapple Building)
13 Haus Tomakala (Talair)
14 Germania Club
15 PMV Stop
16 Teachers College
17 Gordon Market
18 Wards Theatre
19 Islander Hotel

To University & Gerehu

Magani Crescent

Independence Drive

Melanesian Way

John Guise Drive

Godwit Road

Woodcock Rd

Lapwing Drive

Waigani Drive

Road

Cameron

Gordon Circuit

To Boroko

Waigani

0   200   400 m

there is no shade. The Bootless Bay area (south-east of Moresby) and the other islands around the harbour are also popular.

Many expats have boats and the yacht club is busy on weekends. If you play your charm cards right, you may get asked out for the day.

Idler's Bay, on the Napa Napa peninsula just east of Moresby, is a popular beach. It's a pleasant drive out beyond here to Rea Rea, a large coastal village which you get to by crossing the creek on a dugout canoe 'ferry' service. Napa Napa was once a nautical training centre and is now a fisheries research station.

Close to Napa Napa is Lolorua Island which is also known as Double Island because during WW II it was neatly chopped in two by a bomb. Also nearby, Gemo Island was established as a leper colony in 1937 but the colony was later moved to Laloki. Tatana Island, between Hanuabada and Napa Napa, is joined to the mainland by a causeway and has a village on the north-west side.

Basilisk Passage is the deep, narrow entrance to the harbour of Port Moresby and was named by Captain Moresby after his ship HMS *Basilisk*. Next to it is Nateara Reef on which the ship SS *Pruth* was wrecked in 1924. An attempt to sink it during WW II broke its hull in two. Sinasi Reef is a very beautiful reef outside the passage and is joined to Daugo Island, also known as Fisherman's Island. There are some very pleasant white sand beaches and it's a popular excursion from Moresby.

Things to Do

The *Times* weekly newspaper has a useful 'What's on Where' page that lists films, discos, activities and clubs of all kinds. There are often films at the University Theatre, especially on Saturday nights, for 50t.

In mid-June (the Queen's Birthday weekend) there is a Port Moresby show

with spectacular displays of traditional dancing.

Clubs Clubs in PNG tend to have high membership turnovers so they can be hard to track down. You could start looking in a number of places: the Yellow Pages of the telephone directory, which has a far from complete list; the *Times'* 'What's on Where' section lists some club meetings; and *Port Moresby – a Guide to the Capital* has a thorough list of clubs – from Friends of the Earth and the PNG Bird Club, to rugby and basketball clubs, to all the service clubs you would expect.

The PNG Bushwalkers Association (tel 27 2423), Mark Rosen, President PNGBWA, PO Box 1335, Boroko, has regular weekend walks, which would not only give you a chance to see something, but also to meet some nice people.

The Hash House Harriers, the Hash House Harriettes and the Port Moresby Road Runners are popular in Moresby; they advertise their venues in Friday's *Post Courier* and the *Times*.

It's reasonably easy to join boat crews if you hang around the Royal Papua Yacht Club. There are some serious yachties here who've done very well in international blue-water races. Water-skiing, scuba diving and game fishing are other activities which are organised from the yacht club. Hiri canoe races often take place along the coast.

The Port Moresby Sub Aqua Club organises regular weekend dive trips to nearby reefs. Try contacting them through the Dive Shop at the Yacht Club.

Tours Pacific Expeditions (tel 25 7803) run a number of day and weekend trips around Port Moresby. They run half (K15) and full day tours (K25) that include Parliament House, the Museum, Hanuabada, artefact shops and a drive out to Sogeri and the Variarata National Park. Their weekend trips include rafting the Vanapa and Angabanga Rivers, sailing a traditional hula along the coast, fishing and a fly in/fly out trip to the Myola Lakes on the Kokoda Trail.

Bob and Dinah Halstead at Tropical Diving Adventures (tel 25 7429), Divers' Den, Turumu St, Boroko, have good value weekend diving trips and diving lessons. Their base charge for a trip is K12, the rest depends on what equipment you hire and how many dives you make. They are worth contacting even if you just want to snorkel.

Most diving is around the Tahira Marine Park or Horseshoe Reef. There are two small wrecks here, both scuttled in 1978; one is a 65 foot government trawler/patrol boat and the other a 40 foot work boat. These are home to two popular TV stars – Nessie, a two-metre moray eel, and Gobble, a huge tame groper. Both like to be fed and fussed over! There are plenty of coral gardens and interesting fish.

The Loloata Island Resort (tel 25 8590) offers day trips out to their island from Moresby for K20 including lunch. The boat leaves from the Tahilla Boat Centre on the road to Kopiango, about 20 minutes from town. The island offers swimming, diving, snorkelling and a licensed restaurant.

The owners of the MV *Boulli*, which is fully equipped for picnics and snorkelling, were planning to start regular, scheduled island trips. Telephone 21 2616 to find out what is happening.

Places to Stay

Places to stay are scattered around the suburbs and are generally pretty expensive. You'll find places near the airport, in Boroko, Waigani, Koki, Ela Beach and the town centre.

If you have a car, it doesn't matter where you stay, but if you are dependent on PMVs, Boroko is the most convenient location, followed by Koki.

There is no shortage of expensive accommodation, but it is worth booking for the cheaper places. They are only small, so they can fill fast.

If you're in Moresby for a weekend, it would be worth thinking about getting out to Yule Island, north-west of Moresby, where there are a couple of reasonably priced guesthouses, or to Loloata Island, to the south-east, where there's a slightly more expensive resort. Nothing much happens in Moresby on weekends. See the sections at the end of this chapter.

Places to Stay – bottom end

The *Salvation Army Hostel* (tel 25 3744), PO Box 4070, Badili, is conveniently located in Koki near the market and on the main PMV route from town to Boroko. Everything is very well maintained and there are kitchen facilities. The 15 rooms cost K15 per person. With a student card this drops to K10. Highly recommended.

The *Country Women's Association* (Jessie Wyatt House) (tel 25 3646), PO Box 1222, Boroko, is on Taurama Rd right across from the hospital and next door to the Red Cross. The address is Boroko but it's a little way from the Boroko shopping centre. The easiest way to get there is by PMV. Most PMVs run to or from town via Three Mile Hill and the Hubert Murray Highway, but some detour to the east through Korobosea (running right past the CWA on Taurama Rd), Kila Kila and Badili. Catch a PMV marked 'Kila Kila' and ask for the hospital. There are four rooms and cooking facilities and the cost is K14 per person. Booking ahead is advisable.

The *YWCA Hostel* (tel 25 6604), PO Box 1883, Boroko, is at the top of Three Mile Hill between Koki and Boroko. PMVs run past regularly between town and Boroko. There are four rooms for visitors, men are welcome, otherwise it's all permanent residents. It costs K16/25 for singles/doubles and a child is K5. The tariff includes breakfast and there are excellent cheap lunches (K1) and dinners (K3). This is a friendly spot and, for Moresby, the value is hard to beat. The craft shop is worth looking at even if you're not staying. During the week there's a

10.30 pm curfew, at weekends 12 pm, but as you'll discover, Moresby's nightlife is unlikely to make this a problem.

At the *University* out on Waigani Drive you can often get a room. Your best bet is during vacations, but there can be spare rooms anytime. Rooms are K14, but they are likely to be less costly if you have a student card or at least say you are a student. Contact the Warden of Students before 4 pm (tel 25 1690); the office is upstairs in the central complex. There's a cheap cafeteria but it may not be open during the vacation period. The surroundings are pleasant and it's a good place to meet local people.

The *Institute of Applied Social & Economic Research* (tel 25 3200), PO Box 5854, Boroko, is on the left past the University. You'll see a sign on Waigani. They have singles for K15 and doubles for K28.

One more possibility is staying at the *In-Service Teachers' College* just across from the Ward's Cinema and Drive In, near Waigani. Accommodation here is K20 including meals, but you have to book ahead, in writing. Write 'Hostel Bookings' on the front of the envelope and address it to The Principal, Port Moresby In-Service College, PO Box 1791, Boroko.

You may hear of cheap, self-contained flats in Boroko. While these are a good bargain, they have generally been set up for volunteer and church workers, not travellers.

Places to Stay – middle

Moresby's medium price range is an odd assortment, much closer in price and style to the bottom end than the top. Three of these are located very conveniently in Boroko.

The *Civic Guest House* (tel 25 5091), PO Box 1139, Boroko, is highly recommended and many volunteers and foreign workers on local wages put up here when in town. It's also popular with travellers and can sometimes be booked out by lower civil servants attending a conference. There is

a pleasant garden with a swimming pool and a pet bird whose squeak is heard intermittently throughout the day. It's on Mairi Place just around the corner from Angau Drive in Boroko. They offer a free airport pick-up. There are 22 rooms with singles/doubles at K34/54 including a good, filling breakfast; they also serve lunches and dinners. The bathrooms are shared but spotless.

Also in Boroko, but more expensive and not particularly pleasant, is the *Boroko Hotel* (tel 25 6677) on Okari St, PO Box 1033, Boroko. There are 37 rooms, singles are K39 to K45, doubles K49 to K55. The rooms are fine, if plain, air-con and fitted with a sink. Some are self-contained. However, the bar in the hotel and the one next door have live entertainment on weekends and the noise carries into the rooms. Guards in the hotel keep patrons in line but venture out with caution. The hotel restaurant is reasonable.

Apart from the Civic Guest House, the best alternative is the *Granville Motel* (tel 25 7590), PO Box 1246, Boroko. It's an easy walk from the airport on Dagura Rd but they also do free pick-ups and drop-offs. It's ideal if you have to catch an early flight. It was built for the Ok Tedi mine workers so the rooms are fairly spartan, but they're more than adequate and everything is spotlessly clean. There's a pool, a tennis court, a *haus win* (house wind or open air bar) and the meals are reasonable. Single, using the communal bathroom, is K30; with private facilities, K35 to K40. Doubles range from K45 to K59.

The venerable old *Papua Hotel* (tel 21 2622), PO Box 122, Port Moresby, in downtown Moresby is on a downwards slide and is not recommended. It's now painted a shocking pink and seems to function mainly as a rowdy drinking hole. During the war, General MacArthur used the hotel as his headquarters, but its days are numbered – there are plans for a new five-star hotel on the site. The hotel entrance is on Douglas and there are a variety of rooms, some air-conditioned, some with fans. Singles are K50 to K55, doubles are K65.

Places to Stay - top end

The prices at this end of the market are simply outrageous. But it seems there are people who will pay them, however unwillingly. If a new hotel is built on the site of the Papua, competition should start to bring some reality into the situation.

The *Port Moresby Travelodge* (tel 21 2266), PO Box 3661, is the top-rated place to stay in Moresby. It's conspicuously located in town at the corner of Douglas, May and Hunter Streets – right across from Australia New Guinea House. Along with ANG House, it dominates the town. The rooms offer some appropriately stunning views over Moresby and the prices are similarly sky-high. Naturally the Travelodge offers all the features you'd expect – air-conditioning throughout, restaurant, bars, souvenir shop, conference facilities, swimming pool and entertainment. It's also said to be the most expensive hotel in all the Pacific! There are 188 rooms with singles at K110!

The *Davara* (tel 21 2100), PO Box 799, Port Moresby, looks out over Ela Beach from Ela Beach Rd, a short stroll from the town centre, but it's starting to show its age. Built in the late '60s it is still well equipped with a swimming pool and a popular bar and restaurant. Singles are K55 to K74, doubles K65 to K84. There are also some cheaper four bed 'bunkhouses' where the charge is K25 per person.

The *Islander* (tel 25 5955), PO Box 1981, Boroko, is in Hohola between the Waigani government complex and Boroko. It's similar to the Travelodge, but the location means it has more space and less spectacular views. Built in the mid '70s it's not quite as expensive as the Travelodge with singles at K95, doubles at K105. The restaurant serves Melanesian and western food.

There are two places close to the

airport. The new *Airways Motel* (tel 25 7033), PO Box 734, Port Moresby, has singles from K55 to K65, doubles from K65 to K70. They also have a K35 day rate. It overlooks the airport from Jackson's Parade and provides top quality facilities. There's an open air bar overlooking the runways and a Greek restaurant.

The final top drawer hotel is the *Gateway Motel* (tel 25 3855), PO Box 1215, Boroko, right beside the airport – you see it when you walk out the doors. It would certainly be convenient for your flight out, but otherwise it's a rather dull establishment. There are 35 rooms, with prices from K68 to K92. There's a bar/ restaurant with reasonably priced grills at lunch times.

Places to Eat

There are more food alternatives in cosmopolitan Moresby than anywhere else in the country. This will be your last chance to eat Japanese, Greek or Italian food, but unfortunately you'll look long and hard for indigenous cuisine. Most restaurants are closed except at meal times and on Sundays they are often closed all day.

Places to Eat - bottom end

There are very few cheap, reasonably good quality places to fill the void between kai/ sandwich bars and expensive restaurants. If you are on a tight budget and can't stomach the thought of a staple diet of greasy fish and chicken your best bet is to stay somewhere that either supplies good, cheap food (YWCA, University) or has cooking facilities (Salvation Army, CWA). Most of the kai bars close fairly early, so by about 7 pm your options have shrunk to the hotels, clubs and restaurants.

Boroko has a large selection of kai bars, but they're all pretty similar. The *Corinthian*, on the corner opposite Steamships, offers sandwiches for around 90t, chicken for around K2. One of the best of a bad lot is beneath the Rex Restaurant, opposite the Police Station – it's clean and efficient and has a more varied menu than most, including fried rice for around K1.

Another to check out is *Luigi's Fast Food* on the shopping centre side of the pedestrian footbridge. It's a bustling place with a prime location and reasonable prices; they'll release half a chicken and chips into your care for K2, a piece of fish for 60t.

Upstairs from the Corinthian and a few doors closer to the post office is the *Oyster Bar* in the Hugo Building. Run by a Filipino family, they offer fish & chips, other seafood dishes and hamburgers for between K2 and K6. You can look out over Angau Drive while you dine.

The *Yellow House* is a busy, friendly place opposite the Steamships store in the section of Angau Drive that has been turned into a mall. It has a varied blackboard menu and reasonable prices and is crowded at lunchtime, but you can usually get a seat and something decent to eat for less than K5. The *Tropicana Restaurant* (tel 25 3841), on Boio St, East Boroko, not far from the International High School, about 1½ km from the post office, offers set lunches Monday to Friday for K5.

American-style fast food has arrived in Moresby in the guise of two drive-in *Big Roosters*. There's one in Boroko on Waigani Drive, a short walk from Highway intersection and another in Koki on the main drag. They're not cheap but they're open till 8 pm and offer standard variations on the chicken-in-a-box theme: a quarter barbecued chicken, salad and chips for K3.39; half a chicken for K3.95. Combined with some fruit from a market, this is not too bad.

In town, the best bet is probably *Tasty Bite* next to the PNGBC. Like most kai bars it closes in the evening, but during the day you can get decent sandwiches for 80t, a hamburger for K1.20. You can get drinks and snacks at a couple of places at the town end of Ela Beach – this is a pleasant place for lunch.

There are a few kai bars around Waigani, but the best options are the snack bar under the forecourt of the Parliament Building, and one on the ground floor of the first high-rise office from Waigani Drive, Haus Tomakala, opposite the Pineapple Building.

The best-value place for a sit down meal is the *University Coffee Shop* and it's also a good place to meet people. If you come in the main university entrance it's to your left past the mural. It's open Monday to Friday from 9 am to 3.30 pm and you can get a hot meal for about K2, as well as sandwiches and milk shakes.

Sandwiches, meat pies, pasties and the like are available from counters in Steamships and Burns Philp stores all around PNG. A pie, pasty or sandwich sells for around 60t. These are very often the best value in town, and they're usually fresh because they have such a rapid turnover. The supermarket sections sell a comprehensive range of, well, supermarket things. Mostly, they're imported from Australia, so they're not cheap, but cooking for yourself will obviously still save many kina.

Don't forget the markets. Locals claim the market at Gordon is the best, but the one at Koki also has a good variety of fruit and seafood. There are a couple of smaller markets, including one at Boroko at the end of Okari St, and another on the corner where you turn left to the airport. Often the prices are clearly displayed, but even if they're not, you're unlikely to be ripped off. Bargaining is out. At Koki you can pick up a fresh fish (big enough for three) for about K1, a bunch of bananas for 80t, an apple for 20t.

Places to Eat – middle

The winner in this section is undoubtedly *The Captains Table* (tel 21 2270) at the yacht club, a short walk around the harbour from town. If you control your alcohol consumption you could enjoy a pleasant meal for less than K5. On the basis of price it could have fitted in the

Top: Carvings from the Blackwater Lakes region, East Sepik Province (RE)
Left: Sepik masks (TW)
Right: Malanggan carvings New Ireland (TW)

Top: Wahgi Valley, near Mt Hagen, Western Highlands (RE)
Left: Parking lot, Mt Hagen Airport (RE)
Right: Traditional housing, near Mendi, Southern Highlands (RE)

previous section, but it's a cut above in quality, and you can spend more if you choose to. It's upstairs at the club and you have to ignore a sign saying 'Members Only' (I'm not sure why it is there, visitors are welcome).

You can eat in or take-away (eating in is more expensive); the menu is Chinese/Australian with an emphasis on fresh seafood. The servings are generous – a small serve will do for two people. A 'small' serve of prawns and a 'small' serve of fried rice will cost K5.80, then divide by two . . . . Barramundi and chips cost K4.50; a steak, K5. It's open every day for lunch and dinner (12 noon to 1.30 pm and 6 to 9 pm).

There's also a good lunch available Tuesday to Friday at the *Golf Club*. The Golf Club lies behind the National Museum, so if you're walking, climb up the hill with the flag pole (Independence Hill) and you will see the club about 10 minutes walk away on the other side. A generous steak and chips costs K4.50 and there are also seafood dishes. Rather than risk a long walk to find their hours have changed, telephone 25 5367. It's also best to be in a group if you're wandering around behind Waigani.

Spaghetti House is at the eastern end of Angau Drive, about a mile from Boroko shopping centre, next door to the bowling and tennis clubs. You can get a decent pizza for K6.50 and they also have pasta dishes.

The best-value meal you can have in Boroko is at the *Rex Restaurant* (tel 25 6447) opposite the police station. In fact, there are few places in PNG to compare. Not only is it reasonably priced, but the surroundings are pleasant and air-conditioned, the service is good and the food delicious. The menu is largely Chinese, but there are some interesting PNG-based dishes as well. If you don't lose control over the alcohol, you could get away for well under K10. There are some vegetarian dishes (amazing!) for around K5, curries and satays for K6, while the

main meat and poultry dishes vary between K6.50 and K8.50. It's open for lunch from Tuesday to Friday (12 noon to 2 pm) and for dinner from Tuesday to Sunday (6 to 10 pm).

The restaurant in the *Boroko Hotel* has passable (only just, the day I was there) food at reasonable prices in a cool, quiet setting. At lunch main courses of fish, lamb or beef are around K6.50, and they sometimes serve what they describe as a *mumu*, which refers to the traditional ground oven (baked sweet potato, vegies in coconut milk and meat). The menu at dinner is the same but prices increase about 25%. On Fridays there's a lunchtime smorgasbord.

The *Green Jade* (tel 25 4013) has a good reputation for Chinese food. It's in Boroko just off Lakatoi Arcade which is left off Tabari Place (there's a South Pacific Bank on the corner). Look about halfway down the arcade on your right. It's on the ground floor down a short, enclosed walkway.

There are a couple of options in town and, amazingly, the best is the *Travelodge Coffee Shop* which is open for breakfast, lunch and dinner. The surroundings are Travelodge-antiseptic and there are an embarrassing number of waiters and waitresses clad in matching lap-laps and padding around barefoot but, aside from this, the food is good and the prices are reasonable. Don't confuse the Coffee Shop with the upstairs restaurant (I got burnt just picking up the menu). There are light meals for K5, vegetarian dishes for K4, burgers for K5 and more substantial stuff for K8. Breakfasts cost K5.

While you're in the building check out the Girl Guide's Shop (interesting books and some crafts) and the local glitterati in the upstairs bar.

It's only open for lunch, but *Munch Junction Coffee Shop*, on the corner of Hunter St and Champion Parade is quite pleasant. Amongst other things, they offer fish & chips for K5 and spaghetti marinara for K6.50.

The Papua Hotel, long a favourite with local businessmen, is now declining fast. *Flynn's Hideaway Bistro & Bar*, enter from Douglas St opposite Steamships, is pleasantly gloomy and cool if you want to escape from the world for a cold ale (the bar is not pink inside!), but the food did not look inspiring. Admittedly I arrived a bit late.

Places to Eat - top end

The Travelodge's *Rapala Restaurant*, as the flag carrier for the top hotel in town, has the good, varied menu you'd expect, at the prices you would expect – from K12 for a main course. The Friday buffet – including a beer or a glass of wine and a choice of seafoods, meats, salads and desserts – is good value at K12.50.

The Islander also has a pricey restaurant and a more reasonable coffee shop, the *Sanemare Restaurant* – has a daily lunchtime smorgasbord and the coffee shop sells steak sandwiches for K4.50, fish for K7. They have a barbecue smorgasbord on Sundays for K8.50 and a seafood smorgasbord for Friday lunches for K13.50. You might be anywhere in the world, but the Islander is nonetheless a pleasant oasis.

The Davara's *Tapa Restaurant* has starters for K5 and meals for K10. Diners get free admission to the Firehouse Disco (a saving of K7.50), so if you are making a night of it, this is worth considering.

The *Granville Motel* is convenient to the airport and serves a three-course meal for K10. It's not exactly an inspiring meal (soup, choice of meat or fish and three vegies, ice cream and coffee) but it's decent, filling and not *bad* value.

A number of the clubs have restaurants/dining rooms. One that gives reasonable value is the *Golden Bowl* at the Germania Club on Waigani Drive. The decor is functional, and the Chinese food is fair to good. There's a rather muddy fish tank whose inhabitants look as though they are there on a temporary basis. Expect to pay around K10 per head by the time you've

had a beer. The steamed fish (K7 to K12) are particularly good. There's a disco on Tuesdays, Thursdays, Fridays and Saturdays; entrance is K5 for men, free for women.

For Chinese, the *Kwangtung Village* (tel 25 8997) on Boio St, East Boroko, has good food – the best Chinese in Moresby it's said. It is moderately expensive and if you have driven it is not a bad idea to tip the guy outside to watch your car.

If you're not counting the kina too carefully and you've got an excuse for a special occasion (like a farewell dinner) try the new *Airways Motel*. It overlooks the airport, and has an attractive open-air bar. This is an ideal spot to sip a drink on a balmy tropical night or wait for a flight – they plan to install a television link to the airport so flight information can be displayed. Their downstairs restaurant is excellent, with a Greek-oriented menu. They've even got a traditional wood-fired oven to make the pitta bread. Some dips, grilled fish and salad, and good coffee will set you back around K15.

Depending on what demands your taste buds are making, there are a number of other top-end alternatives. I was assured that the *Daikoku Japanese Steak House* (tel 25 3857), between Boroko and Three Mile on the Highway, is very good; the posh looking *Shanghai Gardens* (tel 25 3634) in Korobosea is recommended for Cantonese cooking; and *Coyles Bistro* (tel 21 2353) on the ground floor of Cuthbertson House in town is also meant to be OK.

Things to Buy

Pacific Expedition's office is actually in the corner of an amazing artefacts warehouse, *PNG Arts* on Spring Garden Rd on the Gordon side of Waigani Drive, and not far from the reasonably priced *Hanuacraft*. These are two of the best artefact shops in PNG and a visit is a must. Go before you start travelling so you have an idea of what to look for and what to pay (discounting the considerable mark-up), and then visit again when you get back so you can buy what you missed.

There are a number of other artefacts shops of varying quality – if you are keen, get to as many as you can – you never know where you will find the mask of your nightmares.

The YWCA at Three Mile Hill has artefacts, Niugini Arts is past the hospital in Korobosea, and there are two shops at Koki; Pacific Arts and the Girl Guides' shop.

Getting There & Away

Port Moresby is the hub for a great deal of PNG travel, particularly air travel and most international arrivals and departures.

There are numerous flights to major centres all over the country – Lae, Goroka, Mt Hagen, Wewak, Rabaul, Kieta and so on. If you want to fly to smaller places in Milne Bay (including the Trobriands), the Gulf and the Northern District, then Port Moresby will generally have to be your starting point.

Although most travellers fly out of Moresby there are other ways to get to the rest of the country, although some of them are not exactly easy.

You could, for example, walk the Kokoda Trail to Popondetta then fly (K99) or catch a boat with Lutheran Shipping (K18 deck class) to Lae. Or you could fly to Wau (K69) with Talair then either catch a PMV down to Lae, or walk to Salamaua, a short boat ride from Lae. Or you could travel by boat to Kerema in the Gulf Province (K34) and walk or fly north from there. Or you could get to Kerema by taking a PMV to Iokea, then a motor canoe to Malalaua (leaves Friday night and takes five hours), then catch a PMV to Kerema.

You might, if you're lucky, find a ship from Port Moresby right around the eastern end of Papua New Guinea to the north coast – there are no regular voyages and, unfortunately, when I looked around there was no eastbound passenger ship at all.

Jackson's Airport Jackson's Airport, or Seven Mile as it is sometimes called, is a sudden introduction to PNG. The heat hits you the moment you step off the plane; slow-moving queues form for Customs formalities as you stand under slow-turning fans in the arrival shed; and when you're spat out into the car park you're surrounded by crowds – family groups patiently waiting in the shade, fierce looking young men with dreadlocks, tribespeople looking around in bemusement, sophisticated young office workers strutting about . . . .

Until a tourist counter is established, the best place for information is the Air Niugini counter in the domestic section of the terminal. There are security officers on the doors to this section who manage to keep some of the crowd at bay. The outside phones are noisy and often have queues, so if you have to make a phone call, try the bank of phones by the Air Niugini counter – the crowd is usually thinner and the atmosphere is calmer.

The airport has a bank that opens for all incoming flights (normal banks close at 2 pm Monday to Thursday, 5 pm on Friday) and there's a snack bar, a well-stocked newsagent and offices for the three major car-hire companies. The Air Niugini counter is open Monday to Saturday from 5 am to 4 pm (yup, some of those early flights are a lot of fun) and on Sunday from 5 am to 7 pm.

There are usually plenty of taxis hanging around outside the main terminal, the exception being early in the morning; a ride to Boroko will cost about K5, to town about K12. Departures are frequent between 6.30 am and 6 pm and a single journey anywhere in town costs 40t. PMVs don't enter the airport proper, but turn around at the end of the road before the flight tower. If you're going further than Boroko you'll probably have to change at Boroko, which could be a struggle if you've packed the kitchen sink. If you arrive at night, the only safe option for a newcomer is a taxi. It's much easier if you arrive in daylight, especially if you're a woman travelling solo.

Getting to the airport very early can be difficult. Consider staying nearby or book a taxi for the airport the night before. They usually show up, but often much later than you requested. They know the flight schedules and will race you to the airport and arrive with a comfortable two minutes to spare!

In contrast to the arrival shed, the international departure lounge is *air conditioned*, has a bar and a duty-free shop and comfortable chairs, so it's worth going through immigration as soon as they let you.

There is a K10 departure tax for all international flights.

Air If you want to get comparative schedules and prices, the best place to go is the airport.

The domestic airlines, Air Niugini, Talair, Douglas and MAF have separate offices and terminals at Jackson's – as you come out of the main International/Air Niugini terminal, they're to the right, obscured by the Air Niugini workshop, up a slight hill. Qantas' head office is in town in ANG House (tel 21 1422). I didn't manage to discover any signs of life in the shed that is allegedly MAF's home. MAF is useful for many third level airfields in the Highlands and their head office is in Mt Hagen. Douglas has the best connections in Papua and Talair has good links to the islands.

The prices for flights to most centres from Moresby are given in their appropriate Getting There & Away sections, but to give you an idea of straight fares from Moresby:

Lae	K76	Air Niugini or Talair
Popondetta	K49	Air Niugini or Talair
Mt Hagen	K110	Air Niugini or Talair
Wewak	K150	Air Niugini
Rabaul	K157	Air Niugini
Alotau	K85	Air Niugini or Talair
Woitape	K44	Douglas

Air Niugini has branch offices in Boroko (tel 25 3541) on Okari St, in town (tel 21 2888) on Douglas St and in Waigani (tel 25 1932) at the Government Centre; for domestic reservations and reconfirmations phone 27 3555, for international reservations and reconfirmations phone 27 3444. Talair has offices in town (Champion Parade, tel 21 4766) and at Waigani (Haus Tomakala, tel 25 7877); for reservations and confirmations phone 25 5799. If you don't find life at the MAF hanger try phoning 25 2668.

Sea The Burns Philp shipping office (tel 21 2233) is on Musgrave St down by the wharf. They have two vessels that go to the Gulf: the MV *Purari* and MV *Malalo*. One or the other leaves every Tuesday or Wednesday. If you depart on Tuesday, you arrive at Kerema on Wednesday morning for K34, Ihu on Thursday for K40 and Baimuru on Friday for K46. It may be worth seeing if Steamships have anything going, but they weren't interested in passengers when I asked.

Getting Around

PMV Moresby has an efficient Public Motor Vehicle (PMV) service with frequent connections on all the routes between 6.30 am and 7 pm (usually a bit later). PMV fares are a standard 40t for any trip in town. Pay the driver's assistant when you leave, but do not try to pay with large bills.

The PMVs get very crowded at peak hours; and especially on Friday evenings when everyone is doing their weekend shopping, so its worth avoiding them then, if you can.

Destinations are displayed inside the windscreen; yell 'stop' when you want to get off. In town there are established stops indicated by yellow roadside poles. The main interchange point, which can degenerate to a complete shambles, is either side of the pedestrian overpass at Boroko. The markets are always the best place to find long-distance PMVs, but if you head off in the direction you want to go, you can always flag one down. Gordon Market is the best place for PMVs to Sogeri and Bomana.

Around town there are two variations to the standard routes to watch out for. Most PMVs travel along the Hubert Murray Highway between Boroko (Four Mile) and town, but some head east through Kila Kila (useful for the hospital and the CWA Guesthouse) and some head west through Hohola to Gordon or Gerehu, avoiding the traffic snarl around Boroko. Unless Kila Kila or Hohola are on signs on the PMV windscreen you can assume it is going through Boroko.

Outside peak hours (before 8 am and after 4 pm), few PMVs run directly to the Waigani offices; those that do are marked 'Office' or 'W'gani Office'. At other times look for PMVs marked 'Gerehu' that run along Waigani Drive past the government offices and the University to the suburb of the same name. They'll drop you off on the main road, a short walk from the offices.

If you're going to town, look for PMVs going to 'Kone' (Konedobu, the old government centre between town and Hanuabada) or 'H'bada' (Hanuabada). PMVs to the airport usually show a '7 Mile' sign.

Taxi Taxis are readily available at the airport, the big hotels or on the streets, and they are all metered. Central Taxis (tel 25 2646), Radio Taxis (tel 25 5577) and Loaloa Taxis (tel 25 1118) are the main companies. From Boroko it's about K5 to Waigani and K6 to K7 to Moresby centre. Taxi fares are theoretically 45t a km, plus 40t flag fare.

Car Hire There are several rent-a-car places in town. See the Getting Around chapter for more details. Costs are high and for a smallish car (say a Ford Laser) you're looking at K34 per day plus 26t per km, plus insurance at around K12. The three main operators all have desks at Jackson's Airport, Port Moresby.

Avis-Nationwide
    PO Box 3533, Boroko (tel 25 8299)
Budget
    PO Box 503, Boroko (tel 25 4514)
Hertz
    PO Box 4126, Boroko (tel 25 4495)

Around Port Moresby

Moresby is the centre for a limited road network so there are a number of car or PMV trips you can make. There are also some interesting spots you can reach with short, relatively inexpensive flights. Douglas Airways are the most useful company for this region.

If you continue out on the Hubert Murray Highway, past the airport and turn right just before the Moitaka Showground & Speedway, a sealed road takes you along the Sogeri Gorge up to the cool Sogeri Plateau, the beautiful Rouna Falls, Variarata National Park and the beginning of the Kokoda Trail.

If you continue past the Moitaka Showgrounds, the road becomes the unsealed Hiritano Highway and turns north-west through Brown River, passing several attractive riverside picnic spots, continuing past the turn-off to Poukama (where there's a ferry to Yule Island) and on to Bereina and Iokea.

To the south-east, the unsealed Magi Highway runs past Bootless Inlet and the Loloata Island Resort and many fine beaches.

SOGERI ROAD
The trip out to the Sogeri Plateau is one of the most popular weekend jaunts for Moresbyites. It's only 46 km all the way to Sogeri, but there is quite enough to see and do to make it a full day trip. You can get out there by PMVs which run regularly from Gordon Market and Boroko. The fare is K1. The road is surfaced to Sogeri and all the way down to the national park.

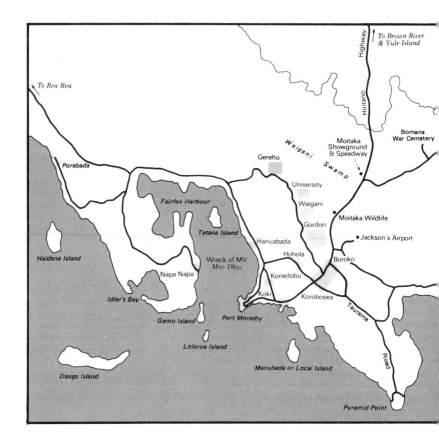

Head out of town on the Hubert Murray Highway and turn right about two km past the airport. There's a crocodile farm just before the turn-off and the Bomana Cemetery is after the turn-off.

Moitaka Wildlife

A few km out of Moresby, before the turn-off to Sogeri, is Moitaka Wildlife. Unless you make prior arrangements, it is only open to the public on Friday afternoons between 2 and 4 pm. This is also feeding time – crocodiles are hearty but infrequent eaters. In between those big feeds they lie there waiting for the next meal. There are a whole series of enclosures, from those for small crocodiles crowded in on top of one another, to a large, empty looking pond that houses the biggest, ugliest, meanest looking pukpuk you ever saw. The big crocs have neat little numbered flags tacked on their backs – you feel like the keepers should yell 'come in number five, your kaikai is ready'.

The farm also has an enclosure of deer and some native animals and birds, including a Raggiana Bird of Paradise which is quite an amazing show-off. He must wait all week for Friday afternoons when he can put on a non-stop performance

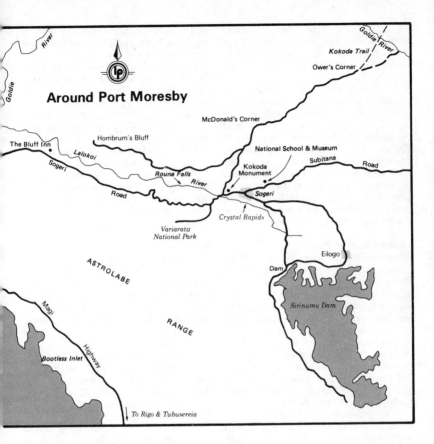

Around Port Moresby

of hopping around, displaying his wings and feathers, calling out, whispering hello, presenting his stomach to be scratched and generally acting the clown.

Bomana War Cemetery

Not far past the turn-off to Sogeri is the large and carefully tended WW II cemetery where 4000 Australian and Papua New Guinean soldiers lie buried. The American soldiers who died in PNG were generally shipped back to the US for burial.

Sogeri

A few km past the cemetery, the road begins to wind up the Laloki River's gorge. On the way you pass the *Bluff Inn*, a pleasant riverside beer garden. You then pass the *Hotel Rouna*. This was once a popular weekend escape but it's now very run-down and depressing; there are plans for it to be remodelled.

The turn-off to the Variarata National Park is past the hotel and, a little further again, there is a look out point for the spectacular Rouna Falls – before the hydro-electric power plants were installed they were even more impressive. There are also good views back towards Moresby. You can have a look at the hydro-power plants and, just before reaching Sogeri, you pass the Kokoda Trail junction.

Apart from its cool climate (thanks to its 600-metre altitude), Sogeri has a pleasant Sunday market with a good selection of fresh vegetables. The road continues beyond Sogeri, via Crystal Rapids, a popular swimming spot, to Musgrave River and the Sirinumu Dam. At Crystal Rapids they charge K2 to enter with a car. If you walk in (it's not far) it's just 30t. The dam controls the water flow to the Laloki River which in turn supplies the Rouna hydro-electric station.

Variarata National Park

The turn-off to the park, the first in PNG, is right after the Number Two Hydro Station on the Sogeri Rd. From this turn-off it's eight km to the park. There is a variety of interesting and clearly marked walking trails in the park and some excellent lookouts back to Port Moresby and the coast. Some of the trails can be quite jungle-like – surprising considering the proximity to Moresby.

From June to November, in the early morning or evening, it is possible to see birds of paradise in a clearly signposted display tree above the circuit track.

Admission to the park, which is a popular picnic spot, is K1 per person, and a map of the walking trails is available at the park entrance. There is an inexpensive lodge where you can stay. See the Places to Stay – Around Moresby section.

Kokoda Trail

Mention walking tracks in PNG and the famed Kokoda Trail is the one most likely to spring to mind. This is a little unfair since the track is far from the most interesting walk in PNG, but its historical connections and its practicality are big attractions.

Linking the north and south coasts, the trail was first used by miners struggling

north to the Yodda Kokoda gold fields of the 1890s, but it was WW II that brought it to the attention of the world.

Following Pearl Harbor in December '41, the Japanese made a rapid advance down the South-East Asian archipelago and across the Pacific, capturing New Britain and the north coast of New Guinea. The Japanese Navy's advance on Port Moresby and Australia was dramatically halted by the Battle of the Coral Sea, but this only led to a new strategy.

The Japanese decided to take Port Moresby by a totally unexpected 'back door' assault. The plan was to land on the north coast near Popondetta, travel south to Kokoda and then march up and over the central range to Sogeri and down to Port Moresby.

They made one serious miscalculation: the Kokoda Trail was not a rough track that could be upgraded for vehicles, it was a switchback footpath through some of the most rugged country in the world, endlessly climbing and plunging down, infested by leeches and hopelessly muddy during the wet season.

The Japanese landed on 21 July '42 and stormed down the trail, battling an increasingly desperate Australian and American opposition. The Allies planned a last-ditch, defensive battle for Imita Ridge, within spitting distance of Port Moresby, and on 16 September this is where the Japanese, their supply lines hopelessly over-stretched, finally stopped.

They had failed to supply their troops by air, their plan to make the trail suitable for vehicles had proved to be unrealistic, and a man could barely carry sufficient food to get himself down the trail and back, let alone carry extra supplies for the front line soldiers. At the same time the Japanese were also being stretched to the limits at Guadalcanal in the Solomons, so they withdrew, with Port Moresby virtually in sight.

The campaign to dislodge them from Buna on the north coast was one of the most bitter and bloody of the Pacific War.

If the two sides didn't kill each other, then disease or starvation did. The fighting was desperate and the terrain and climate were unbelievably hard.

It is impossible to comprehend the courage and suffering of the people who fought here, and it is no wonder the horrors of the Kokoda Trail and the Buna campaign have not been forgotten by either side. Never again did the Allied forces meet the Japanese head-on during WW II. The policy for the rest of the war was to advance towards Tokyo bypassing the intervening Japanese strongholds. Rabaul in New Britain, for instance, was left alone and isolated while the front moved towards Japan.

The turn-off to the trail is just before Sogeri and there's a memorial stone at this junction. The road twists and turns and is rather bumpy, although quite OK for conventional vehicles (so long as it isn't raining).

At McDonald's Corner there is a strange metal sculpture of a soldier; this is where the road once ended and the trail commenced, but the actual trail now starts further on at Ower's Corner (there's a sign).

From Ower's Corner the trail is easy to follow and it heads straight down towards the Goldie River. You can stroll down to the river if you just want an easy taste of what it's like. On the other side of the river, the endless 'golden staircase' crawls up to Imita Ridge, the turning point for the Japanese. See the Walking the Kokoda Trail section at the end of this chapter.

Hombrum's Bluff

A little way down the Kokoda Trail road, a smaller road branches off back towards Moresby, running parallel to the Sogeri road but high above it on the top of the Laloki River canyon wall. It leads to Hombrum's Lookout which was used as a retreat for important military brass during the war. There are excellent views back towards Moresby.

HIRITANO HIGHWAY

The coast west of Port Moresby, which is connected by road all the way to Bereina, is the home of the Mekeo people who are noted for their colourful dancing costumes and face painting. On ceremonial occasions the men paint their faces in striking geometric designs.

You start to escape from the dry climate of Moresby by the time you get to Brown River, a popular picnic spot about 40 km from Moresby. En route to the river you pass through teak plantations. You can get as far as Iokea by PMV.

Brown River

Brown River is a pleasant spot for swimming and a good place for quiet rafting, either on inner tubes or a rubber dinghy. Take the road up the river – it turns off the Hiritano Highway about a km before the bridge. It's best to have two cars, one to leave at the village by the turn-off and the other (preferably four-wheel drive) to drive up the river to another village where you can leave the car right by the water. You then raft down to the bridge and drive back to get the second car.

The trip takes three to four pleasant hours. Don't be tempted to go downstream from the bridge – you can get tangled up in log jams and would, in any case, have trouble getting back to the bridge.

Yule Island

The missionaries who arrived at Yule Island in 1885 were some of the first European visitors to the Papuan coast of New Guinea. Later the island became a government headquarters, from which government and mission workers penetrated into the central mountains in some of the earliest exploration of the country. Today the government centre is on the mainland at Bereina but there is still a large Catholic mission on Yule Island.

One of the early mission workers buried on Yule Island, M Bourgade, was one of France's top WW I air aces. You can still see his grave. Yule Island is a popular place and there is a small guesthouse, Rabao Mareana. Bring your appetite, as Yule is famous for its tasty prawns which are available in large quantities! See the Places to Stay Around Moresby section.

Getting There Turn off the Hiritano Highway approximately 38 km past Agu Vari. From the turn-off, which is signposted, you travel another 20 km to Poukama, where there is a car park (K1 per day) and, if you've warned the guesthouse people of your arrival, a canoe to take you to the island (K1 per person).

Poukama is about 160 km from Moresby, a three hour drive. There's an airstrip at Kairuku, the main village on the island, and Douglas Airways will drop off and pick up on their daily Kerema flight (K49). You can also fly to Bereina for about K45. See Places to Stay Around Moresby for more information.

MAGI HIGHWAY (Rigo Rd)

At Six Mile, instead of turning left to the airport, turn right to Village Arts. The road circles round Bootless Inlet to the small marina (Tahira Boating Centre) from which the ferry crosses to Loloata Island.

Loloata Island

Only 22 km out from Moresby, Loloata Island in Bootless Inlet is another popular weekend escape. Lazing on the beach or skin diving is the order of the day. To get there you drive out on the Rigo road to the Tahira Boating Centre on Bootless Bay, from there you can do a day trip to the *Loloata Island Resort* for K20, including lunch. The resort has snorkelling, diving, fishing and sailboarding facilities and a licensed restaurant. A wrecked, but intact, WW II Boston Havoc bomber is on the reef near the resort. See the Places to Stay Around Moresby section.

Coast

A little further on there is a turn-off to Tubusereia, a Motuan coastal village with houses built on stilts over the water. There are, unfortunately, few reminders of the attractive place it must have been. Corrugated iron, rusting car bodies and rubbish are the 20th-century additions.

The road continues past Gaire and Gaba Gaba, turns inland to Rigo and Kwikila, then back to the coast again at Hula on Hood Bay, another village close to the mouth of the Kemp Welch River. There are many fine beaches all along this road.

TAPINI & WOITAPE

If you want to get a look at the high country behind the coastal strip, or experience one of the most heart-in-mouth airstrips in PNG, or try a lesser known but extremely interesting walk then Tapini is a good place to go. It is a pretty little station at a bit under 1000 metres.

The airstrip is amazing; carved into a hillside, it runs steeply uphill ending in a sheer face so you can only come in one way. When you leave, downhill, the strip drops off sheer at the end. You've got a choice of flying or falling.

There are many interesting walks around Tapini. You could walk to Woitape (three days) and fly out back to Moresby. Woitape is particularly noted for its many orchids. Douglas Airways flies Moresby-Tapini for K56, Moresby-Woitape for K44. Woitape is connected by road to the coast.

There is also a rough road from Tapini to Guari where the once fearsome Kunimaipa people lived. In just 50 km, the road climbs up to nearly 3000 metres and drops down to about 700 metres. Guari is just an airstrip, with no real village, but there are some nice walks in the valley below. You could do a circle trek out to the Kamali Mission.

There's a hotel in Tapini and a guesthouse in Woitape (the guesthouse is much more expensive than the hotel!) – see the Places to Stay Around Moresby section.

PLACES TO STAY AROUND MORESBY

All the following places are too far out of the city for it to be possible to commute. Escaping the city is especially worth considering if you are going to be around for a weekend. Nothing much happens in the big smoke and it's definitely more interesting to be in the country, or near a beach.

The *Hotel Rouna* (tel 28 1146), PO Box 67, Port Moresby is about a km from the Rouna Falls on the Sogeri road and about 34 km from Moresby. The hotel is on a great site, but in its current incarnation it's definitely not recommended. The whole place looks distinctly unloved, and seems to be on the verge of total collapse. Renovations are planned and these may well turn the tide. Until then it's a hotel for thrill-seekers only. A room costs K20, there are no meals but there's plenty of beer.

Also out on the Sogeri road, the *Kokoda Trail Motel* (tel 28 2342), PO Box 5014, Boroko is about 40 km out from Moresby. It overlooks the river and there's an open air bar, reasonable restaurant and a swimming pool. The altitude means that the evenings are cool and invigorating and there is still something of a colonial atmosphere ....

Weekend barbecues are popular; a feature is the crocodile – you eat *it* – it tastes like a sort of sea-foody white steak and costs K8. Other lunches are also around K8. Breakfast costs K3. The Saturday night special is K45 for a room and you can squeeze in as many people as you like. Every second Saturday night a pig is barbecued on a spit and there is a band. Transport to the motel can be arranged. There are 16 rooms and regular costs are K30 for singles, K40 for doubles and K50 for a family.

It's possible to camp in the Variarata National Park but your belongings are not secure. There is, however, the *Variarata National Park Lodge* with small singles for K10, larger rooms for up to four people for K20. Bedding and cooking facilities are supplied but you must bring utensils and food. Ring the ranger at the park on 25 9340 or the Assistant Secretary for Wildlife & Parks on 27 2500.

The *Loloata Island Resort* (tel 25 8590), PO Box 5290, Boroko, has nine twin rooms and the PMV jumping-off point is about 20 minutes from Moresby on the Magi Highway. The daily cost of K50 includes all meals and the launch trip to Loloata Island. You can book a room for the whole weekend – Saturday morning to Sunday evening. Snorkelling, diving, fishing and sailboarding equipment are available on the island.

Yule Island is about three hours northwest along the Hiritano Highway. The *Rabao Mareana Guesthouse* (bookings through Coral Sea Travel Services, tel 21 4422) is recommended. There are seven rooms, most with double beds and the cost is K24 per adult, K6 for children. This includes all meals. The guesthouse overlooks Hall Sound – there's a bar (beer only) and the food (often fresh seafood) is good.

The management makes an effort to be helpful – meal times are flexible, and they can arrange canoes to take guests to secluded beaches and snorkelling spots. There is a car park at Poukama and your car will be looked after for K1 per day. If they know you're coming, they'll arrange a canoe across the Sound for K1 per person.

The small *Tapini Hotel* (tel 25 9280), PO Box 19, Tapini, is just three minutes' walk from the airstrip. There are seven rooms and the nightly cost of K35 includes all meals. The food here has a good reputation.

The *Woitape Guesthouse* (tel 25 7746), PO Box 6036, Boroko, has six double rooms and a daily cost of K75 which, you'll be relieved to hear, includes all meals.

WALKING THE KOKODA TRAIL
The Kokoda Trail is the most popular walking track in PNG. Although there are more interesting walks from a cultural point of view, there are good arguments in the trail's favour; the country it passes through is spectacular, its dramatic role in WW II provides an emotional draw, it is a practical link between south and north coasts – and walking from one end to the other is a feat to be proud of.

The straight line distance from Ower's Corner to Kokoda is about 60 km but for the walker it is a bit over 90 km, but this gives no impression at all of the actual difficulty.

The trail is a continual series of ups and downs – generally steep, exhausting ups and muddy, slippery downs – over the whole trail you gain and lose 6000 metres (nearly 20,000 feet) of altitude. There are villages to stop at along the way and many people spend time looking for war mementos.

The walk can take as little as five (long) days, but it could easily be spread over 10, if you throw in a few rest days. There are between 40 and 50 hours of walking involved so most people average seven days. In 1986 Osborne Bogajiwai set a record of 28 hours, 14 minutes and 30 seconds.

Do not walk the trail during the wet season when the normally muddy trail is dangerously slippery and many rivers are high and hazardous to cross. The best months are usually August and September. Most people walk from south to north. Popondetta (at the northern end) is not a particularly exciting place, so if you're planning to travel along the north coast, bear in mind the *Mamose Express* leaves Oro Bay at 2 pm on Tuesdays.

The trail is generally reasonably clear and a guide is not necessary although, back in 1968, a Canadian woman died of exposure after losing her way.

Before you start out, contact the impressively titled National Emergency & Surveillance Administration & Co-ordination Centre at the Army's Murray Barracks headquarters (tel 24 2480 or 24 2208), PO Box 391, Port Moresby, to inform them of your party's plans and get up-to-date information on the trail. Don't forget to report in at the District Office at Kokoda.

If you want more information you could talk to Pacific Expeditions (tel 25 7803), who run tours over the trail. They have a reasonably priced information service and good contacts with village guesthouses along the way.

Lonely Planet's *Bushwalking in Papua New Guinea* has a detailed description of the walk and there are good maps available in Moresby from the National Mapping Bureau at Waigani. Do not leave without

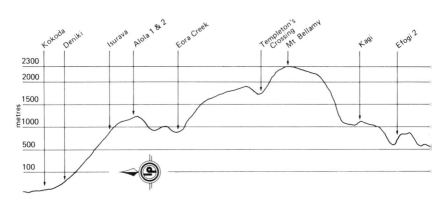

copies of the 1:100,000 topographic maps for Kokoda, Efogi and Port Moresby, and the *Longitudinal Section of the Kokoda Trail*, which has useful descriptive notes and detailed sections of tricky areas.

As you may be starting to appreciate, the walk is no picnic, although anyone with reasonable fitness will be OK, so long as they stay within their limits (there are, as yet, no prizes for speed) and have the right equipment. Comfortable boots are essential and gaiters are recommended. Take wet weather gear and stoves since even in the 'dry' season it can be very wet. When you reach high altitudes it can get quite chilly at night so come prepared; you'll need a sleeping bag. Make sure you take a comprehensive medical kit.

There are guesthouses where you can spend the night in most villages, but take a tent for safety and flexibility. Some of the available shelters are small, so if you meet another party you might have to camp and a tent fly may well be useful to waterproof a run-down shelter . . . . Make sure you pay for village accommodation – it's usually around K5 per person.

There's a guesthouse at Myola, which is a bit off the main trail, and although it costs K15 for food and accommodation, it is recommended; the food is excellent, the 'lakes' are interesting and this is a good spot for a rest day. If you just want a taste of the trail and have some spare cash

(approx K25), it's possible to fly in. Speak to Pacific Expeditions. The guesthouse is built of traditional materials and this is a serene and beautiful spot. There are trout in nearby streams, some beautiful walks and interesting war relics. This would make a great weekend escape from Moresby.

There's also a guesthouse at Efogi and at Naduli (K6). In Kokoda there's a guesthouse beside the museum; ask at the District Headquarters.

Bring enough food for the walk. Villagers will generally sell some fruit to passing walkers but, apart from at the guesthouses, there's not much surplus to spare.

Distances along the trail from Ower's Corner are Imita Gap seven km, Ioribaiwa (an old village site) 12 km, Ofi Creek 16 km, Naoro Village 27 km, Menari Village 36 km, Efogi Village 46 km, Kagi 51 km, Kokoda Gap 62 km, Eora Creek 71 km, Alola Village 75 km and, finally, the Kokoda War Memorial 94 km.

The highest point along the trail is Mt Bellamy at 2560 metres, between Kagi and Kokoda Gap. From Mt Bellamy the trail descends steeply to Templeton's Crossing.

If you want a little taste of the trail without walking the whole distance, you can walk down to Goldie River from Ower's Corner in just an hour or so. If you

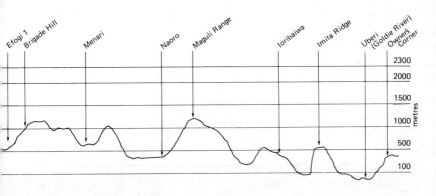

have the energy, struggle up the Golden Staircase to Imita Ridge on the other side. Another option would be to fly in, walk a section and fly out. Between Naoro and Efogi the trail is a little easier and there are airstrips at both villages.

Some advice from recent walkers:

I think most friendly PMV drivers would take you up the road as far as the start of the trail – ask them anyway. Otherwise it's a long and unnecessary walk. From the beginning of the trail you can continue eight km down the old and overgrown army road to Goldie Village. From there we had two volunteer guides take us to where there seems to be a junction with the old trail.

We encountered nothing but friendliness and hospitality all the way along the trail and were able to stay at rest houses in the villages. Make some contribution for this, even when unasked.

Don't walk the trail without the relief map. Some parts are a real maze. If in doubt whether you are on the right trail watch out for rubbish. If there's garbage around you are going the right way.

Detail from a painting by Kauage, a contemporary artist whose work can be seen at the National Art School. His work is represented in museums around the world.

Lae & Morobe

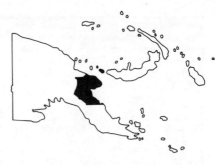

Area 33,152 square km
Population 350,000
Lae 75,000

The province of Morobe curves around Huon Gulf and includes the mountainous Huon Peninsula. The provincial headquarters, Lae, is its focal point and PNG's second largest city. The province's main river, the Markham, bisects the mountains with a broad, open flood plain. Morobe has the best road connections in the country. From Lae you can drive west to the Highlands along the Markham Valley, north-west to Madang, or south to the highland areas around Wau and Bulolo, the centre of the 1920s gold rush.

HISTORY

Some of the earliest remains of human civilisation in PNG have been found in this province; axe heads discovered at Bobongora by students of the University of PNG have been dated at 40,000 years old. It is believed the earliest settlements were in coastal areas. These early settlements were subsequently flooded by rising sea levels (post Ice Age) and therefore most of PNG's prehistory has been lost under the sea. However in some regions, like parts of the Huon Peninsula, these coastal areas have subsequently risen and exposed the remains of these early settlements.

The Leiwomba people occupied the Lae area and the Anga (once widely known as the Kukukuku, a term that was used by the coastal people and is now actively resented by the Anga) lived a nomadic existence in the central mountains in the Menyamya district, but their territory stretched through to the Gulf of Papua. The first contact the coastal people had with Europeans came when the German New Guinea Kompagnie made an unsuccessful attempt to colonise the mainland.

In 1885 the Germans established their first settlement at Finschhafen, and soon started to disintegrate due to the effects of malaria, boredom, alcohol and various other tropical ills. These problems followed them along the northern coast and were only left behind (at least partially) when they transferred to the island of New Britain. The Lutheran Mission arrived when the company was at Finschhafen, but managed to hang on after it departed. Finschhafen is still a major Lutheran base.

After the Australian takeover Morobe became a fairly quiet place. Until the discovery of gold no one cared to disturb the regions' ferocious warriors. At Ho'mki ('outcrop of rocks'), by the Butibum/ Bumbu River, large boulders mark the site of the last raid on Lae by hostile tribes from up the valley. This final clash, in 1907, killed 67 people.

The legendary prospector 'Sharkeye' Park is credited with the discovery of gold close to Wau in 1921. By the mid-'20s the gold hunters were flooding in, arriving at the port of Salamaua and struggling for eight days up the steep and slippery track to Wau, a mere 50 km away. As if the conditions of the track, the wet and often cold climate and tropical diseases were not enough, the miners also had to contend with hostile tribes. Frequent

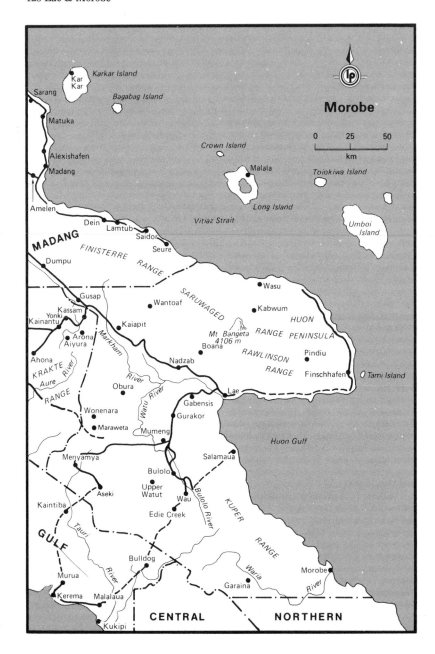

reprisal raids by angry miners hardly helped matters.

In 1926 a richer field was discovered at Edie Creek, high in the hills above Wau. Although miners made quick fortunes here and at the earlier Koranga Creek Strike, it soon became evident to the more far-sighted prospectors that to really squeeze the most out of these gold-rich streams large investments and heavy equipment would be needed.

The rough trail from the port of Salamaua up to Wau, Bulolo and Edie Creek was totally unsuitable for transporting heavy equipment, so the New Guinea Gold Company took the brave step of flying in the equipment. An airstrip was prepared in Lae and a shuttle service began. At one time, more air freight was lifted in PNG than in the rest of the world put together!

The gold fields continued to be productive until after the war when the recovery rate started to drop, gold was pegged at an artificially low price (US$35 an ounce) and the costs of production increased. One by one, the eight huge dredges were closed down, the last one in 1965. Although many people still work the fields it is now a small-scale cottage industry.

Lae, or Lehe as it was originally spelt, was a tiny mission station before the gold rush. It soon became a thriving community clustered around its central airstrip, in true PNG fashion. The history of the town and of aviation remained closely linked. In July 1937 the pioneer aviator Amelia Earhart took off from Lae on one of the final legs of a round-the-world flight and disappeared over the Pacific without trace.

The volcanic eruptions at Rabaul in 1937 prompted a decision to move the capital of New Guinea to Lae, but WW II intervened before the transfer was really under way. Lae, Salamaua and Rabaul became the major Japanese bases in New Guinea.

In early '43, the Japanese, reeling from defeats at Milne Bay and the Kokoda Trail, their naval power devastated by the Battle of the Coral Sea, decided to make one more attempt to take Port Moresby. This time they attacked towards Wau, marching up over the mountains from Salamaua in late January 1943. Australian troops in Wau were quickly reinforced by air from Port Moresby and the Japanese advance was repelled.

A grim campaign to clear the Japanese from Morobe followed. It took six months to struggle through the mud and jungle to the outskirts of Salamaua. Australian troops landed on beaches 25 km east of Lae on 4 September and the next day a huge Allied force parachuted onto Nadzab airstrip, up the Markham Valley from Lae. Transport aircraft then flew vast numbers of men and huge amounts of materials in for the advance on Lae.

Salamaua was captured on 11 September and once Lae was surrounded it was easily taken on 16 September. Many Japanese escaped into the mountain wilderness of the Huon Peninsula and started on the incredible retreat that was to eventually end at Wewak.

Lae, Wau, Bulolo and Salamaua were all destroyed during the fighting and Salamaua was never rebuilt. Today it is just a tiny and very pretty village with a pleasant guesthouse. Although the gold was giving out and Papua and New Guinea were to become a united colony governed from Port Moresby, Lae soon had a new reason for existence.

The road between Wau, Bulolo and Lae was built during the war and work on a road along the Markham Valley from Lae into the Highlands commenced. The Highlands, unknown territory before the war, became the scene for major developments. Important coffee and tea industries were established and the crops were trucked down the Highlands Highway and shipped out from Lae. Lae became the major port and industrial centre in PNG and still has the most important road links into the interior.

GEOGRAPHY

Morobe is an arc of land surrounding the Huon Gulf; it's the hump in the New Guinea 'dragon's' back. The lofty Saruwaged Mountains form the spine of the Huon Peninsula; one of the most tangled and impenetrable rainforests in PNG blankets their lower slopes. The Saruwageds march right down to the sea and pop up again as the backbone of the mountainous island of New Britain.

The mountains in the south-west are equally inhospitable. Here they are part of the central spine of the island and they rise higher and higher towards the centre. Between the two ranges there is the wide, flat, fertile Markham Valley which has become a major cattle-grazing area. Morobe also includes a number of volcanic islands between the Huon Peninsula and New Britain.

PEOPLE

Curiously, there are many parts of Morobe which were virtually uninhabited when Europeans first arrived, including the fertile Wau and Bulolo Valleys. The Leiwomba people, however, were long established in the Lae area and the Anga lived in the central mountains.

Frequently referred to incorrectly and offensively as the Kukukuku, the Anga averaged less than 150 cm (five feet) in height and were renowned fighters. They lived a nomadic existence interspersed with violent raids on more peaceful villages at lower altitudes – or upon each other. Despite the bitter climate in their high mountain homeland, they wore only a tiny grass skirt, like a Scotsman's sporran, and cloaks made of beaten bark, known as *mals*.

J K McCarthy, who between the two world wars made some of the first contacts with these people, describes them vividly in his book *Patrol into Yesterday*. His contact even extended to an arrow in the stomach. The warriors are excellent bowmen who make up for their imperfect aim with an incredibly rapid delivery.

McCarthy also recounts their first sight of an aircraft: Men took turns at crawling underneath it to inspect its genitals, unsure whether the bird was male or female. Their first reaction to McCarthy was less confident. When the first white man arrived in an Anga village, many of these otherwise fearless people literally fainted.

Lae

Lae is a green, attractive place that fits easily into its tropical setting – a striking change if you've just come from Port Moresby in the dry season. It's the second largest town in PNG, with a population of around 75,000.

Unfortunately, it now has a very bad reputation for rascals. The paranoia on the part of locals is intense, and you will need to have a very thick skin not to be affected. Even more unfortunately, the reputation and the paranoia are largely deserved, so there is no point staying any longer than you have to. Make your transport connections and go on to somewhere like Salamaua where things are less tense.

There are few places where the country's terrific potential and its problems are so startlingly obvious. In happier days Lae had a reputation as a garden city and there was no better place to appreciate the reasons for this than at the Botanical Gardens. Today, the gardens are still beautiful, but you would be most unwise to visit them other than in broad daylight, in a large group and preferably with a local guide.

Orientation

Lae is built on a flat-topped headland, although from the centre itself you get few views of the sea. The old Lae Airport, where the airlines have their offices, lies at the foot of the hill to the west. Voco Point, where the shipping companies have their

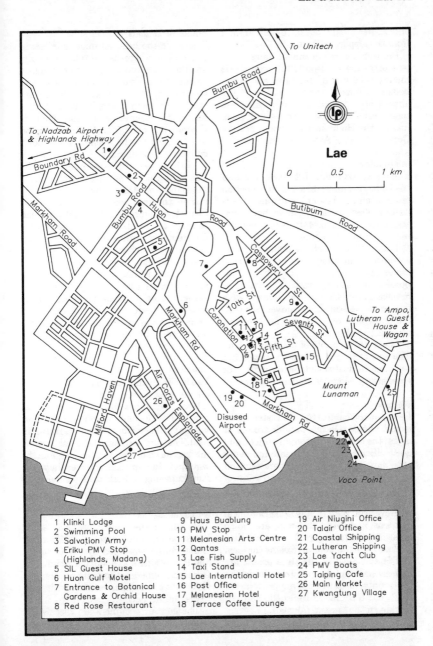

Lae

0   0.5   1 km

1   Klinki Lodge
2   Swimming Pool
3   Salvation Army
4   Eriku PMV Stop
    (Highlands, Madang)
5   SIL Guest House
6   Huon Gulf Motel
7   Entrance to Botanical
    Gardens & Orchid House
8   Red Rose Restaurant
9   Haus Buablung
10 PMV Stop
11 Melanesian Arts Centre
12 Qantas
13 Lae Fish Supply
14 Taxi Stand
15 Lae International Hotel
16 Post Office
17 Melanesian Hotel
18 Terrace Coffee Lounge
19 Air Niugini Office
20 Talair Office
21 Coastal Shipping
22 Lutheran Shipping
23 Lae Yacht Club
24 PMV Boats
25 Taiping Cafe
26 Main Market
27 Kwangtung Village

offices, lies at the foot of the hill around from the airport to the south.

Pre-war Lae sat on the flat land to the west of the town's airport, but today this is mainly occupied by factories and warehouses. Nadzab Airport, which is the airport both Air Niugini and Talair are reluctant to using, is 45 km west of town, just off the Highlands Highway. See the Getting There & Away section.

Information

There's a good Public Library in Lae and the Unitech Library has a good collection of maps and a cheap photocopier. Lae is well supplied with all the major banks and shops, including sports stores (for snorkelling gear) and bookshops.

The post office is efficient and there is a group of public telephones next door that rarely have queues, are reasonably soundproofed and usually work. The excellent newsagent on Coronation Drive has a public notice board that advertises club meetings, lost dogs, prams for sale and other useful things.

There are a couple of dentists in Lae. The only other places where you can find someone to deal scientifically with your gnashers are Moresby, Rabaul and Arawa.

Warning

Be especially careful in Lae. Listen to the locals' advice. Do not wander around at night; the taxis are reasonably priced and quite efficient, so if you're out and about after dark, use them. Avoid wandering off by yourself; stay within sight and sound of other people. If you arrive at night, get your PMV driver to deliver you to wherever you plan to stay. The Botanical Gardens and Mt Lunaman are no-go areas for lone travellers.

There's no problem with using the local PMVs and most of the time people are friendly and helpful, as they are throughout the country. I didn't see any violence or theft, but a couple of times the hair did prickle on the back of my neck.

Botanical Gardens

These are the best botanical gardens in PNG. There are huge trees virtually smothered in vines and creepers, brightly coloured birds that call out raucously and electric green lizards that scuttle through the undergrowth. The garden also boasts an exotic orchid collection that is theoretically open from 10 am to 12 noon or 2 to 4 pm on the weekends, but don't count on the reliability of those hours.

Within the garden boundaries is the Lae War Cemetery with the graves of thousands of Allied soldiers who died during the last war. If the war seems distant and unreal, pay a visit and read some of the headstones. The names are frighteningly ordinary, many of their owners were extremely young, and the places they died lie all around you.

Over the last few years there have been many vicious attacks on people in the gardens, even in broad daylight. Plan to go with a decent-sized group and preferably with a local guide. There are more people around on weekends and it tends to be safer.

Markets

Lae has three markets. The main market on the west side of the airstrip is quite interesting. It has food and a few local curios. The Butibum market is a smaller, village market out of town on the Butibum road. The third market is the Kamkumsung market, just past the Bumbu Bridge on the way out to the Unitech. It serves the whole Kamkumsung suburb and surrounding villages.

Mt Lunaman

The hill in the centre of town – Mt Lunaman or, more correctly, Lo' Wamung (First Hill) – was used by the Germans and the Japanese as a lookout point. The Germans named it Burgberg or 'Fortress Hill', while the Japanese riddled it with caves and tunnels.

The current occupiers are rascals (no doubt they have given it a new name) and it is, once again, a no-go zone – unless you're in a car, with a group, in daylight and preferably with a local guide, it's not worth the trouble.

Unitech

The Matheson Library, at the PNG University of Technology (Unitech), is the largest library of technology in the South Pacific. The Duncanson Hall has 36 Sepik style carved pillars and the coffee house is also built like a traditional haus tambaran. The Unitech also has an artefacts collection that includes many rare pieces. It's the only public collection of artefacts in the Morobe Province. The Unitech is 10 km out of Lae.

Wagan

Eight km from town, across the Butibum River, Wagan is a small village near Malahang Beach which the Japanese used as a landing point. You must ask the villagers for permission to visit the black sand beach where the remains of the landing barge *Myoko Maru* are sinking into the sand.

On the way to Wagan you pass by the Lutheran Mission, Ampo, and the Lae Lutheran Guesthouse. The church was used as a field hospital during the war and was one of the few buildings in the Lae area to have survived the conflict.

Things to Do

The Bulai International Primary School on Huon Rd, past Eriku, has a swimming pool that is open to outsiders on weekends for a small charge.

If you want to try bushwalking around Lae, ring Rod Clarke of the Lae Explorer's Club (tel 42 2276 during business hours) and check the notice board outside the newsagent on Coronation Drive for notices advertising walks.

If you're keen on diving, contact the people from Salamaua Haus Kibung who run dive trips out of Salamaua and Lae. A day trip with rental equipment and lunch costs K45.

Tours Morobe Tours (tel 42 4198) operate air-con bus trips in and around the town. A three hour tour, taking in the local sites and history, costs K50, which is reasonable, I suppose, if you can split it with (quite) a few people. They pick up from the Melanesian Hotel and Lae International Hotel.

Places to Stay – bottom end

Lae used to have one of the best accommodation bargains available in PNG – *Haus Buablung* (tel 42 4412), PO Box 1055. Although it's still cheap, some aspects are now pretty hard to tolerate. On Cassowary St, not too far from the town centre, it's a hostel-style place mainly occupied by young people on a permanent basis. Walk down Hawk St, turn left at the bottom and it's on your left, just over a little bridge; there's no sign.

Clean sheets are provided and the rooms are adequate, although noisy. Rooms do not have fans and can be very hot. The shared showers and toilets rank with some of the filthiest I have ever seen and are, in their own humble way, quite spectacular .... While they are a bacteriologist's dream, for normal travellers the challenge is not to discover a new bug, but to complete normal bodily functions without touching anything!

To round off the negative side, the food that is included in the price is virtually inedible. The pluses are that it is friendly, centrally located, reasonably secure, a good place to meet locals and it only costs K10 per person, food included.

The best option is now the *Lutheran Guest House* (tel 42 2556, 42 3711), PO Box 80, at Ampo on Busu Rd, opposite the Balob Teachers' College. Ampo (pronounced Umpo) is the main administration centre for the Lutheran Church and the comfortable, old, colonial-style guesthouse buildings are about 200 metres on the right from the main road, set in green, attractive grounds. It's K20 for a shared room with sheets and fans, very clean shared bathrooms and lounge rooms with coffee-making facilities. All meals are included and they are excellent.

The guesthouse's priority is to look after people who are associated with the church, so although they welcome travellers, you may be unlucky and find it full. They have quite a few beds, however, so tell them you are a traveller and cross your fingers. The place has a list of regulations that fills a small book (I'm not kidding) but this is understandable considering that they cater for diverse people, among them missionary families, teachers, travellers, convention-goers and locals. If you don't mind making a few concessions, you'll meet some very friendly, interesting people, in a calm, relaxing environment. Ring in advance. The gates are closed between 10 pm and 6 am.

The only drawback is that it's too far out of town to walk, but a taxi only costs about K1.50 and the PMVs are frequent. Catch one from the main PMV station on the corner of 7th St. You want a 'Butibum' PMV, but check with the driver's assistant that it goes to Ampo.

The *Salvation Army Hostel* (tel 42 2487), PO Box 259, is on Huon Rd one km or so from the centre near the Eriku PMV station, but there are only four immaculate rooms. They have cooking facilities so you can save money by fixing your own food. A two bed unit costs K20, and they have weekly rates. If you don't mind roughing it, they sometimes let people camp in the Recreation Hall for K1 per person. There are no cooking facilities.

Close by, on Klinkii St, which runs off Huon Rd, is *Klinkii Lodge* (tel 42 1281), PO Box 192. The rooms are large, very clean and quiet. Free videos are shown every night. Meals are available and served in your room at a cost of K7.50 for lunch and K10.50 for dinner. There are 20 rooms with singles/doubles at K30/38.50, including breakfast.

The *Summer Institute of Linguistics* (SIL) missionary group run a guesthouse (tel 42 3214) on Poinsiana Rd, off Kwila

Rd, which runs into Milford Haven opposite the Botanical Gardens. Rooms are K28/34 for singles/doubles, with cooking facilities only, so it's not a great bargain.

The *Lae School of Catering* (tel 43 6999), PO Box 305, at the Lae Technical College has a few rooms to rent out, but only when school is in session. The nightly cost is K16 per person and meals are also available.

Finally, the *YWCA* (tel 42 1691) has a small establishment on the right hand side of 7th, a short distance from town. They may have space for women at K23 per single.

The famous old *Hotel Cecil*, an establishment that became a South Pacific legend (it was featured in *Return to Paradise* by James Michener) is no more. The site, below town opposite Voco Point, is apparently to become an executive housing estate and the new headquarters for the Evangelical Lutheran Church.

Places to Stay – top end

The *Melanesian Hotel* (tel 42 3744), PO Box 756, is only a minute's walk from the town centre. It has everything you would expect, including a choice of bars and restaurants and a pleasant swimming pool. After 6 pm you must wear a shirt and trousers – enough said? There are 67 rooms with singles/doubles at K66/80. Meals are good and the smorgasbord is excellent value at K8, but otherwise their food is not cheap.

The *Huon Gulf Motel* (tel 42 4844), PO Box 612, is on Markham Rd, right by the old airstrip. It is somewhat smaller than the Melanesian, but is otherwise very similar. Like the Melanesian, all 30 rooms are self-contained and air-con and there's a swimming pool. Singles/doubles are K60/66. The lunch menu includes barramundi, steak or ham for about K10.

The top hotel in Lae is the new *Lae International Hotel* (tel 42 2000), PO Box 2774, a short distance from town. It was, until recently, a gracious, old colonial lodge (it is still often referred to as the Lae Lodge) but it's now a modern and luxurious hotel. It's actually considerably better than most soul-less new hotels, with a friendly atmosphere and an attractive design that actually acknowledges and makes some concessions to its location.

There's an excellent 25 metre pool and an open-sided Haus Win where they have a Friday night disco (K5) and a popular pool side lunchtime barbecue on Saturday and Sunday. There's also a restaurant, coffee shop and sandwich bar. The rooms have air-conditioning and TVs and the cost is suitably 'international'; singles/doubles are K89/99.

Places to Eat

If you are not eating at your hotel, Lae has a small range of alternatives, particularly for snacks and light lunches. If you're in Lae over a weekend, give serious consideration to the pool side barbecue at the *Lae International Hotel* which is very good value at K6.50 to K7.50.

There's a wonderful *Sanitarium* health food shop on the corner of 7th, near the PMV station, that sells delicious sandwiches, fruit juices, cold milk and a full range of Sanitarium products. This provides a rare opportunity to stock up with good food.

The most pleasant spot for a proper meal is the *Lae Yacht Club* which is down on Voco Point. It overlooks the water and they serve lunches, dinners and *cold* beers every day. The outside bar opens from 4.30 pm and there's no better spot to sit and watch the world go by. A roast meal will cost about K5 and something a bit fancier like prawns will cost K7. They also have cheaper snacks.

Togo's Coffee Hut is on 7th St at Coronation Drive in the Central Arcade. It's cool and pleasant with sandwiches, burgers and milkshakes in the K1 to K2 range. Steaks are K5.

The *Terrace Coffee Lounge* on 2nd St is also good. Sandwiches are K1 to K2,

omelettes K3.50. It's open 9 am to 5 pm, Monday to Friday, half a day on Saturday and closed on Sunday.

Raffles Restaurant is also on 2nd, but it's only open at lunchtime. You buy what you want at the takeaway bar and carry it through to a sit down section with a bar. A serve of roast meat and veg is K3.

The best place for hot takeaway food is the *Lae Fish Supply*. It has many more choices than the average kai bar and it's clean and cheap. A spring roll or a piece of fish will cost about 50t, a boiled egg 30t and a good serving of chow mein K1.70.

There are two Chinese places. The *Red Rose Restaurant* on Huon Rd, a bit out of town, has a good reputation and reasonable prices. You can eat your fill for around K8. The *Kwangtung Village* is owned by the same people who own the Moresby Kwangtung Village. The food is good but a little more expensive than the Red Rose, say around K10 per person. It's rather inconveniently located on Mangola Rd, out beyond the market, on the other side of the airport.

The best-value meals in town are served at the *Lutheran Guest House*, but they're for residents only. The *Huon Gulf* and the *Melanesian* both have licensed restaurants, with prices in the K10 to K15 bracket. The *Lae International Hotel* has an expensive restaurant, but the Coffee Shop is quite reasonable – K5 for spaghetti, for instance. They also have a Sandwich Bar that sells open sandwiches for around K2.50, but they are a bit on the small side.

Things to Buy

The Melanesian Arts Centre (tel 42 1604) on 8th St has a good collection of artefacts including many pieces from the Trobriands and the Sepik region. It's easy to walk past without noticing it; it's a weatherboard house, next door to the petrol station. Owned by Robyn Leahy, daughter-in-law of Mick Leahy, it's open Monday to Saturday, from 9 am to 12 noon. Prices are similar, maybe a little better than those in

Moresby and they will ship stuff home for you. The staff are friendly, helpful and knowledgeable. A buying day when local people bring in goods is interesting to see. Ask if one is coming up.

Morobe Arts & Handcrafts is in the building next door to the Melanesian Hotel and it has an interesting collection, including sand paintings. Walk down the passageway immediately in front of the drive and it is on your right. There's a good view over the harbour to the towering Herzog Mountains on the other side.

Small inexpensive crafts are also available from street sellers who spread their wares on the sidewalk around the large downtown department stores, particularly the Burns Philp store.

Getting There & Away

There's a wide choice of transport into and out of Lae, as Lae is the major centre on the north coast, the major north coast port, an important airport and the coastal access point for the Highlands Highway.

There are frequent air connections to all main centres, including to the islands, regular shipping services along the coast and out to New Britain and numerous PMVs plying between the Highlands and Madang. Just to make life difficult, there are two airports and the one currently in use is miles from the town centre. See the following section.

Air The wrangle over the two Lae airports has been going on for years and seems set to continue. The old airport and the airline offices are right in town, but the newer Nadzab Airport, which is now being used by Air Niugini and Talair planes, is 45 km away, just off the Highlands Highway.

This was an important airstrip during the war, and it is much more spacious than the old airport in town. Nadzab was used in the early '80s, but it proved so unpopular that in 1984 the town airport was used for all flights, except those landing after 6 pm.

Nadzab is now back in use and proving to be no more popular than the last time around. The current situation is a mess and may change once again. The problem, as you may have guessed, is transport to and from Lae.

Air Niugini seems to have a slightly greater commitment to the place than Talair. Air Niugini offer a chartered bus service which runs to and from their office at the old airport to meet all incoming and outgoing Air Niugini flights.

The bus theoretically leaves town two hours before Air Niugini flights arrive, giving you more than ample time to check in, but there doesn't seem to be any fixed schedule. There are only one or two buses in the morning and the afternoon, so try and get some idea of what's going on when you reconfirm your flight. Talair does not run a bus. Perhaps they could provide parachutes instead and push passengers out over Mt Lunaman? The Air Niugini bus is free and Talair passengers can use it, but the timing can be inconvenient.

The only other alternatives are PMVs to/from Eriku (in Lae), taxis, hotel courtesy buses and generous locals. Forget the taxi. How does K30 for the journey sound? PMVs cost about K5 and, although some do go to the terminal, there is no regular service. I wouldn't depend on them if I was catching a flight.

In desperation, you could catch a Highlands bound PMV and walk from the Highway turn-off (it's not far). The ritzy hotels send a courtesy bus if they know a customer is coming. If you are staying somewhere else you may still be able to get a lift with them, if you attract sufficient sympathy. Don't arrive at Nadzab late if you can help it, because your options will be reduced.

Nadzab is not an exciting place to spend time, but there is a cafeteria with cold drinks, a phone and car hire is available.

The main airline offices are a short walk from the centre of town at the old Lae airport. Air Niugini (tel 42 1892) has frequent flights to all major centres, Talair (tel 42 2316) has flights to the Wau/Bulolo region, Finschhafen, the Highlands and others areas and Morobe Airways (tel 42 1501) has flights around the province. MAF (tel 42 3804) also has a base, and flies around the region and up to the Highlands.

PMV PMVs to Wau, Goroka and Madang leave Lae between 8 and 9 am every day; there are fewer on weekends. Eriku is the main long-distance PMV stop.

Sea There are frequent connections west along the coast as far as Vanimo and east as far as Oro Bay (Popondetta), and regular connections with New Britain and Manus Island. If any passenger-carrying freighters have to take dangerous cargo (such as petrol), they will not accept passengers. Usually they give a couple of weeks notice, but not necessarily.

Lutheran Shipping (tel 42 1961, 42 2813) and Coastal Shipping Services (tel 42 3179) both have their offices and piers at Voco Point, a short walk from the airport near the Yacht Club. Pacific New Guinea Line (tel 42 1990) is on the other side of the airport in Mangola St.

You might have more success getting on a freighter by talking directly to the ship's captain rather than the office people. You may have to deal with some reluctance to take passengers or pressure to pay more and take a cabin.

To/From Port Moresby Flights from Port Moresby climb up and over the central mountain range. In the old days you flew through, rather than over, the mountains. These days you whistle over the top in 45 minutes, but in an Air Niugini F28 you are still not too high to appreciate the dramatic geography.

Both Air Niugini and Talair have frequent flights to Lae (Nadzab Airport) and the cost is K76. Talair also have a flight to Wau, Monday to Saturday, for

K69. You could then catch the PMV down to Lae (K7), or walk three days to Salamaua and catch a boat (K5), or fly for another K35.

Other alternatives from Moresby include: making your way to Kerema on the Gulf of Papua by boat (K34) and flying across with Talair (K74), walking the Kokoda Trail and flying from Popondetta for K82 or, more economically, catching the *Mamose Express* from Oro Bay for K27 tourist class, K18 deck class. It's very difficult to find a boat all the way from Moresby.

To/From Wau & Bulolo See the Wau & Bulolo section in this chapter for more details on the route. A flight costs K35 and the PMV fare is K6 to K7. It is around 180 km by road to Wau. Money has been allocated to seal the road and once this happens flights will become rare.

To/From Highlands It's possible to fly to Goroka with Talair every day except Sunday for K63.

See the Highlands chapter for details on PMVs and the highway. The fare to Goroka is K8 and it is about 330 km. If you're lucky, you can sometimes deliver cars for Ela Motors who, for reasons best known to themselves, trust travellers (for a couple of days) with vehicles that would otherwise have to be transported. See the Highlands section for more details.

To/From Madang Air Niugini has a daily flight and they'll take you along for K62.

The road is now pretty good, although it's not surfaced once you leave the Highlands Highway. All up, it's about 360 km. When it is open, it can be covered by virtually any vehicle, but when it's closed, even a four-wheel drive won't get through. The problem is, as usual, the many river crossings that have to be made.

PMVs leave from Eriku around 8 am, cost K10 to K12 and take seven or eight hours. After turning off the Highlands

Highway, the road runs through a flat valley cultivated with the cane fields of the Ramu Sugar refinery before climbing over the hills on the approach to Madang. There is accommodation available at the sugar refinery.

The boat trip is much more enjoyable and costs about the same as a PMV. Lutheran Shipping's comfortable, passenger-only *Mamose Express* services all the main north-coast ports. See the Getting Around chapter for a full schedule, but don't forget these things can change.

Currently, it leaves Lae for Madang every Wednesday morning and arrives in Madang at 6 am on Thursday. It doesn't leave until 7 pm Friday, so you get two days in Madang, which is enough time to have a decent look around. Fares are: Lae-Madang, K18/12, tourist/deck class; or straight through from Lae to Wewak, K45/30, but this includes overnight accommodation, with harbour views, in Madang!

Lutheran Shipping also operates less reliable, slower and much less comfortable passenger carrying freighters on the route. By comparison to the *Express* they're not a bargain, but the trip is still enjoyable. The notorious MV *Totol* has a regular schedule to Madang via Finschhafen and Wasu but, because it has to unload cargo, the trip takes at least 18 hours. It costs K11 for deck class and K21 for 1st class. Take deck class (it's covered) while downstairs is crowded and the cabins are sauna baths. Bring your own food and toilet paper.

To/From New Britain Air Niugini has daily flights, except Tuesdays, to Rabaul. The flight costs K131.

Coastal Shipping Services runs two vessels to Rabaul. The *Kimbe Express* departs on Fridays and travels via Kimbe. Check the schedules. There is deck class only and the cost is K44 to Rabaul and K30 to Kimbe.

The MV *Beaumaris* departs on Tuesdays, has two cabins and deck class

and also stops at Bialla and Buluma. Deck class costs the same as the *Kimbe* and cabin class is K80 to Rabaul, K55 to Kimbe. Take your own food and bank on the trip taking around two days to Kimbe, three to Rabaul. It usually leaves Lae at around 6 pm.

The Pacific New Guinea Line's MV *Kris* also does the Lae / Bialla / Kimbe / Rabaul run, leaving Lae on Fridays and costing K44.

Other Virtually all the Madang-bound boats go via Finschhafen. The fare is between K10 and K14. Both Talair and Morobe Air fly this route for K42.

Lutheran Shipping runs a fortnightly boat, the MV *Makaya*, direct to Lorengau (Manus Island), which costs K33.

It's also possible to get boats to Umboi Island or Salamaua. There is a regular weekly boat to Umboi, but other boats also operate to islands of the Siassi group.

There are frequent irregular boats from Voco Point to Labu Miti and Maus Buang villages near the Labu Lakes. The journey takes 60 to 90 minutes and costs K3. Local boats also go to other villages, like Busama, or a little further to Salamaua. Ask around at the bay past Lutheran Shipping. The owners of Salamaua Haus Kibung also organise transport to Salamaua. See the Salamaua section for more details.

Getting Around

PMVs around Lae cost 30t. The main PMV stations are in town, on 7th, and at Eriku on either side of the pedestrian overpass across Huon Rd. Eriku is the place to catch long distance PMVs to the Highlands and Madang. Both stations are chaotic, especially at peak hours.

To make things interesting the urban PMVs don't have destination signs. The driver's assistant leans out the window and calls the destination and the names of stops in a semi-automatic, rapid-fire incantation. Even if you don't understand a word, people will usually point you in the right direction. You can't go too far wrong because the urban PMVs all have circular routes. Sooner or later you'll end up back where you started.

Taxis are pretty cheap. A kina or two will get you to most places in town. Apart from the airport, they can also be found in town along from the PMV station. Jumi Cabco (tel 42 3535) is the biggest outfit.

Hertz (tel 42 3082), Avis (tel 42 2722) and Budget (tel 42 2069) all have desks at Nadzab. In addition, Avis has an office at the Lae International Hotel and Budget has an office at the Melanesian Hotel.

South of Lae

The Labu Lakes, right across the Markham River from Lae, were used to hide ships during the war, but the maze of waterways and swamps are now only home to crocodiles. The beaches on the ocean side are beautiful and they are an important breeding site for the leatherback turtle, incredible reptiles that can live to a great age, weigh up to 500 kg and measure up to two metres in length.

MAUS BUANG & LABU TALI

From the end of November until early February, leatherback turtles come ashore along the beaches around Maus Buang and Labu Tali Villages and dig deep nests where they lay up to 100 eggs, which hatch about two months later. This process is one of the most extraordinary sights in the world, and this is one of the few places where it can be witnessed.

Traditionally the eggs are gathered by people from the villages, but over the years demand for the eggs has increased to the point where the turtles are in danger of dying out. To both save the turtle and improve the villagers' very basic living standards, lecturers from Lae Unitech have convinced the people to set aside the three km beach between the two villages for conservation.

As compensation for the lost food, Unitech has undertaken to raise money, both for the local school and other community facilities and for a bush-material guesthouse near the school. The idea is that visitors will, in long term, supply an alternative income for the villagers and provide them with an incentive to conserve the turtle population.

If you are fortunate enough to see the turtles, please make an effort not to disturb them; some human-being-type animals apparently have an overwhelming urge to torture them by shining torches in their eyes, riding them up the beach, poking them with sticks . . . .

Places to Stay

Until a guesthouse is built, accommodation is on the floor of the school at Maus Buang, and it's necessary to take food and sleeping gear. A village committee has been formed to administer funds and they plan to charge K8 per night. Although this is certainly not cheap, it does include a guide to help you look for turtles, and the proceeds go to important local facilities and contribute to the conservation of the leatherback turtle. Seeing the turtles is worth a lot more.

Further along the coast is pretty Busama Village, where there may still be a guesthouse (care of the District Officer in Lae), then Salamaua.

Getting There & Away

Boats leave frequently from Voco Point in Lae; just go down to the point, ask around and wait. The journey takes one to 1½ hours and costs K3. It is also possible to get a boat across the Markham River and walk along the empty beaches. This takes four or five hours – watch out for crocodiles.

SALAMAUA

The picturesque peninsula has little to indicate its role in the gold rush days when it was the largest town on the north New

Guinea coast, or the part it played in WW II.

Today, two laid-back villages occupy the site: Kela and Lagui. Close by, there's excellent diving, good walks and a few interesting war relics. It's a popular place for Lae people to escape to and there is now an excellent place to stay – Salamaua Haus Kibung.

The original town cemetery is disappearing under the bush, but it can still be reached by following a rough path that begins in the north-west corner of the school oval. This path also leads past a small reef which is good for snorkelling. Near the start of the path is the entrance to a Japanese tunnel. A steep path leads up the hill to four Japanese gun emplacements and there's a great view.

You can also visit Coastwatchers Ridge where Australians were stationed to report on Japanese shipping and troop movements and, if you want a full day's walk, Mt Tambu has spectacular views and a huge battlefield where the Australians met the Japanese advance towards Wau. Local guides are available.

Most people just relax, fool around with a snorkel and take in the scenery!

Places to Stay

Salamaua Haus Kibung (tel 42 3782), PO Box 343, Lae, has accommodation for 32 people in two and four-bed bungalows that shelter under the palm trees. The rates are a bit steep at K15 per adult, half that for children under 12. It's best to take your own food, but there is a local market near the school open from 7 to 8 am on Wednesdays and Saturdays where you can get fresh fruit and fish and a trade store.

Depending on your energy level and interests, you can hire canoes and windsurfers (K5 per hour), go diving with a fully equipped dive boat visiting local reefs, islands and wrecks for K45 per day, or organise a guide and go bushwalking. It can get busy during the weekend with Lae refugees.

It used to be possible to stay in a bush hut at the Community School for K2 and locals used to rent out bush huts for similar prices. Ask around.

Getting There & Away

There's an interesting three day walk down from Wau. Boats run from Voco Point in Lae and will probably cost around K5. The local PMV boat is not entirely reliable but, most days, there will be something running, probably leaving Salamaua early and returning from Lae in the afternoon.

It's possible to get off in other villages along the way, like Maus Buang, where you can watch leatherback turtles (see the previous section). You can walk from Busama to Salamaua along the beach in about five hours.

The Haus Kibung people (tel 42 4428, 42 5692) have two boats the *Barbarian* and the MV *Huon Chief* which leave from the Coastal Shipping wharf. They definitely run down to Salamaua on Friday evenings and back on Sundays. The cost is K10 return.

Eastern Highlands

WAU & BULOLO

Wau and Bulolo were the sites for New Guinea's gold rush of the 1920s and '30s, but the gold began to peter out by the start of WW II and the mines never got back into full swing afterwards. The construction of a road down to Lae on the coast during the war has permitted timber and agricultural industries to develop. If you're interested in gold mining history, the mountains and their people and superb bird life, Wau and Bulolo are well worth a visit.

Gold is still mined by the New Guinea Gold Company near Wau, but the quantities recovered today are much smaller than in the the '30s. There are many Papua New Guineans working

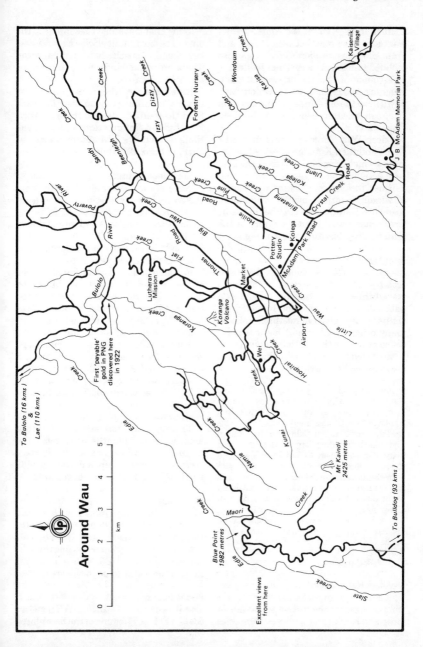

Around Wau

smaller finds – you'll see some of their work along the road between Bulolo and Wau. European residents of Wau are also inclined to have an occasional fossick.

A couple of the old pre-war dredges, weighing 2500 tons, all of which were flown in by the old Junker tri-motors from Lae, can be seen near Bulolo. Between Bulolo and Wau the road winds through the deep Wau Gorge, crossing first Edie Creek and then Kotunga Creek – the two creeks which formed the basis of the gold rush activities.

Edie Creek is about 20 km from Wau by a winding, rather heart-in-the-mouth road. Mt Kaindi, towering behind Edie Creek, has a small hut – enquire at the Wau Ecology Institute about using it.

Errol Flynn

In about 1930, a young, adventure-seeking Errol Flynn arrived in PNG and stayed three years. He first worked as a patrol officer, but was soon into trading, shipping and general hustling. Like so many others, gold caught his fancy. He did some prospecting and later, apparently, he managed a claim. Much of his time was spent in the Wau area.

I met a wacky, engaging, machinating Californian who had with him a treasure map he'd been given by an American old-timer and one-time New Guinea hand and soldier. This old guy, now living in California, had known Flynn and befriending the guy I met, gave him a map indicating where to find Flynn's old gold stash. Apparently it fills an old tank's gun barrel and lies rusting along some old track in the Wau area. Anyway, the fellow knew all about downed planes in the area and small village names and who knows? Only thing was he was broke and the visa department was on his case and Jesus this chewin' tobacco's gotta be better than that red stuff everybody's workin' on . . . .
– Mark Lightbody

McAdam National Park

This 20 square km park was established in 1962 to preserve the last virgin stands of Hoop and Klinkii pine and over 200 species of birds that have been recorded in the area. The bird life includes cassowaries, eagles and 10 species of bird of paradise. There are also orchids, ferns, butterflies and tree kangaroos.

Unfortunately, there are no tourist facilities yet, but you can view the park from the road adjacent to the boundary. For further information contact the Ranger-in-charge, McAdam National Park, PO Box 127, Bulolo.

Wau Ecology Institute

A privately funded research institution, the Wau Ecology Institute is both an excellent place to stay (see the following Places to Stay section) and interesting in itself. It was originally founded by the Bishop Museum in Hawaii which remains one of the principal benefactors.

Research projects include investigations of seed dispersal patterns by birds and ways of regenerating soil exhausted by too frequent burning off and cropping. This form of 'shifting' agriculture is still very common in Papua New Guinea.

The institute has a small museum and a zoo with tree kangaroos, cassowaries, a crocodile and a hornbill amongst other animals. Below the zoo in the rainforest is a display tree where you can see birds of paradise – if you're lucky! The whole area is renowned for its bird life.

There are many interesting walks in the area on local footpaths or through the neighbouring coffee plantations. It takes several hours' walk, up and over the hills north of Wau, to the Edie Creek area.

War Relics

About a four hour return walk to the south-east of Wau along a good path, there's a surprisingly intact B17 bomber. It was shot down by Zeroes during the war. An upside down DC3 with a jeep still inside is also said to be in the area.

Places to Stay

The *Wau Ecology Institute* (WEI) (tel 44 6341), PO Box 77, is one of the best places in PNG for budget travellers. It's a couple of km out of Wau on a hillside overlooking the town, so get a ride or ask your PMV to take you to the 'ecology' – you'll have a hard walk if you don't.

The institute undertakes a variety of research projects and they provide accommodation for visiting researchers. Ring ahead and check if they have room for casual visitors.

The nightly cost is K10 per person and blankets and sheets are provided. There are five houses, all with cooking facilities. One of them will sleep up to nine people. There is also a 10 room hostel; each room will sleep four. The hostel is an excellent place for meeting people but you have to fix your own meals – facilities are provided.

WEI also has several huts up in the mountains which they'll let you use for K5. Someone from WEI goes up to the hut on Mt Kaindi every Monday; you can walk back downhill in four hours. There's also a hut on Mt Mission – great for birdwatching – that they visit on Thursdays; it's a hard two day walk back. Take your own food. If you plan to do some walking in the area, somebody at WEI should be able to suggest a reliable guide.

If WEI is full, you may get a room at the *Wau Lodge* (tel 44 6233), although it's at a boarding school and gives priority to parents and church workers.

The *Pine Lodge Hotel* (tel 44 5220), PO Box 26, in Bulolo is owned by Melanesian Tourist Services, the people who run the Melanesian Explorer, so the hotel is suitably luxurious. There are 14 comfortable, furnished bungalows, each with a private balcony overlooking the Bulolo Valley. It has a a swimming pool and aviaries in landscaped gardens. All this has a price: singles/doubles are K75/85. Tours are arranged to the surrounding district.

Remember that in Wau or Bulolo you're up about 1200 metres and come prepared for chilly nights.

Getting There & Away

If you fly between Wau and Lae with a small carrier, you've got a fair chance of making some additional stops. Aseki is a tiny airstrip approached through spectacular limestone outcrops. On one you can see a cleft in the side of the rock where villagers left the smoked bodies of their dead.

Wau airstrip has nothing to remind you of its former level of activity. It's one of the steepest airstrips in Papua New Guinea, falling 91 metres in its 1000 metre length. Very definitely one way!

Talair fly direct to Wau from Moresby, Monday to Saturday, for K69, then on to Lae, via Bulolo, for another K35. Alternatively, you could catch a PMV down to Lae (K7), taking four or five hours, or walk three days to Salamaua and catch a boat to Lae (around K5). Morobe Airways and MAF also fly to Wau, and if you had a group you could consider a charter.

The unsealed road to Wau splits off the Highland Highway only a few km out of Lae. Money has been allocated to seal it and once this happens flights will become rare. The road crosses the wide Markham River on a single lane concrete bridge, then twists, turns and winds up into the hills. Mumeng, around the mid point, is the only town of any size it passes through.

It's easy to find a PMV out of Lae – just ask around at Eriku, there are lots of PMVs shuttling back and forth.

MENYAMYA & ASEKI

Menyamya is in the heart of the old Anga country and is now a coffee growing centre; it's not particularly interesting in itself. Some people still wear traditional dress and the area has been recommended for bushwalking.

The Anga used to smoke their dead and leave the mummified bodies in burial caves. They now practise Christian burials. It is possible to see some of these mummified bodies at Aseki, but the landowners now charge you K5 for viewing them. There is also a smoked body at Pangapo Village three or four hours walk from Menyamya.

The market days in Aseki are Tuesdays, Thursdays and Saturdays and at Menyamya, Mondays, Thursdays and Saturdays. You can see people in traditional dress, but ask permission before taking photos; they'll probably charge you.

Places to Stay

If you want to stay up in the Menyamya district, contact the German Development Agency (tel 44 0211), or the District Office (tel 44 0218) which has a lodge that costs around K10.

Lutheran missionaries have established a guesthouse in Aseki at K3 per night. It has a bucket shower, sink and pit toilet, but it's not very comfortable.

Getting There & Away

A road runs from Bulolo up to Menyamya then on to Aseki through some extremely rough and absolutely spectacular country. There are PMVs on the route, although they may not run every day; Bulolo to Menyamya will cost about K12.

People have walked in from Kerema on the Gulf, but this would definitely not be a picnic stroll. You can fly Douglas Airways or Talair between Kerema and Kaintiba for around K30, walk to Bema Mission, then to Tawa (eight to 10 hard hours), then to Aseki (another 10 hard hours). MAF fly to Aseki from Wau for about K40.

WALKING IN THE REGION

There is some good, if difficult, walking in the Wau area. One thing to enquire about is whether the clans in the area you plan on visiting are currently displeased with one another, that is, thumping each other.

Bushwalkers sometimes follow the old gold miners' route between Wau and Salamaua. The path is in reasonable condition and it takes about three days of hard walking. Don't consider walking up from the coast, walking from that direction takes more like a week.

You can stay in villages along the way for around K2 a night, but take your own food. After a couple of days recovering at Salamaua Haus Kibung, catch a boat to Lae.

The old WW II Bulldog track, intended to link Wau with the south coast, runs on from Edie Creek. The track never actually got to the coast – from Bulldog you had to travel by river. Since the war, the track has deteriorated and been cut by landslides and slips in many places.

Even walking the track is a long hard slog today and by vehicle, even a motorcycle, it would be impossible. But good walkers, preferably with a guide, can walk to Bulldog in about three days from where you *may* be able to get a boat down river to the south coast. Serious planning is required and this walk should definitely not be undertaken lightly.

Walking in the Menyamya-Aseki-Kaintiba-Kanaben area has been recommended by travellers. As a slightly easier alternative to the Bulldog Track, it is possible to walk between Kerema, on the Gulf, and Aseki. See the previous Getting There & Away section.

These walks are 'adventures', not mere treks. Guides are highly recommended and you should expect a hard slog and be properly equipped. Ask the people at WEI to recommend a guide.

RAFTING THE WATUT

PNG has countless rivers ideally suited for white water rafting, but Sobek Expeditions pioneered rafting in this country on the Watut.

The five-day trip is now handled by a local company, Niugini Adventure (tel 75 1304), PO Box 295, Kundiawa, Chimbu Province, which still has close links with Sobek. Sobek markets the trip in the USA and provides experienced river guides.

The trip starts from Bulolo where you

float down the Bulolo River, a tributary of the Watut, passing the rusting reminders of Wau and Bulolo's gold rush days.

The Watut turns sharply west into the 3000 metre Kuper Range and commences to tumble down towards sea level. It drops at the rate of 20 metres a km and rushes through something like 150 rapids. For white water enthusiasts the Watut is a classic.

After several days rafting through soaring gorges, past tangled jungle, under suspension bridges and past remote villages you finally reach the wide Markham River, which flows down from the Highlands. It's then only a short distance to Lae.

ZUMIM

Still in Morobe Province, although a fair way up the Markham Valley on the Highland Highway, this small village to the left of the road, has an interesting local pottery industry where you can buy crudely fired pots.

East of Lae

FINSCHHAFEN

The town of Finschhafen was the German New Guinea Kompagnie's first, unsuccessful, attempt at colonising New Guinea. Between 1885, when they arrived there and 1892, when they moved west to Stephansort, the Germans had a miserable time and died like flies from malaria and assorted tropical ills.

They did not do much better at Stephansort and soon moved to Madang and then to Rabaul, where they finally found peace from the mosquitoes. Today Finschhafen is an idyllic coastal town.

The modern town of Finschhafen was moved from its original site after WW II. Little remains of the original town apart from one old Lutheran building, which is now used by holidaying missionaries. Its tower was once used as a lookout.

Towards the end of WW II the town was used as a staging post for American troops and vast numbers of GIs passed through. The war's abrupt end left them with millions of dollars of purposeless aircraft and equipment, so the whole lot was bulldozed into a huge hole. There are a number of well-preserved sunken ships and downed aircraft offshore. Salamaua Haus Kibung organises diving trips in the area.

Nearby Malasiga Village was settled by Tami Islanders and it is possible to buy the famous Tami Island bowls – ask for the 'stor bilong carving'.

Places to Stay

Dreger Lodge (tel 44 7050), PO Box 126, five km from Finschhafen, was built and is run by Dregerhafen Provincial High School. It consists of three chalets, each with room for four people and the cost is K10 per person. There are communal cooking facilities – no food is provided so bring it from Lae. The lodge is five km from the town centre, at the school. There is good snorkelling nearby. A reader told us of a guesthouse at Logaweng Senior Seminary.

I heard talk of other places you can stay, so ask around.

Getting There & Away

The Lutheran Shipping boats, including the *Mamose Express*, all stop in Finschhafen. Tourist class from Lae costs K14, deck class K9 and the journey takes about seven hours; from Madang it is an overnight journey of 14 hours costing K18 and K12.

You can fly from Lae with Talair, Morobe Airways and MAF for K42. See the Getting There & Away section for Lae.

During the war a road was pushed through all the way to Finschhafen from Lae, but it has since disappeared. A road is being constructed now, mainly for new logging projects, but in a piecemeal fashion and major river crossings are liable to delay completion for many years. There's a road from Finschhafen to Sialum and roads to Pindiu (50 km) and Wasu, past Sialum, are being worked on.

It's possible to walk to Lae from Finschhafen; students from Dregerhafen High regularly do this walk. See the headmaster for advice. The walk along the coast, sometimes on the beach, takes three days.

ISLANDS

The beautiful Tami Islands, offshore from Finschhafen, can be a little expensive to visit – even though they are only 12 km from the coast. The Tami Islanders are renowned for their beautifully carved wooden bowls. Malasiga Village is a good place to look for transport and there is a guesthouse for K5.

There are other islands off the coast, particularly the Siassi Group between the mainland and New Britain. Umboi Island (Rooke Island) is the largest with a total area of 777 square km and a number of settlements. Siassi is the main village; there are two good boat anchorages at Marien Harbour and Luther.

Slightly north of Umboi is the sometimes violently volcanic island of Sakar, only 34 square km in area. Tolokiwa, a little to the west, is wooded and inhabited but it too has a conical volcano 1377 metres high. All these islands are in the volcanic belt which extends through New Britain and down to the north coast of New Guinea.

The Highlands

Area 65,248 square km
Population 1,270,000

The great Highlands area, which is now divided into five separate provinces (Chimbu, Eastern Highlands, Enga, Southern Highlands, Western Highland), is the most densely populated and agriculturally productive region of PNG. Strangely, it was the last part of the country to be explored by Europeans: the first Highlands tribes were not contacted until the 1930s. Until then it was thought that the centre of PNG was a rugged tangle of virtually unpopulated mountains.

It was definitely a shock when a series of populated valleys, stretching right through the country, was discovered. Little development occurred before WW II which, fortunately for the Highlanders, almost entirely bypassed the region, so it was not until the 1950s and '60s that the Highlands were really opened up.

Today, this is a dynamic and fascinating part of PNG. The people's lives are changing quickly, but many aspects of their traditional culture remain, particularly in terms of social organisation. Clan and tribal loyalties are still very strong. It is possible to see dramatic sing-sings and warriors wearing ostentatious traditional dress, but in most parts of the Highlands, and especially in the main towns like Hagen and Goroka, the people have taken on the trappings of the west – more particularly, *sekonhan klos* (second-hand clothes).

Although some individuals and even some tribes are exceptions to the rule, traditional dress and decorations are now most usually reserved for rare ceremonial or festive occasions, which, as a tourist, you will be very lucky to see. Some of the big hotels organise theatrical sing-sings, but these are usually rather sad and listless affairs.

The Highlands are not a lifeless, open-air museum specially designed for amateur photographers, but home to a number of vital, rapidly changing cultures that are maintaining some things, adapting others, and adopting still more with wholehearted fervour.

The Highlands have the most extensive road system in the country, half-a-dozen major towns and a growing cash economy based on coffee and tea, soon to be joined by oil wells and gold mines. The countryside is dramatic and beautiful, with wide, fertile valleys, countless streams and rivers, and endless saw-toothed mountains.

HISTORY

Most of the Highland valleys were settled 10,000 years ago and the presence of shells amongst archaeological deposits show that by this time people were also trading with the coast. Some sites that have been excavated date to much earlier.

Kuk Swamp in the Wahgi Valley (Western Highlands Province) has evidence of human habitation going back 20,000 years, but even more significantly there is evidence of gardening beginning 9000 years ago. This makes Papua New Guineans among the first farmers in the world. The main foods that were cultivated are likely to have been sago, coconuts, breadfruit, local bananas and yams, sugar cane, nuts and edible green leaves.

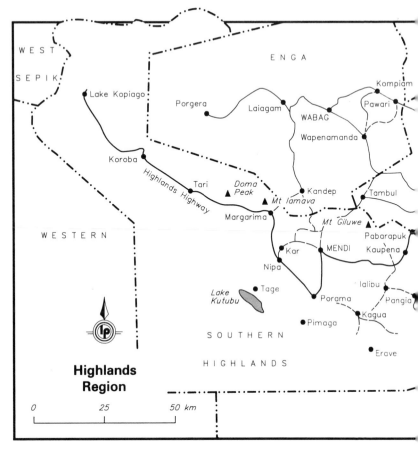

Highlands Region

```
0        25        50 km
```

It is still uncertain when the pig and more productive starch crops (Asian yams, taros and bananas) were introduced but it is known that this occurred more than 5000 years ago, maybe as much as 10,000. Domesticated pigs – which continue to be incredibly important, ritually and economically, in contemporary society – and these new crops were probably brought to PNG by a later group of colonists from Asia.

The sweet potato was introduced to the Indonesian Spice Islands by the Spaniards in the 16th century and it is believed Malay traders then brought it to Irian Jaya, from where it was traded to the Highlands. The introduction of the sweet potato must have brought radical change to life in the Highlands – it is still the staple crop. Its high yield and tolerance for poor and cold soils allowed the colonisation of higher altitudes, the domestication of many more pigs, and a major increase in population.

As with the rest of PNG, there was tremendous cultural and linguistic diversity. The largest social units were tribes numbering in the thousands and the area

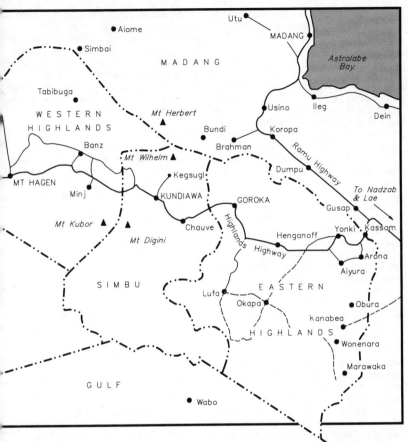

that a single group controlled was usually small. There were apparently no empires or dynasties. Despite the political fragmentation there were extensive trade links with the coast.

The evidence relating to the real history of the Highlands before the arrival of white men is extremely scarce, and it is unwise to assume that the situation that existed when the patrols entered the fertile valleys perfectly reflected the past. Highlands societies were certainly not static. It is difficult, for instance, to assess the impact of the introduction of the sweet potato. It is also known that some steel knives and axes had been traded from the coast in advance of the patrols, and this may well have changed patterns of labour and warfare in advance of the white man's arrival.

When the whites did arrive minor warfare between the tribes was common, but the number of fatalities was probably relatively low, in part because of the weaponry – bows, arrows and spears. Two of the most striking characteristics that were encountered were the intensive and skilful gardening, and the fantastic personal adornment of the men, which was the most striking form of 'artistic' expression.

The first direct European contact with the Highlands came as a result of the gold rush in the Wau/Bulolo region, which created speculation there would be more gold further afield. In 1930 Mick Leahy and Mick Dwyer set off south to search for gold in the region they believed formed the headwaters for the Ramu River. To their amazement the streams they followed did not turn north-west to join the Ramu, but led southwards through the previously undiscovered Eastern Highlands.

When they finally reached the Papuan coast they discovered that they were at the mouth of the Purari River. Rather than starting on the southernmost flanks of the Highlands the streams that formed the Purari started just the other side of the towering Bismarck Range from the Ramu (on the map, less than 25 km from the Ramu and around 80 km from the north coast) and ran through populated valleys all the way to the south coast.

In 1933 Mick Leahy returned with his brother Danny and this time they stumbled upon the huge, fertile and heavily populated Wahgi Valley. After an aerial reconnaissance they walked in with a large well-supplied patrol.

The first patrol built an airstrip at Mt Hagen and explored the area, but the hoped-for gold was never discovered in any great quantities. Jim Taylor, the government officer who accompanied this patrol, was one of the last direct links to those extraordinary times. He died peacefully, at his farm outside Goroka, a PNG citizen, in 1987.

The film documentary *First Contact* includes original footage by Mick Leahy and is a priceless record of the first interaction between Highlanders and Europeans. See it if you can; the people at Ambua Lodge and and the Madang Resort Hotel often screen it in the evening.

Missionaries soon followed the miners and the government and missions were established near present day Mt Hagen and in the Chimbu Valley, near present day Kundiawa. Equally predictably, two missionaries managed to get themselves killed. In response, a government patrol post was set up at Kundiawa and the whole Highlands area was declared a 'Restricted Territory' with controlled European access.

WW II intervened, and once again the mountains largely protected the Highlanders from outside forces. It was the 1950s before major changes were really felt and many areas remained virtually unaffected until the '60s and '70s.

The construction of the Highlands Highway had a major impact on the area, as did the introduction of cash crops, particularly coffee. The Highlanders have adapted to the plastic-age with remarkable speed, perhaps due in part to western capitalism meshing with their existing culture; they have always understood the importance of land ownership, and they are skillful gardeners and clever traders. Material wealth, while handled very differently to the way it is in the west, was still of crucial importance in establishing the status and wealth of a big man and his clan.

The dense population of the Highlands and the cultural differences between this and other parts of the country have caused more than a few problems. Ritual warfare was an integral part of life in the Highlands and to this day *payback* feuds (to revenge both real and imagined injuries) and land disputes can erupt into major conflicts.

Population pressures have pushed many Highlanders out to other parts of the country in search of work, where they are often resented and held responsible for rascal activity.

Over the aeons the Highlanders and the coastal people have distrusted each other and this mutual suspicion still exists. The energetic Highlanders believe the coastal people are lazy and unfairly dominate government bureaucracies. The coastal people see the Highlanders as aggressive, their numbers as threatening and feel that the Highlands have had a disproportionate share of the development pie.

GEOGRAPHY

The Highlands are made up of a series of fertile valleys and rugged intervening mountains. The mountains form the watershed for some of the world's largest rivers, in terms of water flow (the Ramu, the Sepik, the Strickland, the Fly, and the Purare) and form a central spine the length of the island. While there are higher mountains on the Irian Jaya side of the island, there are a number of mountains that exceed 4000 metres in height and Mt Wilhelm is 4509 high.

For administrative purposes, the Highlands are divided into five provinces – Eastern Highlands (around Goroka), Chimbu or Simbu (around Kundiawa), Western Highlands (around Mt Hagen), Enga (around Wabag) and Southern Highlands (around Mendi).

PEOPLE

The Highlanders are usually stockier and shorter than the coastal people. There are a large number of different tribes, language groups and physical types.

Mogas

If you need to be convinced that 'keeping up with the Jones' and accumulating and displaying wealth are not peculiarly modern preoccupations, a visit to the Highlands should soon do the job. Wealth is enormously important in establishing status and men of consequence in a village, the big men, are almost invariably men of affluence. Just being rich, however, is not enough – other people have to know you are rich. As a result, much of the ceremonial life of the Highlands is centred around displays of wealth – ostentatious displays.

The most vivid demonstrations are the

mogas – in Enga Province the *tee* ceremonies are very similar. Within many Melanesian cultures, and especially in the Highlands, the approved method of establishing just how rich you are is to give certain important goods away. This ceremony, which is part of a wider circle of exchange and inter-clan relationships, is known in the Highlands as a moga.

In fact, wealth is never really given away, at least not in the western sense. Your gifts both cement a relationship with the receiver (a related and allied clan perhaps) and pacify potential enemies. The receiver is effectively obliged to return the gifts and, if possible, the receiver will attempt to outdo the giver's generosity. One way or another, the giver expects to have at least an equivalent number of pigs and kina shells returned.

The moga ceremonies flow from village to village with one group displaying their wealth and handing it on to the next. Even enemies are invited, in hopes that they'll be impressed by how much is given away.

During these festivals literally hundreds of pigs are slaughtered and cooked and all present indulge in an orgy of eating. Each clan attempts to surpass their neighbours by producing as many pigs as possible. Some indication of the economic significance of these feasts can be gauged by the fact that a decent-sized pig is worth around K200 to K300 and a sow can be worth even more.

You'll see the ceremonial grounds where these feasts occur as you drive the Highlands Highway, especially past Mendi in the Southern Highlands. They are distinguished by a fenced quadrangle, covering up to an acre or so, surrounded by long houses (shelters where the guests sleep) with long pits dug in straight lines and filled with cooking stones (for cooking the pigs). Attempts to convince the Highlanders, many of whom live on the borderline of protein deficiency, that pigs could be rationed more sensibly, rather than used in this feast or famine manner, have been largely unsuccessful.

Bride Price

Marriage is another occasion that is used to prove just how much you can afford to pay: the bride's clan has to be paid a bride price by the husband's clan. Although local councils have tried to establish price controls, the going rate in the Highlands is now around 20 pigs plus K600 or more in cash and it's increasing.

Bride price varies throughout the country and is usually higher in the cities: in Moresby, the average is now more like K12,000, with wealthy people paying many times more. An interesting earlier description of the tense negotiations to establish a bride price, and the related issue of prestige, can be found in Kenneth Read's book *The High Valley*.

The old shell money has been seriously devalued since European contact, both because it has become more readily available and modern currency has been widely accepted. Pigs still retain their value – a pig is not just food, it's the most visible and important measure of a man's solvency. Cassowaries are also extremely important in the Highlands although they're much less edible!

Payback

Compensation claims may also make demands on a clan's wealth. An eye for an eye is the basic payback concept (it is virtually a greater sin to fail to payback than to have committed the initial wrong), but sufficiently large payments of pigs and cash will usually avert direct bloodletting. Pigs have traditionally been used to negotiate an end to conflicts of many kinds and naturally the government and the courts prefer this kind of solution.

In a society where the clan is of much greater significance than the individual a whole clan is held responsible for an individual's actions: in the case of a killing, revenge will be taken by the aggrieved clan, preferably by killing the murderer but, if that proves too difficult, anyone in the murderer's clan will do.

To this day, violence will often only be averted by very substantial financial compensation, whether or not western-style justice has also been done. Car accidents are now becoming an increasingly rich source of payback feuds.

Sing-sings

Although these are not an everyday occurrence you should definitely try to see one while you're in the Highlands. Around Hagen they are still quite frequent, but finding where they are and getting to them can be a problem. Many parts of the Highlands are still inaccessible to vehicles, and the sing-sings are often in remote areas.

A sing-sing can be held for any number of reasons – it might be associated with paying off a bride price, a moga ceremony or even some more mundane activity like raising money for a local school or church. Whatever the reason, the result will be much the same – a lot of people, brilliantly costumed, singing and dancing around. Take plenty of film if you're keen on photography.

Other Highland ceremonies you may come across are the courting rituals known as 'Karim Leg' (Carry Leg) or 'Turnim Head'. Ceremonially dressed young couples meet in the long houses for courting sessions where they sit side by side and cross legs (Carry Leg) or rub their faces together (Turn Head). While you may not get to see them 'for real', they are sometimes staged for tourists.

Arts

The Highlanders do not carve bowls, masks or other similar items; their artistic talents are almost always expressed in personal attire and decoration or in the decoration of weapons.

The best known weapons are probably the fine ceremonial axes from Mt Hagen. The slate blades come from the Jimi River area north of Hagen on the Sepik-Wahgi divide and are bound to a wooden shaft with decorative cane strips. They were never intended for use as weapons or tools.

'Killing sticks' from Lake Kopiago had an obvious and practical use: the pointed fighting stick is tipped with a sharpened cassowary bone to make a lethal weapon in close fighting. Beautifully decorated bows and arrows are also sold throughout the Highlands.

Other traditional items you may see are the fine kina shells made from the gold lip pearl shell. A good example is still likely to be expensive, costing anything between K8 and K20. *Aumak* necklaces, which are made of bamboo rods and were used to record how many pigs the owner had given away, are also sold, but they're much cheaper than a kina shell. In the Western Highlands, kina shells are sometimes mounted on a board of red coloured resin; at traditional wealth displays, such as the moga ceremonies, long lines of these are formed on the ground.

People also sell excellent basketry incorporating striking geometric designs (trays, baskets and so on) from stalls along

Ceremonial Axe

the Highlands Highway, but once again they are not cheap, reflecting the amount of work that goes into creating them.

Hardly traditional, but extremely attractive nonetheless, coarse-woven woollen blankets, rugs, bedspreads and bags are available in several Highlands centres.

GETTING THERE & AROUND
Air
Air Niugini and Talair have regular connections to and from Goroka, Mt Hagen, Wewak, Madang, Lae and Port Moresby. In addition there is a comprehensive third level network around the Highland centres. The chart details some of the connections and fares.

The major third level carrier, Talair, has its headquarters in Goroka (tel 72 1355), PO Box 108, Goroka and has some convenient flights to the Sepik River or south to the Gulf and Western Provinces. If you are going to Bensbach Lodge in Western Province you'll find it as easy to get there from the Highlands as from Port Moresby.

MAF has an extensive network to many out-of-the-way places and their headquarters is in Mt Hagen (tel 55 1434), PO Box 273. They have strips dotted all over the Highlands and the Sepik region. If you're planning a walk, find out if and when they fly in your direction, just in case you need to take an easy way out.

Remember that MAF flies small planes, so don't expect to get away with too much over the 16 kg baggage limit. Bad weather can also play havoc with their schedules. For information about flights to the Western and Sepik Provinces you may have to call their office in Wewak (tel 86 2124).

Road
The Highlands Highway The most important road in PNG starts in Lae and runs up into the central Highlands. Where the highway ends depends on your definition. As a decent road it now continues to Tari, in

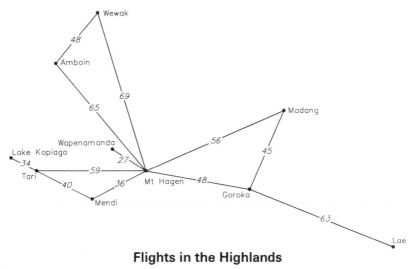

Flights in the Highlands

Fares in Kina

rougher condition to Koroba and in still rougher condition on to Lake Kopiago. The highway is now sealed as far as Mt Hagen and in parts between Hagen and Mendi. New branches off the main road are being developed, although their condition varies widely.

From Lae the road runs out through the coastal jungle then emerges into the wide, flat Markham Valley. Shortly after leaving Lae a road branches off to the left, crosses the wide Markham River and then twists up to Bulolo, Wau and Aseki. If you can, pause at the interesting pottery village of Zunim, about 130 km from Lae and 15 km past Kaiapit.

It's a rather hot, dull stretch to the base of the Kassam Pass where the road starts to twist, turn and climb. At Watarais, before the pass, the Madang road branches off to the north-west and runs along the Ramu Valley. At the top of the pass there are some spectacular lookout points across

the Markham Valley to the Saruwaged Mountains. The road continues through rolling grass hills to Kainantu, the only reasonable sized town before Goroka.

From Goroka the road continues through the valley to Asaro, then climbs steeply to the 2450 metre high Daulo Pass, about 25 km from Goroka. It continues twisting, turning and generally descending all the way to the Chimbu district and Kundiawa, about the mid-point between Goroka and Mt Hagen.

From Kundiawa the road descends to the Wahgi Valley and it's a fast run to Mt Hagen past the turnoffs to Minj and Banz. The road from Hagen to Mendi is spectacular; you skirt Mt Giluwe, PNGs second tallest mountain at 4362 metres, and go through some beautiful valleys. On good days you can also see Mt Ialibu to the south of the road. Along the way, you'll see some enterprising people selling woven walls of bamboo or pitpit leaves – sort of pre-fabricated housing. There are also likely to be some road side stalls selling attractive, though expensive, basketry.

The road becomes even more interesting after Mendi, as you pass ceremonial grounds, a suspension bridge over the Lai River, and through the stunning Poroma Valley. It's a narrow gravel road in good condition, but you can't go too fast and you have time to soak in the views as you go through Nipa and Margarima. After Poroma you climb the high (2900 metre) pass overlooking the wide and fertile Tari Basin. It's then a quick run past the Ambua Lodge, through the Wigmens' intensively cultivated gardens to Tari.

The road deteriorates after Tari and again after Koroba. If you're aiming for Lake Kopiago, you'll be lucky if you don't have to do some walking. There's very little transport, especially after Koroba: it's only a one hour drive to Koroba, but a two day walk from Koroba to Kopiago. Beyond Kopiago it's definitely walking only. Koroba and Kopiago are not of particular interest in themselves, but you will see some interesting people at their Friday and Saturday markets.

Other Roads Between Goroka and Mt Hagen there's the 'old' Highlands Highway that parallels the new road for part of the distance. An 'old' road also runs to Mendi from Mt Hagen, on the other side of Mt Giluwe to the 'new' Mendi road. The new road runs through Kaupena; the old road goes through Tambul.

A reasonable road runs north from Mt Hagen through the spectacular Baiyer Gorge to Baiyer River and a good road branches off the Mendi road and continues on to Wabag and Porgera. From Wabag, there's a loop through Laiagam to Kandep and down to Mendi. It may not be passable due to washed out bridges and slides. From Kandep another branch goes down through Margarima, half-way between Mendi and Tari. This is not often used and its condition varies, though it's never great.

There's a breathtakingly precarious road north from Kundiawa to Kegusugl if you're intending to climb Mt Wilhelm.

Self Drive You can drive yourself, at a suitably high price – see the Getting Around chapter. Rental firms often have restrictions on 'out of town' use, which particularly applies in the Highlands. An alternative is to deliver a car up to the Highlands from Lae. If your timing is right, Ela Motors may give you a vehicle to be taken to either Goroka or Hagen. If you do strike out with them, it would be worth trying others.

Although an early start and late finish, plus non-stop driving, could get you from Lae to Mt Hagen in a day (443 km), what's the hurry?

Because of the risk of being held up by a roadblock manned by rascals, very few people drive at night. Roadblocks can even happen during the day, although this is rare. If you are forced to stop (don't unless you have to, and be very sceptical if you are waved down), don't panic. They'll just want your money. This warning is not intended to induce fear and loathing. Talk to people and they'll fill you in on the current situation: you are very, very unlikely to have any problems if you heed local advice. News travels very quickly and if there is trouble, it is usually part of a wider, well-known disturbance.

PMVs PMVs are frequent between all the major centres. Just about all long distance PMVs are comfortable, fairly new minibuses that make a trip quite pleasant – they're no hardship at all. There isn't a lot of space for luggage though and if you have a large bag it may be on your lap most of the way.

PMVs generally make their first trip early in the mornings around 8 am, sometimes earlier. The best place to look for them is usually at the markets. Although there will often be some later in the day, their deadline for reaching a destination is sunset, which is around

6 pm; bear in mind breakdowns can add unforeseen hours and give yourself some leeway if you have a deadline.

Many PMVs make return journeys within daylight hours, for instance they'll leave Lae early and leave Goroka for Lae (K8, four to five hours) around midday. PMVs will meet a demand, if it's there, so work out what the local people require and you'll get some other ideas. There will, for instance, be very early PMVs to get people to Saturday markets, and returning PMVs after the markets; there'll be PMVs between Kundiawa and Hagen (K3, two hours) later in the day after people have had a chance to shop, and so on.

Your safest bet is to be early. In addition, it's not a good move to wander around Lae or most Highland towns at night looking for accommodation; try to arrive in daylight, but if you don't, get the PMV to deliver you to the place where you plan to stay.

Expats frequently criticise PMVs and rarely use them, but those who do find them comfortable, cheap and safe. They present a great opportunity to meet locals. Bad drivers are rare (I suppose they don't last) and most are very cautious. On less important routes, say to Baiyer River, trucks are still used as PMVs and these are obviously somewhat more spartan.

Lae-Kainantu	K5	3 hours
Kainantu-Goroka	K3	1½ hours
Goroka-Kundiawa	K3	2 hours
Kundiawa-Mt Hagen	K3	1½ hours
Goroka-Mt Hagen	K7	4 hours
Mt Hagen-Mendi	K8	3 hours
Mendi-Tari	K12	4 hours
Wabag-Laiagam	K4	3 hours
Laiagam-Porgera	K3	1½ hours

Prices change, but over the past few years improved road conditions and competition have tended to counterbalance increased costs. Times are a different matter: if you get a straight run, times can be less than those shown, but if you have numerous stops for passengers, or a flat tyre, they can be much longer.

Walking

The best way to see the Highlands is to walk – and there are networks of tracks everywhere. It is also possible to walk to the Highlands from the coast (probably combining walking with PMVs and planes) although with the exception of the route between Kegsugl and Madang, these routes are not for the faint-hearted.

Most tour companies (see the Facts for the Visitor chapter) have walks in the Highlands, but if you're reasonably well equipped, don't mind roughing it and don't tackle anything too radical, there is no reason why you shouldn't do it yourself. This is a volatile, rugged area however, so it is important to talk to locals and local government officers, especially the District Officers (*Kiaps*) before you set out, and in most cases guides are necessary.

To/from the Coast Although you end up in Morobe Province, you can walk from the south coast to the Wau/Bulolo region at the eastern end of the Highlands (see the Wau/Bulolo section in the Lau & Morobe chapter). And you can also walk from Kegsugl to Brahman, near Madang. See the Simbu Province section of this chapter.

Around the Mountains There are any number of walks you can do around and about the Highlands region, ranging from days to weeks in length. A couple to consider, which are briefly covered in this chapter, are climbing Mt Wilhelm (Chimbu Province section), walking to Lake Kutubu (Southern Highlands section), or to Oksapmin, or even Telefomin from Lake Kopiago (Southern Highlands section).

Talair and MAF both fly from the Highlands to the Sepik region (for instance, Talair flies from Oksapmin to Green River, and MAF flies from Oksapmin to Ambunti).

Eastern Highlands

Area 11,706 square km
Population 310,000

The Eastern Highlands have had longer, more extensive contact with the west than other parts of the Highlands. The people have abandoned their traditional dress for day-to-day use, although you'll still occasionally see traditional dress at the Goroka market. Their villages are recognisable for their neat clusters of low-walled round huts. Although the province is heavily populated, the Eastern Highlanders are a less cohesive group than the people in other parts of the Highlands.

Goroka is the main town and is one of the most attractive places in PNG, a green, shady, well-organised city with decent shopping, transport and facilities. Kainantu, near the border with Morobe Province is the second largest town.

The steep and rugged mountains of this province form the headwaters for two of PNG's most important river systems: the Ramu which runs parallel to the coast to the northwest, and the Wahgi and Aure rivers which run south and enter the Gulf of Papua as the Purare. The highest point is Mt Michael at 3750 metres, but most of the population lives between altitudes of 1500 and 2300 metres. There are large areas of rolling kunai-grass covered hills.

KAINANTU

The major town between Lae and Goroka, Kainantu is an important cattle and coffee production region. There was also some gold found in this area and very minor production still continues. The town is basically strung along the highway, 210 km from Lae and 80 km from Goroka. Evenings can be quite cool because the town lies at 1600 metres.

The Eastern Highlands Cultural Centre (tel 77 1215), PO Box 91, which is on the Lae side of town on the highway, is well worth visiting. They sell reasonably-priced traditional crafts from the eastern Highlands, such as pottery and flutes, and there's a small museum and coffee shop. The centre also trains people in handicrafts like print-making, dressmaking and weaving. They're open Monday to Friday from 8 am to 4.30 pm, Saturday from 10 am to 5 pm and Sunday from 11.30 am to 5 pm.

Places to Stay

The *Kainantu Lodge-Motel* (tel 77 1021), PO Box 31, is on a hill overlooking Kainantu on the other side of the disused airfield parallel to the highway. It's signposted and is about a 20 minute walk from the PMV stops. It's quite pleasant and has 17 rooms with singles/doubles at K35/42 with shared facilities, K48/64 with private facilities. There are a variety of discounts for larger groups and they also offer generous weekend specials – like a 50% discount for staying Friday and Saturday nights – but ring ahead to check the current offer. There are a couple of bars and meals are available – breakfast or lunch is K3.50, dinners around K7.50.

The *Salvation Army Flats* (tel 77 1130) are a cheaper possibility, but their policy on renting to visitors fluctuates. Certainly at times visitors have been most unwelcome. All you can do is ask.

Getting There & Away

PMVs from Lae to Kainantu cost K5 and take three hours, from Kainantu to Goroka they cost K3 and take 1½ hours.

AROUND KAINANTU
Summer Institute of Linguistics

The headquarters of the American-founded Summer Institute of Linguistics is about a 15 minute drive from Kainantu in the Aiyura Valley, which is a pleasant place for day walks. There is a large school and expat community.

SIL is a missionary organisation whose primary objective is to translate the Bible into every PNG language. The good side of this is that they do record many languages, some of which are dying out and might otherwise be lost. I suspect that their translations must be fairly free. The mind boggles when you wonder how they represent various things like camels, Romans and deserts, let alone the rest.

Other complications come to mind: in the Trobriands the people do not believe there is a connection between intercourse and pregnancy, which would rather spoil the impact of the virgin birth . . . .

Yonki & the Upper Ramu Project

Situated 212 km from Lae and just 23 km from Kainantu, Yonki is the support town for the Upper Ramu hydro-electric project. Commissioned in 1979, the project was financed by a K23 million World Bank loan and supplies power for Lae, Madang and much of the Highlands. You can arrange a free tour of the project which is four km from the town.

Okapa

Okapa, south-west of Kainantu, is notable for the disease known as Kuru which was unique to this area. No recent cases have been recorded. Kuru was dubbed the laughing disease since it attacks the central nervous system and the victims die with a peculiar smile. One particular language group was, apparently, decimated by Kuru. It appears to attack women more often than men. It is thought there could be a correlation between this disease and ritual cannibalism of dead relatives.

GOROKA

The town of Goroka has grown from a small outpost in the mid-'50s to its current position as a major commercial centre with a population around 25,000. It's still a typical PNG town clustered around the airstrip, but it's also spacious and attractive and conveys a sense of civic pride and community that is rare in PNG. The town is small enough to walk around and the atmosphere is much more relaxed than at Mt Hagen or Kundiawa.

At an altitude of 1600 metres and 297 km from Lae, the climate is a perpetual spring – never too hot, never too cold.

Information

The town has an adequate range of facilities, including reasonable shopping, banks, a post office and the Raun Raun Theatre, an interesting local arts complex. This is Talair's headquarters, Air Niugini and MAF also have offices here and the three major car rental firms are represented. There's a council swimming pool just below the Minogere Lodge that is open 9 am to 6 pm daily.

Highland Shows

During the 1950s, as the Highlands first came into serious contact with Europeans, the Highland Shows were instituted as a way of gathering the tribes and clans together and showing them that the people from across the hill weren't so bad after all. They were an amazing success and grew from the original concept of a local get-together into a major tourist attraction. As many as 40,000 warriors would gather together in the show arena in a stomping, chanting dance that literally shook the earth. Drums thundered, feathers swayed and dancing bodies glistened with paint, oils and pig grease. It was like nothing else on earth.

Unfortunately, over the last few years the shows have suffered a serious decline. The Highlanders are increasingly sophisticated, so the curiosity-value of the gatherings for the participants themselves has declined, along with their pride in their traditional finery. In addition, with improved transport and better roads it is no longer such an effort to get from place to place, so people don't need to save up for an annual gathering.

Still, the shows go on and if you can see one, you're unlikely to be disappointed. It will certainly be one of the best available opportunities to get an overview of PNG's extraordinary cultural diversity.

The shows used to take place on even

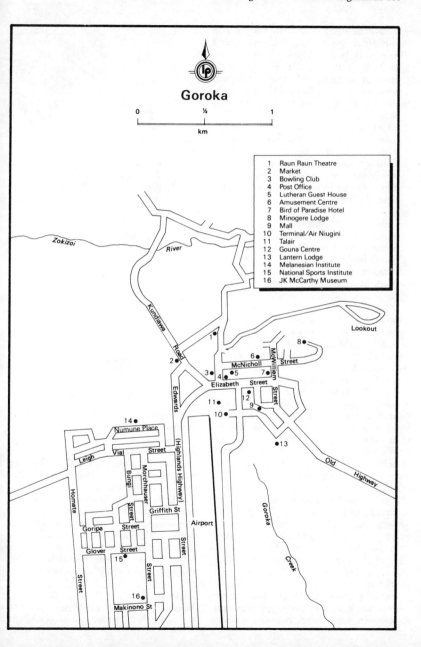

Goroka

0   ½   1
km

1   Raun Raun Theatre
2   Market
3   Bowling Club
4   Post Office
5   Lutheran Guest House
6   Amusement Centre
7   Bird of Paradise Hotel
8   Minogere Lodge
9   Mall
10 Terminal/Air Niugini
11 Talair
12 Gouna Centre
13 Lantern Lodge
14 Melanesian Institute
15 National Sports Institute
16 JK McCarthy Museum

numbered years in Goroka and on odd numbered years in Mt Hagen, most frequently in mid-August. This changed in 1988, with the Mt Hagen people deciding to make their show an annual event and bringing forward the date to the end of July. The Goroka event may also become annual.

Contact the National Tourist Office or the respective provincial governments for more information. For some reason the Goroka show seems to be the better of the two. Make sure you book accommodation if you will be in either town around the time of the festivities.

JK McCarthy Museum

McCarthy was one of PNG's legendary patrol officers and he wrote one of the classic books on New Guinea patrolling – *Patrol into Yesterday*. The museum that bears his name is off to the side of the airstrip, a reasonably lengthy walk from town. This is the only rival to the National Museum in Port Moresby, and it should definitely not be missed.

Among the exhibits, there are a variety of pottery styles, weapons, clothes and musical instruments, even some grisly jewellery, including a necklace of human fingers! Perhaps the most interesting feature is the fascinating collection of photos, many of which were taken by Mick Leahy when he first reached the area in 1933. There are also some relics from WW II, including a P-39 Aircobra left behind by the USAF after the war, which is behind the museum.

There is a shop with a selection of artefacts and handicrafts, including some striking modern paintings. It's open 9 am to 12 noon and 1 to 4 pm on weekdays, 2 to 4 pm on Saturdays and 10 am to 12 noon on Sundays. Admission is free but there is a 50t charge to take photographs.

Market

Saturday is, as usual, the best market day. You'll see fruit and vegetables, rats, possums, ferns, fungi, pigs and feathers.

Highland man with aumak

Despite all this, it's not as colourful as the Hagen market.

Raun Raun Theatre

If you have a chance, it is well worth seeing a performance by the Raun Raun Theatre (tel 72 1166), PO Box 118, Goroka. This highly successful Goroka-based theatre company undertakes national tours and has also performed internationally to high acclaim. The theatre building itself, in the park opposite the market a short walk from town, is an interesting and successful example of modern PNG architecture.

Lookout

Wisdom St, beside the post office, leads to a track that climbs to an excellent

Top: Huli women (Southern Highlands) at market with their bilums,
     the all-purpose string bags used throughout PNG (RE)
Left: Crowds at a sing-sing (TW)
Right: A chilly warrior at the Mt Hagen market (TW)

Top: Elizabeth Sowerby Orchid Park, Madang (ML)
Bottom: Poinsettia growing wild near Goroka (ML)

lookout, Mt Kiss Kiss. It's a long, steep walk if you haven't got wheels, but the reward is an excellent view over the valley. Unfortunately, this has at times been off-limits to visitors because of rascal activity. Check the situation with a local.

Places to Stay – bottom end

There are only two real choices, but fortunately they're both good. The Sports Institute and the Lutheran Guest House both give the mid-range hotels a very good run for their money and they have a fair number of beds.

The *Lutheran Guest House* (tel 72 1171), PO Box 44, is right in the centre of town, behind the post office and is recommended. It's clean, comfortable, convenient and friendly; some rooms even have private facilities. Bear in mind this is a church-run establishment and you will probably have to make some concessions. Bed and an excellent cooked breakfast is K16 and dinner is usually available.

Some people prefer the modern *National Sports Institute* (tel 72 2391, 72 2019), PO Box 337 and it certainly is a good place to stay. It's a bit out from town, about a 20 minute walk from the post office, on Glover St near the museum, but it's convenient if you want to catch an early PMV to Lae. It's on the site of the old showgrounds, which are still shown on some maps. There are 100 rooms at K12 per person. All rooms are singles and guests can take advantage of hot showers, satellite TV, tennis courts, the gym and other sports facilities. Good meals are also available: breakfast is K4, lunch K4 and dinner K6. The receptionists will sign you in between 7.30 am and 7.30 pm, Monday to Friday, or you can call either Andrew Bacam or Oscar Miller after hours on 72 2436 or 72 2615. Transport is available to and from the airport.

The *Teachers College* (tel 72 1039, 72 1257) sometimes has cheap rooms available, but it's a long way from town and not really worth the trouble.

Places to Stay – top end

The *Bird of Paradise Motel* (tel 72 1144), PO Box 12, on Elizabeth St in the centre of town is the top hotel in Goroka. It's only a few minutes' walk from the airport. All rooms have private facilities and all mod-cons, and the prices for singles/doubles are K63/88. They also have a bunk room for K21 per person. Breakfast will set you back another K6. The 'Bird' has a pool and a licensed restaurant (K8.50 and up) and a bistro (K5.50 and up).

They enforce dress regulations in the evening; no hairy legs allowed. Rejected, I went for a drink in the public bar on the corner and found the company much friendlier and more hospitable than the long-trousered type inside, although it would probably be a bit hectic on pay Fridays.

If there is a drawback it's probably the central position; people in the lower level front rooms may find the street noise annoying. At lunchtime the rooftop *Flight Deck* has hamburgers and salads or other light meals from around K3.50. Tours to see the Asaro mud men cost K17.50 per person.

The *Lantern Lodge* (tel 72 1776), PO Box 769, is equally close to the airport, but is both a bit cheaper and considerably more run-down; it certainly looked neglected. Singles/doubles are K50/70; meals are extra with breakfast at K5, lunch at K5 and dinner in the restaurant from around K10.

Goroka's third hotel is the *Minogere Lodge* (tel 72 1009), PO Box 2. It is run by the local town council and, regrettably, looks like it. There are 57 rooms at K30/40 in the hostel section and K40/50 in the motel section. Breakfast is included in the tariff, but the hostel rooms are spartan, without private facilities or even a wash basin in the room. The motel rooms are better equipped.

The Minogere does have a pleasant outside patio area where a good (K5) barbecue lunch with smorgasbord salad is served on Sundays. The complete fixed price dinner at K8.50 is reasonably good value and the pleasant outdoor patio has beer at K1.20 a stubby. The council swimming pool is just below the patio area. The hotel now has TV in the lounge every night. It's a short walk from town up a steep hillside, but a bit far from the airport if you have much luggage.

Places to Eat
Apart from eating in the hotels there are the usual kai bars and the unusual *Goroka Coffee Shop* which has a pleasant outdoor courtyard. It's right in the centre of town in the Gouna Centre, behind the ANZ Bank. They offer good sandwiches for K1 to K1.50, plus luxuries like home made chocolate cake, banana bread, yoghurt and even smoothies. Breakfasts are also served. Unfortunately it's only open until 4.30 pm on weekdays and between 9 am and 12 noon on Saturdays.

Things to Buy
Some artefacts are sold from the footpath in front of the Bird of Paradise Hotel. There usually isn't anything of much of quality and the prices are high but negotiable. It's worth a look; there are spears, bows and arrows and assorted necklaces and other items.

The art department at the Goroka Teachers College produces and sells prints, paintings and so on using western tools and traditional concepts. They also have some artefacts for sale.

Getting There & Away
You can fly to Goroka directly from Port Moresby, but most travellers arrive from Lae, either by air or road. See the introductory Highlands Highway section for details on the road.

Air Talair (tel 72 1355) has its national headquarters at the airport. Air Niugini (72 1211) and MAF (tel 72 1080) also have offices at the airport. Flights to Moresby cost K96, to Lae K45.

PMVs The main PMV station is at the market, but if you're going to Lae or planning to stay at the Sports Institute, you may find the PMV stops on Edwards St, parallel to the airport, more convenient. A PMV from Lae will cost K8 and take four or five hours, to Kundiawa will cost K4 and to Mt Hagen will cost K7 and take around four hours.

Car Hire Budget (tel 72 1488) has an office at the Steamships store, Hertz (tel 72 1710) is at the Westpac bank on Fox St and Avis (tel 72 1084) is at the Air Niugini terminal. Apparently Avis will give you a discount if you book ahead through Air Niugini.

Getting Around
It's easy enough to walk around Goroka and, consequently, there don't seem to be any taxis or urban PMVs. The Sports Institute has transport to the airport and the Bird of Paradise Motel runs a tour to see the mud men.

AROUND GOROKA
You can easily arrange visits to coffee plantations or coffee processing plants around Goroka. Try to line up a trip with a coffee buyer; some of them can speak English and it is an interesting way to visit a Highlands village.

Lufa
Lufa is south of Goroka and is a good base for climbing Mt Michael, named after those two original Highland 'Michaels': Mick Dwyer and Mick Leahy. There is a cave near Lufa with some interesting prehistoric cave paintings.

Bena Bena
About 10 km out of Goroka on the old road to Kainantu (it must have been a hard trip once) is the village of Bena Bena with the biggest Highlands weaving set-up. Curiously, the hand looms are all operated by men, quite the opposite of most South-East Asian countries where

weaving is a woman's skill. A couple of women do weave shoulder bags in an adjoining hut. The men weave pleasantly coarse rugs, bedspreads and place mats.

They're not cheap – rugs start from K20 and go up towards K100. There are other weaving centres around the valley, but the prices are fairly standardised.

The Rothman's tobacco factory is also interesting. After seeing gammune twist tobacco rolled you can take a swim in the nearby river. The manager will guide you around the factory and point you towards the river. Start from Goroka early so you have time to get back before dark.

Kotuni

There is a trout farm at Kotuni – about 15 km out of town off the Hagen road. Trout are bred for consumption or to be released as fingerlings into the many excellent, well stocked Highland streams. Apart from putting trout on the local menus, the trout farm is a popular weekend spot as it's very beautiful – a rocky little river splashes through the jungle close to the fish tanks.

Admission is free and the trip up from Goroka, past villages, tropical vegetation and coffee plantations, is fun. They'll also catch and grill a trout for you right there if you feel like a barbecue.

Mt Gahavisuka Provincial Park

This is an area of around 80 hectares set in beautiful mountain scenery. It is 11 km from Goroka and one km higher, and is reached by a four-wheel drive road (dry weather only) that turns off Highlands Highway on the Mt Hagen side, opposite the Okiufa Community School (look out for the sign).

The Park includes a botanical sanctuary, where exotic plants from all over PNG have been added to the local, natural orchids and rhododendrons. There are clearly marked walking tracks and a lookout at 2450 metres with a spectacular view. Facilities include two car parks, picnic shelters, two orchid houses and an inform-

ation centre. There is no admission fee. You can contact the ranger on 72 1203.

Asaro Mud Men

Many years ago, so the story goes, the village of Asaro came off second best in a tribal fight. Someone at Asaro had a bizarre inspiration and the revengeful warriors covered themselves with grey mud and huge mud masks before heading off on their inevitable payback raid. When these ghostly apparitions emerged from the trees, their opponents scattered.

The mud men recreate this little caper for tourists, but unfortunately it has become rather commercialised and dull. The number of mud men appears to be in direct proportion to the number of kina-paying tourists.

It would be much better if the mud men were to perform, say, once a month and really make a show of it rather than continue the current half-hearted, 'if there's a tourist bus coming' affair. Mud men tours are arranged by the Bird of Paradise Motel for K17.50 per person, and by Trans Niugini – see the Hagen section.

One traveller wrote that Komiufa, about five km from Asaro on the Highlands Highway, was a good place to see, very briefly, the mud men. Payment of K10 could persuade four men to don their masks and dance around for a couple of minutes. Resist further requests for photo payments.

Daulo Pass

The road out to Hagen is fairly flat through Asaro, but it then hairpins its way up to the 2450 metre high Daulo Pass. The Pass is cold and damp but the views are spectacular, particularly if you're heading down from the pass towards Goroka. This has become a notorious spot for rascals to stop and rob vehicles. Very few attempt the trip after dark.

Simbu (Chimbu) Province

Area 8476 square km
Population 200,000

Travelling west from Goroka, the mountains become much more rugged and the valleys become smaller and less accessible. Some of the highest mountains in PNG are in this region, including Mt Wilhelm, at 4509 metres, the highest of them all.

The province's name is said to date to the first patrol into the area. The story has it that steel axes and knives were given to the tribespeople and that the recipients replied that they were *simbu* – very pleased. The area was accordingly named Simbu, which was temporarily corrupted to Chimbu, and finally changed back to Simbu.

Despite its rugged terrain, Simbu Province is the most heavily populated region in PNG. The Simbu people have turned their steep country into a patchwork quilt of gardens that spreads up the side of every available hill. Population pressures are pushing them ever higher – to the detriment of remaining forests and, consequently, the birds of paradise.

Kundiawa, the provincial capital and site for the first government station in the Highlands, has been left behind by Goroka and Hagen. It has a spectacular airstrip, but its attractive location, on steep hillsides, may well have inhibited its development.

The Simbus have a reputation for being avid capitalists who keep a good eye on their coffee profits and also for being great believers in the payback raid. Minor warfare is still common in the Simbu region and aggrieved parties are all too ready to claim an eye-for-an-eye. The old customs are breaking down, but at one time all the men in a village would live in a large men's house while their wives lived

in individual round-houses – with the pigs.

KUNDIAWA

Although it's the provincial capital, you can cover most of Kundiawa in half an hour – and you won't be much better off for your efforts. There's a PNGBC bank, a post office, some rather limited shopping, one handicraft store and that's about it. Most people go straight through to Mt Wilhelm, Goroka or Mt Hagen. One of the main problems is the absence of reasonably priced accommodation.

The most convincing reason to stop is if you are interested in rafting or bushwalking – this is the base for a local company called Niugini Adventure (tel 75 1304), contact Murray Fletcher, PO Box 295, Kundiawa, which handles rafting trips on the Watut (see the Wau & Bulolo section) and Wahgi Rivers (see Around Kundiawa) and a variety of caving and bushwalking trips, including the walk to the top of Mt Wilhelm.

Places to Stay

There are only two places to stay in Kundiawa and neither is cheap. The garish *Simbu Lodge* (tel 75 1144), PO Box 191, right by the airport has 20 rooms with singles/doubles at K70/90. They also have a bunkhouse for K30, but if you're not careful you'll spend a fortune on meals. The restaurant is expensive: breakfast is around K6, lunch is K12.50 and dinner is K15. The bar is popular with expats living in the area and one traveller reported that the disco is good fun, especially on pay Fridays.

The *Kundiawa Hotel* (tel 75 1033), PO Box 12, is rather cheaper with 10 rooms at K30/40 for singles/doubles. It can be a bit of a hell-house on drinking nights.

Things to Buy

The *Simbu Women's Handicraft Shop* has an interesting selection of artefacts. It's next door to the Agriculture Bank on the way to the Chimbu Lodge and is open from 7.45 am to 4 pm Monday to Friday and from 8 am to 12 noon on Saturdays.

If you're looking for food supplies, the best stores are *Sika* or *Collins & Leahy*.

Getting There & Away
Air The airport is quite spectacular as it's on a sloping ridge surrounded by mountains. Air Niugini (tel 75 1273) and Talair (tel 75 1034) have offices but not many flights service Simbu. Most travellers use Mt Hagen or Goroka airports.

PMVs Goroka/Kundiawa is K4, Kundiawa/ Mt Hagen is K3 and Kundiawa/Kegsugl for Mt Wilhelm is around K4 (they leave from the Shell Service Station - beware of overcharging), and each of these sectors takes around two hours. It's a relatively easy two or three day walk to Kegsugl from Brahmin Mission near Madang. See the following Madang Walk section.

AROUND KUNDIAWA
Rafting the Wahgi River
Many people have enthused about the rafting trip on the Wahgi. It was pioneered by the American adventure company Sobek, and is now run by Niugini Adventure. The scenery is excellent: the river goes through deep chasms, under small rope bridges and there are several good stretches of rapids and waterfalls. Unfortunately the trip is not cheap, although everything, even food, is included. A one-day trip costs K60.

Pari Hill
There's a good walk up Pari Hill behind Kundiawa - it takes about four hours to get up and down. At the top there are some interesting old graves and some modern ones surrounded by empty beer bottles. There are also some burial caves with the dried remains of warriors killed in battle.

The award for commercial enterprise must go to Benson & Hedges - just after the start of the walk, at the bottom of the hill, there's a tomb flanked by two large

Benson & Hedges adverts, one of which has been stuck on upside down. The start of the ascent is near a blue wooden church with a corrugated iron roof.

Caves
There are a number of caves around Kundiawa that are used as burial places. Other large caves, suitable for caving enthusiasts, are only a few km from Kundiawa while the Keu Caves are very close to the main road near Chuave. The Nambaiyufa Amphitheatre is also near Chuave and is noted for its rock paintings.

MT WILHELM
Climbing to the 4509 metre summit of Mt Wilhelm is, for many people, the highlight of their visit. On a clear day you can see both the north and south coasts. Even if you don't intend to tackle the summit, it is well worth considering staying near the base at Herman's Guesthouse or Niglguma Village. Both places are very pleasant and are reached after a spectacular drive from Kundiawa through classic Simbu country. You could explore the area and walk some of the way up the mountain.

There are a number of ways of tackling the climb, depending on your wealth, health and available time: you can go with a trekking company (Pacific Expeditions or Niugini Adventure) who will provide a guide, porters, food and equipment; you can hire guides and porters yourself; or you can do it all yourself.

The last option is entirely feasible if you're reasonably fit and have some warm gear - and want to go as fast or as slow as you like. The path to the summit is clearly marked (a guide is not necessary) and no technical climbing is required.

You will find people are keen to offer their services as guides and porters. A porter will cost about K5 a day, a guide about K12. If they overnight with you at Pindaunde Lakes you must supply them with food and blankets. Alternatively, you can arrange for them to leave you there and, if you wish, come back for you later. Porters from Niglguma will do this for K5 each way – ask for Anton or Maria Kaugla, they'll recommend someone trustworthy. You can contact Anton, c/o Catholic Mission, Denglagu, PO Box 34, Kundiawa, Simbu, about porters, or the Niglguma Guesthouse. Herman Sieland, Herman's Guesthouse, PO Gembogl, also arranges guides and carriers.

A mountain this high should never be underestimated. It can get very cold on top and can easily become fogbound and even snow. Climbers can suffer from altitude sickness, sunburn and hypothermia (hopefully, not all at once). See the Health section in the Facts for the Visitor chapter. It is vital that you have sufficient food and warm clothing and that you assess the weather and your physical state realistically. You would be most unwise to tackle it alone.

In addition, make sure you have a hat and sun cream (you burn deceptively quickly at high altitudes), water containers (there's no water on the last stretch past the lakes), a torch with a spare globe and strong batteries, gloves, candles and a small stove.

The first stage of the climb entails walking up to the Pindaunde Lakes from the high school and disused airstrip at Kegsugl. The track takes off from the top end of the airstrip. After climbing fairly steeply through dense rainforest, the track turns into the Pindaunde Valley and continues less steeply up the hummocky valley floor.

After about four hours you'll reach the Pindaunde Lakes. These are at about 3500 metres and there are a couple of huts; it can get very cold. At this height you have reached the zone where you could suffer altitude sickness. The huts cost about K4 per person and contain beds and a kerosene lamp. The lamp isn't guaranteed, hence the candles on your shopping list. It costs K15 to camp! See the ranger at Kegsugl for the keys before you leave, although it's possible he'll be somewhere on the trail. If

he is around at Kegsugl, he'll let you leave extra gear with him, otherwise you could leave stuff with Herman.

You are likely to be offered strawberries for sale along the first stretch of the walk, and if you are, buy them. They're the sweetest strawberries I've ever tasted and apparently they grow all year round – perhaps because of the altitude and all the UV radiation.

From the huts it's a long, fairly hard walk to the summit, taking about five hours. Some walkers reckon it is better to spend a day acclimatising at the lake huts and exploring the area before attempting it. After the lakes, water is difficult to find, so carry your own. It can become very cold, wet, windy and foggy at the top. The clouds roll in around 9 am or even earlier so it is wise to start from the huts as early as possible.

Most people recommend starting at 3 or 4 am – hence the torch on your shopping list. The ascent and descent will probably take you all day (coming down to the huts will take about three hours), but some people do go all the way back to Kegsugl.

While you're in the Mt Wilhelm area a visit to Niglguma Village or Gembogl is worthwhile. You can walk to Gembogl from Kegsugl in a couple of hours and on the way you pass through half a dozen villages, including Niglguma which is at the junction of two streams and has a guesthouse. Gembogl has suffered the inroads of corrugated iron construction, so Niglguma is more interesting.

One possible (leisurely) itinerary would be: day one from Hagen or Goroka to Kegsugl, day two to the Pindaunde Lakes, day three acclimatising, day four to the summit and back to the lakes, day five to Niglguma, day six to Mt Hagen or Goroka.

Places to Stay

Over the years *Herman's Guesthouse* has become a veritable institution, a refuge for exhausted walkers, and deservedly so. It stands alone, alongside the road that leads up to the airstrip at Kegsugl – you can't miss it. It's not exactly luxurious, but it's homely, very clean and there are hot showers and cooking facilities. Bring your own food. There's room for 14 people in two rooms with raised sleeping platforms and it costs K5 per person. Herman Sieland, the expat German who runs the place, can be contacted through PO Gembogl. Hopefully he'll have had success with his plans to organise a PMV.

If you are interested in staying in a village – and I recommend you do – there's a good set-up at *Niglguma Village*, which is at the junction of two streams on the Gembogl-Kegsugl road. This guesthouse has been built in traditional style by a Christian group. Ask for the 'Kristian Mamas' Hut'; there's a flagpole in the front yard.

There's room for 12 people and they charge K5 per head. There aren't too many luxuries, but there are cooking facilities, a toilet and a beautiful rushing stream. Bring your own food, although you may be supplied with some fresh vegetables. If you're lucky, the friendly locals may cook a mumu and maybe even bring out their bamboo flutes for a small sing-sing. If you want porters or a guide, ask for Anton or Maria Kaugla. Niglguma is a pretty spot and it would be worth visiting even if you aren't a mountain climber.

Getting There & Away

Kegsugl, at the foot of the mountain, is about 57 km from Kundiawa along a road that has to be seen to be believed. You can get there by irregular PMVs that cost K4 or K5 and take a couple of hours. They leave from the Shell Service Station in Kundiawa. The Bundi road branches off to the right over a bridge, just before Kegsugl. The airstrip at Kegsugl, once the highest in PNG at 2469 metres, has been shut down.

WALKING TO MADANG

The turn-off for the Bundi road, and the trek to Brahmin (and Madang) is between Gembogl and Kegsugl. You turn right over a bridge, instead of left to Kegsugl. You can walk right down to Madang – but most people catch a PMV at Brahmin.

It's a relatively easy, though sometimes hot trek, because you follow a four-wheel drive track. Some vehicles have apparently gone through. A reasonable pace would get you to Madang in three fairly long days. Bring your own food, although you can get meals at Bundi.

The first stretch is largely up hill and there are very few villages. The first village you come to, Bundikara, is about a five hour walk. There's an attractive waterfall and you can apparently stay in the village. There are great views from lookout points along the way.

It's another 3½ hours to Bundi where there is a group of lodges known as the *Mt Sinai Hotel*. These cost K8 per person, including dinner. From Bundi it's 2½ hours to War, which is just after a suspension bridge and from War it is a 3½ hour climb to Brahmin Mission. A PMV from Brahmin to Madang will cost K5 or K6 and takes about 1½ hours. Brahmin is about 25 km from the Lae-Madang road.

Western Highlands Province

Area 8288 square km
Population 300,000

Continuing west from Simbu Province you descend into the large Wahgi Valley. Although almost half the province was restricted or uncontrolled until the '60s, traditional dress is now rarely worn. You will still see some of the older men dressed traditionally, especially for market days and sing-sings.

Mt Hagen is the provincial capital and

although it is not particularly attractive it does have the somewhat out-of-control energy of a frontier town. The surrounding countryside is worth exploring.

The province's terrain varies between swamps just above sea level and a number of peaks that are over 4000 metres high, including Mt Giluwe at 4360 metres and Mt Hagen at 4026 metres. Forest only remains on the mountain slopes and the valleys and lower hills are grass covered. This is the result of human activity: shifting slash-and-burn cultivation and hunting fires. Gardens and stands of casuarinas are scattered through the hills and large tea and coffee plantations now dominate the most fertile valley floors.

The men usually have beards and their traditional clothing is a wide belt of beaten bark with a drape of strings in front and a bunch of tanket leaves behind. The leaves are known, descriptively, as *arse-tanket*. The women can be just as decoratively dressed, with string skirts and cuscus fur hanging around their necks.

Today, that attire is usually reserved for sing-sings and bright lengths of printed cloth and T-shirts are more likely to be the everyday wear. Naturally, traditional dress is more likely to be seen in the smaller towns and villages than in main towns. At sing-sings both sexes will have beautiful headdresses with bird of paradise plumes and other feathers.

The Wahgi people keep carefully tended vegetable gardens and neat villages, often with paths bordered by decoratively planted flowers, ceremonial parks with lawns and groves of trees and colourful memorials to deceased big men.

Sing-sings are still an integral part of life and you should make every effort to see one. This is, unfortunately, not all that easy to do, but keep an ear to the ground, especially if you're walking through the region.

BANZ & MINJ

These two towns are mid-way between Kundiawa and Mt Hagen in the Wahgi Valley; Banz is a few km north of the Highway and Minj is a few km south.

This is an unstable part of the world; sadly, the provincial high school at Minj was closed at the end of 1987 after a series of deliberate fires and the murder of the school cook. Bush-material accommodation for travellers and a cultural centre/museum were amongst the buildings destroyed. There is very little to attract the traveller now, although there is an excellent golf course at Minj.

Places to Stay

There are small hotels in both Minj and Banz. In Minj, *Tribal Tops* (tel 56 5538), PO Box 13, is operated by Tribal World who also run the Plumes & Arrows Hotel at Hagen and the Sepik International Hotel at Wewak. It is surrounded by a high wall, and has an attractive garden and swimming pool. Like the other places in the chain, it is liberally decorated with Sepik art, much of which is for sale (it ain't cheap). The normal rate is K82, but if you're a tourist and book and pay 14 days ahead, this drops to K45. They have a bunk room for K17 per person. A continental breakfast will cost about K4.50 and main meals range from K10 up.

In Banz the *Kunai Hotel* (tel 56 2245), PO Box 16, seems to be concentrating on beer sales.

Getting There & Away

A PMV from Hagen to the Minj turnoff is K2 and a further 20t will get you to the town centre, such as it is.

MT HAGEN

This is the provincial capital for the Western Highlands, and although it is now commercially more important than Goroka, it is not nearly as attractive. It lies 445 km from Lae and 115 km from Goroka.

Mt Hagen was just a patrol station

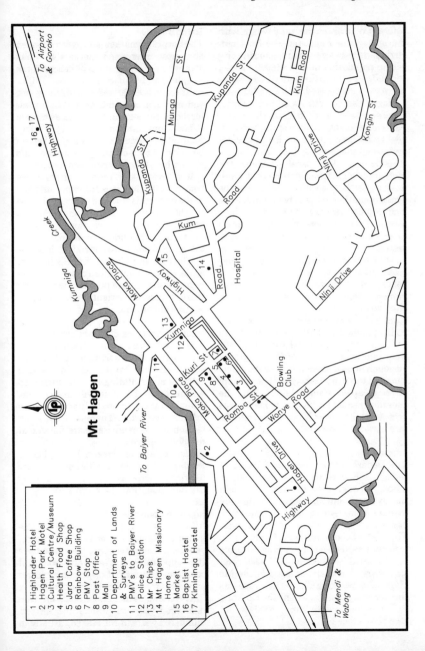

Mt Hagen

1 Highlander Hotel
2 Hagen Park Motel
3 Cultural Centre/Museum
4 Health Food Shop
5 Jara Coffee Shop
6 Rainbow Building
7 PMV Stop
8 Post Office
9 Mall
10 Department of Lands
   & Surveys
11 PMV's to Baiyer River
12 Police Station
13 Mr Chips
14 Mt Hagen Missionary
   Home
15 Market
16 Baptist Hostel
17 Kimininga Hostel

before WW II, but in the last 20 years, with the opening of Enga and the Southern Highlands, it has grown into a unruly city with a population of over 40,000 people. It's quite a shock to find a PNG city where the streets are packed with people.

Hagen can sometimes be quite tense; there's a 'wild west' feel to the place. Payrolls for many businesses in the region now go by helicopter because trucks are ambushed so often.

Aside from the rascal problem, the more traditional tribal warfare continues, exacerbated by the value of coffee and the over-population of the best land. The local Papua New Guineans are the best source of information about which areas to avoid at any given time. Don't walk around at night.

The town acquired its name by a rather roundabout route. It is named after nearby Mt Hagen, which in turn was named after a German administrator, Kurt von Hagen.

In 1895 two Germans started off on a badly planned and ill-fated attempt to cross the island from north to south. They were murdered by two of their carriers, although one wonders if they would have survived the trip in any case. The carriers later escaped from custody. In the subsequent hunt for them, von Hagen was shot and killed near Madang in 1897; he was buried at Bogadjim.

Information

The Department of Lands & Surveys at the end of Kuri St has a good selection of maps, although they are less likely than the National Mapping Bureau in Moresby to have complete stocks. All the main banks have branches, as do the airlines. This is the headquarters for MAF.

Forster's Newsagent on Hagen Drive has a good collection of books and stationary. Look out for signs of the Mt Hagen Bushwalking Club – their base was the Christian Bookshop along the Highway from the Rainbow Building, so this would be a good place to ask.

The Market

The Saturday market is one of the biggest and most interesting markets in PNG and, if you're lucky, you will still see some people in traditional dress. You're unlikely to see plumed headdresses, but you may notice young men with leaves, feathers or flowers in their hair as a more subtle continuation of the tradition. Snapping a picture of anyone is likely to be followed by a demand for money – it's always best to ask permission first.

It is even rarer for women to dress traditionally than it is for men, but they make up for this with the sheer brightness of their dresses and bilums. Add a brilliant kerchief, several flowing scarves in various colours, traditional facial tattoos and you have a striking sight.

Don't forget to look at what is for sale; aside from a superb range of fruit and vegetables, there are pigs and, when I was there, a cassowary tightly trussed up in lengths of bamboo.

Western Highlands Cultural Centre

The centre, also known as the museum, is a bit tatty, but it's worth a visit. Although small, it has quite an interesting collection, including a reconstructed village hut. The staff will answer any questions and explain the functions of the articles on display. There is also a small section where handicrafts are for sale at reasonable prices.

It's upstairs off Hagen Drive, beside Forster's Newsagent and it's open Monday to Friday, 9 am to 12 noon, 1 to 4 pm. They ask for a donation of a kina or so.

Highland Shows

Although the Highland shows are no longer as spectacular as they used to be, you should definitely go to one if you have the opportunity. They are colourful occasions and a great opportunity to get an overview of all the different tribes.

The shows used to take place on even numbered years in Goroka and on odd numbered years in Mt Hagen, usually in mid-August. In 1988, the Mt Hagen people decided to make their show an annual event and bring forward the date to the end of July. The Goroka event may also become annual, but in 1988 it will, as usual, be in mid-August.

Contact the National Tourist Office or the respective provincial governments for more information. For some reason the Goroka show seems to be the better of the two. Make sure you book accommodation if you will be in either town around the time of the festivities.

Other

In the dusty open space beside the PMV stop at the end of Kuri St, the men play a curious gambling game, one man standing in a roped-off area, another holding money and playing cards pasted to a piece of cardboard. I couldn't figure it out.

Places to Stay – bottom end

The *Kunguma Haus Poroman* (tel 52 2722, 52 1957), PO Box 1182, should not be missed, especially by budget travellers. Not only is it reasonably priced, but it's clean, comfortable and an interesting, friendly place to stay. Why aren't there more places like this?

It's usually just called Haus Poroman, which means 'house of friends'. In Kunguma Village, about seven km from town, it perches on a ridge, with superb views across Hagen and the valley to the mountains. Staying out of town is a distinct relief; Liz, the manager, will pick you up from town or the airport.

Keith and Maggie Wilson, the owners, also run the excellent Jara Coffee Shop in town and this serves as a convenient meeting place if you arrive by PMV. The lodge itself is well designed and built in traditional bush materials, with an open fire, a well-stocked library and a range of videos (some made by Maggie) about PNG. Facilities are shared and, although it's not the Hilton, it is comfortable – and it costs K12. You can also stay in a traditional hut nearby for K5.

The food is excellent: people drive out from Hagen just to eat here. Breakfast is K3, lunch K3.50, dinner K5.50. Traditional mumus are sometimes organised.

There are also plenty of things to do in the surrounding area: there's a marked trail through the rainforest; you can visit the nearby village and watch traditional crafts being made; make a three hour trek through the Nebilyer Valley, through forest and past villages to the Leahy's coffee plantation; make a one day walk to the huge Kum Caves; search for gold at Kuta Ridge; or visit Baiyer River Bird Sanctuary (K25, including lunch). Guides are available. This is a good place to meet other travellers and to get information, especially on the Highlands.

If you decide to stay in town there are a number of reasonable options.

The immaculate *Kimininga Hostel* (tel 52 1865), PO Box 408, is on the Goroka side of town, about 10 minutes' walk from the centre, past the market. If you are coming from Goroka by road, get off before you get into town. The food is good and the rooms are comfortable, although they don't have private facilities. There are 37 rooms, K20/32 for singles/doubles in the old wing, K28/40 in the new wing, all including breakfast. There's a lounge with coffee, free, on tap in the evenings and a free laundry. Lunches cost K6 and an excellent three-course dinner is K12.

Right next door, the *Baptist Hostel* (tel 52 1003), PO Box 103, is used mainly by locals, but travellers are welcome. You need your own bedding and food, but there is a kitchen that you can use. It's a bit grubby, but the cost is very reasonable at just K7 per night.

The *Mt Hagen Missionary Home* (tel 52 1041), PO Box 394, across from the hospital, a short walk from town, is a reasonably-priced, homely place and is recommended. It's run by a friendly American family and is spotlessly clean. Shared rooms are K15 per person with breakfast, K20 with dinner too. Lunch is K4.

Places to Stay – top end

The *Highlander Hotel* (tel 52 1355), PO Box 34, is just a hundred or so metres from the town centre. It has two wings and rooms in either wing have private facilities and tea/coffee making equipment. The newer rooms have all mod-cons. Singles are K60 to K70, doubles are K70 to K80. Food is extra: breakfast is K6.50, lunch is around K9.50 and dinner is around K12. The Highlander is surrounded by pleasant gardens with a heated swimming pool; it's quiet and peaceful, but a little colourless.

The *Hagen Park Motel* (tel 52 1388), PO Box 81, is rather noisy and active and starting to look a little run-down. The rooms here are quite large: a budget room costs K30 and a deluxe room (with TV and fridge) costs K52. The food is also a bit cheaper than at the Highlander.

The *Plumes & Arrows Inn* (tel 55 1546), PO Box 86, is a bit inconvenient for town, but only a three minute walk from the airport. It has a high stockade fence (to pursue the wild west analogy) and it feels like a fortress, but there are some attractive gardens and a swimming pool inside. This is the headquarters for Tribal World, a company that organises up-market tours in the Sepik region and around the Highlands. The rooms cost K82 but there's a substantial discount if you are a tourist and book ahead. There's a bunk room at K17. The food is good with breakfasts at K4.50 and main meals K10 and up. The lounge/dining room area has Sepik art for sale.

Places to Eat

In the Hagen Plaza, the *Plaza Coffee Shop* has sandwiches, omelettes, milk shakes and so on – a lunch will cost from K1.50 to K3. The outdoor patio under the umbrellas is a good place to relax. It's closed on Sundays and after 4 pm.

The *Jara Coffee Shop* is the official meeting place for people going out to Haus Poroman. It's just across the Hagen Drive from the post office, right on the corner with Kuri St. They have good homemade food: quiche and salad for K1.50, hamburgers around K2, sandwiches around K1 and milk shakes for 90t.

There's a Chinese restaurant called the *Apollo* where you can get a reasonable meal for around K8 or K9. *Mr Chips*, with the huge sign opposite the police station, has takeaway hamburgers, hot dogs and french fries that are said to be the best in PNG.

The health food store on Hagen Drive opposite the provincial government offices is a good place to stock up if you're going walking.

Steamships is the best supermarket.

Getting There & Away

Air Air Niugini (tel 52 1122) and Talair (tel 52 2465) have offices in town and MAF (tel 55 1434) has its headquarters at the airport. The airport is about 10 km from town, so you have to catch a PMV (K1). It's a couple of km off the highway on the Goroka side of town. If you're looking for a PMV to town, walk towards the Plumes & Arrows Hotel, until you see a couple of shops and a straggly market – this is where the PMVs turn around. Haus Poroman and the Highlander pick up and drop off passengers, and there are taxis. Make sure you leave yourself plenty of time if you're using PMVs to catch a flight.

Hagen has extensive air links to the north coast (eg Wewak K69, Madang K56), the rest of the Highlands (eg Mendi K36, Tari K59, Goroka K48), the south coast (eg Port Moresby K110, Kerema K103) and other destinations like Tabubil (near OK Tedi in the Western Province) for K124.

MAF flies twice weekly to literally dozens of third level airstrips. If you're planning a walk, and want to know where along your route you could bail out, or how you could make some short cuts, go and talk to them. Most of their flights are reasonably priced and they also offer a 25% student discount.

PMVs PMVs heading to Simbu, Enga or the Southern Highlands come and go from the end of Kuri St on the Highway, near the distinctive rainbow building. There are regular connections to Mendi (K8, three to four hours) and to Goroka (K7, three to four hours). PMVs to Baiyer River (K2, around 1½ hours) leave from the corner of Moka Place and Kumniga Rd.

Tours If you plan to stay at Ambua Lodge near Tari, you may be able to ride up with a Trans Niugini (tel 52 1438) vehicle, which will give you a chance to stop along the way. Their head office is on Kongin St behind the hospital and quite a walk from town. They have tours around the area and to see the mud men of Asaro. They have regular buses between Hagen and Goroka. Haus Poroman (see the Places to Stay – bottom end section) also arranges tours.

Getting Around

Most of Hagen is accessible by foot, so there don't seem to be any urban PMVs. There are a couple of taxi companies that might come in handy if you have an awkward flight to the airport: Kops Taxi (tel 52 2893) and Tais Escort Taxi Service (tel 52 1458).

BAIYER RIVER

The 120 hectare Baiyer River wildlife sanctuary is 55 km north of Mt Hagen and it *used* to be one of the best places in the Highlands to visit and to stay. Sadly, it is now quite run-down. Even more unfortunately, in recent times it has become quite unsafe. Apparently there are major problems in the surrounding region and, the rascals are so active that even the missionaries are pulling out of the area. Tribal World and Trans Niugini no longer organise tours, mainly because robberies on the Baiyer River Rd have been so depressingly frequent.

This situation could quite conceivably change, and if it does, a visit is still recommended. Ask around in Hagen to get the latest information. The Jara Coffee Shop would be a good place to start, because Haus Poroman still does tours when it's possible, and you could try phoning the sanctuary's superintendent on 52 1482. The Police may also be helpful, but they'll more than likely try to dissuade you if there is even the remotest risk.

If you do visit, and everything has been maintained in the intervening period, you'll find the largest collection of birds of paradise in the world, nature trails through the forest, display trees used by wild birds of paradise and a decent self-service lodge. Don't forget birds of paradise moult between January and March. Admission is K1.

There are many animal and bird enclosures dotted around the rainforest and some good picnic spots. Not only are there birds of paradise, but also hornbills and parrots. There are some cassowaries, but they're in cages – a good thing, too, because they're downright mean looking! They also have a large collection of possums and tree kangaroos.

A garden has been established with special plants to attract butterflies – over 84 species, including the famous Ulysses, have been sighted.

Like many other zoos and wildlife sanctuaries, it would be better if there were fewer animals in larger enclosures. But even if cages get you down there can still be magic moments, like when a bird of paradise swoops through the trees high above you. The rainforest in the area is also a treat.

Places to Stay

There is a reasonably priced lodge at the sanctuary, the *Baiyer River Bird Sanctuary Lodge* (tel 52 1482), PO Box 490, Mt Hagen. There are seven rooms at K10 per person, K4 for students. There is no food, but there are cooking facilities.

Getting There & Away

Haus Poroman makes day tours for K25 per person, when it's feasible, and if the situation with the rascals improves, it is possible some of the other operators will start up again. A PMV from the corner of Moka Place and Kumniga Rd will cost K2 or K3. On the way you pass through the spectacular Baiyer River Gorge. The PMV trip takes about 1½ hours and would be safer than driving yourself.

Southern Highlands Province

Area 25,988
Population 270,000

The Southern Highlands are made up of lush, high valleys between impressive limestone peaks. This region is particularly beautiful and many of its people retain their traditional ways and dress. The headwaters of some mighty rivers, the Kikori, Erave and Strickland among them, cross the province and Mt Giluwe, 4362 metres high, is the second tallest mountain in PNG.

This most remote region of the Highlands is still relatively undeveloped. Even in the past, it was at the end of the trade route from the Gulf of Papua to the Highlands.

Beyond the Wahgi/Hagen area, both to the south-west past Mendi and north-west around Wabag, is the country of the Wigmen – these are the Huli, the Duna and a number of other tribes whose men are famous for the intricately decorated wigs that they wear.

The proud Huli men of the Tari Basin, in particular, still wear their impressive traditional decorations. The Huli are the largest ethnic group in the Southern Highlands with a population of around 40,000 and a territory exceeding 2500 square km.

The Wigmen do not live in villages, but in scattered homesteads, dispersed through their immaculately and intensively cultivated valleys. Their gardens are delineated by trenches and mud walls up to three metres high, broken by brightly painted gateways made of stakes. These trenches are used not only to mark boundaries and control the movement of pigs, but also to secretly deploy large troops of warriors in times of war. War was and, to some extent, still is a primary interest of the men.

The Mendi area is now the most developed part of the Southern Highlands but it was not explored by white men until 1935 – these early explorers called it the Papuan Wonderland.

It was 1950 when the first airstrip was constructed and 1952 before tribal warfare was prohibited. Not unnaturally the Mendi tribesmen turned their energies to attacking government patrols who were still fighting them off as late as 1954. The discovery of the beautiful Lavani Valley in 1954 set newspapers off with high-flown stories about the discovery of some lost Shangri-la.

The Southern Highlands is starting to attract caving expeditions as the limestone hills and the high rainfall is ideal for the formation of caves. Some caves of enormous depth and length have already been explored and it is a distinct possibility that some of the deepest caves in the world await discovery in this region.

Mendi is the attractive provincial capital and Tari is another thriving centre.

CUSTOMS
Wigs
The striking decorative wigs that distinguish the Wigmen are made from human hair. Wives and children, who are consequently often short-haired, have to donate their hair for the men's elaborate wigs. The whole design is held together by woven string. It is possible to tell which tribe a man comes from by the way he wears his hair or decorates it.

The Huli wigmen cultivate yellow everlasting daisies especially to decorate their wigs and they also use feathers and cuscus fur. They often wear a band of snakeskin on their foreheads, a cassowary quill through their nasal septa and their faces may be decorated with yellow and red ochre.

Pan pipes are a popular form of entertainment.

Brides in Black

Mendi brides wear black for their wedding – they are coated in black *tigaso* tree oil and soot and they continue to wear this body colouring for a month after the wedding. The tigaso tree oil comes from Lake Kutubu and is traded all over the area.

During this time neither the bride or the groom work, nor is the marriage consummated. This gives the bride time to become acquainted with her husband's family and for the groom to learn 'anti-woman' spells to protect himself from his wife.

Throughout the Highlands, women are traditionally distrusted by men, who go to extraordinary lengths to protect themselves and maintain their status. Sexual relations are not undertaken lightly. Contact with women is believed to cause sickness, so the two sexes often live in separate houses and the men often even prefer to cook their own food. The boys are usually removed from their mothers houses at very young age.

Women travellers should bear these customs in mind, because in many places they are still strictly upheld. Violence against PNG women is widespread.

Widows in Blue

A dead man's wife, daughters, mother, sisters and sisters-in-law, coat themselves with bluish-grey clay while in mourning. The wife carries vast numbers of strings of the seeds known as 'job's tears'. One string a day is removed until eventually, with the removal of the last string, the widow can wash herself of her clay coating and remarry. This is usually about nine months after the death.

Women's Houses

The walls of women's houses are about four metres tall with kunai thatched roofs and walls of pitpit cane on the outside. The women sleep in semi-circular sleeping rooms at each end of the house, and the pigs sleep in stalls along one wall. The sitting and cooking area is in the centre.

Long Houses

Long houses known as *haus lains* are built along the sides of Mendi ceremonial grounds and used as guesthouses at singsings and pig kills. They can be up to 150 metres long, although 70 metres is the usual length and they are built beside stone-filled pits where the pigs are cooked.

Warfare

Land ownership is highly complex and very important, so disputes over land are often at the root of conflicts. In general, a man inherits land rights, not just from his father, but from any known ancestor on both his mother's and his father's side. All the descendants of a man who planted a tree might have rights to its fruit; and a man will probably have rights to a number of widely scattered pieces of land.

Fighting arrows are carved from blackpalm and are traditionally tipped with human bone. The tips were made from the forearm of a male ancestor so that his spirit could 'guide' the arrow to an enemy. Although casualties are fairly rare in traditional warfare, the men are fine bowmen and can shoot over long distances. They also carry bone daggers carved from the leg bone of a cassowary. Fights are still quite common.

Food

The highlanders are highly skilled subsistence farmers, largely dependent on the sweet potato. This is grown in neat round mounds about a metre and a half in diameter (in the Wahgi Valley they're square). The mounds are fertilised with ashes and can have very high yields.

Bananas, sugar cane, greens and yams are also traditional crops which are now supplemented by many more familiar western vegetables. Hunting is relatively unimportant, but the pig is vital, both for protein and as a symbol of wealth.

Face Decoration

Imbong'gu girls paint their faces red and their lips white for sing-sings. Their heads are crowned with a great range of bird feathers, including several Raggiana Bird of Paradise feathers. The men wear their wigs and blacken their faces with soot, whiten their beards and eyes and colour their lips and noses red.

MENDI

Despite being the capital of the Southern Highlands, Mendi is just a small town, built around an airport. It shelters in a long green valley, surrounded by beautiful limestone peaks. It has a population of around 6000 and, although it can supply all essentials, there is not much to keep you hanging around.

The Westpac and PNGBC banks have branches and Air Niugini, Talair and MAF have offices here. There is a handful of shops, supermarkets and kai bars, a post office, a hotel . . . . It's really just the starting point for a trip to the Tari Basin or to Lake Kutubu.

Saturday, when tribespeople crowd into town from the surrounding country, is the best day to visit Mendi. There's an artefacts shop near Mendi Motors on the other side of the main road, that sells hand-loomed products, baskets and weapons. It's not cheap, but the wares are of reasonable quality; it's open 9 am to 3 pm Monday to Wednesday, 9 am to 4 pm Friday and 9 am to 12 noon on Saturday.

There used to be a small museum, and there is talk of re-establishing it. Ring the Department of Commerce & Tourism (tel 59 1033) to see if anything has happened.

Places to Stay

The *Mendi Hotel* (tel 59 1188), PO Box 108, is the only hotel in town. It's pretty uninspiring, but comfortable and it has a licensed restaurant. Considering this is PNG and the hotel has a monopoly on visiting salesmen and bureaucrats, the prices aren't too bad: singles/doubles with breakfast included are K45/60, plus a budget dormitory for K20 and discounts for PNG residents. The food is good. For lunch you can get toasted sandwiches for around K2.50, fish & chips for K5 and dinner for between K10 and K15.

There are two good alternatives for those who choose to live a little cheaper and scorn luxury: the Menduli Guest House and the Pentecostal Guest House, both of which are run by church groups.

The *Menduli Guest House* (tel 59 1158), PO Box 35, is a 20 minute walk from town and costs K8. You walk out the old Hagen road past Mendi Motors, take the left fork after the bridge, pass the large Menduli Trade Store and it's further up the hill on your right. There are plenty of rooms, it's clean, there are cooking facilities and the cost is K8. Olivier Meric de Bellefon established the Lake Kutubu Lodge and now, amongst other things, he manages this place. You can contact him about Lake Kutubu on 59 1158.

The *Pentecostal Guest House* (tel 59 1174), PO Box 15, is next door to the church and closer to town and the airport. When you walk out of the airline terminals, look across the road and you will see the Pentecostal Church. It only has five rooms and church workers have priority, so it's sometimes full. The rooms are clean and there's a kitchen (supply your own cooking gear). It costs K6 per person per night.

The *Educational Resource Centre* (tel 59 1252) also has reasonable value rooms with meals and cooking facilities.

Getting There & Away

Air Talair and Air Niugini fly between Mendi and a number of major centres: to

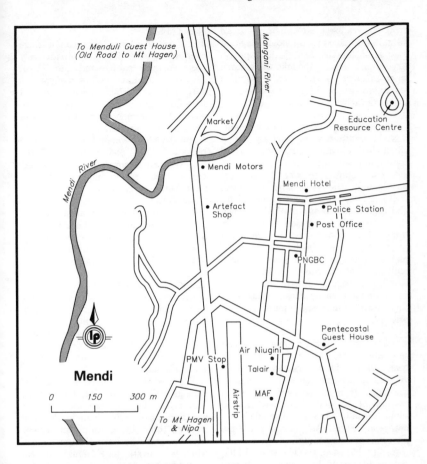

To Menduli Guest House
(Old Road to Mt Hagen)

Mangani River

Mendi River

Market

Education
Resource Centre

Mendi Motors

Mendi Hotel

Artefact
Shop

Police Station

Post Office

PNGBC

Pentecostal
Guest House

Air Niugini

PMV Stop

Talair

Mendi

MAF

Airstrip

0   150   300 m

To Mt Hagen
& Nipa

Tari for K40; Mt Hagen for K36 and Port Moresby for K114. Talair flies to Lake Kopiago for K60. MAF flies to a number of smaller airfields and has daily flights (except Saturday and Sunday) to Pimaga for K24, which is the starting point for the walk to Lake Kutubu. Talair may also start flights to Pimaga.

PMVs PMVs run back and forth between Mt Hagen and Mendi with reasonable regularity, taking three hours or so and costing K8. The road to Tari goes via Nipa

and is a spectacular four hour drive costing K12. The PMVs cruise town looking for passengers, but there's a PMV station on the main road below the airfield.

LAKE KUTUBU
South of Mendi, Lake Kutubu has some of the Highlands' most beautiful scenery and an excellent lodge. The lake is beautiful, the surrounding country is home to friendly people who still live a largely traditional life. Butterflies and

birds of paradise are common. You can swim in the lake and visit local villages or just soak up the beauty and peace. According to legend the lake was formed when a fig tree was cut down by a woman looking for water. Whatever the tree, its trunk, branches or roots touched, turned to water.

The lodge is an interesting development: it is a local initiative and profits are being channelled into agricultural projects and community services.

One of the initial reasons why the local people built the lodge was to control visitors. They are still quite traditional, and segregation is maintained between the sexes – this segregation, among other things, was undermined by travelling couples who stayed in the villages. (The men's houses are impressive buildings built on stilts that are 150 to 200 metres long.) The lodge means that the people can now more easily accept visitors on their own terms, and maintain their privacy.

If you do visit Lake Kutubu, remember you are a guest of the people and tread carefully – try not to damage this beautiful spot. Do not try and stay in the villages – this would defeat the purpose of the lodge. It is OK to swim in western costume at the lodge, but elsewhere you should swim in a lap-lap. Women should not wear shorts. Ask before you take photos or enter buildings.

As is the case elsewhere in PNG, generosity should be reciprocal. If you accept a gift it is expected you should give something in return. Don't turn the children into beggars by handing out sweets or pencils. If you do want to make a practical gift, talk to the lodge manager – he's bound to have some ideas.

If you want further information, contact Olivier Meric de Bellefon (tel 59 1158), at Mendi, Lake Kutubu Lodge, c/o Menduli Pty Ltd, PO Box 35. Olivier helped set up the guesthouse.

Places to Stay

The *Lake Kutubu Lodge*, on a ridge overlooking the lake, is attractively designed and constructed from bush materials. You have two options: you can stay in the comfortable lodge proper and have full board for K20, or you can stay in a more basic bunk house for K6 and cater for yourself. You can also pay separately for meals: K5 for dinner, K2 lunch and K3 breakfast. The food is good and the quantities are generous. Kutubu's perfect climate means there is never a shortage of fresh fruit and vegetables. There is also a trade store.

The lodge has a motor canoe and they arrange tours to some of the beautiful rivers and waterfalls that run into the lake. The cost depends on how much fuel is used, but will probably be around K15.

Getting There & Away

There are two ways of getting to Kutubu, so you can come and go by different routes. If you have the time and inclination, the ideal solution would be to walk in from Nipa and fly out from Pimaga. Both methods end up costing much the same.

The easy method is to fly from Mendi to Pimaga with MAF (tel 59 1091). They fly Monday to Friday, depending on the weather. It costs K24. There is a lodge at Pimaga (built by Kutubu Enterprises, who also own the Lake Kutubu Lodge) where you can stay for K6 a night and eat for K3 for each meal.

From Pimaga you walk about 22 km on a dirt road to the south-eastern tip of Lake Kutubu and an attractive village called Gesege. This takes four or five hours and a guide isn't necessary. From Gesege you catch a motor canoe to the lodge at Tage Point for K20.

The alternative is a three day walk from Nipa, on the Tari-Mendi road. Go to Nipa and the Tilliba Mission where an American, Vic Slaughter, can recommend guides he has trained, or you can walk three hours to Ungubi where Pastor Tom may also be able to organise a guide. A guide will cost K10 a day and you supply the food. It's an interesting walk that crosses several large rivers and there are specially built bush huts along the way.

TARI

Tari is the main town for the Huli wigmen and the centre for the beautiful Tari Basin. The main attractions are the people and the surrounding countryside, but there's a PNGBC bank, a post office and, of course, an airfield, which is serviced by Air Niugini, Talair and MAF. Saturday is the main market day, but there are smaller markets between Wednesday and Saturday. The superb Ambua Lodge is just off the Highlands Highway, overlooking the Basin, about half an hour from Tari.

A Huli Wigman painting himself

Places to Stay

Perhaps the nearest equivalents to the *Ambua Lodge* would be some of the famous African game park lodges. At 7000 feet the lodge has a superb view of the land of the Huli below and a refreshing mountain climate. The dining/lounge/bar is the kind of place you could relax in for hours, just watching the clouds roll by. There's even an outdoor spa.

Guests are accommodated in individual, luxury, bush-material huts. Every hut has a great 180° view and they are surrounded by flower gardens with a backdrop of mossy forest. It is a little incongruous to find such opulence in such rugged circumstances, but it's certainly impressive. Needless.

Needless to say, it isn't cheap, but they do have some special weekend rates. The price of K125 twin share does include transfers and tours around the valley to visit villages, watch birds of paradise (10 species are found in the vicinity of the lodge) and so on, but its still pricey for real people.

If the price is a worry, you can get a taste of all this a lot cheaper. There's a very basic bush hut for K5 per person per night, and you can buy your meals or use the bar after 8.30 pm. They show a *First Contact* video every night. There are also some pleasant walks that have been put in through the forest to a couple of nearby waterfalls. Ambua is operated by Trans Niugini (tel 52 1438), PO Box 371, Mt Hagen, who also run the Karawari and Bensbach lodges.

A little more down to earth, the *Tari Guest House* (tel 50 8017), PO Box 12 – sometimes also known as the Huli Traders Guest House – is not far from the airport and charges K12 per person. There are hot showers and cooking facilities and the people who run it can give you some good tips about things to do in the valley. There is also a *Catholic Church Hostel* (tel 50 8092), PO Box 14, that charges K10/15 for singles/doubles.

Getting There & Away

Air Air Niugini and Talair fly to Moresby for K128. Talair flies to Mt Hagen (K59), Kopiago (K34) and from Amboin (Karawari, near the Sepik). Many points through this and other more remote regions are serviced by MAF, including April River for around K55.

PMV PMVs to Tari from Mendi cost K12 and take four hours. PMVs also run from Tari to Koroba. Beyond this, most transportation is by plane or foot, although the road is being pushed through to Lake Kopiago. At present traffic tends to be light.

KOPIAGO TO OKSAPMIN

From Lake Kopiago, you can walk to Oksapmin in the West Sepik Province in four or five days. This is a very hard and potentially dangerous walk, so don't undertake it unless you are pretty fit. The walk passes through the spectacular Strickland Gorge, a staggeringly rugged and awe inspiring stretch of country – so it's worth the effort. The tracks are very steep and slippery, even in the dry season, which is definitely the best time to walk. Guides are essential; expect to pay them around K5 per day.

There's a Uniting Church Mission Guesthouse at Kopiago about 30 minutes from the town. On the first day, you walk six to eight hours from Kopiago to Kaiguena where there is a small guesthouse for K2. Day two takes you on a hard eight to 10 hours' walk from Kaiguena through beautiful rain forest to Yokona where there is a haus kiap. On day three you can either walk from Yokona to Gawa in one very hard 10 or 12 hour day or break the walk by camping at the Strickland River.

It's a steep and dangerous three hours down the Strickland Gorge to a bridge across the river. You can camp in a cave near the bridge. The next stretch is to Gawa where there is a small hut you can use. It's a steep, unshaded, uphill walk

A Huli Warrior, Tari

that takes six or eight hours. If you overnight at the river you can start early in the morning and avoid the worst of the heat. The last day's walk is a reasonably easy three hours to Oksapmin. There's an Agricultural Centre at Oksapmin run by the Peace Corp and there are plans for a guesthouse: expect to pay around K5.

If you are really keen, you can continue walking to Tekin, Bak, Bimin and down to Olsobib in the Western Province, or to Telefomin. Talair flies from Oksapmin to Green River on the Upper Sepik for K73, to Telefomin for K33 and to Vanimo for K109. See the Sepik chapter for more information on Oksapmin and Telefomin.

Enga Province

Area 10,790 square km
Population 190,000

Beyond Mt Hagen to the north-west the roads deteriorate and the country is less developed although, as elsewhere in the Highlands, coffee is an important local industry. This situation is changing, especially with the development of the giant gold and silver mine at Porgera in the west. When it becomes fully operational in the early 1990s Porgera will be the largest gold mine outside South Africa.

Even in the '60s much of this region was still virtually independent from government control, and it was a part of the Western Province until 1973. Control may have arrived, but tribal warfare can still occur. You may occasionally see circular, fenced areas filled with green and purple tanget bushes. These are the burial places of victims of tribal fighting.

Wabag is the provincial capital but, it is still more an outlying town to Hagen than a major centre in its own right. The province is made up of rugged mountains and high valleys and the main rivers are the Lai and the Lagaip. The people are fragmented into small clans, but the Enga language-group covers most of the province; some tribes have close similarities with the people of the Southern Highlands.

WABAG

From Mt Hagen the Wabag road starts out in the same direction as the Mendi road, then branches off north-west. It climbs over the Kaugel Pass, which is nearly 3000 metres high, before Wapenamanda.

Wabag has a large cultural centre in the valley that cuts the town in two. It's open from 9 am to 4 pm on weekdays and has an art gallery and museum. The gallery has a workshop where you can see young artists making 'sand paintings', the principal artwork on display in the gallery. Different coloured sands are mixed with glue and applied to a hard surface, usually plasterboard, with striking visual effect. The adjacent museum has a large number of war shields, wigs and masks from many parts of PNG as well as Enga Province.

Places to Stay

Although it's not in Wabag itself, the *Kaiap Orchid Lodge* (tel 52 2087), PO Box 193, is not far away, and it is recommended. About 2700 metres above sea level, it is built from local bush materials and is surrounded by gardens, with more than 100 species of orchids and 13 species of rhododendron. There are walks you can do in the local area and, with luck, you may well see birds of paradise.

It's a friendly informal place with a bar, lounge, a log fire and good food. It is also very good value – accommodation is K13, dinner is K7 and lunch and breakfast are K5 each. They also arrange good-value Highland treks.

To get there, take a PMV from outside the Christian Bookshop in Mt Hagen to Wabag. You can then either ring the Lodge and get picked up or you can catch another PMV to Sari Village, a couple of km from town, along the road to Laiagam. From there it's a tough but pleasant 1½ to two hour walk on the road up to the mountain ridge. The road crosses the Lai River, passes gardens and houses and there are good views along the climb to the mountain ridge.

The *Wabag Lodge* (tel 57 1069), PO Box 2, has 14 rooms, in Polynesian roundhouse style, and will arrange tours out of Wabag. Singles/doubles are K27/37. The *Malya Hostel* (tel 57 1108), PO Box 237, is out of town on the road to Mt Hagen and is run by the provincial government. Singles/doubles are K12/30 and meals are available at a reasonable price.

Getting There & Away A PMV from Mt Hagen to Wabag costs K4, Laiagam to Kandep is K3. The scenery on the three to four hour trip from Hagen to Wabag is magnificent, but the road is brutal. The road crosses one river nine times and another river, the Lai, three times. The Lai eventually joins the Sepik. The road to Porgera has been upgraded for gold-mine traffic and is now good.

AROUND WABAG
Wabag to Mendi

If you have a sturdy four-wheel drive you can continue beyond Wabag to Laiagam and down to Mendi. It's hard going and the road from Laiagam to Mendi is often closed between Kandep and Mendi due to poor road conditions and washed away bridges. If it is closed, you have an interesting 54 km walk along the highest road in PNG ahead of you. It may be possible to stay at the mission about half-way along the road at Pingerip.

Laiagam

Laiagam has the National Botanical Garden with a huge collection of orchids.

Kandep to Margarima

There's a road from Kandep to Margarima, about half way between Mendi and Tari. It runs through magnificent scenery with extensive marshes and high mountains, inhabited by many relatively isolated people. The road is often washed out so transport can be hard to find. You'll probably have to walk.

Lake Rau

Lake Rau is a crater lake at nearly 3000 metres in the centre of Enga Province. It's a day's walk from Pumas, above Laiagam and you will need a guide.

Madang

Area 27,970 square km
Population 240,000

Madang Province consists of a fertile coastal strip backed by some of the most rugged mountains in New Guinea – the Adelbert and Schrader Ranges to the north and the Finisterre Range to the south. Offshore are a string of interesting, and still active, volcanic islands. More or less in the middle of the coastal stretch stands Madang – quite possibly the most beautiful town in the whole country, even, some claim, in the whole Pacific.

HISTORY

The Russian biologist Nicolai Miklouho-Maclay was probably the first European to spend any length of time on the mainland of PNG. He arrived on Astrolabe Bay, south of the present site of Madang, in 1871 and settled in for a 15 month stay before leaving to regain his health, which was badly affected by malaria. His interest in New Guinea led to two further, equally lonely visits.

Unlike many explorers who followed him, his relations with the local tribes were remarkably good and his studies still make fascinating reading. He was suitably amazed by the large, two-masted, sailing canoes of the Madang people and named the islands in Madang Harbour the 'Archipelago of Contented Men'. It is thought the name of this stretch of coast, the Rai Coast, is a derivation of his name Maclay.

The German New Guinea Kompagnie turned up 13 years later, but their stay, although longer, was rather less successful. As Maclay had found to his cost, the northern New Guinea coast was unhealthy and rife with malaria and the disease followed the Germans as they moved first from Finschhafen to Bogadjim on Astrolabe Bay and then on to Madang. If malaria didn't get them then Blackwater Fever usually did.

From 1884 to 1899 a total of 224 officials worked for the company, of whom 41 died and 133 either resigned or were dismissed. Gavin Souter's book *The Last Unknown* depressingly describes the sheer misery of working for 'the bloody bone' as the company became known.

On the point of failure, the German Government took over and moved to the healthier climate of Kokopo near Rabaul on New Britain, but the coast still has many German names and mission stations, although gravestones are almost the only reminders of the old company.

In WW II the Japanese soon took Madang, but after the recapture of Lae, Australian troops slowly and painfully pushed the Japanese along the coast to their final defeat at Wewak. The bitter fighting for control of 'Shaggy Ridge' and the route over the Finisterre Range to Madang, started in late '43 and it took a full month to push the Japanese down to the coast and on towards Wewak.

Madang was virtually demolished during the war and had to be totally rebuilt. Even the old German cemetery bears scars from the vicious fighting. Madang's importance as a major north coast port, from where freight was flown up to the Highlands, was drastically changed when the Highlands Highway shifted business to Lae.

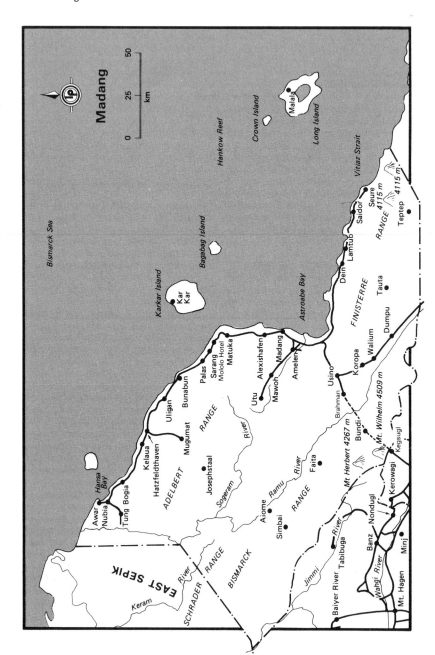

Timber cutting development has since rejuvenated the town which is also an important ship building and repair centre. Madang is now linked to the Highlands by road, but the road is still not sealed and can be cut by floods. The long projected, but still distant, direct road to Kundiawa in Simbu Province will have to be built before Madang is conveniently 'on-line' to the Highlands.

GEOGRAPHY

The Madang area is composed of strips of lowland and mountain. Along the fertile coast, coconuts and cocoa have been grown since the German days. Inland, mountain ranges rise parallel to the coast then slope down to the Ramu River valley which also parallels the coast. This is productive cattle country and home to the Ramu Sugar Refinery, which meets almost all of PNG's sugar requirements. Only a low divide separates the Upper Ramu from the Markham Valley, in which the Highland Highway runs to Lae.

Inland from the Ramu, the Bismarck and Schrader Ranges rise to the highest peaks in the country, including Mt Wilhelm which stands on the border with Simbu Province. The volcanic islands off the Madang coast are still periodically active.

PEOPLE

The diverse geographic nature of the Madang Province is reflected in the make-up of its people who can, by virtue of lifestyle, be broken into four distinct groups: islanders, coastal people, river people and mountain people. These groups are alike in physical appearance, apart from the small-statured Simbai tribes who inhabit the foothills of the Highlands.

Traditional dress is rarely worn, but the majority of people still live in villages and at a subsistence level. The coconut is used extensively, except in the mountains. Islanders depend on seafood; the coastal people grow a variety of different root crops, bananas and tropical fruits; the river people's staple is sago; and the mountain people base their diet on the sweet potato, although this is now supplemented by many western vegetables.

The Manam islanders live around the base of a volcano and their society is dominated by a hereditary chief, known as the *Kukurai*. Although there are different language groups, the Manam clans are related to the people who live along the lower sections of the Ramu River, the north coast of the province and the lower Sepik. The artefacts produced on Manam are not unlike those produced on the Sepik.

There are even closer artistic links between the Ramu and the Sepik. The mighty Ramu is almost linked to the Keram, and thence to the Sepik, so there was probably extensive trade and cultural interchange for thousands of years. The way of life is similar, and the Ramu people are also great wood carvers.

The nearby coastal villagers of Yabob and Bilbil are famous for the earthenware pots they make and, like the Motuans of the Port Moresby district, they once traded these items far up and down the coast in large trading vessels known as *lalaoika*. Their attractive houses are made from sago and toddy palms, usually without nails. The walls and fold-out windows are made from sago palm leaf stems tied into frames and panels with sago palm leaves, either intertwined or sewn into long shingles.

Madang

The title of 'prettiest town in the Pacific' may not be an official one, but it is often applied to Madang and many people think it's justified. The town of 20,000 is perched on a peninsula jutting out into the sea and is liberally sprinkled with parks, ponds and waterways.

The warm, wet climate and fertile soil lead to luxuriant growth and many of the huge shade trees, planted by the Germans, survived the war and still tower over Madang's gently curving roads. A scatter of perfect islands around the town's deep-water harbour completes the picture.

Madang is the most tourist-oriented city in PNG and this, fortunately, translates into a wide range of facilities but falls short of being overwhelmingly plastic. It is not, however, the place to come if you want to see untouched local cultures. By far the greatest attraction is what lies beneath the surface of the sea. It is also possible to find some excellent places beside the sea, and these are not necessarily five-star hotels.

Until recently Madang seemed to be immune from rascal problems – people fondly imagined that it was just too beautiful for such things! Although there is nothing like the unfortunate atmosphere in Lae, and houses are not fortresses in disguise, it is now wise to be a little cautious. Madang is relaxed and easy going, but women should not wander off alone, and western swimming costumes should be worn with discretion.

Orientation

Madang is built on a peninsular; on the south-eastern side, Coronation Drive faces across Astrolabe Bay to the beautiful Finisterre Ranges and on the north-western side, the town faces across the still waters of Binnen and Madang Harbours to the airport and the palm-lined coast.

The main shopping area is to the right at the end of Modilon Rd, the main road that runs the full length of the peninsula. Unfortunately the airport is at least seven km from the main area of town (you have to cross the Wagol River and skirt Binnen Harbour) and is too far away to walk. See the Getting There & Away section.

Information

The Madang Visitors Bureau (tel 82 3199), PO Box 2025, Jomba, is on Modilon Rd, just near the intersection with Coronation Drive. They produce a rather limited range of information on the province, but they will definitely be able to help you out if you have any queries. The Bureau adjoins a small museum, which is worth a visit (see the following section).

The shopping in Madang is not as extensive as in Lae, but you'll have no problems with essentials. There's a post office, banks and Air Niugini, Talair and Lutheran Shipping all have offices here.

Museum & Cultural Centre

The Museum adjoins the Madang Visitors bureau. Although it is rather small and the range of exhibits is limited there are some interesting items. There are statues, shields, spears, jewellery and musical instruments from the period of German occupation, and there are examples of contemporary carvings and paintings.

The most interesting exhibits are the models of traditional local boats. The *lalaoika*, a one-mast canoe, and the *balangut*, a two-mast canoe, are beautiful vessels. They were used in trading fish and pottery along the coast. *Lalaoika* were once made at Bilbil Village but they became obsolete with the arrival of roads, PMVs and outboard motors. One was built in 1977 for a royal visit, but it has since rotted away.

The museum is on Modilon Rd, very near Smugglers' Inn. It's open Monday to Friday from 8 am to 12 noon and 1 to 4 pm. Admission is by donation.

Cemetery

In the centre of town, right behind the market, is the old German cemetery. Madang was the New Guinea Kompagnie's last attempt at a foothold on the mainland before they packed it in and moved to New Britain. The malaria in Madang was extremely virulent and this rather bleak little cemetery attests to that fact.

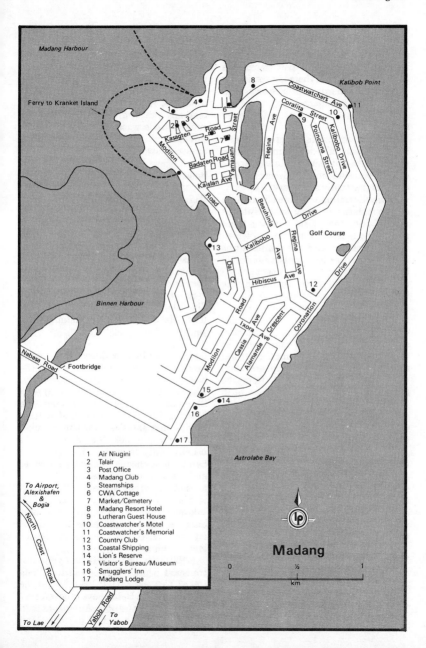

Madang Harbour

Ferry to Kranket Island

Kalibob Point

Coastwatchers Ave

Coralita Street

Regina Ave

Poinciana Street

Kalibobo Drive

Kasagten Road

Street

Tamauani

Modilon

Badaten Road

Kaislan Ave

Road

Beauhinia Drive

Golf Course

Kalibobo Road

Dal Cr

Hibiscus Ave

Regina Ave

Ave

Binnen Harbour

Ixora Ave

Crescent

Coronation Drive

Nabasa Road

Footbridge

Modilon Road

Cassia Ave

Alamanda Ave

To Airport,
Alexishafen
&
Bogia

North Coast Road

Astrolabe Bay

To Lae

Yabob Road

To Yabob

1	Air Niugini
2	Talair
3	Post Office
4	Madang Club
5	Steamships
6	CWA Cottage
7	Market/Cemetery
8	Madang Resort Hotel
9	Lutheran Guest House
10	Coastwatcher's Motel
11	Coastwatcher's Memorial
12	Country Club
13	Coastal Shipping
14	Lion's Reserve
15	Visitor's Bureau/Museum
16	Smugglers' Inn
17	Madang Lodge

Madang

0   ½   1

km

Market

Behind the cemetery is Madang's colourful and popular market which is at its busy best on Saturdays. Apart from the vegetables and fruit, there is a section for handicrafts and artefacts. The local shell jewellery can be a bargain.

Parks

Madang has some delightful park ponds – one of them liberally decked in water lilies – but all with ominous signs to warn you of crocodiles. However, nobody can seem to remember actually seeing one.

When the Germans decided, in 1904, to attack malaria by filling in the swamps around the town, thus creating these ponds, the locals did not take to forced labour. A plot against the Germans was stifled by the drastic action of rounding up the ringleaders and shooting them. They were buried on Siar Island in the harbour.

Coastwatcher's Memorial

This 30 metre high beacon is visible 25 km out to sea, a reminder of those men who stayed behind the lines during the last war to report on Japanese troop and ship movements. The coast road from the memorial is one of the most pleasant in Madang, fringed by palm trees and poincianas and backed by the golf course with fine views across Astrolabe Bay towards the Rai Coast.

Lion's Reserve Beach

Just north of the Smugglers' Inn, this small beach has excellent coral and tropical fish just a few strokes from the shore. It's not so good at low tide, however, when sea urchins and sharp coral wait for the unwary foot.

Things to Do

You can get out on Madang's exceptionally beautiful harbour by yourself using local boats, or with a cruise operated by Melanesian Tours (Madang Resort Hotel) or Jais Aben Resort.

Two islands that are commonly visited are Kranket and Siar; both are easily accessible for day trips. See the Around Madang section for more information; it's possible to stay cheaply on both these islands. This is a must for budget travellers. Wherever you stay, you must take advantage of the harbour and the superb underwater scenery, whether through glass viewing boxes, snorkelling or skin diving.

Harbour Tour The Madang Resort's tour departs every morning at 9 am and costs K17.50. You get picked up from your hotel and taken to see the rusting wreckage of Japanese landing craft, Kranket Island where you can view the fish and coral formations through glass bottomed viewing boxes and Siar Island where you get a chance to wander around or snorkel for an hour or so.

Smith Kinan, who runs a guesthouse on Siar Island, also does harbour tours for K10. Make sure you understand what you're getting.

Do-it-yourself Harbour Cruises If you want to organise your own voyage around the harbour you can do it easily and cheaply. Wander down behind the Lutheran Shipping office, or just behind the Madang Club, and you'll find a ferry service that shuttles across to Kranket Island for just 30t. It's irregular, but usually fairly frequent, and you could hardly do it cheaper. Sundays are quiet and the boat makes fewer trips.

Another method is to take a PMV round to Siar Village for 40t, then negotiate a ride across to Siar Island. It's only a short distance, but they still charge K1 and will try for more. You can also find canoes for longer cruises.

A third alternative is to rent your own transport. The Diving Specialists of PNG (tel 82 2707, ext 287), PO Box 337, at the Madang Resort Hotel, have canoes for K7 a half day, K14 a full day. Afternoons tend to get windy, stirring up waves and making it hard to paddle, but this is a great way to get around. Definitely take a T-shirt and suntan lotion: you can really fry out there! They have Hobie Cats and windsurfers too. Smith Kinan and Saimon Tewa also hire canoes for around K5.

Rooke's Marine Repairs (tel 82 2325), PO Box 427, rent a larger motor cruiser that would be suitable for sport fishing and longer trips, and the Madang Marine Centre (tel 82 2252), PO Box 8, has a six berth houseboat for hire at K34 per head.

Swimming Apart from Lion's Reserve, there are several spots along Coastwatcher's Drive and also at the inlet by the CWA Cottage. Other favourite spots are Siar Island, Kranket Lagoon, Pig Island (an exceptionally beautiful little island, despite the name) and Wongat Island.

Snorkelling & Diving The snorkelling and diving are excellent, and the area is justifiably world famous. There is excellent visibility, superb coral, and if you're diving, many WW II wrecks.

You can hire gear from Diving Specialists of PNG (tel 82 2707, ext 287), PO Box 337, at the Madang Resort Hotel. Snorkel gear is K5 and for K10 they'll take you along with divers, perhaps dropping you off at beautiful Pig Island. Skin diving gear is K10 per day and two dives (you don't have to do them both in the same day) are K40. There is a wide range of different dive locations within 15 minutes of Madang. Courses are also available. Highly recommended.

Diving Specialists also organise trips to Hansa Bay, a beautiful spot 220 km north of Madang, within sight of the frequently active volcano on Manam Island and where there are some superb wreck dives. They accommodate people in an attractive, bush-material guesthouse. Non-divers can go along for K60 all inclusive per day. See the following section on the North Coast Highway.

If you are just snorkelling, have a word to them about possible locations. There are even corals and fish just off from the dive shop itself. Other good places are Lion's Reserve, Siar Island, the reef in Kranket Lagoon, Pig Island and around Sinaub Island. If you take a dugout out from Siar or Kranket to dive further from shore never do it alone. There are very strong currents in some places and the boat could easily drift away, leaving you stranded.

Smith Kinan, on Siar, will hire snorkelling gear for K3, as will the caretaker on Kranket, for K2. Apparently, you can miss out on equipment at Siar, so you're probably best to rent in Madang.

A short drive north of Madang, the Jais Aben Resort (tel 82 3311) specialises in diving. If you have a meal you can use their facilities, including their swimming pool. They hire small boats for K25 per day and snorkelling gear for K3. They organise a harbour cruise and village tour and have windsurfers. It's an interesting place that combines tourism and diving with serious marine research. See the North Coast Highway section.

Places to Stay - bottom end
There are some good choices in Madang but the best is the *Lutheran Guest House* (tel 82 2589), PO Box 211, on Coralita St, about midway between the Madang Resort Hotel and the Coastwatcher's Motel. It's friendly, clean and the rooms all have their own fans and bathrooms. It can get busy on weekends so it's worth booking ahead; solo travellers may be asked to share a room. Accommodation is K12, lunch is K3, dinner is K4. The guesthouse also rents a car for 40t a km; this is good value and feasible if you can get a group together.

Smugglers' Inn (see the top end section) is not only one of the country's top hotels, but it also offers a reasonable bargain. They've taken out the air-conditioners in one of the older wings (leaving the shower, toilet, fridge, the view of Astrolabe Bay and the use of the swimming pool) and are offering the rooms for just K30 for singles (hmmm), K40 per double (better) and K50 per triple (not bad). For a good view, ask for room eight or nine.

The *CWA Cottage* (tel 82 2216), PO Box 154, is still popular with travellers, but it's not great value at K14.70 per night. It's between the Madang Club and the Madang Resort Hotel, close to the town centre. There are just four rooms and booking ahead is not a bad idea. The friendly woman who runs the place is only there from 8 am to 12 noon, so call then to book. If she's not there try phoning 82 2188 (before 8 pm). No meals are served, but there are good kitchen facilities available. Budget travellers will find a useful notice board.

The *Madang Lodge* (tel 82 3395), PO Box 969, is a little characterless, but it is clean, comfortable and reasonable value. A notch above most of the bottom end accommodation, it's still fairly spartan. It's on the coast on Modilon Rd not far from Smugglers' Inn. There's a rocky little cove where you can swim and snorkel. Rates, including breakfast, are K24/28 for singles/doubles, lunch is K4.50 and a three course dinner is K9. They also hire out 10-speed bicycles for K6 per day, which would be great for visiting some of the local villages. They do airport transfers for K2.

Madang also has a *Lutheran Hostel* on Dal Crescent, but it is usually reserved for local people only and it is very grubby. A bed is K2 or you can camp on the lawn, but either way you can't lock up your stuff.

There are two other alternatives: Siar Island and Kranket Island. Siar has two competing village guesthouses and Kranket has self-catering lodges. The conditions at Siar are not luxurious, but the cost is low, you get a close-up view of village life and a chance to laze in the sun and snorkel – for many this is a highlight of their PNG trip. See the Around Madang section.

Places to Stay – top end

The *Smugglers' Inn* (tel 82 2744), PO Box 303, has long had a reputation as one of PNG's top hotels – certainly it would be hard to beat its delightful setting. Built on the waterfront on Modilon Rd, the open air restaurant offers superb coastal views and breezes and an outdoor bar area juts out into the water. There's a swimming pool or you can snorkel at the Lion's Reserve beach only 50 metres away.

There are 50 rooms in four categories. The most costly have sea views, but they all have private facilities. Singles run K30 to K70, doubles K40 to K80. Dinners are about K10 for main courses – a favourite dish is the seafood platter served in a huge shell and costing K25 for two. You can also get a hamburger with French fries and salad for K3.50.

The *Madang Resort Hotel* (tel 82 2655), PO Box 111, has a setting virtually as good as Smugglers'. The competition between the two hotels is keen, and it would take a brave person to declare a winner. The Madang also has a swimming pool and a haus win (open air restaurant) right by the water. The rooms range from K35 to K115 for singles, K45 to K125 for doubles. What you get is what you pay for: the top end is luxury, self-contained waterfront bungalows; the bottom end (which is not too bad at all) is a motel-type room with a TV and coffee-making facilities.

The grounds are really quite superb and include the Elizabeth Sowerby Orchid Collection and cages with cuscus, hornbills, cockatoos and other wildlife. Diving Specialists of PNG have their shop by the water, and there's a jetty for the *Melanesian Explorer* which journeys to the Sepik and around Milne Bay.

Breakfasts are K4.50 and lunches are K1.50 to K3. The food at dinner is of the high standard you would expect with main courses around K12. On Sundays there's a barbecue lunch for K8 with a self-serve salad bar.

The *Coastwatcher's Motel* (tel 82 2684), PO Box 324, is on Coastwatcher's Avenue, near the Coastwatcher's Memorial. It is a smaller, more modest hotel/motel with just 14 family-sized rooms. All rooms are air-conditioned, have fridges, TVs and telephones and there's also a swimming pool. Rooms cost K44/51 for singles/doubles, including breakfast, which is very reasonable for PNG. The restaurant offers good-value counter lunches for around K3 and dinners for K10 – their Chinese steamboat is recommended. The bar is a friendly spot for a cold beer and can get quite lively in the evenings. There's a happy hour at 5.30 pm on Wednesdays and Fridays.

The *Jais Aben Resort* is a luxury resort, strongly oriented to diving. It is about 14 km from Madang just north of Nagada Harbour. See the North Coast Highway section.

Those with sea legs should consider hiring a six-berth houseboat from *Madang Marine Centre* (tel 82 2252), PO Box 8, for K34 per head.

Places to Eat

Consider spoiling yourself with a meal at the Smugglers' Inn or Madang Resort Hotel haus wins – they're not cheap, but it is quite magical sitting out by the water on a balmy tropical night eating good food.

Apart from the hotels and hostels, the Madang Club's *Tipsy Fish Restaurant* offers plain food at reasonable prices. It's officially 'members only', but someone will be glad to sign you in. Everything is under K5, lunch is from 12 noon to 2 pm, dinner from 6.30 to 8 pm. The Club is a popular spot for an evening drink. It's next door to the CWA Cottage with a nice view over the harbour. You can still see some old German steps nearby.

At the *Country Club* (read golf club), along Coastwatcher's Ave, you can get cheap meals from Tuesday to Saturday and snacks like pies and sandwiches. You have to be signed in. It opens from 4 pm Monday to Friday and 12 noon on Saturday and Sunday. There is also a bar, of course.

Steamships and *Burns Philp* both have the usual lunchtime sandwiches and milkshakes, but BP have the superior range.

Things to Buy

The clay pots from Yabob and Bilbil villages are the most interesting traditional local items. If you buy them, make sure they are very carefully packed as, like other PNG pottery, they are extremely fragile.

There are thriving artefacts workshops and marketplaces at Smugglers' Inn and the Madang Resort Hotel, mostly dominated by women from the Sepik and the Ramu. There are excellent selections of bilums, shell jewellery and carvings. Don't rush into your purchases, and remember there is a 'second price'.

Getting There & Away

Air The airport is about seven km from town, which is too far to walk unless you are very keen. During the day you will be able to pick up a PMV on the North Coast Rd for around 30t, but if you get in after dusk you'll be dependent on taxis (tel 82 3319). A taxi should cost around K2.50, but there are stories of the unwary paying many times more. Make sure you fix the price before you get in. All the big hotels pick up and drop off passengers, so you may be able to get a lift with them, or a local, if you're lucky.

Air Niugini is at the airport (tel 82 2255) and Talair (tel 82 2757) has an office in town. There is talk of another international airport opening in PNG and there is a very strong lobby for Madang. Currently, there are flights from Port Moresby (K108), Lae (K62), Mt Hagen (K56) and Wewak (K75). Talair flies from Goroka for (K45) and to a few smaller places like Bundi (on the way to Mt Wilhelm, K39), Saidor (east along the coast, K32) and Karkar Island (K30).

The flight from Goroka is very brief and quite interesting as you climb up and over the southern fringe of the Highlands, then over the Ramu Valley and drop down to the coast. Flying to or from Wewak, you can see the mouths of the Ramu and Sepik Rivers as they meander and loop to the coast, joined by many tributaries.

Road Madang is linked to the Highlands Highway by the Ramu Highway which is unsealed and can be closed by floods (see To/From Highlands) and roads run in both directions along the coast. The North Coast Highway runs nearly 250 km to the west, virtually to the mouth of the Ramu River and east to Saidor.

There are PMVs on all these routes. Heading northwest, Bogia, near the end of the North Coast Highway, is K5, Malolo is K1.50 to K2, Alexishafen is 70t, Riwo/Jais Aben is 60t and Siar Village is 40t. Heading south, Yabob Village is 30t, Bilbil Village is 40t and Ramu is K7. PMVs all leave from the vicinity of the market; Bogia PMVs leave from the oval area under the big fig tree. Trucks are still sometimes used on the north coast route.

Sea Madang is on the main north coast shipping route that is so well serviced by Lutheran Shipping (tel 82 2577), PO Box 789, on Modilon Rd. Poroman Shipping (tel 82 2636), PO Box 486, also has some interesting, though irregular voyages, and there are boat connections with Manam and Karkar Islands. Every couple of weeks the Manus Provincial Government has a boat, the MV *Tawi*, to Lorengau.

Once again, the most important option is Lutheran Shipping's *Mamose Express*. On its eastward bound schedule it arrives in Madang at 6 am Sunday and leaves for Lae at 7 pm, so even if you go straight through you get a day to sample Madang. Westward bound, you arrive in Madang at 6 am on Thursday and leave at 7 pm Friday, so you get two days in Madang, which is enough time to have a good look around. Fares are: Madang-Lae, K18/12, tourist/deck; Madang-Wewak, K27/18, tourist/deck. Straight through from Wewak to Lae is K45/30, but this includes

overnight accommodation, with harbour views, in Madang!

Lutheran Shipping has a number of considerably less comfortable freighters that also call in to Madang, including the MV *Umboi* and MV *Nagada* which go through to Vanimo from Lae.

Poroman Shipping is just off Modilon Rd, before town and they have two boats: the MV *Deaniel* and the MV *Doilon*. Do not expect any luxuries – these are small working freighters. They sail irregularly to Manus for K14, to Karkar for K7 and up the Sepik. See the River section.

There's a regular speedboat trip out to Karkar on a vessel called the *Trimanta*. It leaves Madang at 8 am Monday to Friday and at 9 am on Saturday. It costs K13 and takes 1½ hours.

The Manus Provincial Government Shipping Officer (tel 40 9088), PO Box 111, operates the MV *Tawi* to Lorengau, but it's an irregular service, departing roughly once a month.

River Poroman Shipping makes trips up the Sepik River as far as Green River for K40 (6 days); to Ambunte is K25. There are local motorised dugouts on the Ramu River, which very nearly joins the Keram, which joins the Sepik near Angoram.

To/From Highlands The Ramu Highway joins the Highlands Highway at Watarai, and while the Ramu Highway is now quite OK, it can still be closed by floods. See the Highlands chapter for details on the Highlands Highway. PMVs leave from the Madang Market.

There are direct PMVs to Lae or Goroka for around K12, although you may have to change PMVs at Watarais if you're going to the Highlands, since there are fewer PMVs to Goroka. You should get to Watarai for K8 and to Goroka from Watarai for another K4 or so.

It's an interesting drive to Watarais, passing through many isolated villages, past beautiful mountain and jungle scenery. There are still some unbridged

Top: Saturday morning market, Madang (ML)
Bottom: Spear fishing, Kranket Island lagoon, near Madang (RE)

Top: Coastal view from Nobanob lookout, north of Madang (ML)
Bottom: Siar Island, near Madang (RE)

rivers to be forded. You also pass Ramu Sugar, where accommodation is available, and Usino, where you may be able to find shoestring accommodation (see the Inland section).

It is possible to walk from Brahmin Mission via Bundi (Talair flies there for K39) to Kegsugl, at the foot of Mt Wilhelm, where you can catch a PMV to Kundiawa in Simbu Province. This would probably take a minimum of four or five days. See the Walking to Madang section under Simbu Province in the Highlands chapter.

To/From Wewak There are daily 40 minute flights with Air Niugini to Wewak for K75. Travelling on the *Mamose Express*, you leave Madang at 7 pm on Friday evening and arrive in Wewak at 10 am on Saturday morning. Fares are K27/18 for tourist/deck class.

To/From Lae See the To/From Madang section in the Lae & Morobe chapter.

Getting Around

There are frequent PMVs around Madang with a standard 30t fare in town. There are also plenty going further out at pleasantly low fares. See the Getting There & Away section. The market is the PMV hub.

Kubai Taxis can be phoned on 82 3319, and they run 24 hours Monday to Saturday; K1 will get you to most places in town; K2.50 should get you to the airport.

Avis Rent-a-Car has a desk at the airport and at the Madang Resort Hotel (tel 82 2804) and Budget operates from Smugglers Inn (tel 82 3044). Lastly, the Lutheran Guest House (tel 82 2589) rents a car for 40t a km.

One thing you can do in Madang, which you may wish was possible in many other PNG towns, is hire a bicycle. The Madang Lodge (tel 82 3395) hires 10-speed bikes for K6. They're good for a jaunt out to Yabob Village or even further.

Around Madang

SIAR ISLAND

Siar Island is a popular spot for picnics, barbecues and snorkelling, and it's just a short boat ride from town. On the beach you can see some large chunks of aircraft wreckage and the totally rotted remains of a Japanese barge. With a fellow amateur aircraft expert we decided it was American, WW II of course, twin-engined, possibly a B-25 or a P-38. Any answers?

Somewhere on the island are the graves of those unfortunate victims of the anti-swamp-filling conspiracy. There are reefs on both sides of the island.

The most exciting thing about Siar is the possibility of cheap and interesting accommodation, which allows you to make the most of the beach and reefs and learn something about village life.

Places to Stay

Two local people have set up simple, basic accommodation for budget travellers. The conditions are not luxurious, but they are adequate – even families stay. For many people this is a highlight of their PNG trip.

The men who run these two places are serious, even bitter, rivals in the competition to attract foreign shoestringers. *Saimon Tewa* (tel 82 2885), PO Box 887 or contactable through the Madang Club, PO Box 2, is the originator and takes credit for the enterprise. His is the better known place because it has been going for quite a while. It has the nicer beach and the facilities are OK. Unfortunately, Saimon has a somewhat a disreputable reputation, but he has his defenders as well as his detractors. Accommodation is in a bush-material dormitory house. Saimon picks up people from the Madang Club for K1, or you can get across from Siar Village (40t by PMV) for around K1.

Smith Kinan PO Box 792, Madang,

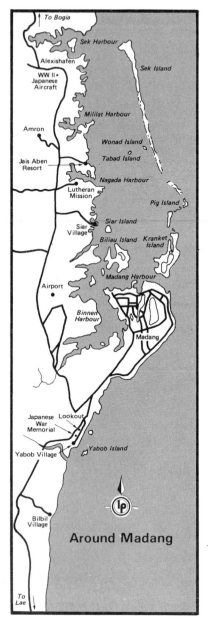

Around Madang

the upstart, has a place further up the island in his family's compound area. Smith and family are more reserved, perhaps even shy, and pretty much leave you alone unless you make the effort. There are three twin rooms in one traditional palm roof, woven-leaf-walled, bamboo-floored house. Beware the pet hornbill, Tommy, who collects anything left lying around – you can usually repossess your belongings at the base of his breadfruit tree. Smith will pick you up from the airport if you write ahead.

Both places cost K6 (plus 25t bed tax) a night including breakfast and a dinner of local food. The fare is simple but good, especially if you get rice cooked with coconut milk, but it's worth bringing some of your own food for lunch or to supplement what can be a limited menu (rice and tinned fish).

You can *usually* rent a mask and snorkel although you're taking a chance on quality and availability – renting in Madang is a safer bet. Smith rents canoes for K5, and I imagine Saimon probably does too . . . .

Getting There & Away

Saimon drops in to the Madang Club almost daily to see if anyone wants to go to Siar. Smith does the same, but at the CWA and the Lutheran Guest House. They'll charge a kina to take you out – a nice trip.

Alternatively you can take a PMV to Siar Village for 40t, and catch a boat for the short ride from there. Saimon's contact in the village is Komian Kuneng (dugout) or Tabb Tamlong (outboard). Smith's contact is Paul Muz and he charges K1. To get to the Jais Aben Resort for diving or a meal costs around K2.

KRANKET ISLAND

Kranket is a much larger island than Siar with several villages, and an absolutely beautiful lagoon. Once you're on Kranket you can wander around, swim, snorkel, or find somebody to take you further out on an outrigger canoe. It's a short hop to the island across the harbour and there are two excellent accommodation options.

About a 45 minute walk from where the ferry lands, on the eastern side of the lagoon, there's an immaculately cared for picnic area, with mown lawns and swept paths. It's private land, owned and cared for by the Dum (pronounced 'doum') Clan and they charge K1 to use the facilities. The caretaker also hires snorkelling gear for K2; the lagoon is good.

Places to Stay
The Dum Clan also operates the lodges and hostel, which adjoin the picnic area. The cheapest option is the *Hostel*, a large bush-material house with four or five bedrooms, a pleasant, shady lounge and a kitchen with a gas stove and refrigerator. This costs the princely sum of K5 for adults, K2 for children. You supply food and cutlery.

Kranket Island Lodge consists of two well-built, traditional-style bungalows, both with private bathrooms, septic toilet systems, running water, gas stoves, kerosene fridges and hot and cold water. Each has a dining room, a bedroom with four or five beds, plus a large, furnished lounge room overlooking the water. The all up cost is K60 per night – and you really get all the comforts of home. You can book through the Madang Resort Hotel (tel 82 2655) who will organise transfers for K4.

Getting There & Away
You can catch local ferry boats from behind the Lutheran Shipping office, or near the Madang Club for 30t.

BILIAU ISLAND
There are three wrecked Japanese freighters and a small landing barge on Biliau Island, the large island right in the middle of the harbour. More Japanese barges can be seen further to the right. You can reach the island by dugout or canoe while staying at Siar or from the Madang Hotel.

YABOB VILLAGE
If you take Modilon Rd out of town, shortly before the right turn to the airport and north coast road, a road branches off left to Yabob village. You pass a lookout point and a Japanese war memorial on the way to this pretty little village. There's an island nearby, which you can easily arrange to visit by canoe.

Long before Europeans arrived in the area, Yabob was well known for its fine clay pots which were traded far up and down the coast. You can still buy them today as it's a continuing craft.

BILBIL VILLAGE
This is another attractive village where pottery is still produced. Take the first road on the left after the Gum River, off the Ramu Highway; this loops back to the highway. A PMV from the market will cost 40t.

BALEK WILDLIFE SANCTUARY
This is to the right of the Ramu Highway if you're coming from Madang. The Sanctuary ends with the bitumen at the Gogol River. Backtrack to where the power lines cross the road and you'll see a sign. There's a 50t charge payable at the group of houses on the left.

There's a strange, fish-filled, sulphurous stream bubbling from a cave and more interesting vegetation. There are apparently more extensive walks (including a 'remarkable' five hour jungle tramp), caves and good views, but you'd need sturdy clothes and boots, and a guide. There are cassowaries and bird of paradise in the bush.

North Coast Highway

The road runs a long way north-west of Madang and will eventually reach all the way to Wewak – it already runs to the Ramu River although the last stretch is not too good. It's expected to meet the

Sepik somewhere downstream from Angoram where vehicles will cross the river by ferry. A road already runs from Angoram into Wewak. The final section from the Ramu to the Sepik is still a long way in the future.

There are a few places where you can stay: Jais Aben Resort, which is about 16 km from Madang; the Malolo of Madang, which is 42 km from Madang; and the Bogia Hotel, which is 197 km from Madang. PMVs run as far as Hansa Bay.

North Coast Diving There's more good diving along the north coast from Madang. An hour's drive brings you to a spot where the water drops off 60 metres only a stone's throw from the land. In 35 metres of water, the sunken wreck of the minesweeper *Boston* is a favourite dive. There's a wreck of US freighter *Henry Leith* near the Jais Aben Resort.

At the 'water hole' a lagoon is connected to the open sea by a large underwater tunnel. It's beyond the Plantation Hotel and the enclosed lagoon has sand and is safe for children as well as offering dramatic snorkelling. At Bogia Bay there's a Japanese Zero fighter upside down in the water several hundred yards directly out from the jetty. Hansa Bay has some spectacular wreck dives.

NOBANOB & NAGADA

A little beyond the Siar Village turnoff on the north coast road, about 14 km from Madang, there are turnoffs to the left and right. The rows and rows of dead coconut trees, killed by 'medicine' to make way for cocoa and coffee, are a landmark to watch for. The right hand turn leads to the Lutheran Mission on Nagada Harbour. The left hand turn leads up to Nobanob Mission out-station and was used as a Japanese lookout during the war. There is a fine view over the north coast, Madang and the harbour from up here. The road to the lookout takes 15 to 20 minutes' driving.

JAIS ABEN & AMRON

Just north of Nagada Harbour the Jais Aben Resort specialises in diving and has equipment rentals and boat tours to good dive sites. A couple of km further north, 16 km from Madang, the Japanese WW II HQ at Amron is off to the left of the road.

Places to Stay

About 16 km from Madang, off the main road on the waterfront, the *Jais Aben Resort* (tel 82 3311), PO Box 105, is the newest competitor for Madang's tourists. Managed by an American, Diane Christianson, the resort features spacious grounds, self-contained units (half with their own kitchens), a swimming pool, restaurant and dive centre, all on the sea front. It's an attractive spot. They also undertake serious marine research.

There are boats for hire and all water sports are offered. They have diving equipment, windsurfers and canoes and offer diving trips, game fishing and water skiing. Most people buy a package that includes diving, but the rooms themselves go for around K55/65 for singles/doubles.

Lunches are good value, from at K1.50 to K8, and the dinner menu ranges from K6.50 to K8.50. Weekend barbecue buffets are K8. If you buy a meal, you can use the facilities.

Getting There & Away

A taxi from town costs about K6 or you can take a PMV to the turn-off for about 60t. You can take a dugout canoe from Siar Island for about K2.

ALEXISHAFEN

Alexishafen Catholic Mission is off the road to the right, 21 km north of Madang. Like so much of the area it was badly damaged during the war, although the old graveyard still stands as a firm reminder of the number of early missionaries who died for the cause. There is a fine teak forest along the north coast road. The timber is totally unusable since the trees were riddled with shrapnel during the war.

A little beyond the mission you can see the site of the old mission airstrip, now virtually overgrown. The WW II Japanese airstrip is a little off the road to the left, between the mission airstrip and Alexishafen. You can easily recruit a couple of kids from the villages to guide you to some of the Japanese aircraft still standing close to the strip. The rotting wreckage of one Japanese twin-engined bomber is only a wingspan away from the bomb crater which immobilised it. Closer to the north coast road is the fuselage of an early Junkers mission aircraft.

MALOLO

The road continues north to the Malolo of Madang, a hotel, 42 km up the coast. There are magnificent views of Karkar Island.

Places to Stay

The *Malolo of Madang* (tel 82 3176), PO Box 413, can be reached by PMV for around K2, but if they know you're coming they'll pick you up from Madang. It's a relaxing place and the hotel and its seafood restaurant have a good reputation. There's a swimming pool and good snorkelling (gear is provided). It's not bad value either, especially if there's a group of you. The cost, including a continental breakfast, is K30.50/36.50 for singles/doubles and K68 for a family cottage that holds up to six.

BOGIA

Bogia, 200 km from Madang, is the departure point for Manam Island. The road peters out a short distance before the mighty Ramu River. There's a black sand beach and about 10 km beyond Bogia, towards Hansa Bay, is Kabak where there is a very nice beach at the old plantation. The reef at Kabak has plenty of colourful fish.

Places to Stay

The small *Bogia Hotel* (tel 83 4422), PO Box 855, Bogia, has a motor boat for hire. There's good swimming, snorkelling and diving. There are four rooms and singles/doubles cost K35/45. Book ahead. Some people have stayed with locals.

Getting There & Away

Bogia Company Trucks go to Madang on Monday and Thursday and you might catch a ride with them either way. In Madang ask at Boroko Motors on Modilon Rd where they refuel before heading back. It's more than three hours' drive. You can also get to Bogia by PMV for K5. The PMVs leave from the oval area under the big fig tree not far from the Madang Club.

HANSA BAY

At this popular diving spot past Bogia the wreckage of 35 Japanese freighters and US aircraft litter a shallow harbour. Although some are too deep to inspect without scuba equipment others are in only four to six metres of water. They've all been there since a US raid in November 1942. You can rent a dugout from a local village; the usual cost is K1 per diver per day. Either go to the black sands beach at Awa Point or to the village of Sesemungam.

Get your guide to take you to the *Shishi Maru* – the upper deck is only six metres below the surface. Two anti-aircraft guns on the bow point towards the surface. Brass shell castings litter the deck and forward holds. Two fire engines are sitting in the hold, just before the bridge, where they were once waiting to be unloaded. The *Shishi Maru* is about 60 metres long and would have been about 6000 tonnes. Before diving here ask the villagers' advice – there are sometimes sharks in the shallows.

Both Jais Aben and Diving Specialists of PNG bring divers to Hansa Bay. Diving Specialists have a bush-material guesthouse.

Inland

There are also some isolated and interesting places inland towards the Highlands. Simbai and Bundi are the main stations, but both are very remote. Bundi is wedged between Mt Wilhelm and Mt Herbert in some of the roughest country in PNG. Some of the people living in these areas are almost small enough to be termed pygmies. Dumpu was the base from where the attack on Shaggy Ridge was launched during WW II. The Ramu is one of PNG's great rivers, but it has never been popularised like the Sepik, although it is also home to wood carving cultures.

USINO
There is an interesting place to stay near Usino for keen outdoor people – low-key, village-style accommodation for about four people, not too far from the Ramu. It's run by Martin, Kupile and their daughter Marianne. It's necessary to contact them in advance (Martin Borkent, PO Box 230, Madang). Unfortunately, they don't have a phone, but if you have a contact number in PNG, Martin will ring you. The other option is to ask at the Lutheran Guest House in Madang; they'll probably have up-to-date information. Bed, breakfast and a light afternoon meal is K8.

Martin has been trading in the area for many years and knows it like the back of his hand. Visitors can explore the rainforests and swamps, which are full of wildlife, and since the guesthouse is about a 1½ hours' walk from the Ramu for a reasonable charge they can also get out on the river.

To get to Martin and Kupile's camp catch a PMV from Madang or Lae to Usino Junction for K4 or K5, then ask for 'camp bilong Martin'. There are two alternative routes, a main track which will take about 1¾ hours and a 'draiwara short cut'. You'll need a guide for the shortcut.

RAMU SUGAR REFINERY
This is a major industrial development designed to make PNG self sufficient in sugar. There is reasonably priced accommodation organised by the refinery and you can use the impressive sporting facilities that have been developed for the employees (golf, tennis, swimming).

BUNDI & BRAHMIN
Bundi is about a six hour walk from Brahmin Mission and Brahmin is about 25 km from the Lae-Madang road. A PMV from Madang to Brahmin will cost K5 or K6 and take about 1½ hours. There are a group of lodges at Bundi known as the *Mt Sinai Hotel*. The cost is K8 per person and this includes dinner. You can continue walking from Bundi to Kegsugl, near Mt Wilhelm, and then catch a PMV to Kundiawa. See the Walking to Madang sub-section of Simbu Province in the Highlands chapter.

Islands

MANAM ISLAND
The island of Manam, or Vulcan, is only 15 km off the coast from Bogia. The island is 83 square km in area and is an almost perfect volcano cone, rising 1829 metres high. The soil is extremely fertile and supports a population of about 4000, but from time to time the entire population has had to be evacuated as the volcano is still active. At night the volcano tip glows and occasionally spurts orange trailers into the sky. There is a seismological observatory on the side of the cone.

There is a German mission on the island and if you manage to make it over there you will enjoy an incredible welcome by the local people, particularly the children. Ask your boat crew for somewhere to stay and bring your own food. Recently, there have been some thefts from travellers – the modern world has arrived.

Getting There & Away

Manam is 193 km from Madang and not easy to get to. Bogia is the normal departure point; take a PMV from Madang for K5. Apparently, government and private boats leave Bogia for Manam virtually daily, although there is no schedule so you might end up waiting a few days; check at the District Office. Be careful with your possessions on the boats.

KARKAR ISLAND

William Dampier, the English pirate-explorer whose visit to the west coast of Australia preceded Captain Cook's visit by nearly a century, made an early landing on the 362 square km island. Later Lutheran missionaries had a hard time both from malaria and the local natives. The island has a population of 25,000, a high school and 20 community schools. It's one of the most fertile places in the country.

A volcanic eruption temporarily evicted the missionaries, but they came back and today Karkar has both Catholic and Lutheran missions as well as some of the most productive copra plantations in the world. The volcanic cone is just two metres higher than Manam's at 1831 metres; it's a full day's walk up to the crater and back. The volcano erupted violently in 1974, leaving a cinder cone in the centre of the huge, original crater. It erupted again in 1979, killing two vulcanologists. Since then climbing must be authorised and you must be accompanied by a vulcanologist. Enquire at the local government office in Madang.

A road encircles the island and it takes four hours to drive right round. You can also walk around the island, but treat the river crossings with great caution. When it rains on the mountain water comes down the rivers like a wall. A year or two back some unwary Australians were killed crossing a river. There are also river crossings to be made when climbing the volcano. Karkar also has good beaches and places for snorkelling.

Places to Stay

There is no real accommodation on the island although there is talk of establishing a guesthouse. As yet nothing has materialised. The high school will sometimes offer you a place for K10 or you can try the hospital. The school is near Kulili wharf. A friend of Saimon Tewa, Stahl Salum, has a plantation on the northern side of the island – Gaum Plantation. Prices are negotiable for full board and he'll run you around the island, but that can be expensive.

Getting There & Away

There are passenger and cargo boat services from Madang to Kurum wharf or Kulili wharf on the nicer side of the island. Frequent boats go from Madang.

There's a regular speedboat trip out to Karkar on a vessel called the *Trimanta*. It leaves Madang at 8 am Monday to Friday, and 9 am on Saturday. It costs K13 and takes 1½ hours. Poroman Shipping (tel 82 2636) is just off Modilon Rd, and makes irregular trips to Karkar for K7, taking four hours.

Talair flies every morning except Sunday for K30.

BAGABAG ISLAND

Bagabag encircles a sunken crater 36 square km in area and is inhabited. During the war the Japanese used the 'fjord' to hide ships.

LONG ISLAND

The largest of the volcanic islands, Long, is 414 square km in area and 48 km off the coast. It has two active craters, one of which contains a lake surrounded by crater walls up to 250 metres high. The population only totals about 600, but the island is renowned for its prolific bird life and the many fish which swarm around its surrounding reefs. Turtles come ashore to lay their eggs at certain times of year. Getting here isn't easy as there is no regular boat service. MAF flies from Madang.

The Sepik

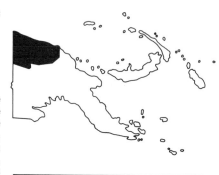

Area 74,915 square km
Population 380,000

The Sepik region is quite possibly the most fascinating area of PNG. There are islands, a long stretch of open coastline with good beaches, a number of fair-sized, coastal towns and some rugged mountain ranges. It is the mighty Sepik River, however, that commands the most attention.

The Sepik is one of the largest rivers in the world in terms of annual water flow and although it is rivalled in size by the Fly River in the south of the country it is far more significant as a means of communication and in terms of its cultural and artistic heritage. The region is a centre for thriving artistic skills.

The Sepik has the same relevance to PNG as the Congo to Africa and the Amazon to South America. River-boating down the Amazon is an amazing experience, but people say the Sepik is even better. Do it!

This chapter is divided into three sections: West Sepik Province, East Sepik Province and, although the Sepik flows through both provinces, The Sepik & its Tributaries, which includes river-side towns and villages.

HISTORY

Very little archaeological evidence has been found to shed light on the early history of these provinces. Since most people are likely to have lived along shifting rivers or the coastline (which has flooded since the last ice age) it is unlikely much will ever be found. The area was, like other parts of PNG, fragmented into numerous different language groups and clans, and violence between these groups was commonplace. Most languages are spoken by less than 2000 people. The main language group of the Middle Sepik is

Iatmul (with over 10,000 speakers), in the Maprik area there are 30,000 Abelam speakers and along the coast around Wewak there are around 35,000 Passam speakers.

The Sepik's first contact with the outside world was probably with Malay bird of paradise hunters; the feathers from these beautiful birds were popular long before European ladies of society had their fling with them during the last century. The first European contact came in 1885 with the arrival of the Germans and their New Guinea Kompagnie. Dr Otto Finsch, after whom the German's first station – Finschhafen – was later named, rowed about 50 km upstream from the mouth and named the river the Kaiserin Augusta, after the wife of the German Emperor.

During 1886 and 1887 further expeditions, using a steam boat, travelled 400 km upriver and then, when the river was higher, 600 km. These early expeditions were soon followed by more mercenary explorers, traders, labour recruiters and, inevitably, the missionaries – for here was a whole new parcel of country waiting for the word.

The Germans established a station at Aitape on the coast in 1906 and in 1912-13 sent a huge scientific expedition to explore the river and its vast, low-lying basin. They collected insects, studied the tribes and produced maps of such

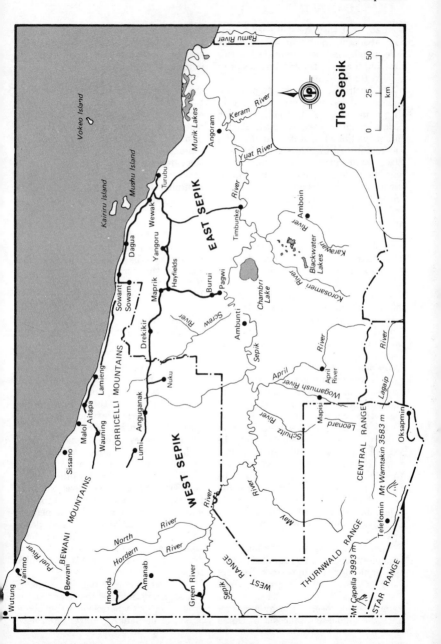

accuracy that they are still used to this day. Angoram, the major station in the lower Sepik, was also established at this time, but the arrival of WW I put a stop to activity for some time.

The Australian administration of New Guinea suffered from very tight purse-strings and an area like the Sepik, with little economic appeal, was pushed to the end of the line. The station at Ambunti was established in 1924 and in the early '30s a small flurry of gold rushes in the hills behind Wewak and around Maprik, stirred further interest. Then WW II arrived and once more development and exploration of the Sepik went into reverse.

The Japanese held the Sepik region for most of the war but the struggle for control was bitter and prolonged. As the Australian forces pushed along the coast from Lae and then Madang, the Japanese steadily withdrew to the west. In early '44 the Americans seized Aitape and an Australian division started to move west from there. When a huge American force captured Hollandia (Jayapura in Irian Jaya today) in April '44, the Japanese 8th Army was completely isolated.

The enormous number of rivers and the extensive coastal swamps made the fight along the coast a drawn out struggle. It was over a year later, in May '45, before Wewak fell and the remaining Japanese troops withdrew into the hills behind the coast. Finally, with the war in its last days, General Adachi surrendered near Yangoru. He was so weak he had to be carried on a chair. The formal surrender took place a few days later on 13 September '45 at Wom Point near Wewak. Of 100,000 Japanese troops only 13,000 survived to surrender.

Since the war, government control has been re-established and extended further upriver although the uppermost limits of the Sepik are still amongst the most unchanged and isolated parts of the country. It has been a touchy area ever since the Indonesian takeover of Dutch

New Guinea, although the border was jointly mapped and marked in 1968. On several occasions large numbers of refugees have fled into PNG.

In 1984 over 100 Melanesian soldiers in the Indonesian Armed Forces deserted to the OPM (the Irian Jayan rebels) sparking a major Indonesian operation, which in turn drove over 10,000 Papuans into PNG. Years later these refugees, and those that have come both before and since, remain a political football. Only a small number have shown any interest in returning to Irian Jaya, so the PNG government has belatedly decided to settle them permanently. Unfortunately for the refugees PNG doesn't have the necessary funds, and Australia has refused to help. In the meantime they live in extremely basic conditions in camps close to the border: Blackwater, near Vanimo, and Green River, near the Sepik River, are two of the largest camps.

GEOGRAPHY

The Sepik River is 1126 km long and is navigable for almost that entire distance. It starts up in the central mountains, close to the source of the country's other major river, the Fly, which flows south. The Sepik flows in a loop, first west across the Irian Jaya border, then north on the Indonesian side before turning east across the border again. It then runs through two PNG provinces: West Sepik Province, with its capital at Vanimo, and East Sepik Province, with its capital at Wewak.

At its exit from Irian Jaya the Sepik is only 85 metres above sea level and from there it winds gradually down to the sea; a huge, brown, slowly coiling serpent. It has often changed its course leaving dead-ends, lagoons, ox-bow lakes or huge swampy expanses that turn into lakes or dry up to make grasslands in the dry season.

As an indication of its age and changing course, along much of the river there is no stone or rock whatsoever within about 50 km of its banks. Villages often have 'sacred stones' that have been carried in from far away and placed in front of the village *haus tambaran* (spirit house).

The inexorable force of the river often tears great chunks of mud and vegetation out of the river banks and at times these drift off downstream as floating islands – often with small trees and even animals aboard. There is no delta and the river stains the sea brown for 50 or more km from the shore. It is said that islanders off the coast can draw fresh water straight from the sea.

For much of its length, the Sepik is bordered by huge expanses of swamp or wild sugar cane known as pitpit. Further inland there are hills and eventually the Sepik climbs into wild mountain country near its source. Between the river and the coastal plain the Bewani and Torricelli Mountains rise to over 1000 metres. There are no natural harbours on the whole Sepik region coastline.

ARTS

Traditional art was closely linked to spiritual beliefs, indeed Sepik carvings were usually an attempt to make a spirit visible and concrete, although decorations were also applied to practical, day-to-day items, like pots and paddles.

Carving is now rarely traditional – it is now more likely to be a mixture of traditional motifs, the individual's imagination, and commercial good sense. (Sound familiar Michaelangelo?) Originally each village had its own distinctive style, but a pan-Sepik style is now emerging.

Carving has become a vital part of the river's economy and without it some villages would probably cease to exist. In many river villages it is literally the only significant source of cash, which is needed for clothes, store food, education, petrol, utensils .... Coffee is grown in the Maprik region, but on the river there are no cash crops, no paid employment and rarely any agricultural surplus.

If a group arrives in a village, a market will materialise instantly. Considering the amount of labour and skill that goes into a carving the prices are very low. Depending on the size and quality of the piece prices will of course vary – you can buy hooks and carvings for as little as K1, a mask for K3, all the way up to K20 and more.

The mark-up by the time these things reach the west is absolutely unbelievable – admittedly they aren't easy to transport and there are numerous middlemen, but how can they justify 1000% and 2000% increases? You may see artefact buyers with huge heavily-laden canoes doing their rounds; a single buyer may spend thousands of kina in a village.

There is some degree of haggling, but bargaining in the Asian sense is unknown. The people are too proud – it is not wise to denigrate someone's carvings. You can, however, ask for a 'second price' and sometimes even a 'third price'. There are no prizes for taking a villager down.

As you will soon discover, if you are a keen collector, you can very quickly end up with a lot of very heavy *diwai* (wood). Bear in mind that the airlines have baggage limits and particularly in the case of light aeroplanes there simply may not be room for a three-metre statue! Although the airlines seem to be fairly flexible, especially on the F28s and Dash 8s, the official limit is 16 kg and there just isn't much room for flexibility on the smaller planes.

You must also bear in mind the PNG Government's restrictions on exporting some items, and import restrictions in your country of origin and any other country you may be visiting on your way home. See the Customs section in the Facts for the Visitor chapter.

There are a couple of alternative methods for dealing with a lot of wood. Air Niugini has special discount rates for flying artefacts from Wewak to Moresby – any parcel over five kilos is only 64t a kilo. Overseas from Port Moresby the rates are quite a bit steeper: to Sydney, K2.71 per kilo, minimum K30; to Los Angeles,

K9.23 per kilo, K40 minimum; to Paris, K12.08 per kilo, minimum K55. Shipping would be much cheaper. Mail is generally more expensive than air (except for small parcels) and the maximum acceptable length is one metre.

GETTING THERE & AWAY
Air
The standard way to get to the Sepik is to fly to Wewak from Madang or from Jayapura (Indonesia) via Vanimo. There is now an increasingly popular trans-Pacific flight from Los Angeles to Jayapura with Garuda (the Indonesian international airline) – see the Vanimo section and the Getting There chapter.

Air Niugini flies between Madang and Wewak every day of the week for K75 and there's a flight from Mt Hagen which goes through Wewak, on to Vanimo and then Jayapura (using a Douglas Airways plane) on Wednesdays (K114). On Saturday Wewak is linked to Manus (K100).

Talair has a daily flight to the Highlands from Wewak; more often to Mt Hagen (K69) than to Goroka. They also have many flights around the region, as do Douglas and MAF, so there are a number of 'back door' entries. You could, for instance, fly or walk to Oksapmin from Lake Kopiago (see the Southern Highlands section) and then fly with Talair from Oksapmin to Green River (K73). Or you could fly Talair to Amboin (near the Karawari Lodge on the Karawari River) from Hagen on Mondays and Wednesdays (K65), or to Tari from Wewak. It would be worth talking to the MAF people if you are looking for even more exotic permutations and combinations.

Sea
Wewak is the most westerly port for the trusty *Mamose Express*, but other Lutheran Shipping (tel 82 2577), PO Box 789, Madang, vessels continue on to Vanimo. See the Getting Around chapter

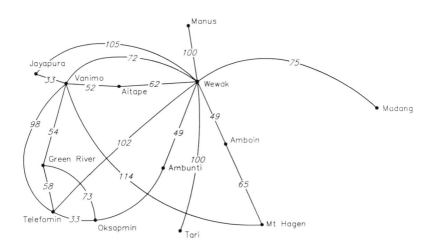

Flights in the Sepik

Fares in Kina

for a complete schedule and list of fares for the *Mamose*; it leaves Madang on Friday evening, arrives on Saturday morning and costs K27/18, deck/tourist class.

The *Melanesian Explorer*, which is a small, luxury cruise ship operated by Melanesian Tourist Services (tel 82 2766), PO Box 707, Madang, sails regularly from Madang to the Upper Sepik. As you would expect, it's not cheap, but if you have limited time and like a reasonable degree of comfort, this could be a worthwhile option.

The MV *Tawi*, which is operated by the Manus Provincial Government (tel 40 9088), Shipping Officer, Manus Provincial Government, PO Box 111, Lorengau, plies between Lorengau, the outer islands of Manus, Wuvulu Island, Wewak and Madang. Wewak or Madang to Lorengau takes from five to seven days and there is a return voyage every couple of weeks. There's no straightforward schedule and Wewak-Manus is about K30. I heard of the *Joseph Wyett*, also operated by the Manus Government, which apparently goes between Wewak and Manus every three weeks.

Poroman Shipping (tel 82 2636), PO Box 486, Madang, has two boats, the MV *Deaniel* and the MV *Doilon*, that make voyages from Madang up the Sepik River as far as Green River (K40, approx 10 days) via Ambunte (K25, approx six days). Do not expect any luxuries – these are small, working freighters – and they are designed and operated with the transport of cargo in mind, not western tourists. Bring your own food and toilet paper.

GETTING AROUND
Air
Talair, Douglas Airways and MAF (particularly MAF) have quite a wide range of connections through the Sepik provinces. Both Douglas and Talair have daily flights between Vanimo and Wewak (K72) via some isolated airstrips in the Bewani and Torricelli Mountains and Aitape (K52) – this is much more

enjoyable than streaking over the top in a F28 and some of the landing strips are really interesting! MAF has bases in Anguganak and Telefomin that are contacted through Wewak (tel 86 2500), PO Box 666, Wewak, and they service most airstrips twice a week.

Talair (tel 86 2012), PO Box 47, Wewak, flies from Wewak to Amboin (Karawari Lodge – K48) and Tari. Douglas (tel 86 2098), PO Box 155, Wewak, flies to Wuvulu Island (K83), Ambunti (K49) and Telefomin (K102).

From Vanimo Talair (tel 87 1180), PO Box 25, Vanimo, and Douglas (tel 65 9069), PO Box 39, Vanimo, also fly north to Telefomin (K98), Oksapmin (K109) and Green River (K54). MAF has an interesting flight from Oksapmin to Ambunti.

Sea
Lutheran's somewhat basic cargo freighters, the MV *Nagada* and MV *Umboi*, continue on to Vanimo from Wewak; one makes the voyage each week for K17.50/24, deck/1st class; half that to Aitape. 'Deck class can be OK. Food, of a kind, is available on board and you eat with the captain – which is no special thrill as he eats where everyone else eats!'

River
There is a wide range of alternative methods for getting out on the big, brown Sepik and its tributaries. There is no right way or wrong way; the factors to consider are your finances, available time, and last, but not least, your capacity for roughing it. The spectrum of travellers ranges from the dedicated shoestringers who buy canoes and paddle from village to village, to those who prefer a tour using motorised canoes, and finally at the luxury end, those who prefer to stay on a cruise ship or at a comfortable lodge. See Getting Around in The Sepik & its Tributaries section for a more detailed discussion of the options.

Road

The road links in the Sepik provinces are quite limited, but where there is a road there will be PMVs. The roads are rough, even the one to Angoram, which is, in relative terms, a good, all-weather road. The roads to Pagwi and Timbunke are real teeth rattlers and in the wet they must be a nightmare, sometimes impassable. When they are dry, conventional vehicles will survive, but four-wheel drive is essential after rain. The North Coast Highway runs west past Aitape.

PMVs Except on major routes like from Wewak to Angoram and Maprik, PMVs are quite infrequent. Starting very early and being relaxed about arrival times is more important than ever. The PMVs are usually trucks and are often very crowded. Hitching is possible – most private cars act as de facto PMVs anyway – so if you're waiting on the side of the road, wave down anything that comes by (thumbing is unknown). You may well be expected to contribute an equivalent to a PMV fare, but you'll also meet some exceptionally generous people.

Hire You can hire from Budget, Hertz and Avis in Wewak, but remote area surcharges apply. This means a four-wheel drive utility (a ute to Australians, pickup to Americans) will cost around K56 a day plus 32t a km.

East Sepik Province

Area 43,770 square km
Population 250,000

The East Sepik Province is much more developed than its western counterpart and includes the most visited and heavily populated sections of the Sepik, as well as several large tributaries. Wewak, the provincial capital, is a thriving, important commercial centre, separated from the Sepik basin by the Prince Alexander Range.

WEWAK

Wewak is an attractive, bustling town where you can happily spend a day or two in transit to the Sepik or Irian Jaya. Apart from good shopping and some reasonable accommodation options, there's an attraction that is rare for PNG coastal cities – golden sand, backed by the proper swaying palm trees, right next door to town. Beautiful beaches stretch all along the coast.

Wewak is built at the foot of a high headland that overlooks the coast and nearby islands of Kairuru and Mushu. Cape Wom, to the west, is the place where General Adachi finally surrendered to the Allied forces near the end of WW II. To the east is Cape Moem, an army base.

The hills behind the town climb steeply, so you don't have to travel far to enjoy a very good view.

Orientation

The headland overlooking Wewak is largely residential, although this is the site for the Sepik Motel and the Wewak Hotel. The main commercial area is at the bottom of the hill behind the beach. The rest of town stretches eastwards towards the airport which is about seven km away. Like a number of other PNG towns, Wewak is irritatingly spread out; fortunately, there's an excellent PMV system.

Wewak is not a particularly well-sheltered harbour. There's a small wharf for local fishing boats and canoes, right by the town centre, and a longer one for larger ships to the east of the Sepik International Motel, midway along along the bay formed by Wewak and Boram Points; the main coastal road does a loop around it.

Information

There is an East Sepik Tourist Board (tel 86 2112), BMS Freemail Bag, Wewak, and although they are not really set up for dealing with the public they will certainly be able to tell you if there are any cultural events in the area, and advise you about getting to places like Cape Wom and Kairiru Island.

Although Wewak is much more relaxed than Lae, it is not without its problems, so you should exercise a moderate degree of caution. There are some quite large squatter camps and some accompanying crime. You are not likely to have any problems during the day and most people are particularly friendly and helpful. Walking around at night would be asking for trouble, and women should not wander off alone. Discretion should be used when swimming in western costume, but the beach in front of the Sepik International is fine.

All the banks and airlines are represented, and this is the spot to stock up for a Sepik expedition. If you're going on to Irian Jaya get some rupiah (Indonesian currency) in Moresby, as the banks here occasionally have small amounts, but don't carry a permanent stock.

The local Hash House Harriers run on Mondays; ask around at the banks or the Yacht Club. Someone will take you along and after the run there's food and drink.

Things to See

Near the main wharf the rusting remains of the MV *Busama* are rotting away in the sand. Further down at Kreer, on the road to the airport, there's a market and the wooden hulk of a Taiwanese fishing junk that was seized a few years ago for infringing PNG's coastal fishing limits.

There are five markets, in descending order of importance: Taun (at the end of the main street), Dagua (good for PMVs, not far from town), Kreer (on the airport road, just before it turns inland), Nuigo (not very interesting) and Chambri (really just an artefact stall on Boram Rd).

You can spend a pleasant couple of hours climbing the headland for views, then visiting the Sepik Arts & Cane Interiors shop on the corner diagonally opposite to the Post Office, watching the

village boats at the small wharf, and, finally, downing a cold beer at the Yacht Club.

The view from the hills behind the town is superb. Those staying at Ralf Stuttgen's guesthouse don't have to go any further than their bedroom window to see it, but if you are staying in town it's worth the drive. There's a fair amount of traffic.

The Sepik coastline is unprotected, so in season, from September to January, there can be decent surf, including board-rideable waves to the east towards Turubu. Dabiar Beach at Forok Village has been recommended.

War Relics

Wewak's most vivid legacy of the bitter fighting in WW II is the bomb craters that pockmark the area. They are still visible around the Boram airport runway and the now disused Wirui airstrip (closer to town).

Near the Windjammer Motel there's a serene and simple Japanese/PNG Peace Park. At Mission Hill there's a Japanese War Memorial; the remains of the many troops buried here in a mass grave were later exhumed and returned to Japan. Someone in the know could lead you to old gun emplacements.

Places to Stay – bottom end

Ralf Stuttgen's (tel 86 2395), PO Box 154, place has become an institution, and every budget traveller that visits the Sepik ends up staying here. It's a great place for meeting all sorts of weird and wonderful people, and getting up-to-date information on the river. It's fairly basic, and completely chaotic, with all sorts of people and children virtually hanging from the ceiling of a small house.

Ralf is a German expat and he knows the Sepik. If you can pin him down for a conversation he has a wealth of anecdotes and facts –. he's kept pretty busy delivering kids to and from school, cooking, shopping, painting the house and, while I was there, finding an alsatian

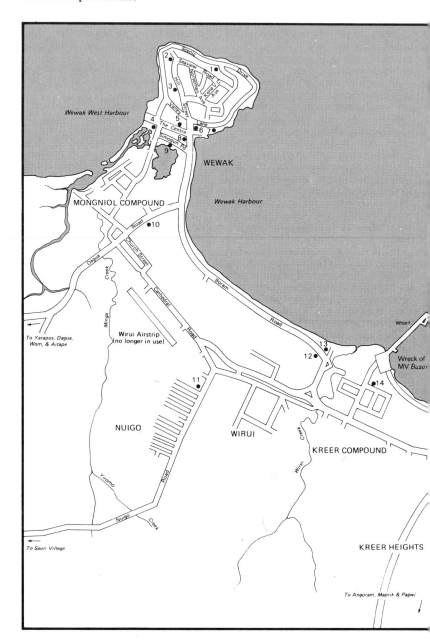

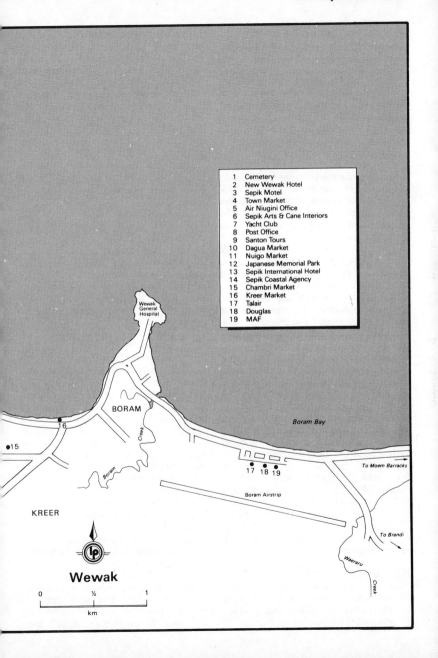

1 Cemetery
2 New Wewak Hotel
3 Sepik Motel
4 Town Market
5 Air Niugini Office
6 Sepik Arts & Cane Interiors
7 Yacht Club
8 Post Office
9 Santon Tours
10 Dagua Market
11 Nuigo Market
12 Japanese Memorial Park
13 Sepik International Hotel
14 Sepik Coastal Agency
15 Chambri Market
16 Kreer Market
17 Talair
18 Douglas
19 MAF

Wewak
General
Hospital

BORAM

Boram Bay

16

●15

17 18 19

To Moem Barracks

KREER

Boram Airstrip

To Brandi

Waeraru Creek

Boram Creek

Wewak

0   ½   1
km

to mate with one of his bitches .... There's also an excellent multilingual travellers' notebook, to which I am indebted.

He can squeeze about 10 people into two bunk rooms, and I'm sure he'd make room for more. It's a homely, friendly place and it only costs K8 per night. Cheap meals and good breakfasts are also available, as well as an endless supply of coffee.

It's on the ridge overlooking the coast, just below a radio mast, on the right-hand side of the main road running to the Sepik, about six km from town. Although this makes it a bit inaccessible it also means there are great views, and it is (at 400 metres elevation) markedly cooler than in town. It's really too far to walk, as it's a steep climb, but it's on the main Sepik road so there's plenty of traffic. If you're expected, Ralf will pick you up. He can then explain the system with the PMVs (30t to/from the turnoff and 30t up the hill) and hitchhiking. He goes in and out of town so frequently you can often get a ride with him anyway; he charges a small amount to help cover petrol costs.

Ralf's is a good spot to start your Sepik trip because all the PMVs go right past. This means you don't have to hang around the markets, and you can sit under the shady tree at the bottom of Ralf's driveway and enjoy the view while you wait. Even if you miss the early morning PMVs you'd stand a good chance of getting a ride in the early afternoon.

In town, not far from the Sepik International Motel, you may be able to stay with Peter Ulai (tel 86 2137), PO Box 342. This is just a house, with space to roll out a mattress and fairly basic facilities. Plan on supplying your own food. Peter will pick you up from the airport, and he'll charge just K5.

Places to Stay – top end

There are three hotels in Wewak. Two of the hotels are close together on Hill St, on the Wewak headland above town, and one is right beside the beach.

The *Sepik Motel* (tel 86 2422), PO Box 51, is the first place up the hill from town and has a swimming pool and 16 family rooms, all with air-con, videos and private facilities. It's due for renovations, but it's comfortable and efficiently run. There's a haus win, with excellent views over the western harbour and across to the hills. The food is good too, with a changing menu that sometimes includes a large pizza for K5. Other main meals are around K10. Singles/doubles/triples are K72/90/100, including breakfast. They'll store stuff for you while you're out on the river.

The *New Wewak Hotel* (tel 86 2155, 86 2554), PO Box 20, right at the top of the hill overlooking the sea, has 16 singles and 17 twin, some air-con, some with fans. Singles/doubles are K68/85; breakfast costs K4, lunch and dinner to K10. It's very run-down, and has quite a depressing atmosphere, despite the views. There are plans afoot for a long-overdue, major redevelopment.

The third place, the *Sepik International Hotel* (tel 86 2548), PO Box 152, is three km round the bay from town towards the airport, with an enormous wooden crocodile encircling the swimming pool and Sepik carvings at the entrance. It has the best location if you're interested in being right on the beach – it's only a couple of steps into the sea from the rooms at the front – this can be a distinct disadvantage if there's a surf running and you're trying to sleep.

It's a popular local eating place at lunch and dinner (although it sells meals all day) and it's a good place for a beer. There is a reasonably-priced snack menu, with various hamburgers and the like for around K2.50. A lunch or dinner main course will be around K10. The bar is open from 10 am to 10 pm.

It's worth visiting just to see the carvings that have been incorporated in the interior, including a magnificent crocodile bar. They have masks for sale, and local people gather to sell their trinkets every afternoon. You could spend a pleasant couple of hours alternating between the beach, bar and artefacts.

There are three classes of rooms, becoming more expensive the further you are from the beach: C-class is pretty ordinary and you share bathroom facilities – K40 for the first person, then K10 for each person after that; B-class has fans and private facilities – K50 for the first person, then K10 for each person after that, up to four; A-class has air-con doubles for K90.

The hotel is run by Tribal World (tel 55 1555), PO Box 86, Mt Hagen – who also have hotels in Minj and Mt Hagen, and organise tours around the region, including the Sepik. These cost about K95 per day, per person. There was talk about constructing a guesthouse at Timbunke.

Places to Eat

There aren't too many options apart from the hotels and the standard kai bars in the shopping centre. You can get some snacks at the *Yacht Club* and on Tuesday and Friday nights they have good meals for about K5. The Yacht Club overlooks the harbour and has a pleasant haus win, and cold draught beers for 90t.

The Garamut Supermarket has an excellent hot bread kitchen, where you can fill up on delicious fresh cakes and soft drink for less than a kina.

Things to Buy

The *Sepik Arts & Cane Interiors* has a collection of masks, carvings, weapons and cane-work. There is some interesting work and the prices are reasonable, although naturally a bit more expensive than in the villages.

A group of artefacts sellers set up a market at the Sepik International Motel every evening. They sell jewellery and smaller pieces that are fairly commercial, but there is occasionally something interesting. It's worth a look. The motel also sells masks and carvings; they have a large collection, but the prices are high.

There's also a small stall on Boram Rd with attractive, though expensive woven bags and a few carvings (if you're coming from town, it's just off Boram Rd on the left, before the turnoff to the Sepik and Ralf's place). It's known as Chambri Market.

Getting There & Away

Air Wewak is a major hub for air transport around the Sepik, and has frequent connections to Madang, Vanimo and the Highlands. The main Air Niugini office is in town (they also handle bookings for Douglas), and Talair also has offices in town and at the airport. Douglas flies to Ambunti for K46. The MAF office is at the airport. See the introductory transport sections for details and addresses.

Sea Wewak is the westernmost port of call for the *Mamose Express*, but other Lutheran Shipping vessels go on to Vanimo. Sepik Coastal Agencies (tel 86 2464) handle Lutheran's bookings (you can buy tickets in advance) and will have up-to-date arrival and departure times. Their office is not far from the wharf (coming from the wharf take the first turn on your left) and it's open from 1 to 4 pm Monday to Friday, and 9 to 11 am on Saturdays.

There are also links to Manus, Wuvulu and Kairiru Islands. See the introductory transport sections.

PMVs Roads run west along the coast as far as Aitape through the Torricelli Mountains and into the Sepik basin. The markets are, as always, the best places to get PMVs, particularly Dagua. If you're going to the Sepik, Ralf Stuttgen's place is also a good spot to start. They leave early, but to Angoram you can often get PMVs in the early afternoon. Aitape is K10; Angoram, 2½ hours, K5/6; Timbunke, three hours, K5; Maprik, three hours, K6; Pagwi, four or five hours, K10.

Getting Around

PMVs are frequent and cheap, which is just as well, since everything is so spread out. They charge 30t for anywhere in town. There are major PMV stops at all the markets and one opposite the post office. A few run all the way along Boram Rd, but they are more frequent along Cathedral Rd. They run right past the airport – you can see the road and a shelter from the terminal. If you're going to Ralf's, get off at Chambri market and start walking up the Sepik Rd. Try hailing any passing vehicle.

The PMVs stop at dusk, which can mean you can be stuck at the airport, especially if you come in on the Air Niugini evening flight. The best solution is to let someone know you're coming – all the 'Places to Stay' pick up from the airport. There are no taxis, but there are hire cars – see the introductory Getting Around section for addresses.

AROUND WEWAK

There are some good beaches for swimming and diving at Cape Moem, past the airport, but the cape is an army base so you have to get permission to enter from the commanding officer (tel 82 2060). Get a PMV to Moem Barracks, then walk a km or so along a dirt road to the right. Unless you're a keen diver, it's not really worth the effort.

At Brandi High School, to the east of Cape Moem, the students have built a traditional village within the school grounds. There's also a collection of Japanese war relics.

Cape Wom

Cape Wom, about 14 km to the west of Wewak, is the site of a wartime airstrip and this is where the Japanese surrender took place. It is an atmospheric spot. There's a war memorial flanked by flag poles on the spot where Lieutenant General Adachi signed the surrender documents and handed his sword to Major General Robertson on 13 September 1945. On the west side of the cape there's a good reef for snorkelling and a nice stretch of sand for swimming. It would be a very pleasant place for a picnic and there are good views across to the islands.

There is some debate about how safe Cape Wom is to visit, as there have been some thefts and assaults. I was assured that the local people have cleaned up the problem, and there was no hint of trouble when I was there. You would be wise to take care of your belongings, and if you have any doubts, call Peter Waliawi, the Secretary of the East Sepik Tourist Board (through the Wewak Town Development Commission on tel 86 2112), for up-to-date advice.

There is a ranger at the gates, which are open from 7 am to 6.30 pm, and there's a fee to enter (K2 per car). If you don't have a vehicle, catch a PMV at Dagua market bound for Dagua (a small village further to the west) and get off at the turnoff to the cape (there's a small village known as Suara). The PMV will cost around K2. From the turnoff it is a hot three km walk.

Kairiru Island

There are a number of islands just off the coast from Wewak. Kairiru sounds particularly interesting, as there are a number of villages and the western end is volcanic – the sea has apparently broken into an active crater. There are hot springs, waterfalls and, at the eastern end of the island, an enormous Japanese gun. It's an untouched place and a good escape from Wewak.

Places to Stay There are apparently places where you can stay with local people – a first-hand report would be gratefully accepted. Peter Waliawi, the Secretary of the East Sepik Tourist Board (contact through the Wewak Town Development Commission, tel 86 2112) may be able to arrange accommodation at St Xavier's High School. Take your own food.

Getting There & Away The *Tau-K* goes between Kairiru and Wewak on Tuesdays and Fridays. It arrives in Wewak about 9 am and leaves around 2 pm – don't rely too heavily on these times. The journey takes about two hours and costs K2.50. It docks at the small pier across the road from the post office. There are probably also outrigger canoes going every day.

WUVULU ISLAND

Wuvulu is less than 200 km from Wewak and is according to all descriptions the perfect tropical island. There are no rivers or creeks discharging into the sea so the water is incredibly clear. The diving and snorkelling is superb, with coral, numerous turtles and sharks. The Wuvulu islanders are closely akin to Micronesians and still make distinctive canoes, some large enough to hold 40 people. Officially the island is a part of Manus Province.

There are two villages on the island and the *Wuvulu Lodge* which is operated by the islanders. There is accommodation for 12 people at K40 for full board. The meals are good, and there's diving equipment and bicycles for hire.

Douglas Airways flies to the island from Wewak on Mondays and Saturdays for K83, and the Manus Government's MV *Tawi* (contact the Shipping Officer, Manus Provincial Government, tel 40 9088, PO Box 111, Lorengau) also visits the island, although there's no straightforward schedule. For information about the lodge, or bookings, contact the Lus Development Corporation (tel 86 2331), PO Box 494, Wewak.

MAPRIK AREA

The Maprik area, in the Prince Alexander Mountains, overlooking the vast Sepik basin, is noted for the Abelam peoples' distinctive haus tambarans, their yam cult and their carvings and decorations.

The population around Maprik is quite dense and there are many small villages, each with a striking, forward-leaning haus tambaran, a unique architectural style

that has been echoed in such modern buildings as the National Parliament. The front facade of the Maprik haus tambarans is brightly painted in browns, ochres, whites and blacks and in some cases they are 30 metres high. Inside, the carved spirit figures are similarly treated.

Maprik Haus Tambaran

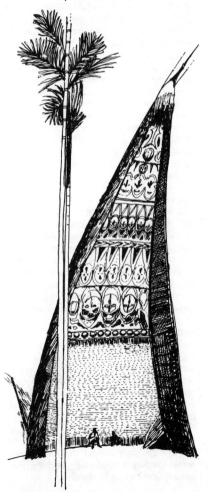

Yams are a staple food in this region and they also have cultural significance – you will see them growing on their distinctive, two metre, cross-like trellis. Harvesting entails considerable ritual and you may see yam festivals or sing-sings during the July/August harvest time. The woven fibre masks, which are the region's most famous artefacts, were originally used in a ceremony where the yams were decorated like human beings, establishing a ritual link between the clans and their crops.

There are some interesting back roads between Maprik and Lamu linking villages, some with spectacular haus tambarans and good carvings. Ask permission before entering villages and then see the head man. Ask before taking photos, and don't assume you can wander into the haus tambaran at will, especially if you're a woman. Haus tambarans were traditionally exclusively an initiated man's preserve, although these days the rules are sometimes bent for western tourists.

Places to Stay

The *Maprik Waken* (tel 88 3011), PO Box 104, in Maprik has six rooms with costs of K25 per person. You can also book through the Angoram Hotel. The price seems erratic and the hotel doesn't have a very good reputation. It used to be possible to stay at Maprik High School two km from Hayfields, towards Pagwi, but closed indefinitely in 1987 due to rascal activity.

Getting There & Away

From Wewak the road climbs up and over the Prince Alexander Mountains then continues 132 km to Maprik. Maprik is actually eight km off the Wewak-Pagwi road; the junction is called Hayfields, where there is a petrol station, a couple of trade stores and an airfield. A PMV from Wewak to Maprik costs K6, Maprik to Pagwi K4, or you can get one direct to Pagwi. The last stretch to Pagwi goes across the Sepik flood plain, and it would be very hard going in the wet.

On the way from Wewak, watch for large mesh nets spread between tall trees. Flying foxes (bats) fly into the net, become entangled, and end up in the cooking pot.

Roads will eventually link Lumi with Aitape. A road already continues to Lumi, although missing bridges and deep rivers can make it hazardous. 'Always get out and walk the crossing before trying to drive across', suggested one visitor, 'or join the Lumi yacht club'. A road link to Ambunti is also planned, but for the time being you'll have to fly.

West Sepik Province

Area 31,145 square km
Population 130,000

West Sepik, known also as Sandaun (sundown, or west) is little developed, but agricultural activity in the Telefomin District and timber development around Vanimo, the provincial capital, have nonetheless brought rapid change.

VANIMO

Vanimo is on a neat little peninsula that is reminiscent of Wewak. The similarity continues because there are beautiful beaches on both sides. It is however, much smaller and quieter, with invariably generous and hospitable people. In Vanimo everything is within walking distance, but I'd no sooner start out on foot than someone would offer me a lift! In PNG smaller is better.

Vanimo is only 30 km from the Indonesian border so it is virtually within earshot of the trouble that sporadically flares up between the Indonesians and the Irian Jayans. The last influx of refugees was in 1984 and these people are still a major, sometimes resented, presence in town. Their camp is at Blackwater 20 km to the east. The situation along the border is now quiet.

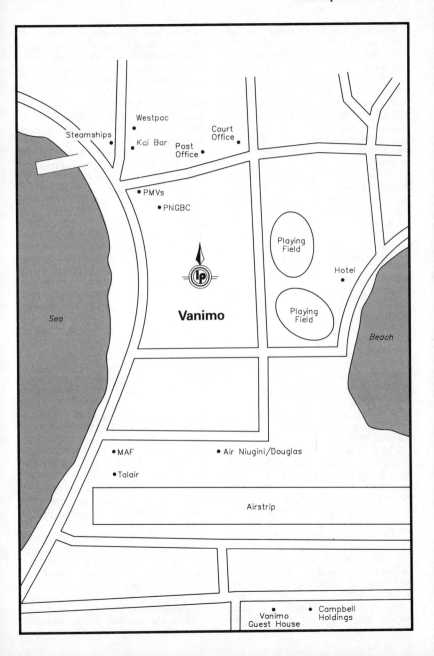

The town has all the essentials: there are Westpac and PNGBC banks, a post office, a couple of reasonable supermarkets and a pub.

Unfortunately, there's nothing too inspiring in the accommodation department. If there were some reasonably-priced village guesthouses, you could hardly imagine a better place to escape to.

If you're adequately protected from the sun and carry some water, you can do a pleasant two hour walk around the headland. You're bound to find some good spots to snorkel. There's another good walk west along the beach from the airport. After about 40 minutes you come to a limestone headland draped with vines; wade around it to the beautiful beach on the other side. There's a rusting Japanese landing barge just offshore.

Places to Stay

There is a hotel and a guesthouse. The *Island Narimo Hotel* (tel 87 1102), PO Box 42, is nicely sited on the eastern side of the peninsular, right next to the beach, with a fine view, but it's a bit run-down. It's perfectly clean and comfortable, just not very inspiring. It has 12 rooms with communal facilities and two with private facilities. Rooms are air-con and there's satellite TV. If you pay cash, or with Amex, it costs K45 for bed and breakfast, which by PNG standards I suppose isn't bad.

The food is excellent (the manager is something of a gourmet) with lunches from K3.50 to K6, main dinner courses from K9 to K14. They can arrange for a vehicle if you contact them in advance and they may also have fishing trips.

The *Vanimo Guest House* (tel 87 1113), PO Box 82, has four twin rooms and can be rather cheaper than the hotel. Officially it's K33 but at this rate you'd be much better off at the hotel – the rooms are small and hot and the toilets and showers leave a lot to be desired. Speak to Brian Callinan at the Air Niugini desk at the airport about student discounts and

suchlike at the guesthouse. Dinner is cheap at K2.10 and there are cold beers and a pool table. It's a bit of a walk, from the other side of the airstrip to town, but you're bound to be offered a lift.

Getting There & Away

Air Air Niugini, Talair and Douglas all fly from Wewak for K72. It's much more interesting to fly in a small plane, because the views are great and you put down at Aitape (K52) and a couple of interesting airfields in the mountains. The Air Niugini planes now turn around at Vanimo, but on Wednesdays Douglas Airways continues to Jayapura for around K33 – the complete trip to Jayapura from Wewak costs K105. Many people then connect with a Garuda flight which leaves Jayapura on Friday and flies to Los Angeles. There is a K10 departure tax for international flights. See the Getting There and Away chapter and the Visas section in the Facts for the Visitor chapter.

Talair and Douglas also fly north to Green River, a large station a three hour walk from the Sepik, most days of the week for K54. On Mondays and Fridays Talair flies to Telefomin (K98) and Oksapmin (K109).

Sea Lutheran Shipping's somewhat basic cargo freighters, the MV *Nagada* and MV *Umboi*, continue on to Vanimo from Wewak; one or the other makes the voyage each week for K17.50/24, deck/1st class; and half that price to Aitape. In Vanimo you get tickets at the wharf prior to departure. Don't count on arriving in town in time for the Jayapura flight – there are inevitably delays.

I once met an adventurous young English couple who arrived in PNG from Irian Jaya by the highly unofficial method of getting a local fisherman to drop them off just across the border; from there they got a ride into Vanimo. This is probably completely illegal but they got away with it. With the touchier border situation

I wouldn't recommend it today, and definitely not if you're heading to Indonesia. Christina Dodwell in her book *In Papua New Guinea* also arrives in PNG by this route.

Getting Around

Everything in Vanimo is within walking distance. PMVs to the surrounding district congregate at the market or near the PNGBC near town. Apparently it's easy to get out to the border, especially on Fridays. You can probably hitch.

AROUND VANIMO

There is a good road along the coast from Vanimo to the Irian Jaya border which is marked by the PNG patrol post of Watung. Here you can see one of the 14 markers which the joint Australian-Indonesian border mapping party erected in 1968. On the way to the border you'll pass some tidy little villages such as Mushu and Yako and some superb white beaches.

The road to Bewani is passable and there are good views and several waterfalls.

The Border

The border between Papua New Guinea and Indonesia (Irian Jaya) is a typical example of good colonial thinking. A ruler-straight line was drawn across a totally unknown area of the world, with no regard for who might be living near it, or on it. There have been a whole series of Dutch-English, Dutch-German, Dutch-Australian and most recently Indonesian-Australian attempts to define exactly where the border is and today it is pretty clear just which unfortunate villages straddle the line.

For many years, PNG villages near the border were under much more Dutch influence than Australian for Hollandia was close while Wewak was a long way away. Many people close to the border still speak Bahasa Indonesian, the lingua franca of Dutch rule. Apart from their other insecurities, villagers within 20 miles of the border on the PNG side are not allowed to grow coffee or raise cattle due to fears of diseases being spread across the border and eventually reaching the productive PNG coffee and cattle industries. Further

south in the Sepik region the high Star Mountains of Irian Jaya continue across the border to form the watersheds for both the Sepik and Fly Rivers.

AITAPE

Aitape is a tiny, picturesque little town that has retained evidence of its long, by PNG standards, colonial history. The Germans established a station here in 1905 and the jail they built in 1906 still stands above the town. It was used by the Japanese during the war.

There are some bits of aircraft wreckage near the wartime Tadji airstrip, the first place captured by the Allies in their advance on the Sepik district. In 1974, 48 dumped aircraft were counted and in a six-week operation many of them were shipped back to the USA for eventual restoration and display at an aircraft museum in California. A Japanese war memorial is between the town and the Santa Anna Mission.

The offshore islands, about 15 km from the coast, are interesting.

Places to Stay

There are single and double rooms at the *Tamara Inn* (tel 87 2060), PO Box 72, Aitape. The quality apparently varies considerably with who is running it at the time, but the rates aren't too bad at K45 (fans), K50 (air-con) including meals.

Getting There & Away

A road links Wewak to Aitape. It's a bit rough without much traffic and it can be impassable in the wet. PMVs run from Wewak for around K10. Douglas and Talair come through every day on their way to or from Vanimo and Wewak for K52.

TELEFOMIN

The remote and tiny station at Telefomin was only opened in 1948 and it's still one of the most isolated places in the country. Despite its inaccessible location high in the central mountains, however, the area is changing quickly and traditional dress is now rare. The Baptist Mission has established a museum with wicker masks, arrows and displays of local flora and fauna. There is a coffee shop run by some volunteers and this would be a good spot to get information about accommodation. There are some dramatic caves in the Oksapmin Valley – guides are necessary.

Places to Stay

There is village accommodation in the region, but talk to the District Officer-In-Charge. Some of the missions in the region accept visitors, but advance notice is a very good idea.

Getting There & Away

Talair flies from Telefomin to Green River on the Upper Sepik for K58, to Oksapmin for K33 and to Vanimo for K109. You can also fly in from Hagen or Port Moresby, via Ok Tedi. MAF also flies to many airfields. It is possible to walk from Oksapmin in five days, but this is very tough and should not be undertaken lightly. Guides are necessary.

OKSAPMIN

Although it was only established in 1962 this remote station is now seeing a fair bit of development and changing quickly.

Oksapmin is the main centre for people around the area where the Southern Highlands Province meets the Western and West Sepik Provinces. This is a beautiful region with the Om and Strickland Rivers and their spectacular valleys. It's driest in November and December, but it can be very wet anytime.

Places to Stay

It is possible to stay in villages around the area, but you should contact the District Officer-In-Charge first. Volunteers have a guesthouse at Tekin, two hours' walk away. There's an Agricultural Centre at Oksapmin run by the Peace Corp, and there are plans for a guesthouse; expect to pay around K5.

Getting There & Away

If you were really keen, you could continue walking to Tekin, Bak, Bimin and down to Olsobib in the Western Province, or to Telefomin. There's a road link to Tekap, a three day trail to Framin (where there's an Aid Post), and another two or three days to Telefomin. Don't attempt this without a guide and make sure you contact the police or the District Officer-In-Charge before you set out. It's another tough five

Huts on the Telefomin Plain

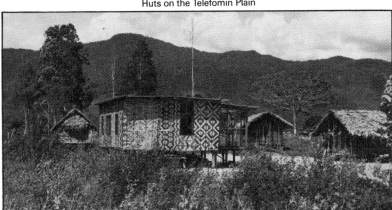

day walk to Lake Kopiago - see the Highlands chapter for more information.

Talair flies from Oksapmin to Green River on the Upper Sepik for K73, to Telefomin for K33 and to Vanimo for K109. There are also flights to Hagen and Moresby. MAF flies to Ambunti (on the Sepik River), Bimin, Tekin and Oksapmin from Telefomin, Mt Hagen (where their headquarters are) and Wewak.

AROUND OKSAPMIN

There are now trade stores in the area with the usual tinned fish, rice, sugar and so on. The district is becoming important for the vegetables it grows and supplies to the Ok Tedi mining project nearby. Other cash crops like coffee beans have also been introduced. This was a protein-deficient area and even spiders, grubs and beetles were eaten before the ubiquitous *tin fis* was introduced. In the evenings you can still sometimes see torches around the valleys as women search for frogs, mice and snakes.

An interesting circular walk can be made through the villages around Oksapmin to the west and back along the Arigo River. North of town there are very few people but around town and to the south in the five high valleys of Bimin, Bak, Tekin, Teranap and Gaua there are over 10,000 people. For the most part their homes and gardens are at about 2000 metres. There's a sub-district office in the Teranap Valley. Bimin is the most isolated of the valleys though it does have an airstrip. Gaua, too, is isolated, but it is only a few hours' walk over the mountains south of Teranap office. The other three valleys are linked by a 32 km road from Terenap to Tekin, up the valley to Tekap through the gap to Bak Valley and down to Daburap. This is known as the Opiago Road. Eventually it will run down to the Strickland, go up the valley of the Tumbudu River and to Lake Kopiago.

The Highlands Highway will eventually extend all the way to Oksapmin. Hopefully by then the Strickland Valley and Gorge will have been designated as a National Park.

Both the Om Valley and Upper Leonard Schultze Valley now have two airstrips and three aid posts, but they are still very isolated. Baptist Missions are found in Telefomin and Tekin and Seventh Day Adventists have moved into the Om River area.

Socially, the entire district is different to the Highlands. There are no ceremonial exchanges and no bride price transactions. 'Big Men' don't exist in the same way and there are few leaders of any lasting duration. The societal system is based on sharing, with power more or less distributed equally. Traditionally, wars were rare and small in scale and sorcerers held the most power. Male and female initiation, along with platform burial and certain forms of dress, have virtually died out, and traditional dress is now only worn on special occasions.

Oksapmin area people are known as having a shame rather than a guilt culture. When people for any number of reasons are shamed they often blame themselves. Apparently a very high percentage of deaths is attributable to suicide. Difficulties in marriage and problems with witches are major causes, but the most important reason was bereavement. Family members used to kill themselves at the loss of loved ones, but this no longer occurs.

Modern development and the problems caused by men leaving to work in other districts and then returning home have resulted in difficulties and disillusionment for people in the region, but it remains quiet and peaceful.

Sheldon Weeks of The University of PNG has collected and edited various studies of the area into *Oksapmin, Development & Change*, available inexpensively at the university in Moresby. This work supplied much of the information for this section.

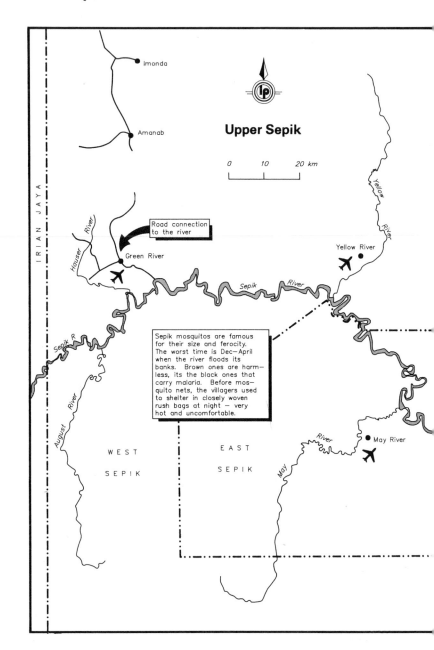

Upper Sepik

0   10   20 km

Road connection
to the river

Green River

Yellow River

IRIAN JAYA

Imonda

Amanab

Hauser River

Sepik R

August River

WEST SEPIK

EAST SEPIK

Sepik River

May River

May River

Yellow River

Sepik mosquitos are famous
for their size and ferocity.
The worst time is Dec–April
when the river floods its
banks. Brown ones are harm-
less, its the black ones that
carry malaria. Before mosquito nets, the villagers used
to shelter in closely woven
rush bags at night — very
hot and uncomfortable.

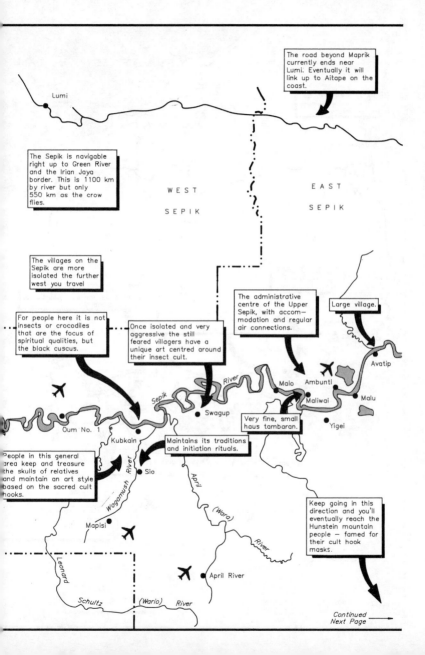

The road beyond Maprik currently ends near Lumi. Eventually it will link up to Aitape on the coast.

The Sepik is navigable right up to Green River and the Irian Jaya border. This is 1100 km by river but only 550 km as the crow flies.

WEST SEPIK

EAST SEPIK

The villages on the Sepik are more isolated the further west you travel

The administrative centre of the Upper Sepik, with accommodation and regular air connections.

Large village.

For people here it is not insects or crocodiles that are the focus of spiritual qualities, but the black cuscus.

Once isolated and very aggressive the still feared villagers have a unique art centred around their insect cult.

Avatip

Maio   Ambunti

Maliwai   Malu

Sepik   River

Swagup

Very fine, small haus tambaran.

Yigei

Oum No. 1

Kubkain

People in this general area keep and treasure the skulls of relatives and maintain an art style based on the sacred cult hooks.

Maintains its traditions and initiation rituals.

Sio

Wogamush River

April

(Wara)

Mapisi

Keep going in this direction and you'll eventually reach the Hunstein mountain people — famed for their cult hook masks.

River

Leonard

April River

Schultz   (Wario) River

Continued Next Page

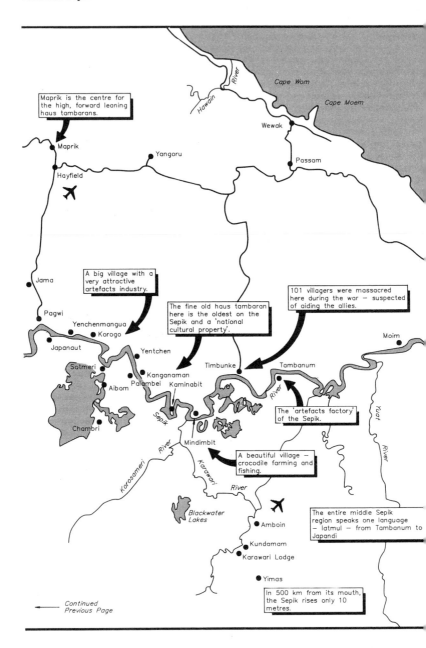

Maprik is the centre for the high, forward leaning haus tambarans.

A big village with a very attractive artefacts industry.

The fine old haus tambaran here is the oldest on the Sepik and a 'national cultural property'.

101 villagers were massacred here during the war — suspected of aiding the allies.

The 'artefacts factory' of the Sepik.

A beautiful village — crocodile farming and fishing.

The entire middle Sepik region speaks one language — Iatmul — from Tambanum to Japandi

In 500 km from its mouth, the Sepik rises only 10 metres.

Continued Previous Page

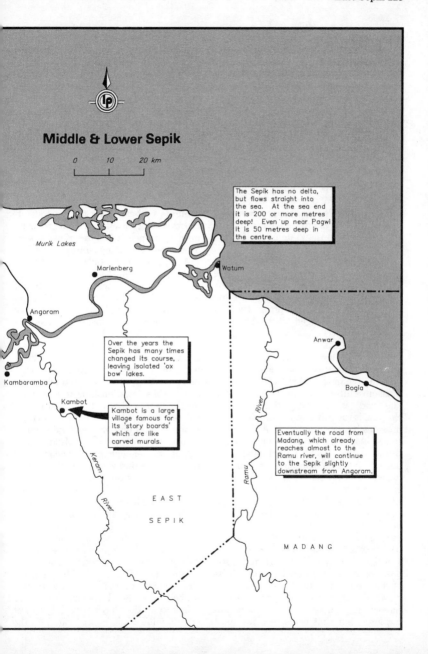

Middle & Lower Sepik

0   10   20 km

The Sepik has no delta,
but flows straight into
the sea. At the sea end
it is 200 or more metres
deep! Even up near Pagwi
it is 50 metres deep in
the centre.

Murik Lakes

Marienberg

Watum

Angoram

Anwar

Over the years the
Sepik has many times
changed its course,
leaving isolated 'ox
bow' lakes.

Bogia

Kambaramba

Kambot

Kambot is a large
village famous for
its 'story boards'
which are like
carved murals.

Eventually the road from
Madang, which already
reaches almost to the
Ramu river, will continue
to the Sepik slightly
downstream from Angoram.

Keram River

Ramu River

EAST

SEPIK

MADANG

The Sepik & its Tributaries

The mighty Sepik (pronounced 'sea-pick') reverted to its local name when the Australians took over from the Germans and Kaiserin Augusta had her name withdrawn from the river. Some people say 'Sepik' means 'great river', but nobody is certain. There are few exploitable natural resources so the Sepik has attracted little development, despite the relative density of the population. On the surface, most villages still appear relatively untouched by western influences and the art is still vigorous and unique, although rarely traditional.

The art itself makes a visit worthwhile. The scale of the river, the impressive architecture of haus tambarans, the beautiful stilt villages, the long canoes with their crocodile-head prows, the bird life, the flower-clogged lakes, the misty dawns and spectacular sunsets make a visit unforgettable.

Nowadays, however, there are many western influences. The Sepik peoples have a dynamic, living culture, not a museum culture, so change, both good and bad, is not surprising. Western clothing is the rule and the impact of the missions has been profound. Although in some villages there has been a revival of traditional ceremonies, including male initiation, this is alongside, or somehow mixed with, Christianity and western-style education. Many of the young men leave the villages and if they do survive the shanty towns in the cities and return, they bring with them both visible and invisible baggage. Travellers and artefact buyers have also left changes in their wake.

Although the Middle Sepik in particular is one of the most frequently visited parts of the country it is not by any standards crowded with tourists. The largest single impact is made by the *Melanesian Explorer*, but that aside, you are most unlikely to be in a village at the same time as any other traveller. You may see the odd group sweeping past in a canoe or river boat, and perhaps a trader or missionary, but that will be about it. Only a small but steady number of travellers stay in the villages, especially independently.

Bear in mind that although in photos Sepik villages look idyllic the photos do not show the heat and humidity (which can be extreme), the mosquitoes (which can be unbelievably numerous and vicious), the village food (which is, at best, monotonous and tasteless), or the housing conditions (which in terms of western comforts are basic). Nor do they indicate the rewards of travelling at your own pace, meeting the people and experiencing such a rich and fascinating culture!

As a general rule, you're best not to try and do too much. Resist the urge to cast yourself unrealistically as a heroic explorer. Although there are differences between the villages' carving styles, their organisation and appearance does not change significantly. Rather than exhaust yourself paddling for days in the middle of a huge monotonous river you would be better off to give yourself time in a village, preferably a bit off the beaten track, so you can establish relationships and get a feel for the people's lives. This is difficult if you're looking at the world through a fog of sunburn, mosquito bites and exhaustion. Two or three villages on the Middle Sepik will be quite enough for most people, and many people find they enjoy themselves more when they get off the main river.

In order to see the Sepik you must either grit your teeth and spend a considerable amount of money, or have plenty of time and persuasive ability – see the Getting Around section following. There is road access to the Sepik at only three points: Angoram on the Lower Sepik, and Timbunke and Pagwi on the Middle Sepik. The alternative is to fly in to airstrips like Amboin on the Karawari River, or Ambunti on the Upper Sepik. The most artistic villages are concentrated on the

Top: Mendam Village, Murik Lakes, near the mouth of the Sepik (ML)
Left: Children, Middle Sepik (RE)
Right: The Sepik finally meets the sea (TW)

Top: The *Melanesian Explorer* cruises the Sepik and the north coast (TW)
Left: Bridges often link different sections of straggling Sepik villages;
    this one is in Timbunke (ML)
Right: The Chambri Lakes, Middle Sepik (TW)

Middle Sepik and the most spectacular scenery is on the lakes or tributaries. If you want to see a reasonable amount of the river at not too considerable a cost, Angoram or Pagwi are the best bases to use although Timbunke and Ambunti are also worth considering.

The Upper Sepik extends from the river's source to just below Ambunti, the Middle Sepik covers from above Pagwi to just before Angoram and the Lower Sepik is the final section from Angoram to the coast.

WHEN TO GO

July to November is the dry season, with the main wet season being December to April. The region gets over 300 inches of rain a year, so it can rain anytime, though it rarely does during the day. Temperatures and humidity can be high, but it's usually pleasant on the river, where you're more likely to get a breeze. The dry season is the best time to visit, since the mosquitoes are less numerous. By August the river level can drop significantly, and this may make negotiating some tributaries and barats difficult. In the dry season the Chambri Lakes can get very smelly: they shrink, fish die and weed rots. The people start gardening in June (when there is little likelihood of floods) and they harvest vegetables from September to November (which must be a relief from sago).

WHAT TO TAKE

Whether you're going in a dugout canoe or on the *Melanesian Explorer*, you must plan carefully what to take although if you're travelling independently the issue becomes vital.

Everyone

You need light cotton clothes – light enough not to be too hot, long enough to protect you from the sun and heavy enough to prevent mosquito bites (they'll bite through fine cheese cloth). If you don't burn easily (remember you'll spend a lot of time on a reflective surface) shorts and T-shirts will be sufficient while you're on the river, as the mosquitoes are only a problem ashore. You'll appreciate being able to tuck a long pair of pants into socks to protect your ankles from probing proboscises, especially in the evenings.

A broad-brimmed hat, sun cream, sunglasses and insect repellant are essential. People talk about their insect repellants on the Sepik with much the same professional interest that travellers in India bring to bear on their stomach condition, but all the major brands seem to work.

A swimsuit is worth packing, although it won't be much use if you're staying in a village since most villagers are very prudish. For men a pair of shorts will be appropriate, women may find a laplap best. Tennis shoes that you don't mind getting wet and muddy are ideal footwear; thongs or sandals are nearly as good.

Bring plenty of film if you're a photography freak and binoculars if you're interested in birds. Make sure this sort of equipment is in a bag or case that is at least rain and splash-proof, preferably fully waterproof. A rain-cape is a good multi-purpose tool (ground sheet, cargo and person protector), and in the wet season, or if you burn easily, an umbrella would also help.

Although the bank at Angoram changes travellers' cheques it is advisable to organise your money in Wewak, Vanimo or Tari. Make sure you have plenty of small denomination notes – especially K2s – as you will find the village people will rarely have change.

Staying in Villages

Those staying in villages will need a torch (flashlight) for night excursions. It's ideal if the torch casts a wide beam, because you may need it for cooking at night. Take a spare globe and batteries. Candles are useful.

It is essential to sleep well if you're going to survive the heat, food and mosquitoes in good humour. That means you must have a mosquito net (nets will probably be supplied for tour groups) and a sleeping mat. There is an art to organising a mosquito net, but first you must ensure that it is large enough to allow you to sleep without touching the sides (a two-person net gives you much more room: if you're large it's essential) and the mesh size must be very fine (around one mm). A well-ventilated inner section from a hiking tent is ideal, as it also gives you a bit of privacy.

You will need a supply of cheap string or twine so that you can suspend the net from handy beams and walls. Sepik long houses have no internal divisions, so your net becomes your bedroom. If you've hung a net and you're not using it, drape the sides across its roof. Make your entry as swiftly as possible, tuck the bottom edges of your net underneath your mat, and then make sure you've killed any *natnats* that have come in with you. The mat is not just an optional extra. The floors of Sepik long houses are made of the outer casing of a palm, which is smooth, springy, airy, and definitely not mosquito proof. The mat will also be very useful as a cushion in your canoe.

You must take at least some food. Although there are infrequent trade stores they usually only sell tinned fish, rice and tobacco. The local people will often offer you a meal (not always), but most of the year this will only consist of sago (*saksak*) and smoked fish (*makau*). The sago is, in most forms, vaguely suggestive of tasteless Plasticine and the smoked fish, while good, quickly loses its appeal. Coconut and banana (the starchy, cooking type) can liven the picture a little, and there are taros and introduced vegetables late in the dry season.

It is an unbelievably monotonous diet, and you will be hard pushed to look that smoked fish in the eye for the 10th consecutive meal. If you do eat the locals' food and have nothing else to give in return, you should pay a kina or so per meal. Instead of paying, however, the best

idea is to have packet soups, biscuits, jam and other western-style food that you can share and trade. If you stay with families, there will always be a cooking fire, but if you end up in a haus kiap you'll need some sort of stove.

Villages often have rainwater you can drink, and it's handy to have a water bottle. The Sepik water may look a bit muddy, but it's quite OK, so long as it hasn't been taken directly downstream of a town. The volume of water is so huge and the number of people living alongside is so small that there aren't any problems. If you want to be absolutely confident take along some purification tablets.

Make sure you have some good maps. The river changes quickly, however, so they are all out of date. An ox-bow becomes the main stream, or the main stream becomes an ox-bow very quickly, and smaller channels can be blocked by floating islands. *Wewak, the Gateway to the Sepik* is a reasonable map and it is available in Wewak at the Christian Bookshop; the spelling is more accurate than most.

There are aid posts along the river, but you should have a medical kit to cope with emergencies. It's easy for a mosquito bite to become infected for instance, and if you are planning a long trip, you should research how to treat malaria.

POINTERS

The Sepik people can often be fairly indifferent, even suspicious, when you first meet them. Younger men particularly, often adopt a tough-guy image. It can take a while to get beyond this barrier. Perhaps this is partly due to pushy travellers who rush in, grab a pile of carvings, struggle bitterly to save every toea and leave without making any contribution. And I'm not just talking about money, but being friendly, taking time to talk, sharing food and maybe even a song.

Try to behave in accord with local customs – watch and learn. Dress and act conservatively, taking your cue from people around you. If you're in a village and want a swim, ask when and where the locals bathe; there will often be separate times for men and women and it will be considered extremely rude if you watch or take photos.

Most Sepik villages are rigidly patriarchal. Western men should be cautious about talking to women – you'll often embarrass them and may cause jealousy – talk to middle-aged men. And western women should be cautious about talking to men – this may be misinterpreted – talk to the women. It is always difficult to read peoples' characters, but watching their faces and learning their names will be a good start. Don't over use their names in normal speech.

It is immensely preferable to stay with a family, rather than isolated in a haus tambaran or haus kiap. It will be more enjoyable and more secure. When you're looking for somewhere ask around among middle-aged men, not children. Try to get to a village reasonably early in the afternoon so you've plenty of time to establish yourself.

The amount you are expected to pay for accommodation varies, so it is worth establishing a figure in advance. As a general rule don't argue or haggle; the Sepik people avoid direct conflict, so if you're quoted a price that is obviously too high, be low key when you suggest a more reasonable figure. Somewhere between K2 and K5 will be usual, plus a couple of kina for food, if you don't have anything to trade. You will normally be expected to pay the man of the house, but this is not always the case. Don't pay in advance.

Ask before you take photographs. *Never* take a picture of or in a haus tambaran (even if it is only under construction) before gaining permission from the men who are inevitably sitting around underneath. The nearest equivalent in western society is a church, so you should show respect. Ask before you enter, even the ground floor, and remove your hat. Women may not be allowed to enter,

especially upstairs, although this rule is usually bent for westerners. Sometimes there will be a charge (usually K1 or so).

On the Middle Sepik you will usually be able to find someone who speaks a little English – often one of the children – but in most cases you will be very restricted in your communication without some knowledge of Pidgin. Beyond the Middle Sepik, Pidgin will be even more important.

Travel Times

The travel times given in this chapter should be used as very rough indicators only. There are many variables that can significantly alter times: the length of a canoe, the weight of cargo, the size of a motor, the skill of the driver, the number of stops you make, how hard and efficiently you paddle, whether you get lost, the height of the river, whether there's a head wind and whether there's any wind at all (chop will slow most canoes down considerably).

The river flows between three and five knots per hour so travelling upstream will be slower and more expensive (more fuel is needed) than travelling downstream. Although the locals can paddle upstream it is unrealistic for westerners to consider doing so.

The motor canoe times given in this chapter are for a large canoe (12 metres) with a 25 hp motor and a full load travelling downstream in good conditions. Canoe times are for solid paddling. As a general rule, 30 minutes in a motor canoe will equal two or three hour's paddling. Add about 30% for upstream times. Flat-bottomed aluminium boats are much quicker, especially in windy conditions.

SAFETY

Basically, it is safe to visit the Sepik, but you should be a little cautious and use your brains. Once you are out on the river you are a long way from help. There have been reports of robberies, and although these are rare, most locals don't like to travel alone. You do have to watch your belongings, so you are best off leaving non-essentials like passports at somewhere like Ralf's place in Wewak. A pile of interesting things left in your canoe while you go for a wander will soon disappear.

Mixed groups of men and women will always be safe to approach, but you should be sceptical about small groups of men. Several homosexual attacks on lone male travellers, after they have trustingly paddled ashore in response to a friendly greeting, have been reported. There have also been stories of children threatening to tip canoes. As always, women should dress conservatively and be doubly careful.

There are still crocodiles on the Sepik, although they are hunted heavily and are very leery of human beings. They are not a problem. Their territories do not extend any great distance from the edge of water – you are most at risk if you are a long way from human habitation, within 20 or 30 metres of a river, at dusk, and you have returned to the same spot several times. A number of people have been bitten by venomous snakes, mostly at night stumbling around in the dark – take a torch and in long grass flick the ground ahead with a handy stick. Check the location of the toilet, which will be a separate shack a short walk away, and the layout of the washing place in daylight.

SEPIK GLOSSARY
Barets
Barets are man-made channels that are built as shortcuts across loops in the river (sometimes saving many arduous miles of paddling) to link adjoining lakes to the river or, when the river's course changes, a village with the river.

Haus Tambarans
Tambarans are spirits so the haus tambaran is the house where they live – or at least where the carvings that represent them are kept. You may also hear them referred to as 'spirit houses' or 'men's houses', since only initiated men (and tourists) are allowed to enter. Once upon a time a woman who ventured inside met instant death – and although western women are

usually allowed inside, times have probably not changed for the village women.

Every clan has to have a spirit house and although they may have lost some of their cultural importance they are still very much the centre of local life. On the Sepik, men while away the day lounging around in the cool shade underneath, carving, talking or just snoozing. On the Blackwater Lakes during the nine month lead up to their initiation, the initiates live in the upstairs section of the haus tambaran, and are only allowed out at night when the rest of the village has gone to sleep.

Haus tambaran styles vary: the high, forward leaning style of the Maprik region is probably best known, but some on the Sepik are equally spectacular. They can be huge buildings on mighty, carved piles, 40 to 50 metres long with a spire at each end stretching 25 metres into the air. When the missionaries first arrived some zealous individuals burnt down haus tambarans to destroy the village 'idols'. One brave district officer actually took the commendable action of charging a missionary with arson and these days a more enlightened attitude is usual.

Head Hunting
The Sepik people were once fierce and enthusiastic warriors, but with the arrival of Europeans the frequent inter-village raids came to an end. Traditionally, no man could take his place in the tribe until he had killed – it didn't matter who, an old woman or a small child was just as good as a rival warrior. The skull was brought back and hung in the haus tambaran and the warrior was then allowed to wear an apron of flying fox skin as a mark of distinction. No haus tambaran was erected without a human skull under every post. Some of them had a lot of posts.

Initiation
In most villages the traditional initiation for young men is no longer practised, but in a surprising number of places it has been re-established – Michael Somare, PNG's first prime minister, underwent initiation on the Murik Lakes. Sometimes there is a significant departure from strict forms of the ceremony, particularly in the amount of time initiates are trained, and the skin-cutting may be carried out over a number of 'operations'. Some people argue that it has lost its true significance and become simply a 'macho' exercise, and it is

difficult to imagine how it is integrated with Christianity and western educations.

After a long period of confinement, training and education the initiation ceremony culminates in a skin-cutting ceremony. The initiates' arms, shoulders and upper bodies are patterned with cuts. These cuts are between one and two cm long, quite deep (they don't just break the skin) and arranged in swirling patterns. The cuts are now most usually made with a razor blade, in place of the traditional bamboo knives, and the whole process takes about an hour. Clay and ashes are rubbed in to the cuts to ensure they heal as raised keloid scars – like crocodile scales. During the ceremony the haus tambaran is totally shielded off by a high fence and the drums, flutes and bull roarers play continuously.

Makau

The most commonly caught fish on the Middle Sepik is the Makau, a small fish similar in size and shape to a bream. They are smoked over a pottery hearth for preservation, then wrapped in banana leaves and cooked. They make good eating and are the usual accompaniment to the sago pancake. They seem to be prolific and they are netted in large numbers by the women. I was told that fish (perhaps only makau?) were introduced to the Sepik by the Germans – does anyone know?

Natnat

Natnat is Pidgin for mosquito. The Sepik variety isn't particularly big or vicious, but they make up for this with their numbers. Walking through Sotmeri one morning I looked up to see the back of the person in front of me completely black with hitchhikers.

They aren't a problem while you're in the middle of the river, but once you're on the banks they descend in hoards. They are particularly bad in the evenings. The dry season (July to November) is much better than the wet, which is impossible to imagine. The mosquitoes are not such a problem once you get up the tributaries, either. Higher altitudes, cooler weather and faster flowing water might explain it, although the Blackwater Lakes seem particularly free.

The Sepik people have developed a number of strategies to cope. The simplest is to wave a plaited fan/whisk, an action that soon becomes completely reflex. Perhaps the greatest contribution the west has made is the cotton

mosquito net. Before these were available finely woven wicker baskets, which must have been unbelievably hot, were used. The other technique is to drive them away with smoke. Special aromatic, smoky woods are used (if possible) and fires are lit under the long houses, so the smoke can drift up through the floor. This makes the long houses smoky, as well as hot, but anything is better than the mosquitoes. Wherever people sit around, fires are lit. The Sepik is the only place I have been where smoke from a fire hasn't followed me – and the only place where I wanted it to!

Penis Gourds

In the Upper Sepik region men traditionally wore a long, decorated gourd on their penises, and not much else. Western clothes have now been adopted. Some villages on the Middle Sepik sell penis gourds to tourists.

Pitpit

Pitpit is a wild sugar cane that crowds up to the bank of the river and grows up to three metres high. Much of the Middle and Lower Sepik is densely lined with this monotonous weed.

Pukpuk

Pukpuk is Pidgin for crocodile. Crocodiles still have enormous cultural and economic importance on the river. In their initiation rites, young men are scarred so that it looks like they have crocodile scales on their arms, legs and trunk. Incisions are made in patterns, and mud is rubbed in to make raised scars that men wear with pride. The process must be unbelievably painful, although the initiates are somehow trained to cope.

Crocodile heads are still carved on the prows of the handsome Sepik dugout canoes. And, of course, crocodiles are still one of the most important sources of cash for the Sepik villagers.

Saksak

Saksak is Pidgin for sago, which is the staple food for the Sepik people, and in fact for people who live throughout the swampy areas of PNG.

The preparation of sago is a long process and the end result is neither very appetising nor very nutritional. It is basically pure starch, but in a land where it is often too swampy to grow anything else, it is vitally important. Certainly there is no shortage of it, since sago palms grow prolifically. On the Sepik dry sago is usually mixed with water and fried into a rubbery pancake, although it can be boiled into a gluey porridge. Mixed with grated coconut it becomes quite palatable, but by itself it is almost tasteless. Supplemented with bananas, vegetables or fish it will keep you going.

The sago palm is a very ancient food source and it is difficult to imagine how and when it was discovered. First, a sago palm (which looks just like any other palm tree to me) is cut down, the bark is cut away and the pith is chipped and pounded out, producing what looks like fibrous sawdust. That's the men's contribution. Next the women knead the pith in a bark funnel with a rough filter, draining water through the pith to dissolve the starch. The starch-laden water is collected (often in an old canoe) and the starch settles in a orange, glutinous mass at the bottom.

Salvinia

Salvinia Molesta, to give this water weed its full name, once threatened the entire Sepik system with ecological disaster. It could well have forced the depopulation of the region, but it is now, fortunately, under control. Salvinia originated in Brazil, has small, fleshy fan-like leaves and can double in size in two days. You will see small chunks of it floating down the river and anybody who has spent time on the river will be able to point it out to you.

When it was introduced to the Sepik it went wild. At its worst in 1982/83 it covered 60% of the Lower and Middle Sepik's lakes, lagoons and barats, often forming a mat too thick for canoes to penetrate, isolating villages and preventing fishing. Herbicides were clearly inappropriate, and it grew much faster than it could be cut.

The solution was to introduce a weevil, Cyrtobagus. The adult feeds on Salvinia's buds and the larvae burrow through the plant which dies, becomes water-logged and sinks. Widescale distribution of the weevil began in 1983. The results were dramatic, and within months Cyrtobagus was winning the war – and it still holds the upper-hand today.

UPPER SEPIK

Above Ambunti the villages are smaller and more spread out, and the people have had less contact with western tourists and are friendly and hospitable. The missions have had a big impact, however. There is

not nearly the same concentration of artistic skills that you find on the Middle Sepik, but it is still an interesting area – traditionally, different villages had their own cult or focal point for the spiritual world.

From Ambunti the river narrows and the land it flows through becomes more hilly with denser vegetation. In many areas trees grow right down to the water's edge. Large vessels can travel a day or two from Ambunti, but beyond that the twisting river is suitable only for small boats. There are few artefacts after Yessan and there is a long uninhabited stretch between Tipas and Mowi, although there are hunting lodges where you can stay, at relatively frequent intervals.

The Upper Sepik is more isolated than the Middle Sepik, since there are no roads, so a visit requires detailed planning. You should definitely bring your own food. If you want to buy your own canoe, a village up here would be a good place to start.

Green River

This is a sub-district station, close to the Sepik River in West Sepik Province, due south of Vanimo and very close to the Irian Jaya border. It's about a three hour walk to the river, but there is a road and you may get a lift.

You can fly from Vanimo with Douglas or Talair every day except Tuesday and Sunday for K59, but there are also links to Telefomin and Oksapmin. It would be worth talking to MAF. This has been suggested as a starting point for a canoe trip, but you will be undertaking a major project; something like 10 days solid paddling to get to Ambunti.

Swagup

Well off the main stream, east of the April River, Swagup is the home of the insect cult people, who are still fairly isolated and have their own language. Their unique art usually incorporates the figure of a sago beetle, dragonfly, praying mantis or other insect. The ferocious reputation these people earned in former times lives on.

Maio & Yessan

These people have a yam cult, but they have been heavily influenced by missionaries. This area is quite swampy and marshy.

Maliwai

This village is on a small lake off the river. Going up the river one encounters many villages known for their specialised religious cults. Here the cassowary figures prominently in myth and is carved into most things, regardless of function. It is customary to cut off a finger joint when there is a death in the family.

Yigei

The Ulagu Lagoon area is inhabited by people originally from the Hunstein Mountains toward Enga Province. Cult hooks are the most interesting artefacts that are produced. The lagoon is home to many varieties and large numbers of birds.

Yambon

Not far from Ambunti, Yambon has good art and an interesting haus tambaran.

Ambunti

Ambunti is an administrative centre of no great interest, but there is an airstrip, and a couple of reliable people who hire motorised canoes. This is one of the best potential places to start a trip. There are even a couple of places to stay.

Places to Stay The *Ambunti Lodge* (tel 86 29220), run by Santon Tours in Wewak is beside the red trade store. It has eight simple but clean rooms at K30/45 for singles/doubles. The lounge, with beer at K1.10, has numerous Sepik artefacts on the wall. You can also organise canoe trips here.

A cheaper alternative is variously known as *PIM*, for Pacific Island Ministries, or the *Akademi* (tel 88 5925), PO Box 41,

which and has rooms for K10, breakfasts for K1.50, dinners for K3. They will also hire canoes for K10 per day. Don't be too ambitious about paddling upstream.

Getting There & Away There is no road link. Douglas flies to Ambunti on Tuesday, Thursday and Saturday for K49 and MAF has a number of links, including one from Oksapmin.

It is possible to hire motorised canoes. One of the most respected and reliable guides on the river, Kowspi Marek, can be contacted through PIM or PO Box 95. Several members of his family now follow the trade, so if Kowspi is booked up, one of his relatives may be able to help. Joseph Wangan has also been recommended. Expect to pay around K30 a day plus fuel.

See what the lodge can offer and ask around at the stores. Often the owners have been around for a while and can offer good advice. Alan Gallagher at Las Trade Store is helpful, but does not rent boats himself so don't expect him to set everything up.

Some people have bought canoes here for as little as K15, but K30 and up is more likely. In general, they're cheaper here than around Pagwi. If you're having problems it might be worth hiring a motorised boat for a day – you *may* be able to find something in a nearby village.

When you can find one, a PMV moto (communal canoe) will cost about K4 to Pagwi. Travel times to Pagwi are one hour motor, six hours canoe.

Malu

This village, near to Ambunti, is interesting for its variety of fruit trees and flowers.

Avatip

Although this is the largest village on the upper Sepik, it's not very interesting. The Germans burnt it down twice and the old carving skills have been totally lost. The men's house is a dull place. The village has three initiations, the second of which is involved with the yam cult while the third is only for old men. Debating is of great importance. They debate to try to find the meanings of names, information which the owners of the names are very reluctant to part with.

MIDDLE SEPIK

The middle Sepik region starts just below Ambunti and finishes just short of Angoram. This is regarded as the 'cultural treasure house' of PNG and almost every village has a distinct artistic style, although these styles are now tending to merge. The villages themselves are very similar so there is no pressing need to see them all. Although the whole middle Sepik region is of great interest the largest concentration of villages is just below Pagwi. It is possible to visit a number of them on day trips.

Pagwi

Down the road from Hayfields, Pagwi is the most important access point to the Middle Sepik, although there is also a road to Timbunke. There is little of interest in Pagwi, despite this vital role, and it's a rather ugly little place. There are a couple of run-down government buildings and galvanised iron trade stores and that's it. You can buy food (although it is mostly of the tinned variety) and the mark-up isn't too bad.

Places to Stay You can sleep on the floor of the Council House for K2 per night. There are no lights or beds, but there is an outside toilet and water tank. It's OK for a short stay while you wait for a boat. There are rats so store your food where they can't get it. You'll need mosquito nets.

Getting There & Away See the Maprik Getting There & Away section. It is 53 rough km from Maprik to Pagwi and it would be murderous in the wet. From Wewak to Pagwi by PMV will cost K10 or K11. The best time to catch PMVs back to Maprik and Wewak is very early on

Saturday mornings (4 or 5 am); there's a trickle of traffic during the week, but nothing on Sundays.

You can hire motorised canoes here, but use discretion. Steven Buku is highly recommended, but he actually lives in Yenchenmangua, about 30 minutes away by motorised canoe. You can contact him through PO Box 106, Maprik. He's honest and fair and has been doing trips for years. Aldonus Mana from Japandai, a bit upstream, is another local operator who has been recommended. Ken Dowry the store owner may be able to advise you about who is reliable.

An interesting and fairly comprehensive three day tour could be made out to the Chambri Lakes, down river as far as Kaminabit, then back to Pagwi. Day trips can be made to Korogo. Daily costs for a canoe seem to be around K35 plus fuel. Aibom, Palambei, Yentchen and Kanganaman are all interesting and are all within reach. It will take about six hours' running time to Timbunke, and another five hours to Angoram. Depending on your stops and side trips you could do a five to seven day trip down to Angoram for around K300.

People have on occasion paid outrageous prices for canoes here – I'm talking K100, so you may have to make enquiries at nearby villages if you want to get something cheaper.

Japanaut

This small village specialises in trinkets – little black masks or other carvings on shell or seed necklaces. Although every village has its own distinctive style there is also almost always some strange little item which is completely out of character.

Yenchenmangua

Yenchenmangua has an interesting haus tambaran and good artefacts.

Korogo

This is a commercially-oriented village right on the side the river. It is worth visiting, because they are in the process of constructing a haus tambaran, and you can see the dramatically carved central poles – they ask for a contribution to the building costs.

There is a Korogo Village Guest House (contact through Joe Kenni at the Angoram Hotel) at K10 per person. You can make a pleasant two hour walk to an interesting inland village. Travel times from Pagwi: ½ hour motor, three hours canoe.

Sotmeri

Variously misspelt as Swatmeri and Suapmeri, Sotmeri is famous for its mosquitoes, less so for its carvings. There is little for sale, although the village was famed for its orator's stools. I was told the mosquitoes take the pleasure out of carving! Despite all this, it's an attractive village and it is at the entrance to the Chambri Lakes.

You may be able to stay with a friendly family for K2; ask for James Yesinduma. James knows everyone who lives on the the river and speaks reasonable English. It is very difficult to find your way through to the Chambri Lakes along the weed-filled barats, but James will arrange a guide for a couple of kina. Rather than backtrack to Sotmeri, you can follow a channel that brings you out just above Kaminabit. Travel times from Korogo: ½ hour motor, three hours canoe. To Aibom in the Chambri Lakes: 1½ hour motor, nine hour canoe. If you can get a PMV from Pagwi it will cost around K4.

Yentchen

An hour by motorised canoe from Sotmeri, you can stay in a big, clean haus tambaran for K5.

Palambei

You can't see the village proper from the river and it can be easy to miss. There are two or three huts and there may be some canoes on the bank. It's a hot 20 minute walk along a barat (dry in the dry season), but it is worth the effort because the

village is beautiful. Built around several small lagoons, which are full of flowering water lilies, there are also two impressive haus tambarans at either end of a ceremonial green. The ruined buildings, including a haus tambaran, close to the green, were bombed by the Allies in WW II.

Stones, which must have been carried many km, have been set up in the glade. There are also two virtuoso garamut drummers who will bring their hollow-log drums to life in an intricate duet. Ask for Otto and pay K4 for an unforgettable performance. The village women make the best bilums I saw on the river. Travel times from Sotmeri: 1½ hours motor, nine hour canoe.

Kanganaman

A brief walk from the river, this village is famous for the oldest haus tambaran on the river. It has been declared a building of national cultural importance and is being renovated with help from the National Museum. It is a huge building with enormous carved posts.

Kaminabit

Kaminabit is not a particularly attractive village, not least because of the large lodge. There are, however, some good carvings. The lodge is used by a number of tour groups, including Trans Niugini (the Karawari and Ambua people) and is only opened for them. Shoestringers should ask for Anton Bob who has opened a separate guesthouse in another western-style building. It has tank water and a kerosene fridge and costs K5. Travel time from Aibom: one hour motor; six hours canoe. From Palambei: 1½ hour motor; nine hours canoe. If you find a PMV from Sotmeri it will cost about K3.

Mindimbit

The village is near the junction of the Karawari and Korosameri Rivers. The Korosameri leads up to the beautiful Blackwater Lakes region. Mindimbit is entirely dependent on carving and there is some nice work, though there is no proper haus tambaran. This was the home for many years for an Australian; his son Jeff Liversich still spends time in the village and is a wealth of information.

You can stay with a friendly family for K3 or so; ask for Peter Bai. They live in the downstream section of the village, which is spread out along the bank and a half hour walk from end to end. Travel time from Kaminabit via the river: 2½ hours motor; or via the shortcut: one hour motor, six hours canoe.

Timbunke

This is a large town with a big Catholic Mission, hospital and a number of other western-style buildings. There are also some impressive long houses. There is a road link to Wewak, which would be murder in the wet, maybe even impassable, but traffic is fairly sparse at best. A PMV will cost around K5.

You can hire motor canoes; ask around at the trade stores. Felix Sony has been recommended. People have had problems trying to find somewhere to stay, and the mission is not helpful. Philip Laki may be able to help and he has also been suggested as someone who might be interested in buying canoes. Travel time from Mindimbit: one hour motor; six hours canoe. Travel time to Angoram: four hours motor. If you can find a PMV from Mindimbit, it will cost about K2.

Tambanum

This is one of the largest villages on the Middle Sepik, and fine, large houses are strung along the bank for quite a distance. The people are renowned carvers. Margaret Mead lived here for an extended time. Travel time from Timbunke: ½ hour motor.

LOWER SEPIK

The Lower Sepik starts a little upstream from Angoram and runs down to the coast. Angoram is the most important town on the Sepik. The Marienberg Mission station which has been operated by the Catholics for many years is about two hours downstream.

Near the mouth of the river, the Murik Lakes are vast semi-flooded swamp lands, narrowly separated from the coast. Villages along this part of the Sepik are smaller, poorer and generally have had less western contact than many in the middle region.

Angoram

Angoram is the oldest and largest Sepik station, established by the Germans before WW I. It's a pleasant, sleepy place with a bit of frontier town atmosphere. It is the administrative centre for the Lower and Middle Sepik. If you were just wanting to 'see' the Sepik without actually travelling on it then Angoram is the best place to visit – it's much more interesting than Pagwi and Timbunke and the road is much better. It's possible to hire motor canoes and although the most interesting art is around Pagwi, culturally there's not much difference.

Eventually Angoram will also be connected with Madang – slightly downstream from the town a barge will cross the river and a road will be put through to the Ramu River. There are several rubber and cocoa plantations along the road to Wewak; the workers live in Angoram. You can change travellers' cheques at the PNGBC bank, although I'd personally feel more confident doing this in Wewak, and there are a couple of reasonable trade stores.

Haus Tamboran Angoram has a large haus tambaran which is a mixture of local styles. It was built solely for the display and sale of artefacts and is now run-down, but there are items from all areas of the Sepik for sale, including masks, flutes, basketwork, jewellery and an excellent selection of the famous Kambot storyboards from the Keram River. There are also items carved by Angoram's resident

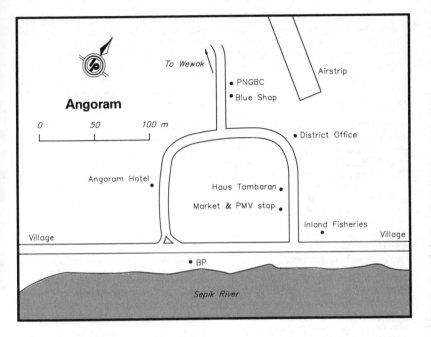

Angoram

0   50   100 m

To Wewak
• PNGBC
• Blue Shop
Airstrip
• District Office
Angoram Hotel •
Haus Tambaran •
Market & PMV stop •
Inland Fisheries
•
Village   Village
• BP
Sepik River

craftsmen. Everything has a marked price, and although prices are higher than on the river they're not too bad.

'Shanghai' Brown Ominously perched right at the end of the rarely used airstrip is a tiny graveyard. Amongst those buried there is the legendary labour recruiter 'Shanghai' Brown who, according to his headstone, 'died in 1956 of Blackwater'. He features briefly in Colin Simpson's book *Plumes and Arrows*.

Places to Stay The *Angoram Hotel* (tel 88 3054), PO Box 35, is a rambling, garishly painted fibro-cement building. The day before I arrived the town had a working bee and cleaned up the paddock in front of the hotel: consequently there was no beer! There *were* refrigerated drinks, a luxury mostly unknown elsewhere on the Sepik. The gardens are well maintained, the rooms are clean and adequate. It's

reasonable value – but it's not exactly the Hilton.

Joe Kenni, the owner, is an important local figure; he also runs the Maprik Waken hotel and is in contact with the Korogo Village Guest House. He's an enthusiastic promoter of tourism in the region and organises tours and rents river transport. One of his employees, Fred, is very helpful and can help organise independent canoe trips. The 40 rooms are air-con, all have attached bathrooms and the rates are from K26 to K31 per person; breakfast is K4, lunch is K6 and a three-course dinner, K12. They may have a student discount.

You can stay with local families further downstream from the Inland Fisheries sheds. One name I was given was Torave Dambui. Another entrepreneur, Peter Dimi, was in the process of building a guesthouse on the other bank, which is not too convenient. He plans to charge K5, but he also runs river boats and canoes so you will come under a fair amount of pressure .... If you're stuck, Ludwig Schulze, a local trader, will be able to suggest somewhere. His crocodile farm and house are about 400 metres downstream from the Fisheries sheds. People sometimes camp at the Police Station.

Getting There & Away The road to Angoram is the shorter of the two access routes to the Sepik. It branches off the Maprik road only 19 km out of Wewak. The 113 km, all-weather road is good by Sepik standards but you still shake, rattle and roll. The traffic is reasonably frequent, but if you're going in to Wewak you will have to start very early – around 6.30 am. PMVs cost about K5 and their stop is near the market. It's an interesting two or three hour journey.

Angoram is a reasonable starting point for Sepik trips, although it is really only relevant to those hiring motor canoes (sooner or later you're going to have to go up stream).

You can book trips at the Angoram Hotel. A river boat with a 40 hp motor and a driver will cost about K80 per day, a canoe about K60. A good day trip is south on the Keram River to Kambot, stopping at either Magendo or Chimondo on the way. These villages are familiar with outsiders and there are no great art bargains, but the river is narrow, winding and the banks are crowded with luxuriant growth. To Kambot by boat/canoe costs about K70/50, to Kambaramba K50/40, to Moin K60/50. You can also make day trips to the Murik Lakes – they're about three hours away.

Prices can vary a lot so ask around. Cletus Smank and Jimmy Yainat have been recommended.

SEPIK TRIBUTARIES
The Sepik River can become monotonous as it winds through its vast, flat plain, with pitpit crowding up to its banks. The most spectacular scenery is on the tributaries

and the villages are generally smaller, friendlier and less visited. In most cases you will have to travel quite a distance upstream and this means you will either have to fly in or use a motor canoe. Most of these areas are more traditional; you should plan your journey with some care and bring food of your own.

May (Iwa) River
May River is a small town more than half way from Ambunti to the Irian Jaya border. There's an airstrip and mission settlement and it's possible to begin a river trip at this point. Canoes can be bought for around K30. The locals and missionaries will discourage you from going alone. The local guides don't like to go alone either – they travel in pairs and ask K10 each a day. The villages in this area are not often visited and relationships between them not always amicable but it could be a great trip.

Talk to the people at MAF or Ralf's in Wewak; they might be able to give you the names of people to contact in the area. It's not a good idea to arrive unannounced and expect to be accommodated.

April & Wogamush River Area
Life on these tributaries continues more traditionally than on the main river with initiation rites and various social taboos and systems still intact.

It is possible to fly to April River (Niksek) from Tari where there's a big mission and new village. For accommodation contact Jacob Walter, Evangelical Mission, CMML, PO Box 72, Wewak in advance. Although there aren't many spare canoes, you might be lucky enough to find one. Expect to pay around K45. There are villages at regular intervals and it will take about 21 hours paddling to get to the Sepik – three or four days. The river splits 2½ hours after Bitaram and the left fork is the quicker route to the main river. From the junction it will take you another three or four days to get to Ambunti.

Chambri Lakes

The Chambri Lakes are a vast and beautiful expanse of shallow water (they partially dry in the dry season, making things pretty smelly). It's difficult to find your way in, as floating islands can block the entrances. James Yesinduma at Sotmeri can organise a guide for a couple of kina. Rather than backtracking via Sotmeri you can continue east and come back out on the river just above Kaminibit.

Indagu is one of the three villages that make up Chambri. There is a haus tambaran here with a huge collection of carvings – mainly in the ' polished Chambri style. There are also many ornamental spears. Aibom, another village on the lakes, is noted for its pottery. The distinctive Aibom pots sell from only a kina or two and the pottery fireplaces used all over the Sepik are made here.

If you're looking for somewhere to stay, ask for Anscar Kui at Aibom, and you may, but don't count on it, be able to stay at the Mission. Jimmy Maik of Kandingai Village, Kandingai, PO Box 106, Maprik, has accommodation.

Travel time from Sotmeri to Aibom is 1½ hours motor canoe, one day canoe; from Aibom to Kaminibit is one hour motor canoe, six hours canoe. It is possible to catch a village boat to Kandingai from Pagwe most days of the week (between 3 and 5 pm) for around K5.

Karawari River

The Karawari runs into the Korosameri (which drains the Blackwater Lakes) and then into the Sepik just near Mindimbit. For the first hour or so the banks are crowded with pitpit but the jungle soon takes over and the river becomes more interesting, with wide sand bars (in the dry), interesting bird life, occasional crocodiles and attractive villages.

Amboin For those with the money, the *Karawari Lodge* (Trans Niugini Tours, tel 52 1438, PO Box 371, Mt Hagen) at Amboin is recommended. It's a luxury base for exploring the Sepik. Built with bush materials and with some of the atmosphere of a haus tambaran, the lodge has dramatic views across the river and a vast sea of jungle. There are 20 twin rooms all with panoramic views. Sitting on the

Aibom Pot

balcony eating fresh, warm scones for breakfast is a surreal and enjoyable experience you will not forget in a hurry. The cost is K125 per day per person, but this does include all meals and tours from the lodge.

Amboin is usually reached by air and from there you travel a short distance up the river to the lodge. Talair flies regularly from Wewak (K48) and Tari (K60). The lodge river trucks will take you to nearby villages like Maraba, Marvwak and Simbut – where the traditional Sepik-style tree houses are still used. There are also tours that utilise the lodge at Kaminibit and some that stay in the villages. Sing-sings and re-enactments of the Mangamai skin-cutting ceremonies are all part of the deal. They also organise special tours for bird-watchers to the Yimas Lakes.

Korosameri River

Mameri, about 40 minutes motor canoe from Mindimbit and just before the turnoff to the Blackwater Lakes, has some of the most accomplished, dramatic and expensive carving I saw; make sure you see some of Ben's work. He will also be able to organise somewhere to stay.

Blackwater Lakes To enter the Blackwater Lakes is to enter a vast water world where villages are often built on stilts and the people pole their canoes through shallow, reed-clogged lakes. The bird life is fantastic. As you get higher, away from the Sepik, the temperatures become cooler and the mosquitoes become fewer. The closer you come to the mountains, the more spectacular the scenery becomes. Lake Govermas is covered in water lilies and surrounded by low hills, mountains, dense forest and three beautiful villages. It is impossible to find your way around the myriad of channels without a guide.

Kraimbit There is a new haus tambaran and the locals are welcoming.

Sangriman This is an attractive, friendly village built on the edge of a reed-filled lake, but there are few artefacts. It may be possible to stay in the Youth Movement Hut. It's about 1½ hours motor canoe from Mindimbit.

Govermas A place of dream-like beauty, Govermas also has one of the most impressive haus tambarans in the region and some excellent carving. It's about 1½ hours motor canoe from Sangriman.

GETTING AROUND
Ships

Poroman Shipping of Madang have a couple of freighters that make irregular voyages from Madang as far as Green River. Although they stop at the main towns, like Angoram, Pagwi and Ambunte, most villages aren't on the itinerary so you spend a lot of time in the middle of the river. As the river is so huge (up to two km wide) and the surrounding area is largely flat, pitpit-covered flood plain, travelling by ship is not as interesting as it might sound. This is more useful as a 'getting there' option – see that section.

The *Melanesian Explorer* is a small cruise boat that is very popular. See the following Tours section.

Village Canoes

The cheapest, most time consuming method of travel is to rely on inter-village, PMV-type canoes with outboard motors and to stay in the villages. Most villages have a club house, a haus tambaran, or *somewhere* where you can stay at a reasonable cost.

There is a reasonably constant movement of boats along the river, with people trading, going to markets and visiting friends and relatives. Predictably, the movement of these boats is entirely unpredictable. You may have to wait many days for someone heading in your direction, and without a reasonable grasp of Pidgin you will find it very difficult to make your intentions clear. There will often be a complete (deliberate?) lack of understanding and people will pressure you to charter a canoe (very expensive) and then load it up with assorted cronies anyway.

If you do get a ride with a *PMV moto* it will be very cheap: around K2 per hour. The best time is Wednesday or Thursday, when people are going to market. Absolutely no boats at all came by on the Friday afternoon or Saturday when I was waiting in Mindimbit and Sunday isn't much better. This is partly because of religion. Some of the Sepik villages (Sotmeri, Mindimbit, Angriman) are Seventh Day Adventists – their sabbath is Saturday and is strictly upheld. Similarly, the Catholics don't travel on Sundays.

The bottom line is that you need a lot of time and patience to travel this way – and even then you just may not have any luck.

Do-it-yourself Canoes

The next step up is to buy a small dugout canoe and paddle yourself. This can be very physically demanding. It is not always easy to find a canoe in reasonable condition for sale at a reasonable price and you will need to have enough time to be open-ended with your plans.

Beyond the obvious advantages of being independent, there are also disadvantages aside from the physical demands. You will only be able to paddle downstream (the current is too strong to fight), and your view of the wide brown river with high grass crowding to its banks, will soon become monotonous. Much of the really beautiful scenery is up the tributaries away from the Sepik flood plain. Without a translator you may well miss out on on worthwhile explanations, and because the river changes course so quickly, some of the most important villages are now quite a distance inland – without a guide you could easily miss them. Look for coconut palms – they almost always indicate human settlement.

Ambunti is a reasonable place to buy

canoes; it's difficult to buy canoes around Pagwi, but the nearby villages are more helpful. Prices vary greatly depending on your negotiating skills and the canoe's condition. Make sure you know whether paddles are being included in the deal, and think in terms of paying K20 to K60 for a canoe. This may sound a lot, but when you see the amount of time and skill that goes into their construction you'll see why. It takes a month of hard work to make a decent-sized canoe. They are an essential tool for the villagers, so usually they'll only want to palm one off if they no longer need it or they can make a profit (ie, the canoe will be old, leaky and expensive). You must check the condition of the canoe carefully. Small cracks can be sealed with mud, but large ones may be a problem.

Depending on your competence with a canoe, you may consider having an outrigger attached (someone in the village should be able to do this at a moderate cost), or even joining two canoes together (although this will slow you down). Although there are no rapids, manipulating an unwieldy dugout in a five knot current can be quite challenging. You must keep your eyes open for floating debris, and for the occasional whirlpool – these aren't big enough to do any damage unless you are caught off balance. The locals paddle standing up, but I don't recommend trying this with your gear on board. A trick that is worth remembering is to lay some sticks across the bottom of the canoe to make a raised base. Use this to keep your luggage out of the water that will inevitably gather in the bottom.

Travellers have suggested Green, May and April Rivers as good places to start, but all these are fairly solid expeditions, not to be undertaken lightly. It will take at least 10 day's solid paddling from Green River to Ambunti, around a week from April River. From Ambunti it will take a solid week to Angoram.

Finally get a good map – *Wewak, The Gateway to the Sepik*, published by Wirui

Press, PO Box 107, Wewak, is an good map that shows the whole length of the river and is more up to date than most. If you're going on one of the tributaries I suggest getting some detailed topographic maps at the National Mapping Bureau in Moresby. Although their detail on the river will not be much help, mountains don't change quite so quickly, so you should still be able to orientate yourself.

Motorised Canoes

It is possible to hire motorised canoes, especially in Ambunti, Pagwi, Angoram and to a lesser extent Timbunke, where there are local entrepreneurs who make their living this way. See the respective sections for recommended guides. Santon Tours in Wewak and the Angoram Hotel also organise canoes and drivers.

This is much more expensive than paddling, but you will be able to work out your own itinerary, travel upstream and the driver doubles as guide. Depending on the driver, this could be good or bad. There are a few rogues who will do their very best to rip you off, and some will virtually force you to do what they think you want to do, entirely disregarding what you say you want to do!

Hiring a canoe will be more feasible if you have a decent-sized group – you may be able to organise this at Ralf's in Wewak. Most of the motorised dugouts will comfortably hold six or seven people and their luggage – they can be over 20 metres long. This kind of trip will also entail staying in villages, although an honest and friendly translator/driver will make life a bit easier and more interesting than if you do it by yourself. You will probably need a couple of days at the beginning of the trip to negotiate a reasonable rate and to find a reliable driver. Talk to as many locals as possible (store owners, district officers, police) and try and build up a picture on who is trustworthy, the going hire rates, how long a journey will take, and how many gallons of petrol will be used.

If you charter a canoe you will also have to pay for the driver to return to his base, whether you go or not. It is, however, much cheaper to travel downstream with a full load, as the petrol (also known as *benzin*) consumption will be considerably reduced. Petrol will very likely be the largest single component of your expense – it's K3 or more per gallon.

There seem to be three ways hire is computed: a per person charge; a daily rate for a driver and canoe including petrol, which is usually around K60 or K80; or a daily rate for a driver and canoe excluding petrol, which is around K30 or K40. To get from Ambunte to Angoram would be a five to seven day trip and could vary between K300 and K400. These costs may seem outrageous, but if you subtract the petrol component and break them down on a daily basis they make sense: K10 for the canoe; K15 for the motor (these are expensive and take a fair battering, pay less for a 15 hp motor); K10 for a driver/guide. These figures will vary depending on your negotiating skills. You will also need to stock up with food, and be equipped to cope with life in the villages.

If you are paying for petrol on top of daily hire, ensure your driver fills up before you start (petrol is more expensive away from the road heads): 15 hp Honda engines are recommended for their reliability and economy. Don't pay in advance for anything except petrol and check the price and quantity delivered. It's possible to hire flat-bottomed river boats in Angoram and they're worth considering if you want to move quickly. They're much faster than a canoe, especially if the river is chopped up by wind – they plane over the top.

As a rule of thumb, bearing in mind that all sorts of factors can have an influence, travelling downstream in a large canoe will take about 1½ hours' running time from Ambunti to Pagwi, about six hours from Pagwi to Timbunke, and five hours from Timbunke to Angoram. You can probably add at least 30% for going up stream. A river boat will be twice as fast. Again as a rule of thumb, 30 minutes in a motor canoe will equal two or three hour's paddling.

You're not going to be superbly comfortable in a canoe but the biggest draw-back is uncertainty – you can arrive at the river and find there are no canoes available and have to hang around for days.

Tours

Depending on where you want to go and your ability to strike a bargain, it may not be much more expensive to join a tour. A number of companies organise groups who travel in large motorised dugouts, and stay in the villages. Prices vary considerably. It would be worth writing to all these people in advance to get an idea of up-to-date costs and options.

Pacific Expeditions, PO Box 132, Port Moresby (tel 25 7803)
    – cover the Middle Sepik and the Blackwater Lakes; motorised dugout canoes and staying in village houses with local families
Niugini Tours, 100 Clarence St, Sydney, Australia 2000 (tel 290 2055)
    – based at Kaminabit & Karawari Lodges
Tribal World, PO Box 86, Mt Hagen (tel 55 1555)
    – mainly day trips from Wewak, but also longer trips
Santon Tours, PO Box 496, Wewak (tel 86 2248)
    – at the budget end, they just organise a motorised dugout canoe and a driver/guide
Angoram Hotel, PO Box 35, Angoram (tel 88 3011)
    – day trips and longer expeditions; dugouts and flat-bottomed river boats
Melanesian Explorer, PO Box 707, Madang (tel 82 2766)
    – a comfortable cruise boat that travels the length of the river
Trans Niugini Tours, PO Box 371, Mt Hagen (tel 52 1438)
    – operator of luxury Karawari Lodge; flat-bottomed river boats; some tours involve staying in villages.

None are particularly cheap but they do take you to places it would be difficult to find yourself, and they do operate to reasonably certain schedules. If you have limited time and want to visit some of the more remote tributaries, this option is worth considering. There are quite large variations between the tours offered, and the costs. Santon and the Angoram Hotel are at the bottom end, Melanesian and Trans Niugini are at the top end.

MARK LIGHTBODY'S SEPIK DIARY

This is my diary of four, probably fairly typical, days I spent on the Sepik River on the *Melanesian Explorer*.

Day 1

We boarded in Madang at 6 pm and had an introductory briefing. Jan Barter, the wife of Peter Barter, who together run the ship and the Madang Resort Hotel, is the tour director. On this trip the ship is just half full with 16 passengers. A young Australian couple, he an economist, she a chemist; two Canadian women on a complete South Pacific tour; an Englishman who once captained out of Hong Kong and his young daughter; a German couple who are both lawyers and travel frequently; two older American couples, one from Hong Kong; a retired gentleman who supplies the humour and an elderly expat who has lived her whole life in PNG but hasn't yet seen the Sepik. And me.

There is a captain, engineer, cook, and several others; including James who seems to do a bit of everything and get along well with everyone. We leave port about 9 pm sailing past Kranket Island among many others off Madang. The stars come out as we head up the coast and watch the flying fish fleeing the ship's wake. Jan promises to wake us at dawn if the volcano at Manam Island is lighting the sky.

Day 2

At 5.30 am most of us are up. Atop the classic silhouette of Manam a red glow lights the sky, occasionally puffing forth a display of sparks and smoke. The peak is at 1829 metres. As day approaches we moor on the beach by a Catholic Mission settlement. The local children are delighted by our appearance and run to the beach in great numbers. Many of them, holding our hands, wander with us as we walk around some of the neat little hamlets.

The common man's houses of wood and leaves are simple and square, those of more important people have a sloping, forward-leaning roof at one end and sometimes a balcony. One large house is for a man and his 25 children. He has five wives as well. Outside the chief's we see some large garamut drums.

Copra is drying over fires of coconut shells. It's sold to barges that come a couple of times a week from Bogia on the mainland. We see the diet staples of taro and cau cau growing as well as mango trees, tapioca, tobacco and betel palms. The lipstick tree supplies the seeds used for red colouring. When a woman has given birth, her head is shaven and coloured with this dye. Back at the ship we join the children in a swim and then move off for the river. The brown flow of the Sepik can be seen spreading out into the ocean long before we reach the mouth.

Anchoring at a baret or channel connecting the river to the Murik Lakes we hop into the speedboats for a 20 minute trip to the village of Mendam. The narrow baret is lined with mangroves, sago and jungle vegetation as well as the birds flapping out of our way. The village is wedged between the shoreline and the swamp and so is often flooded. But it has been dry and beneath the raised houses it's merely muddy.

Upon our arrival the older women, who are wearing nothing but grass skirts, cover themselves up and I wonder how it is they've become self-conscious. In one area of the village sago palm is laboriously cut and pounded to make a food of dubious

value and in another canoes are in various stages of completion. If the whole community works on a dugout it can be done in a few weeks or a month. The carving is particularly fine on the prows and especially remarkable when you see the tools they use.

This village, like many others, lives basically outside the cash economy and trades for goods with its neighbours. One thing you'll notice that money is spent on is radio cassette players. We're offered various carvings for sale including some interesting mortars the old people with no teeth use for crushing up their betel nuts.

Back on board that night, after dinner *First Contact* is screened on the video TV. It contains actual footage from 1930 when Europeans first contacted tribes of the Highlands. The expressions of the people on first seeing the white men and their thoughts expressed in retrospect are priceless in their honesty, depth and humour.

Day 3
The boat starts up about 6 am, breakfast is at 7 am. No progress is made through the night as drifting logs and the winding river make good vision a necessity. Up on deck we see evidence of the river's blight, the weed Salvinia Molesta, every year clogging up the river a little more. Known also as 'Nile Cabbage' this dense, seaweed-like plant is indigenous to parts of Africa and South America. It showed up in PNG in about 1970, one theory being that it was dumped from someone's fish tank and just loved the conditions.

It's particularly bad around the Chambri Lakes where the villages have been completely clogged in for up to 15 months at a time. For people dependent on the river for trade and livelihood this is devastating. The plant gets so thick other plants, even bushes, start to grow in it so obviously attempting to paddle a canoe through it is futile. Various means have and are being used to combat it, including bringing in insects that feed off it. Unfortunately, the rising and falling water levels kill the bugs before they can make any real headway.

By 10.30 am we're in Angoram and it's hot. The haus tambaran is chock full of handicrafts of all types and quality. Unless you're heading down to Kambot village this is the place to get the storyboards as the village is just a few hours away down the Keram River. The overwhelming display is really bringing out the shopper in some people while others walk to the hotel for a cool drink. Over at the open-air courthouse with its richly painted ceiling, groups of people hang around as trials are held.

After viewing a sample of the art found along much of the river we're back on board for lunch. About 1.30 pm we divert from the main river via the speedboats, nine people in each, down a former loop of the Sepik that will one day become cut off, forming an ox-bow lake. Kambaramba is an unusual village in several ways. Built in swamp land, all buildings must be up on stilts. Out front of most houses is a large balcony which in times of flood must house the pigs, chickens and dogs. Because there is no arable land the village had to come up with their own economic solution. Which they did. The women became prostitutes. The government and no doubt the missionaries rather frown on this and there have been moves to relocate the town to higher ground. but home is home and people seem reluctant to go – one factor may be that there are no mosquitoes here for some reason.

The kids and teenagers paddle out from shore at our arrival to look, talk and touch. One of the small boys has a rat on a string that he and his friends are merrily abusing. There's much smiling all round, but eyes reveal that the others' world remains unknown. There's nothing offered for sale, another way the village differs.

Back at the boat there's a film on the kula ring ritual of the Trobriand Islands, then dinner. After passing several small communities we moor for the night not far from Tambanum.

While we eat, villagers from Tambanum come aboard and on the upper deck set up their wares and crafts. Under the lights all the carvings and the chatting villagers make a magical scene. They ask for five volunteers whose faces they will paint in traditional, ceremonial fashion. Four others and I lay still while our faces are covered in clay and then coloured. Later we take pictures of one another looking like the masks we've seen.

Day 4

We're up early for breakfast and after Jan gives us the day's agenda we're off for an 8 am visit to Tambanum. Everyone in the village has been awake for some time and chores are being carried out. It's a very large settlement, but most striking are the tremendous houses. They're easily the biggest we've seen on the river and are all excellently carved. Each houses one family – up to 25 people.

Underneath the houses crafts are being worked on and others have been laid out for display. Tambanum is known for its masks – both highly decorated painted ones and simpler, plain black ones with shells and feathers. Aside from other carved wood items, there are examples of the painted Bioken pottery. The cooking, too, is done beneath the houses.

Each house has carved posts and a broad, firm stairway leading inside. We're given permission to look inside and edge around a dog lying on the steps. Without getting up he snaps at me when I proffer a hand. This draws giggles and guffaws from the neighbours. The interior is very neat, cool and dark. Evenly distributed around the one large room mosquito nets hang to the floor. Various artwork hangs from the ceiling and support beams and posts as well as bilums, clothes and other supplies.

It's a prosperous town and the people are friendly, even low-key, in bargaining over their goods. Despite some obvious western sophistication and dress older traditions live on. We see a woman in mourning covered in white clay to make herself unattractive and several older ladies sitting in just lap laps smoking pipes, quietly contemplating our visit from a distance.

Straight well-defined pathways lead around the village and some of us follow them around for half an hour or so before making our return to the boats.

Next stop is the smaller village of Timbunke with a beautiful haus tambaran that sports crest-like emblems in the peak at each end. Inside, the men of the village are lazing, smoking and sleeping. Clan business is still discussed here but modernization has meant less for the men to do and they idle away much of their time in the men's houses. Slow-burning fragrant logs simmer away in piles on the ground, keeping mosquitoes away and providing a light for cigarettes.

Under the roof on platforms the sacred flutes sit raised so the village women can't see them – they're always in male/female pairs. Alone they have no great importance. Hanging from posts are large masks used only at various ceremonies. Old garamut drums and the orator's stool are also interesting, but aren't allowed to be photographed. There's a large orator's stool in nearly every haus tambaran; the Sepik people are noted for their oratorical skills – it's probably no accident that the Prime Minister is a Sepik man. Orators don't sit on the stools, they stand beside them and slap a bunch of leaves on the seat, placing one down each time they make an important point.

Beside the village is a large Roman Catholic mission with a school and hospital. The mission teaching exists side by side with the traditional ways.

Back on the Melanesian we're having lunch and pushing further upstream. From the upper deck you can see the river winding and the low, swampy plains on both sides of it. Only in the distance are there some hills and mountains. Along the shoreline wild sugar cane and tall grasses grow and occasionally a canoe edges by slowly.

The old *Sepik Explorer I* is moored near Mindimbit, at the mouth of the Karawari River. Once used by Melanesian Tours it was sold off and is used as a floating hotel by Trans Niugini tours. They use it as a stopping point on their trips up to Karawari Lodge. The Barters had at one time planned to use it on the Ramu River but now consider a lodge there a future possibility. The area has few villages but is excellent for the flora and fauna.

A little further along and we're off in the speedboats again, this time for scenic Chambri Lake and Aibom village, famous for the pottery made there. To get there entails following one of the narrow, snaking barets from the river. Unfortunately after just 15 minutes the water is impassable – choked by the weeds. It's so thick the engine stalls and the plant must be pulled off by hand after raising the engine. We reach overboard and draw up hunks of it with roots extending two and three feet. Looking down the baret we can see a surface like a mown lawn; we can only hope some solution is found soon.

As a substitute, it's decided we'll stop in at Kaminabit village. By the time we arrive it's as though they've been expecting us and have laid out all their craft items for sale. There are a few interesting items – this village is noted for figures with horns reaching up from the shoulders or head, but there are more penis gourds and shell jewellery than anything else. The old lodge, an odd-looking creation by a Yugoslavian-American, is all boarded up and without much else of note we don't stay long.

In the evening, people, mostly teenage girls, from the village come to the ship in hopes of selling a few more articles. Actually, just being on the ship with each other and looking at the tourists seems to be the main reason for the visit. One thing worth looking for are the small, finely-carved spirit figures, lucky charms in a sense, that sometimes come in their own mini-bilum. Village elders would be able to explain the story behind the figure, but the younger people often have little knowledge of them.

After a late dinner some of us join James in a speedboat for some croc hunting. Slowly we move along the river's barets and tributaries, James skimming the

Korogo Mask

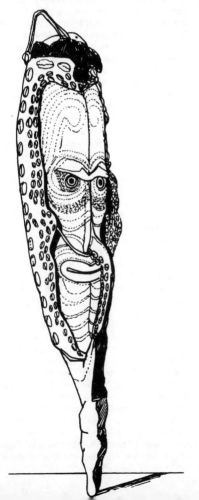

flashlight beam along the water's surface searching for the tell-tale red glowing disk that's a croc's eye. Occasionally he flashes the light in a tree hoping to catch a glimpse of a cuscus.

It takes a while to spot a pair of eyes; they are near the river's edge and silently we move towards them. James intends to grab the little pukpuks by hand; for the possibility of a large one he's brought along a spear. In an hour we've seen about 10, made four or five attempts at capture and have bagged two small ones. After sneaking the boat up to them James has shot his hands into the water grabbed the little rascals behind the head and scooped them up before they know what's happened. On the return to the ship a large one is spotted, judging by the distance between the eyes, but it wisely disappears beneath the waves upon our approach.

Back on board ship the two young crocs are carried flailing and kicking into the lounge for inspection. While somebody boldly holds one, James flips the other on its back on the table. He gently strokes its stomach so it's soon asleep with no need to be held at all. After holding both of them thus suspended he explains the differences between fresh and saltwater crocs and how to identify them. Both are found all the way up the river, but the salt variety can also venture out to sea. They're more valuable due to their smaller scales and better colouring, They also grow larger, but by the end of the trip I still have trouble telling one from the other.

Even these small ones are feisty little devils and will go for you if given a chance, but held firmly they're surprisingly placid. If held down on their backs they soon go completely limp and would eventually die; flipped over they immediately spring back into action!

Crocodiles are still very important commercially although it is now illegal to take ones over seven feet (two metres) – the illegal size is actually determined by girth, not length. A seven foot crocodile is about 20 inches (50 cm) in girth. The skin from a good condition saltwater crocodile can be worth K6 an inch (in girth), a freshwater only K4. Below 10 inches they're worth much less. Many villages have crocodile farms, but they're generally not grown beyond 4½ feet in length (1½ metres) as they take a long time to grow larger than that. The complete hide must be presented for sale, so you can't cheat on the maximum size limit by cutting the skin down. Crocodiles are edible, but only the tail is palatable – the rest is very sinewy. According to the connoisseurs it has a sort of fish-meat taste. Crocodiles won't bite underwater so villagers catch them by feeling in the mud with their feet – I wouldn't want to test that theory! Many are caught in fishing nets.

The specimens are then awakened and taken up on deck where a race is to be held to see which gets down off the table, runs to the side of the ship and dives into the river first. This last bit of novelty garners much banter and hooting most especially from James, himself.

Day 5 Another early start and we're off to Palambei just in front of the 115 HP outboards. The village is not on the river but a pleasant 20 minute walk through the jungle past gardens and a tributary. Here there are two haus tambarans, one at each end of a football-field sized clearing used for traditional ceremonies and dances. Both houses are exquisite examples of the incredible construction techniques employed. The plaited grass trusses used to bind the beams are of particular note. Also interesting are the fertility figures seen above the stairwells.

In between the haus tambarans are the ruins of another one said to have been bombed during the war by the US while Japanese troops were hiding out here. There is a cluster of 'sacred stones' in front of the larger haus tambaran. The wide meanderings of the Sepik has totally swept away all stones for a great distance on either side of the river's present course.

Yet every village has a number of stones that have been there as long as anyone can remember – they've obviously been carried in. Though many artefacts are available here, two of the best are the bilums and ceremonial lime sticks.

From here, it is not far to Kanganaman across the river to where another pleasant walk past lush vegetation leads us to the clean, green attractive village. The magnificent haus tambaran here is said to be the oldest on the river and has been designated a National Historic Site. The final figures on the columns are very well carved and tend to be black and slim in contrast to the painted, squat figures at Palembei. There are interesting combinations of women with crocodiles or birds which relate to many myths linking the two. Despite which the village spiritual life remains a totally male preserve in which women have no part at all.

The villages are fairly close together in this middle Sepik region and in 10 minutes by speedboat we're at Yentchen. It's noon now and quite hot, but the humidity isn't too high. This so-called wet season has been very dry thus far, which accounts for the low water level and the remarkable absence of mosquitoes. After hearing all the stories, I came to do battle and compare their ferocity to those of Canada's north woods. Maybe it was a fluke, but I never opened the repellent jar.

Yentchen has a two-storey haus tambaran – it was copied from photographs taken at the turn of the century by German explorers of the one standing at that time. The top floor is only for initiates, the rest of the men stay downstairs. You climb upstairs between the legs of a graphic female fertility symbol, getting blessed in the process. This is the only way a woman's form is permitted inside the haus. Yentchen is noted for its wickerwork dance costumes – figures of crocodiles, pigs, cassowaries and two-headed men. On the second floor you'll also see life-size replicas of these animals in painted bark.

It's also enjoyable walking through the village, crossing the ditches by log and twine bridges. We pay a quick visit to a captured cassowary. He's fairly young but a mean, aggressive-looking creature who gobbles down small coconuts whole. They don't have the same significance here as they do in the Highlands and villagers sometimes transport them there in order to sell them. A small cassowary I saw for sale in Mt Hagen market was K160.

After the busy morning we're glad to get back to the ship for a break and some lunch. The ship cruises for two hours upstream and moors off Korogo where we find an enormous array of artefacts including the well known Mai masks. The haus tambaran is filled with carvings and the carvers, but it seems many items were done in haste and the quality has suffered. The orator's stools are worth noting.

The village is attractive and strolling along its paths away from the commerce is more rewarding. Here, as in many of the villages, fish and shrimps and shellfish are caught in the lakes behind the village. There are many small lakes all along the Sepik, many of them ox-bows formed when the river once again changed course.

For our last dinner on board we have wine with a very tasty spiced shrimp dish. At each meal Jan appears wearing some of her excellent PNG jewellery collection and tells a little story about the pieces. Now at this last meal many of the passengers also have some interesting items of their own. Friends have been made now and over dinner we discuss the day's sights and what we'll be doing in a few weeks' time.

At 8.30 pm there's another video, this one about a walk from Moresby to Telefomin. Filmed in 1968, it focuses on customs found along the way. The sections on childbirth are fascinating, the woman sometimes goes off alone, makes a little hut and waits for the birth.

The following morning we arrive in Ambunti, the last stop for most passengers, others will continue upstream in another day or two. We take a quick look around and though there is no road here it is certainly more modern than any of the river villages. Ambunti has an interesting open court house perched on the hill over-looking the airstrip. After a drink at the lodge we walk over to the landing strip – a grassy field ending at one end in the side of a hill, at the other the river. As is common around the country the departure lounge is the shade under a big old tree where we wait for our charters to come in.

I'm the first to go and the only one heading to Wewak. The plane comes in – a four-seat Talair job – but unlike some, it seems to be in good repair. My confidence is further increased by the young Australian pilot and his wife who are going to finish the next day. It turns out to be the smoothest flight of my PNG trip. The beaches of Wewak appear marking the end of the Sepik tour.

Western & Gulf

Area 134,000 square km
Population 165,000

The two west-Papuan provinces are amongst the least developed in the whole country. The coastline is broken by a series of river deltas, and huge expanses of swamp run inland before rising to the foothills and then the mountains of the Highlands. In the far west the border with Irian Jaya runs north through the open expanses of seasonally flooded grassland. Two of the greatest rivers in the country, the Fly and the Strickland, run for almost their entire length through Western Province.

HISTORY

The coastal people of the provinces have had a long history of contact with outside influences. The annual Motuan trading voyages along the south coast, known as the *hiri*, were still a regular feature long after the establishment of Port Moresby. The Motuans traded pottery for the gulf region's prolific sago. There were also trade links to the Highlands. Due to their easy access from the sea the coastal villages were also the hunting grounds for representatives of the London Missionary Society who were in operation from the early 1880s.

In 1827, Durmont D'Urville surveyed part of the north-east coast of New Guinea and in 1842 he returned in HMS *Fly* to chart the western side of the Gulf of Papua. He discovered the Fly River and decided a small steam powered boat could travel up this mighty river far into the interior of the country.

It was some years before this idea was put into action, but when the controversial Italian explorer Luigi D'Albertis did make his second and most successful trip up the Fly in 1876, he quickly made up for lost time. In his tiny steamer, the *Neva*, he

travelled over 900 km upriver, far further into the unknown interior of New Guinea than any previous explorer. He returned from this epic voyage with a huge collection of botanical specimens, insects, artefacts and even painted skulls from village spirit houses.

However, his methods for appropriating his collection and his relationship with the villagers have coloured subsequent opinions about D'Albertis. He was a great believer in the philosophy of shooting first and asking questions later and he travelled up the river with a huge arsenal of fireworks, rockets, gunpowder and dynamite. At the slightest sign of any difficulty with the locals he was inclined to launch off fusillades of dynamite loaded rockets! It was certainly not sheer chance that led to so many of his artefacts being found in strangely 'deserted' villages.

When he returned to the Fly in 1877 he found the villagers much readier to attack him than on his previous expedition. He did not manage to penetrate so far up river and along the way he lost five of his Chinese crew, one of whom, it would seem, died at his hands.

Many of D'Albertis' 'difficulties' appear to have been self-inflicted, but later missionaries also had their problems although the best known case, that of the Reverend James Chalmers, was also partially his own fault. Chalmers, one of

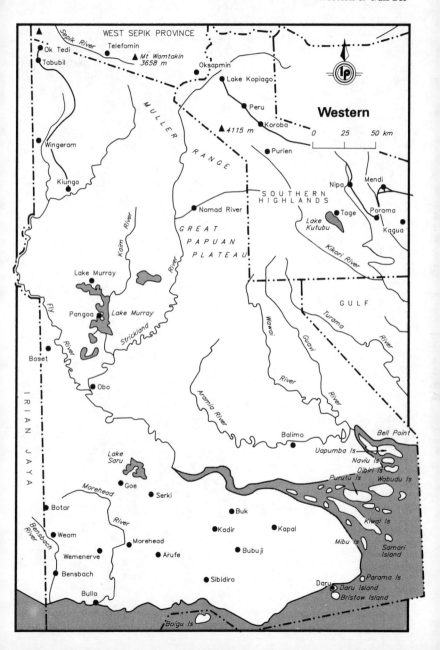

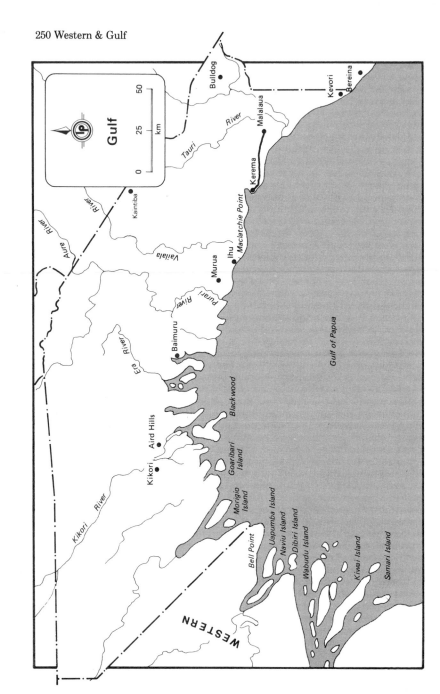

the earliest missionaries in New Guinea, had been involved in some of the first expeditions into the interior, and was a highly respected man. Yet somehow, after 25 years in the country, an act of sheer stupidity led to his death and that of at least 50 others.

In 1901, Chalmers visited Goaribari Island on the Papuan Gulf and his boat was besieged by hostile tribesmen. He eventually managed to persuade them to leave the boat by promising to come to their village in the morning. He must have known that the people were practising cannibals, all too ready to execute captives in their *dobus* or men's house, and any sane man would have departed immediately. Yet next morning, Chalmers, another missionary, a friendly chief and nine local mission students, went ashore – perhaps looking for some sort of martyrdom. They quickly found it, for all 12 had their skulls crushed with stone clubs and were soon cooking up nicely in a sago stew.

The rest of his crew managed to escape and retribution from Port Moresby soon followed. When the government ship *Merrie England* arrived at Goaribari the bill for the islanders' missionary meal was rather more than they might have expected. At least 24 were killed in their first encounter with white justice and 12 *dobus* were burnt down.

A year later Chalmers' skull was recovered and all might have been allowed to settle down had not Christopher Robinson arrived in Moresby in 1903 to become temporary administrator. Robinson decided another visit to Goaribari to recover the skull of Oliver Tomkins, Chalmers' assistant, was in order. As on the first punitive expedition, the visit quickly turned into a massacre and somewhere between eight and 50 villagers were killed. When Robinson returned to Moresby he found Australian public opinion violently against his over-reaction and early one morning, before the official enquiry had commenced, he stood beside the flagpole in the garden of Government House and put a bullet through his head.

Although the Gulf and Western coasts were well charted and the Fly, Strickland and other major rivers were soon comprehensively surveyed, it was not until the late '20s that the mountains north of the coast were explored. In 1927 Charles Karius and Ivan Champion set out to travel upriver from Daru, near the mouth of the Fly, to cross the central mountains and then to go down river on the Sepik to the north coast. Their first attempt failed when they ran out of supplies while trying to find a way through the jagged limestone mountains. A year later they managed to complete their journey, one of the last great exploratory expeditions. In complete contrast to D'Albertis, they did not fire one shot in anger on the whole trip.

Exploration apart, not much happened in the region – there proved to be little agricultural potential due to the frequent flooding. Today there is a massive gold and copper mine, Ok Tedi, high in the central mountains near the border with Irian Jaya, but a very large percentage of the population continues to migrate to other areas, either temporarily or permanently, in the search for work. Ok Tedi has had a major impact on the PNG economy and makes a significant contribution to government revenues.

Most of the Gulf region is just a big, unhealthy swamp and is not terribly interesting. Malaria is at its worst in December and January, while the months of June, July, August and September are very wet and muddy. Round here they call 10 days without rain a drought!

GEOGRAPHY

The border region with Irian Jaya is composed of vast, open, seasonally flooded grasslands to the south, rising up into the mountainous backbone of the country. The Fly River starts from high in this central divide and turns south-east towards the sea where it ends in a huge, island-filled mouth. The Strickland River, nearly equal in size, joins the Fly about 240 km from the coast.

Despite its size the Fly does not have the same importance or interest as the Sepik: it is much more difficult to visit and there is not so much to see. Villages are usually some distance from the river, because it tends to flood so far over its banks. In 800 km to the sea the Fly River falls only 20 metres and flows (slowly) through 250,000 square km of swamp land where mosquitoes appear to be the most successful inhabitants.

From the mouth of the Fly, eastwards to the Purari River, the Gulf of Papua is a constant succession of river deltas, backed by swamps which run 50 to 60 km inland. East of the Purari the land rises more rapidly from the coast, is less subject to flooding and more heavily populated.

The Turama, the Kikori, the Purari and the Vailala are just some of the great rivers that flow into the swampy, delta-land of the Papuan Gulf. Nor is the water just at ground level, the dry climate of Port Moresby and the Central Province gets progressively damper as you move west around the Gulf. When you get to Kikori in the centre of the Gulf the annual rainfall is an astounding 600 cm per year, nearly 20 feet of rain! Between May and October, the worst part of the wet season, the airstrip at Kikori was closed due to adverse weather conditions so often that in 1960 the district HQ was moved east to drier Kerema.

PEOPLE

The people of the delta-land build their houses on piles high above the muddy river banks. As the rivers change their courses they frequently have to move their villages. Each village is centred around the men's longhouse, known as a *dobu* or *ravi*, in which weapons, important artefacts, ceremonial objects and the skulls of enemies were stored. Men slept in the longhouse, women in smaller, individual huts outside.

Today the longhouses are no longer so culturally important; the Gulf people have been bombarded with Christianity for nearly a century and much of their culture and many traditions have been lost – including cannibalism.

Cannibalism had ritual and religious importance, but it is also possible that it was provoked by the endemic protein deficiency of the area. As on the Sepik and the Ramu, the main food is sago, the tasteless, starchy food produced from the pith of the sago palm. There is no shortage of sago, which grows prolifically in the Gulf area, so nobody starves, but where sago is the staple food, severe protein deficiencies are common. Although the villagers supplement their diet with whatever fish they can manage to catch and the small quantity of vegetables their inhospitable land will allow them to grow, this deficiency remains a serious problem today.

Angry protests were once made to the Dutch colonial officials about 'their head-hunters' poaching across the border into British New Guinea. The Tugeri people, whose land once spread across both sides of the border, were ferocious head-hunters who believed they had to collect a head for every child born. But a head was no good unless it had a 'name' to pass on to the child. So their unfortunate victims had first to be persuaded to say something before they were despatched. Presumably even 'don't do it' was good enough.

In the hills behind the coastal swampland live the Anga people, a sparse and scattered tribe once erroneously called the Kukukuku, whose territory stretches right across to the south-eastern Highlands in Morobe Province. They raided villages on the south coast just as often and just as violently as on the north. The last major Anga raid took place at Ipisi near Kerema just before WW II. Today there is a government station at Kaintiba in the heart of their land and all is fairly peaceful.

The Kiwai people, who live on the

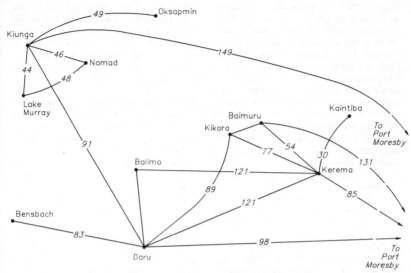

Flights in the Western & Gulf Provinces
Fares in Kina

islands in the mouth of the Fly, are noted for their seagoing abilities and their interesting dances. They have close cultural links with the Torres Strait Islanders off Cape York Peninsula in Queensland, Australia.

ARTS

There are few artefacts created in the Western Province now – the kundu drums of Lake Murray are very rare and the Kiwai people do not often carve – but art is still strong in the Gulf region. Unfortunately, when the missions first arrived in the Gulf area their attitude towards local culture was considerably less enlightened than it became later. Along with abandoning their spiritual beliefs and giving up head-hunting, the Gulf villagers were also pressured to halt their artistic pursuits and in some cases the missionaries actually persuaded them to burn and destroy their best work. Old artefacts still

in existence today are zealously protected.

In the Gulf region, from the mouth of the Fly around to Kerema, seven distinct artistic styles have been categorised. Once upon a time the men's longhouses in the delta villages were veritable museums and although there are no 'fully-furnished' spirit houses left, there is still a busy trade turning out figures, bullroarers, *kovave* masks, headrests, skull racks (every home should have one) and *gope* boards.

Gope boards are elliptical in shape, rather like a shield, and incised with brightly coloured abstract patterns or stylised figures. Once upon a time warriors were entitled to have a *gope* board for each act of bravery or to celebrate each successful conflict. Boards were often cut from the curved sides of old canoes and a board from your vanquished enemy's own canoe had particular significance, transferring some of its previous owner's strength to the victor.

Hohao boards are similar in their original role to gope boards, but can be recognised by their squared off edges, coming to a point at the top and bottom. These were particularly prevalent around Ihu and Orokolo at the eastern end of the Gulf, but greater affluence in this region has caused the skill to virtually die out. It was also in this area that the Hehevi ceremonies once took place, a cycle of rituals and dramatic rites that took a full 20 years to complete. The ceremonies have been halted for 50 years now and the huge masks which were used in dances have also disappeared.

KEREMA

This tiny government HQ town of 3000 people is stationed in Kerema mainly because it has a drier climate than Kikori. Facilities are limited, but there is a PNGBC bank and a sketchy road network, including a link to Malalaua. It is also possible to travel by boat upriver behind the town. This is not a destination, but a place to go through.

Places to Stay

The *Elavo Inn Hotel* (tel 68 1041), PO Box 25, has eight run-down rooms; singles/doubles are K45/70. It's just two minutes from the airport. We have not had any rave reviews. On the other hand, the Catholic Mission near the Catholic Church apparently has decent rooms, showers and cooking equipment (you supply food) for K16.

Getting There & Away

Air Talair has a daily flight that hops to Malalaua (K72), Kerema (K85), Ihu (K98) and Baimuru (K123). Douglas flies the same route for much the same price and then flies on to Kikori (K150). You can also fly to Kaintiba for K30 with Talair.

Sea Burns Philp has two ships that service the Gulf. Their office (tel 21 2233) is in Moresby on Musgrave St down by the wharf. Either the MV *Purari* or the MV

Malalo leaves Moresby every Tuesday or Wednesday. If you leave on Tuesday, you arrive in Kerema on Wednesday morning for K34; Ihu on Thursday for K40; and Baimuru on Friday for K46. It may be worth seeing if Steamships have anything going, but they weren't interested in passengers when I asked.

Other People have walked into Menyamya (north in the Highlands) from Kerema, but this would definitely not be a picnic stroll. You could also fly to Kaintiba and walk from there, picking up road transport into Lae. See the Menyamya/Aseki section in the Lae & Morobe chapter.

The Hiritano Highway from Moresby now goes as far as Iokea, and you can get there by PMV. From Iokea you can catch canoes to Malalaua for K10 (five hours). Apparently, it is also possible to go direct by canoe to Kerema from Iokea for K20. There is a road link between Malalaua Village (which is about two km from the river) to Kerema and there are PMVs for K3. It is also possible to walk along the coast from Iokea at low tide; ferry men employed by the government take people across the rivers; if they're on the opposite side, light a fire to attract their attention. Canoes may not operate during the January to September wet season.

AROUND KEREMA
Malalaua

Malalaua can be reached by air, or a combination of PMV and canoe from Moresby. See the Getting There & Away section for Kerema. You can fly from Kerema with Talair or Douglas daily for K27. This is the southern end of the WW II Bulldog Track which goes through to Edie Creek near Wau. Walking from this end would be extremely difficult; first you'd have to get upriver to Bulldog, and then you'd have a very difficult uphill walk to Edie Creek. Most people come from the other direction (from Wau), but this too is difficult and not to be undertaken lightly.

Ihu

Ihu is the main station between the delta-country and Kerema and it will be the centre for the proposed Purari River power project. A road runs most of the way to the Purari and it is surrounded by beautiful bush. Talair and Douglas fly in from Kerema for K26 and Burns Philp service the port. Canoes apparently travel between Ihu and Baimura and from Baimura to Kikori, although they may not operate between January and September. There's a tractor road along the beach from Ihu to Murua.

Places to Stay There are two places to stay in Ihu, but we don't have first-hand reports on either. They are *Bert Guest House* and the *John Senior Guest House*; both have four rooms and charge K10/15. Contact the Division of Commerce on tel 68 1084 for further information.

Kikori & Baimuru

These two major delta-country towns are set well back from the coastline. Kikori is one of the oldest stations in Papua but Baimuru is now the larger of the two. Both have small airstrips and it is possible to get from one to the other by boat through the maze of waterways. There are some interesting villages along the way. You can also get to Baimuru from Ihu by boat. Talair and Douglas both service the towns (see the Getting There & Away section under Kerema).

Places to Stay The old Gulf Hotel in Kikori has closed down but you can try the *Kikori Guest House* run by the Kikori District Office.

Kaintiba

Kaintiba, in the mountains behind the coast, is in Anga country. There is good walking in the area with frequent villages. Many are within a day's walk of each other and many have some sort of mission where you can put up. The going rate at most of these country missions is around K15, including meals. You can walk from Kerema, or fly with Talair for about K30, three times a week. From Kaintiba it is a tough though interesting walk to Aseki and Menyamya, which are linked by road to Lae. See the Menyamya/Aseki section of the Lae & Morobe chapter.

Places to Stay The *Kamina Guest House* is apparently run by the Catholic Mission and costs K20/25.

DARU

The main town for the Western Province is Daru, on a small island of the same name close to the coast. It used to be a pearl and beche-de-mer trading port and it is still a busy port with a growing fishing industry, but there is not much of interest for travellers. Apparently a local airline donated prizes for a competition: the first prize was one week in Daru, the second prize was two weeks in Daru!

The unfortunate Reverend Chalmers was based here and his 'grave' and that of his wife can be seen, as well as his Tamate Memorial Church, which was built by the Kiwai Islanders and given his native name. Daru is also the town from which the skins of crocodiles, caught in the Western Province, are exported. There's a PNGBC bank.

Places to Stay

There's nothing cheap. The *Daru Guest House* (tel 65 9016), PO Box 62, on Cameron Rd, three km from the centre, has six doubles with nightly costs of K30 per person including breakfast. The latest report says it is very run down.

The *Wyben Hotel* (tel 65 9055), PO Box 121, is the best, indeed the only alternative. For rooms with fans, TV and private bathrooms they charge K55/70 a night. The food is good and features excellent seafood, including crabs, crays, prawns and barramundi. The meals are reasonably priced: breakfast is K6, lunch K3 and dinner K8.50.

Getting There & Away

Talair and Douglas fly from Moresby, Monday to Saturday, for K98. You would think there would be shipping from Moresby, but I didn't hear of any. It would be worth asking around in Moresby; it is likely the Ok Tedi mine has ships, but they probably aren't interested in travellers.

BENSBACH

Only a few km from the Irian Jaya border, Bensbach Wildlife Lodge is the premier tourist attraction in the Western Province – for premier (well-off) tourists! The mouth of the Bensbach River forms the border between Papua New Guinea and Irian Jaya, but the border runs due north while the river bends off north-east into PNG territory. This area is a vast expanse of grassland and swamp, lightly populated due to the effects of heavy head hunting in earlier years.

What it lacks in people it makes up in wildlife – the area is alive with animals and birds, many of them amazingly fearless since they have had little contact with man. The Dutch introduced Rusa Deer into West New Guinea in the 1920s and, untroubled by natural predators, they have spread far into PNG – there are over 20,000 Rusa Deer west of the Bensbach in PNG territory. Wallabies, wild pigs and crocodiles are also prolific and the bird life is quite incredible. It's a photographer's paradise. Keen fishers will also enjoy themselves since the Bensbach River is renowned for the size and number of its barramundi, which feature frequently on the menu at the lodge.

Places to Stay

The *Bensbach Wildlife Lodge* is near Weam, 96 km north of the river mouth, on the east bank of the Bensbach River. The low-lying lodge is built of local materials and has 12 twin rooms, flanking a central bar, lounge and dining room. The rooms are simple, fan cooled rather than air-conditioned (unnecessary in the generally cool climate), and have a refrigerator in each room. There are shower and toilet facilities for each wing. The cost per person per day is K125 for fishermen, K170 for groups of three hunters or more, but this includes all meals, tours, boats, fishing equipment and park entrance fees. Bookings are made through Trans Niugini Tours, PO Box 371, Mt Hagen (tel 52 1483) or in Port Moresby.

Getting There & Away

Talair flies from Daru twice a week for K82. Various charter flights, including to the Highlands, are also possible. You travel by river from the airstrip to the lodge.

OK TEDI

Ok Tedi is a huge gold and copper mine, which was developed in some of the most rugged country and difficult circumstances imaginable. It has not been without controversy, both in terms of its impact on people and the environment. Now fully operational, it is making a significant contribution to PNG's export earnings and to government revenue. Until Porgera in Enga Province takes over, Ok Tedi is the largest gold mine outside South Africa.

The mammoth undertaking began in 1980 and essentially involves chewing up a gold-topped copper mountain with a little silver thrown in. The Australian company BHP and the PNG Government are the two main shareholders. The mine is now processing 30,000 tonnes of ore a day.

The area's remoteness, in the Star Mountains near the Indonesian border, created special problems and solutions as well as very odd juxtapositions. Local men wearing only penis gourds worked beside gigantic modern cranes and bulldozers. In order to service the area, virtually a town (Tabubil) had to be built.

The main supply centre is at Kiunga, south of the site on the Fly River. Roads have been cut through virgin jungle from

Top: Haus tambaran, Palambei, Middle Sepik (ML)
Left: Haus tambaran, Timbunke, Middle Sepik (ML)
Right: Sepik woman in mourning (ML)

Top: Many relics from WW II can be found rusting on beaches (TW)
Left: . . .or in the jungle (TW)
Right: . . .or off the coast (Air Niugini)

here to Tabubil and the mine. Barges take the treated ore downstream to the delta where it is transshipped to waiting cargo vessels. There is accommodation, but few tourists turn up.

Operations were meant to begin in July '84 but a tailings dam, designed to trap waste by-products, collapsed in January '84 making a hell of a mess, raising further environmental concerns and doubts about the project's engineers and planners, as well as costing a fortune to fix up.

In the ensuing months the PNG government was forced to accept a plan for a new interim tailings dam, despite strong misgivings over its environmental impact. To do anything else would have slowed and reduced the flow of much needed dollars.

Places to Stay

The *Kiunga Airport Motel* (tel 58 1055), PO Box 25, has 24 rooms at K55/75 and the *Kiunga Guest Hotel* (tel 58 1084), PO Box 20, has 18 rooms at K70/80.

Getting There & Away

Talair flies from Daru to Kiunga every day except Wednesday and Sunday for K91 and then on to Moresby. There's a direct flight to Moresby on Wednesday for K149. There is a good road between Kiunga and Tabubil, but you can also fly there with Talair. Some fares to Tabubil: from Kiunga – K43, from Hagen – K124, from Oksapmin – K49, from Telefomin – K29.

OTHER

Lake Murray, in the centre of the vast Western Province, is the biggest lake in Papua New Guinea; during the wet it can spread to five times its 400 square km dry season area. There is a crocodile research station at the lake. Nomad, to the north, is one of the most remote and inaccessible patrol stations in the country. There is accommodation available at the *Balimo Lodge*, at Balimo on the Aramai River. With the District Officer's permission you can also stay at the *Gogodala Cultural Centre* here, but the amenities are basic. At Makapa, about 60 km from Balimoa, the *Avanima Guest House* is again care of the District Officer and again is pretty basic.

Northern

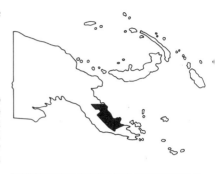

Area 19,827 square km
Population 95,000

Northern Province, known locally as Oro Province, is sandwiched between the Solomon Sea and the Central Owen Stanley Range. It is another little-visited region of the country, but it is physically beautiful and there are a number of areas of interest.

The northern end of the Kokoda trail terminates at the village of Kokoda and from here to the coast, and around the beaches of Buna and Gona, some of the most violent and bitter fighting of WW II took place. Mt Lamington, near Popondetta, is a mildly active volcano that, in 1951, erupted with cataclysmic force and killed nearly 3000 people. In the east of the province there are more interesting volcanoes near Tufi and a section of coast with unique tropical fjords (their origin is volcanic) and a number of guesthouses.

HISTORY

Early European contacts with the Orakaiva people, who live inland as far as Kokoda, were relatively peaceful, but when gold was discovered at Yodda and Kokoda violence soon followed. After the first altercation between the local people and miners a government station was established. The government's results weren't much better since the first officer was killed shortly after he arrived and made peaceful, or so he thought, contacts. Eventually things quietened down and the mines, which were initially some of the richest in Papua, were worked out. Rubber and other plantations superseded them.

The war arrived in the Northern area unexpectedly and dramatically in 1942. The Allied forces were just about to open a base in the area when the Japanese suddenly landed in late July '42 and immediately began to move down to Kokoda from where they intended to climb up and over the Owen Stanley Range to take Port Moresby. This horrific campaign is covered in more detail in the introductory history section and in the section on the Kokoda Trail under Port Moresby. As General Horii withdrew up the trail, lines of defense were drawn first at Eora Creek, mid-way along the trail, then at Oivi, on the road from Kokoda to Buna. Both were taken by the Australians after drawn out and bloody fighting. Horii drowned while attempting to cross the Kumusi River.

If the fighting down and up the trail had been bitter, the final push to retake the beachheads at Buna and Gona was nearly unbelievable. The Australian troops who had pursued the Japanese back up the trail were reinforced by American troops who came round the coast, but the Japanese held on suicidally. Although Kokoda was retaken at the beginning of January it was the end of the month before Buna and Gona had fallen. The Japanese were not so much defeated as annihilated; it has been estimated that of their total force of 16,000 men only about 700 survived.

There are many war relics scattered around the area, most of them considerably overgrown. At Jiropa Plantation, on the Buna road, there is a Japanese plaque commemorating their dead. Oro Bay, now

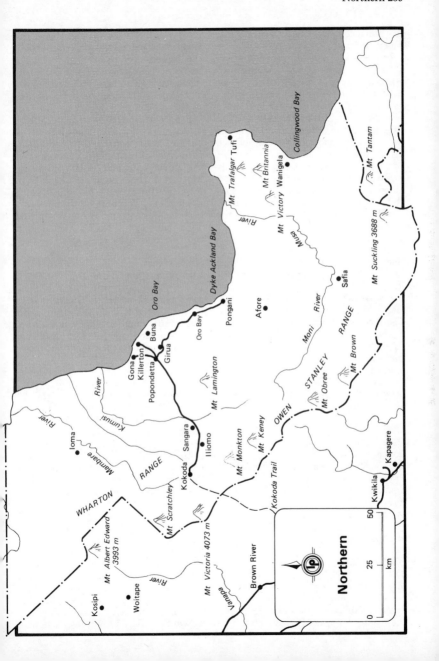

the province's main port, was a major American base.

After the war, rebuilding the region was a difficult task as the damage was especially severe. Strangled by their supply difficulties, the Japanese troops had scoured the country for food, even eating grass and bark off trees in an often vain attempt to prevent starvation. The gardens and plantations were hardly back in operation after the war when Mt Lamington's disastrous eruption totally wiped out Higatura, the district HQ, and killed nearly 3000 people. Today the new HQ town of Popondetta has been established at a safer distance from the volcano.

GEOGRAPHY

The swamps and flatlands of the coast rise slowly inland towards the Owen Stanley Range then with increasing steepness to the peaks which stand at 3500 to 4000 metres at only 90 to 100 km from the sea. The only roads of any length in the district run from the coast, inland through Popondetta to Kokoda where the famous trail starts. Cape Nelson, to the east, is marked by three volcanoes and is famous for its beautiful fjords which have formed between the fingers of lava from some ancient eruption.

ARTS

Tapa cloth, made by beating the bark from a paper mulberry tree until it is thin and flexible, is made in the Northern Province. Natural dyes are used to make dramatic designs on the cloth. Only in the most remote parts is tapa cloth now worn by the local people. It is still made at Wanigela where distinctive clay pots are also fired.

POPONDETTA

The district HQ is not of particular interest except as a base to visit other parts of the Northern Province – Kokoda further inland, the wartime battle sites on the coast, or nearby Mt Lamington. The

town is currently booming because of the Higatura oil palm developments, possibly the largest such development in the southern hemisphere. There is a war memorial with an interesting map of the battle sites and a memorial to the victims of Mt Lamington in the town.

Popondetta may be a safe distance from Lamington, but for travellers it is landlocked and particularly inconvenient. Girua Airport is 17 km from town, just off the Oro Bay road, and Oro Bay, where the *Mamose Express* docks, is 45 km from town. The town itself is just spread along the highway. There are all the necessary basic facilities, including Air Niugini and Talair offices, a PNGBC bank and a couple of reasonable-sized shops.

Places to Stay

The *Lamington Hotel* (tel 29 7152), PO Box 27, has 18 twin rooms. Nightly cost for fan-cooled singles/doubles is K62/76, for air-con K70/82! It's clean, a bit characterless and definitely not cheap. For meals add another K20 or so per person. Lunch in their courtyard costs about K7.

Near the market and the National Broadcasting Commission, the *Popondetta Christian Community Centre* (tel 29 7437), PO Box 26, has reasonable rooms with shared facilities for K25 including breakfast. To find it, walk out the main road towards Kokoda and turn left at the end of the High School, turn right past the market and you'll see the Popondetta Restaurant; the guesthouse is behind this. The restaurant has reasonable food at decent prices.

The *Christian Training Centre* (tel 29 7384), PO Box 126, better known as the CTC, has cheap accommodation for groups of five or more who book in advance – it's primarily a conference centre. It's five km out of town towards the airport. Their rates vary widely depending on what facilities you require, and whether you want meals, but it's good value.

Near the CTC, a 10 minute walk down a

dusty track that actually passes through the CTC grounds, is the *St Mary of the Angels Friary* (telephone through the CTC), PO Box 78, a peaceful spot nestling in the jungle. The Anglican monks lead a quiet but disciplined life, and they may have space for individuals – especially if you have or play a musical instrument! The conditions are spartan, but it is an interesting place to stay. Make a donation.

The *Janita Village Guest House* is also out of town. It's another couple of km before the CTC if you're coming from the airport, on the left just after the second one-lane bridge; there's a sign. They charge K15.

There are also village guesthouses at Emo, Pongani and possibly at Kapruhambo on the road to Killerton. Buna has a guesthouse, *Ase Guest House* (tel 29 7251) that has eight rooms and charges K6/12. Sea travellers should consider the *Bama Guest House* (tel 29 7196) at Oro Bay, which charges K12.

Things to Buy
St Christopher's Diocesan Office, just before the big open Catholic Cathedral on the way into town from the airport, sells tapa cloth.

Getting There & Away
Air No PMVs specifically service the airport, but you will, in time, get one heading to/from Oro Bay along the nearby highway. They are particularly sparse on Sundays. You can get a lift with the helpful Air Niugini staff – and even arrange a lift to get you to your flight out. Otherwise, one of the locals will probably help.

Air Niugini has daily connections from Port Moresby to Popondetta and the short 35 minute flight costs K49. Talair flies from Lae, daily, for K82. They also link with Tufi (K48) three times a week and on Wednesdays and Saturdays they have an interesting flight that hops through Tufi and all the way round to Gurney (Alotau,

in Milne Bay). Douglas flies to Kokoda several times a week for K40.

Sea Oro Bay, 45 km away on the coast, is the eastern turnaround point for Lutheran Shipping's passenger-only *Mamose Express*. The *Mamose* leaves Oro Bay around 2 pm on Tuesdays for the overnight trip to Lae (K27/18, tourist/deck) and continues on as far as Wewak. The freighters *Umboi* and *Nagada* also do the trip though less regularly and comfortably. Carnell Carriers (tel 29 7095) are Lutheran's agents in Popondetta, if you want to check times or make other general enquiries. You buy tickets on the wharf.

PMVs PMVs to Kokoda cost K4.90, to Oro Bay K2.80. They aren't all that frequent so give yourself plenty of time if you're catching a plane or a boat. You'll pick them up on the main highway, but the market (walking out of town, first street on your left past the High School) is a good place to start.

KOKODA
The road from Popondetta has brought Kokoda to within a couple of hours' drive. The Kumusi River is now crossed by a bridge near Wairopi (from 'wire rope' after the earlier footbridge). General Horii and hundreds of other Japanese troops died near here while crossing the river during the retreat from Oivi Ridge. The road climbs steeply over the ridge and then drops into the Kokoda Valley where the walking trail starts. The Owen Stanley Range rises almost sheer behind Kokoda.

The old trail was once used by miners walking from Port Moresby across to the gold fields of Yodda, only 13 km away. For more information on the trail see the Kokoda Trail in the Moresby chapter.

Places to Stay
Accommodation is available at the *Park HQ* for K5 – see the ranger. They'll sell you a certificate for completing the trail for

K5! Some food is available from the trade stores.

Getting There & Away
A PMV to or from Popondetta costs about K5. Douglas flies from Moresby on Monday, Wednesday and Friday mornings (weather permitting) for K40.

MT LAMINGTON
The 1585 metre peak of Mt Lamington is clearly visible from Popondetta but the original HQ was even closer, only 10 km from the volcano. Like many other volcanoes in PNG, Mt Lamington still shakes and puffs a little and the local residents paid no attention to a slight increase in activity in 1951. Then half of the mountain side suddenly blew out and a violent cloud of super-heated gases rushed down, incinerating all before it.

The entire European population of Higatura and many Papua New Guineans died – a total of around 3000 people. It was later estimated that the temperature stood at around 200°C for about a minute and a half and that the gas cloud rolled down at over 300 km per hour. Nearly 8000 people, or about 10% of the province's population, were left homeless. It took a number of years for the region to recover.

Mt Lamington has been fairly calm since and keen bushwalkers can climb it today. You start from Sasenbata Mission, a little way off the Kokoda road. Like most mountains the best time to reach the summit is in the early morning before the clouds roll in; there's a campsite on a ridge line. There is no crater atop Mt Lamington, but the views are excellent. The tribal name of the mountain is Sumburipa. Take water, there's none available near the top and it's thirsty work. Take care, too; it's still active.

TUFI
A suitably patriotic British sea captain named the scenic peninsula where Tufi is sited Cape Nelson after the legendary admiral and dubbed the three mountain peaks on the cape, Trafalgar (site of Nelson's naval victory over the French), Victory (his ship) and Britannia (she's the one who ruled the waves). The beautiful bay to the south he named Collingwood, after one of Lord Nelson's captains.

The cape was formed by an earlier eruption of its three volcanoes and the lava flow down into the sea created the fjords for which it is famous. Unlike the Norwegian originals, the water is always warm and beneath the calm surface of the sheltered bays there is beautiful coral waiting to be inspected. Tufi is one of PNG's best kept secrets, although it is a spectacular place to visit and their are half-a-dozen pleasant, good-value guest-houses. If you can, go.

Places to Stay
The guesthouses at Tufi are all run by local clans and can be booked by writing care of the Post Office in Tufi. They lie between the villages of Angorogo and Sai. They all provide excellent local food, including superb seafood, and this is included in the tariff. All of them charge between K20/25 per person and arrange fishing and diving trips – I don't think it matters much where you end up staying. Outrigger canoes are the standard form of transport. It can get very windy from June through August.

Kofure Guest House is one km from the airstrip and reached by outrigger canoe. The houses, with 18 double rooms in all, are built in the local style.

The *Konabu Guest House* is on the point, a few minutes' walk to the seashore and has seven rooms.

Tainabuna Village Guest House is a one hour canoe away from the airport and has been recommended. The other places are the *Komoa* and *Jebo*.

There is also a hotel at Tufi, the *Laki Hotel* (tel 25 3524), PO Box 6699, Boroko, PtM, with charges varying from K35 to K100.

Further south from the cape on

Collingwood Bay there is a guesthouse at Wanigela. The *Waijuga Park Guest House* has 14 rooms with costs of around K30 per person including meals. Write to the guesthouse at Wanigela Post Office. Canoe trips up the Murin River and glass bottom boat tours to the coral reefs can be arranged.

Manus

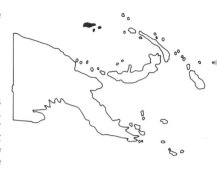

Area 1943 square km
Population 28,000

Manus is the most isolated and least visited province in PNG. It consists of a group of islands known as the Admiralty Islands plus a scattering of low-lying atolls. Manus Island, which gives the province its name, is the largest of the Admiralty Islands.

HISTORY
No significant archaeological research has been undertaken on Manus, so it is uncertain when the first settlers arrived and where they came from. Although the people are Melanesians, they appear to have some Micronesian characteristics. The islanders were sophisticated mariners and fishermen with an extensive trade system. Their large sea-going outrigger canoes were up to 10 metres long, with two or three sails, and their fishing methods included fish traps and kite fishing. Trade linked the islands in the face of their geographic dispersion and the 14 languages of the region. The main social unit was the clan, and warfare between clans and tribes was commonplace.

A Spanish sailor, Alvaro de Saavedra, made the European discovery of the island in 1527, but although various Dutch and English explorers came past in the 17th and 18th centuries it was not until the late 19th century that serious contacts were made. Carteret, an Englishman, dubbed the islands the Admiralty group in 1767 and they were annexed, along with the rest of New Guinea, by Germany in 1885. German law and order, however, did not arrive on Manus until 1911. Some Spanish touches remain – the airport is on an island that is still called Los Negros.

Manus is a rugged, relatively infertile island and this, combined with the fierce independence of its inhabitants, encouraged the German and Australian colonisers to leave it pretty much alone. The Germans did plant coconut plantations on some of the islands, but serious change did not arrive until WW II – and then it was pretty dramatic.

The Japanese occupied Manus in April 1942. In February 1944 American and Australian forces recaptured the island for the construction of a huge base to counterbalance the Japanese forces at Rabaul. Dock facilities were built around Seeadler Harbour and an airstrip capable of handling heavy bombers was built at Momote.

Untold millions of dollars were lavished on the base and at times as many as 600 Allied ships were anchored in Seeadler Harbour. All in all, a million Americans and Australians passed through. A year after the war ended, the Allies had gone, but not before they had scrapped everything. Not surprisingly, this display of western technology and profligacy had quite an impact on the local people, an impact that anthropologist Margaret Mead described in her book *New Lives for Old*.

After the war a remarkable movement led by Paliau Moloat, put paid to old Manus. Although it was first treated simply as a cargo cult, it is now recognised as one of PNG's first post-war independence movements and as a force for modern-

264

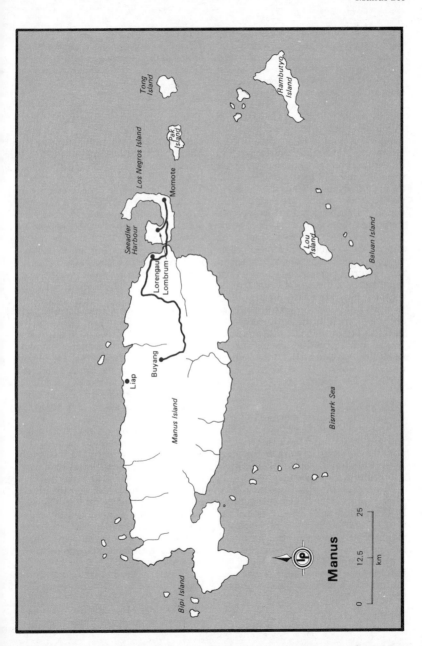

isation. The movement brought together the diverse tribes of the islands in unified resistance to the Australian administration and to the old ways. It did also have a significant religious component and came to be known as the Paliau Church.

Old cults and rituals were thrown over, villages were rebuilt in imitation of European styles, even local schools and self-government were instituted long before the Australian administration belatedly accepted that independence was inevitable. Paliau was imprisoned in the early days but in 1964 he was elected to the House of Assembly. He has not held a seat in the independent PNG parliament.

Perhaps because of their trading prowess and their early realisation of the importance of education, Manus people hold positions of responsibility throughout the country, disproportionate to their small numbers. Because of Manus' fragile economic base, the money repatriated by these workers is most important. Coconuts and copra are still the most significant cash crop on the island, but there is some limited timber cutting, and fishing, in particular, has potential. Of the approximately 35,000 citizens born in the province, 7000 live outside.

GEOGRAPHY

Manus is the smallest province in PNG, both in terms of land mass (2100 square km) and population, but it has a vast sea area (90,000 square km). Its northern boundary is the Equator. Despite this, the daily temperatures are a moderate 24-30° C.

There are 160 islands ranging from Manus which is the largest (104 km long by 28 km wide) and highest (704 metres) to tiny coral atolls, most of which are uninhabited. Lorengau, the provincial headquarters, is on Manus Island. Wuvulu Island, to the far west of the province, has been included in the Sepik chapter, since its most direct transport link is from Wewak.

PEOPLE

The people of the province are Melanesians, although they are not generally as dark as New Islanders, and there has been some intermixing with Micronesians, particularly on the atolls to the west.

The population can be artificially divided into three, although the clan, village and tribal links are much more complicated than this would suggest. The Manus people (sometimes referred to as Titans) occupy the south and south-west islands and share a common language, Titan. These people depend entirely on fishing for their livelihood. The Matangol live to the south, east and north, and although they fish they also depend on some agriculture. The Usiai are coastal and inland people and are exclusively gardeners. There is further specialisation between those who make canoes, nets, pottery, coconut oil, obsidian blades and wood carvings.

Obviously, such specialisation was dependent on trade, which is known as the Kawas system. Although ritual, magic and friendship played an important part, the practical result was that the Manus traded fish and shells for sago and taro from the Usiai and all groups traded their own particular speciality. The obsidian blades from Lou Island were especially important.

Although the Kawas system no longer exists in its traditional form it does continue in some ways. This is partly because of the distribution of land, reefs, rivers and seas which are inherited on a patrilineal system. Although the Manus were allocated some of the German-planted coconut plantations they, and to a lesser extent the Matangol, still suffer from a shortage of fertile land. This is changing, with inter-marriage occurring more frequently.

Margaret Mead first studied the Manus in her book *Growing up in New Guinea* and came back for a second look after WW II. Her studies have been criticised in academic circles, but they still give a fascinating and readable insight into traditional society.

ARTS

Carving has virtually died out in the Admiralties although the people of Bipi still do some – you can see examples in the Lorengau council office. Wooden bowls, stone spears and arrow heads were produced on Lou Island and shields and spears decorated with shark's teeth were produced on the North-Western Islands.

MANUS ISLAND

Since roads are few there is little opportunity to explore the island except by boat or on foot. Manus is heavily timbered, with central hills rising to over 700 metres and many sharp ridges and streams. The airport is at Momote on Los Negros Island and a good road serviced by PMVs connects it with the main town, Lorengau, 27 km away on Manus. A bridge crosses the narrow Loniu Passage. There is a pleasant waterfall and fresh water pool on the Lorengau River about five km upstream from the town of Lorengau.

Apart from rusting remains of the US base and the rugged, but inaccessible interior there is not much to see. Seeadler Harbour, ringed by small islets and reefs, is very beautiful, quite apart from its strategic usefulness.

Los Negros is volcanic and rather more fertile than the main island. Salamei is a particularly good beach.

Things to Do

Ron Knight (tel 40 9159 – mornings), PO Box 108, runs a diving school and has equipment for groups of up to eight people. Bring your own regulator. The diving is, apparently, superb.

Places to Stay

There are a number of places in Manus, but we have no recent first-hand reports. The *Lorengau Hotel* (tel 40 9093), PO Box 89, is a new building with panoramic views over the water, next door to the Lorengau market. Single rooms are K45/55, doubles are K66/76, including breakfast. The meals are reputed to be excellent and feature crayfish for K10; snacks are K1.50/3.50. The hotel has water and land transport and will show visitors around; they can arrange for people to stay in a village.

The *Lorengau Kohai Lodge* (tel 40 9004), PO Box 100, has 12 rooms with singles/doubles at K42/54 – not cheap but it's a pleasant place and the food is good. There's a restaurant and garden bar.

The *Andra Guest House* (tel 40 9088), PO Box 37, has four rooms for K25/30 and *Campbell's Inn Guest House* (tel 40 9224), PO Box 9, has lodge-style accommodation for K30/35. There may be other guesthouses around town.

Tourism in Manus is being actively encouraged and village guesthouses may be opened on Manus and some of the outlying islands. At present, accommodation can be found at village social clubs or private houses. The rates are negotiable, but you won't have to pay more than K10 for a room at a village club. Take some food, partly so you can repay the local hospitality.

See the Sepik chapter for the section on Wuvulu Island and its excellent new lodge.

Getting There & Away

Air A problem. Air Niugini flies to Manus on a Moresby / Lae / Madang / Manus / Kavieng / Rabaul route once a week and there's another flight that includes Wewak. They also come through in the other direction twice a week, and one flight includes Goroka. See the full schedule in the Kavieng section (don't forget it can change). Fares are: Port Moresby K172, Kavieng K89, Madang K90, Wewak K100. If you want to visit Manus you must plan your schedule carefully.

Talair makes a weekly flight with its Dash-8 from Moresby via Madang on Sundays.

Sea Lutheran Shipping's (tel 82 2577), PO Box 789, Madang, MV *Makaya* has a fortnightly voyage to Lorengau from Lae for K33, deck class only, taking 24 hours.

Coastal Shipping Enterprises (tel 92 1733), PO Box 423, Rabaul, runs the MV *Cosmaris* which has one cabin and goes from Rabaul every fortnight; the cabin costs K80, deck class K40. If you join the ship in Kavieng the cabin is K45, deck class K25.

Poroman Shipping (tel 82 2636), PO Box 486, Madang, makes irregular voyages between Madang and Manus for K14 with either the MV *Deaniel* or the MV *Doilon*.

The MV *Tawi*, which is operated by the Manus Provincial Government (tel 40 9088), Shipping Officer, Manus Provincial Government, PO Box 111, Lorengau, plies between Lorengau, the outer islands of Manus, Wuvulu Island, Wewak and Madang. Wewak or Madang to Lorengau takes from five to seven days and there is a return voyage every couple of weeks. There's no straightforward schedule and Madang/Manus is about K30. I heard of the *Joseph Wyett*, also operated by the Manus Government, which apparently goes between Wewak and Manus every three weeks.

Getting Around

PMVs – trucks – cover the entire (limited) road network, including to the old US naval base at Lombrum and airport at Momote.

To get around the coast and to nearby islands you can rent local canoes with 25 hp Johnson outboards for around K30 a day, excluding petrol. If you charter one for 10 days you could make an interesting trip right around Manus. If the south-east winds are blowing you might have to stick to the north coast; the south coast if the north-east is blowing. The fishing is great, particularly along the north coast in the Seeadler Sea. There are guesthouses on some of the northern islands like Andra and Ahus, but on others you can arrange to be put up by asking your captain.

OTHER ISLANDS

The other islands in Manus Province are principally low-lying coral atolls where coconut palms are virtually the only thing that will grow. The main group, scattered hundreds of km north-west of Manus, are known as the North-Western Islands. The people are fine canoeists and, as there are no suitable trees on their tiny islands, they are said to construct their ocean-going canoes from logs that have floated down the Sepik and out to sea.

South of Manus, Lou Island is particularly fertile and beautiful and was once an important source of obsidian blades, before steel arrived. Bipi Island, off the western end of Manus, is famed for its fine carvings.

New Ireland

Area 9974 square km
Population 65,000

New Ireland is the long, narrow island north of New Britain; it's little known and rarely visited, yet it has one of the longest records of contact with European civilisation. European explorers sailed through St George's channel, which separates New Ireland from New Britain, from the early 1600s, and St George's Bay, near the south-east tip, was a popular watering spot for early sailing ships in the region. Later, the Germans developed lucrative copra plantations and the first extensive road network in PNG.

HISTORY
At the same time as they chanced upon the Admiralty Islands in 1516-17, the Dutch explorers Schouten and Le Maire 'discovered' New Ireland, although they did not know it was an island. Later, in 1700, the flamboyant British buccaneer-explorer William Dampier, sailed through the Dampier Straits between New Britain and the mainland and named St George's Bay between New Ireland and New Britain – thinking they were both one island. It was nearly 70 years before Carteret sailed into Dampier's St George's Bay and discovered it was really a channel and New Ireland was separate to New Britain.

It was 1877 when the first missionaries arrived, always an important milestone in PNG. The Reverend George Brown, stationed in the Duke of York Islands between New Britain and New Ireland, arrived at Kalili during that year, crossed over to the north-east coast and after some suitably hair-raising adventures, moved back to safer climes. Not long after, the amazing Marquis de Ray saga took place near the south-east corner of the island – see the separate section in this chapter.

Despite its inauspicious beginnings, New Ireland soon became one of the most profitable parts of the German colony of New Guinea. Under the iron-handed German administrator Baron Boluminski, a string of copra plantations were developed along the north-east coast and a road system, which was long the envy of other parts of the country, was constructed.

Boluminski died of heatstroke before the Australian takeover, and although his road (it still bears his name) was gradually extended, in other respects the island simply marked time. When WW II spread to the Pacific, New Ireland fell almost immediately and Kavieng was subsequently developed into a major Japanese base, although never a rival to Rabaul. Most of the Australians in Kavieng managed to escape but those who chose to stay behind as coastwatchers were gradually captured as the Japanese extended their control over the island.

Like Rabaul, the Japanese held the island right until the final surrender and, again like Rabaul, although the Allies made no attempt to retake New Ireland they inflicted enormous damage. Kavieng, the main Japanese base, was comprehensively flattened, and the Boluminski Highway and its adjoining plantations were severely damaged – the Japanese used it to move supplies down the coast and across to Rabaul. Extensive redevelopment since the war has restored the

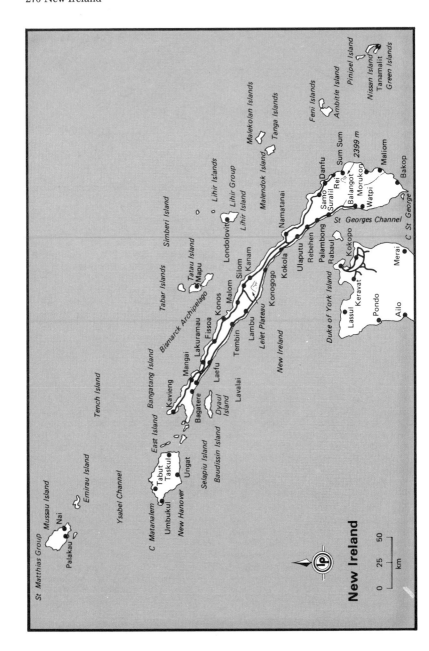

New Ireland

productive copra plantations along the highway and coffee, rubber and timber industries have also developed. Kavieng is also an important fishing port and has a major, Japanese developed, tuna fishing base.

GEOGRAPHY

New Ireland is long, narrow and mountainous. For most of its length the island is only six to 10 km wide with a high spine falling straight to the sea on the southwest coast but bordered by a narrow, but fertile, coastal strip on the north-east coast. It is along this strip that the efficient New Ireland copra producers are based. The highest peak in the central Schleinitz Range is just under 1500 metres. The island bulges out at the south-eastern end and the mountains of the Hans Meyer Range and the Verron Range are somewhat higher: the tallest peak reaches 2399 metres. Despite the narrow channel that separates this part of New Ireland from New Britain there is no comparable volcanic activity in New Ireland.

New Ireland province also includes a number of offshore islands. The major island is New Hanover, also known as Lavongai, off the north-west end. Well offshore from the north-east coast are the islands of Tabar, Lihir, Tanga and Feni. Further to the north-west is the large island of Mussau in the St Matthias Group and the smaller islands of Emirau and Tench.

KAVIENG

Kavieng is a somnolent little town – the very image of a Somerset Maugham south sea island port. It's even hard to pinpoint its centre, although it would have to be Coronation Drive which not only has the hotel and the club but also the Air Niugini office, the post office and, of course, Beeps – Burns Philp if you're new to PNG. The nicest part of Kavieng is the harbour drive, a gently curving road, shaded by huge trees, with most of Kavieng's points

of historical interest dotted along it. You'll notice that even in town most of the men wear lap-laps – a sign of how quiet, isolated and easygoing the island is.

Harbour Drive

Starting from the Coronation Drive intersection you come to a small local market and, on your left, a gentle grassy slope leading up to the District Commissioner's residence. The slope, with a jumble of paving stones along each side, is all that is left of the imposing stairway to Boluminski's residence. The legendary German administrator's home was destroyed during WW II and the far less imposing District Commissioner's residence was built on the same site. A few other stones and bits of paving can be seen on top of the ridge. Further along this waterfront ridge is a large Japanese gun still pointing futilely out to sea.

Down at the shoreline a small, inconspicuous workshop houses another New Ireland relic – the castings to hold the stone, grinding wheel for a mill for the Marquis de Ray's ill-fated project. The wheel itself is in Rabaul but the castings are in remarkably good shape with their date of manufacture, 1852, clearly visible.

The main wharf area looms up next, then an ugly shark proof swimming enclosure. Across the road, and another 100 metres along, is the old cemetery with Boluminski's grave, marked by a plain cross, taking pride of place.

The Harbour

Kavieng has a large and very beautiful harbour and a day can profitably be spent looking around it. The fishing enjoys a good reputation, particularly game fishing, if that's your blood sport. Keep your ears open in the hotel or club and you may get a chance to invite yourself along for a fishing trip. If not, then a wander along the waterfront should turn up a *mons*, the graceful outboard powered canoes, bound for somewhere or other. There are more or

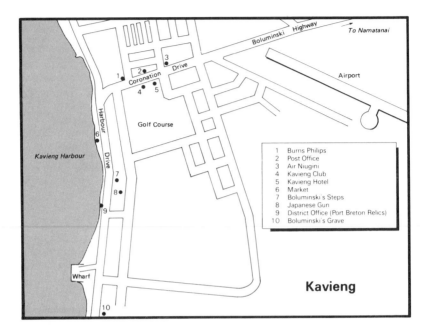

1   Burns Philips
2   Post Office
3   Air Niugini
4   Kavieng Club
5   Kavieng Hotel
6   Market
7   Boluminski's Steps
8   Japanese Gun
9   District Office (Port Breton Relics)
10 Boluminski's Grave

Kavieng

less fixed charges for trips out to various islands or you can arrange a charter or a 'drop me off, pick me up later' trip.

A good place for the latter would be the idyllic little island of Edmago. A tiny dot with palm trees, a white-sand beach all the way round and beautiful clear water over the coral. Finding a way in through the shallow coral to the shore is not easy. On the way out you'll pass the Japanese tuna-processing plant on a large island. The tuna are salted or frozen for export and a large fleet of tuna boats, plus their mother-ship, patrol the waters around New Ireland. Further out is the island of New Sulaman – another popular local picnic spot where you can see copra being prepared by a handful of local families.

Places to Stay

The *Kavieng Hotel* (tel 94 2199), PO Box 4, is a drowsy place straight out of *Tales of the South Pacific*. A large dog, draped across the doorway for most of the day, doesn't even deign to wake up as hotel guests step over him. In fact if you arrive sans-booking you'll probably have a job finding anybody at all. The fan and neon light in my room were similarly relaxed, since they both required a kick to wake them up. There are 34 rooms ranging from fan-cooled (singles/doubles – K20/35), up through air-con rooms (K75/45), to air-con with private facilities in a new motel-style block (K70/75). Full board costs another K24.

The *Kavieng Club* (tel 94 2027), PO Box 62, just a few doors down the road, also offers rooms and is a fun place to hang around for a drink or meal. Many of the island's 'befores', expats of 20 to 35 years duration, regularly drop by for a cold one or a game of darts. It's a good place to hear stories or maybe line up a ride to somewhere else on the island. There are about eight rooms, some with air-con.

Top: Cassowaries are culturally significant and highly valued (ML)
Left: Crocodiles are particularly revered along the Sepik, but they are
      hunted and farmed (TW)
Right: The cuscus is one of PNG's few indigenous mammals (ML)

Top: One of the many coastal villages along the Boluminski Highway,
      New Ireland (ML)
Bottom: What can you say about a beach like this one at Kaibola
      in the Trobriand Islands? (ML)

Listed prices are K15/35. Lunches are available at the bar and the dining room has good-value meals.

Getting There & Away

Air You have to plan your itinerary carefully if you visit Kavieng. Air Niugini's current schedule is quite complex.

Tuesday
Moresby / Lae / Madang / Manus / *Kavieng* / Rabaul / Moresby
Thursday
Kieta / Rabaul / *Kavieng* / Manus / Madang / Lae / Moresby
Friday
Moresby / Lae / Rabaul / *Kavieng* / Rabaul / Kieta / Moresby
Saturday
Moresby / Lae / Madang / Wewak / Manus / *Kavieng* / Rabaul
Sunday
Rabaul / *Kavieng* / Manus / Wewak / Madang / Goroka / Moresby

Some fares are Moresby K195, Manus K89, Rabaul K66 and Lae K169.

Talair flies direct to Kavieng via Rabaul every Wednesday, between Rabaul and Kavieng four times a week (K66), and daily except Sunday to Namatanai (K34). They also have flights to some of the outlying islands.

Sea Kavieng is serviced by two Coastal Shipping Company vessels (tel 92 1733), PO Box 423, Rabaul: the MV *Cosmaris* which sails Rabaul/Kavieng/Manus every fortnight; and MV *Tikana* which sails weekly from Rabaul, deck class only. Fares are K25 for deck class and K45 for the single cabin on the *Cosmaris*.

Pacific New Guinea Lines (tel 92 3024), PO Box 1764, Rabaul, has the MV *Kaum* which sails from Rabaul (departing Monday) to Kavieng for K25. Every second week it goes on to Mussau Island in the St Mathias group and you can go too, for another K11. As with all the coastal

freighters, although basic food is provided, you are advised to supplement this with fresh fruit, and not to expect luxury.

Every afternoon small boats sail from Rabaul to the Duke of York Islands and they sometimes continue on to a small port on New Ireland, opposite Namatanai and connected to it by road. It's worth asking about this because the only alternative is to fly to Kavieng or Namatanai, despite the short distance across St George's Channel.

Road The Boluminski Highway, which runs 270 km from Kavieng to Namatanai and for about 80 km beyond Namatanai, is still in reasonably good shape even for conventional vehicles. See the separate section on the Highway, following.

There are buses between Kavieng and Namatanai, but only once or twice a week. One leaves Kavieng on Tuesdays and costs K10. PMVs run out of each town, but seldom along the entire route, rather they service nearby villages. In the centre of the island the road is very quiet with scarcely a vehicle, let alone a PMV. It is possible to make the trip using a combination of PMVs, paying for a ride on any old vehicle passing by and hitching, but it's best to ask around the hotel or club in Kavieng; people come and go on various work projects. A private car can do the trip in about five hours. Trucks regularly go from Burns Philp – ask them.

There are four main roads crossing from the north-east to the less visited south-west. They run from Fangalawa to Panamefei/Lamusmus, Karu to Konogogo, Bo (near Namatanai) to Labur Bay and from Bo to Ulupatur. Although some of these trans-island roads can be rough or even impassable for conventional vehicles during the wet, the longest is only ll km. It's a narrow island! The south-west coast road is very rough for 40 km in the north and 41 km in the centre.

AROUND KAVIENG

If you've got transport, there are a number

of points of interest within a few minutes' drive of Kavieng. A couple of km out of town along the Boluminski Highway, a little pathway leads off the road to a limestone cave filled with crystal clear water. You have to know where it is to find the trail. During WW II the Japanese used this grotto as a source of drinking water.

At Utu Village the high school has a small museum which you can look around, if you can catch someone with the key to the door. There are exhibitions of Malanggan carvings, ancient stone tools and vessels and a shark catching propeller.

Shark Calling

New Ireland is the centre for the art of shark calling; shark callers can be found at Kontu and Tabar. Certain men have the ability to 'call up' sharks. The unfortunate shark swims up to the caller's boat where they can be speared, netted or even, if they are small enough, grabbed. A variant on shark calling is the shark propeller: a noose is hung with half coconut shells which make a rattling noise, attracting the shark up through the noose. A rope attached to the noose is connected to a wooden propeller which is spun round to tighten the noose and simultaneously pull in the rope. The shark, unable to keep moving, effectively drowns.

BOLUMINSKI HIGHWAY

New Ireland's autocratic administrator, Herr Boluminski, built a road that was not rivalled on the mainland until well into the '50s. When WW I cut short the period of German rule the Boluminski Highway already ran 100 km out of Kavieng along the north-east coast. Under the Australians it was gradually extended and it now reaches about 80 km beyond Namatanai to Rei, before petering out into a four-wheel drive track.

There are also a number of crossings from the east to the west coast but the west coast road is little used and poorly maintained. Several bridges are out so you have to ford rivers which is not always possible in the wet season. Still, New Ireland is extremely well endowed with roads by PNG standards.

Boluminski built the road by forcing each village along the coast to construct and maintain a section. On his tours of inspection, Boluminski would summon the villagers to personally push his carriage over any deteriorated sections and woe betide these villagers if repairs were not underway when he returned.

The highway is paved with koronos, crushed coral, a fine surface for an unsealed road although the glare is rather hard on the eyes in bright conditions and when it's wet it acts like grinding paste on car tyres. Some patches are sealed, others are dirt, but it's all in fairly good shape – and flat. Almost all the way along, the coast is one continuous copra plantation – in places cocoa trees fill the gaps between the palms. Rubber plantations in varying states of prosperity are also interspersed along the route.

There are many villages built beside the road, often right on the palm-fringed beach. Visitors to the island are few, an outsider quickly becomes an interesting diversion. People are friendly, waving and shouting as you drive by, gathering around if you stop. Note how many of the locals have blonde hair – some due to dietary deficiencies, some to an odd genetic strain, as in the Highlands, and sometimes due to good old bleach.

Nearly every village is built near one of the many streams that run down from the central mountains. These streams are cool, clean and delightfully clear and refreshing. Stopping at these to join the villagers in a drink and a dip can make the trip to Namatanai a very pleasant day. It would make a worthwhile trip to walk along either coast road from one village to another; they're often within a few km of each other.

Libba Village, just before Konos, is a good place to look for Malanggan carvings – see the separate section. Konos itself is the approximate halfway point to Namatanai and the only major village along the road. It's also the loading point for Japanese timber ships, which collect logs from the project operating from a little beyond Konos all the way to Namatanai.

About 30 km from Konos, near the Lemerica Plantation, a new road leads up onto the Lelet Plateau where there's an enormously deep limestone cave. Nobody has yet reached its full depth. There are also bat caves near Mongop. The isolated people of the Lelet Plateau will be brought into closer contact with the people along the coast when the new road is completed.

Beyond here the road climbs a couple of times and occasionally deteriorates a little, but in general it continues to hug the coast all the way to Namatanai and beyond. Although there are many fine stretches of white sand, backed by the obligatory palm trees, the swimming is mostly not so good because the water is very shallow and rocky until it suddenly drops steeply away. Pinis Passage, just on the Namatanai side of Konos, is a small, popular beach.

Malanggan Carvings

Twenty years ago it was widely reported that the art of Malanggan carving had completely died out. Now there has been a modest revival although finding carvings for sale can be difficult. One carver making these interesting artefacts, with their American Indian totem pole look, can be found in a coastal village about midway between Kavieng and Namatanai. An American collector prompted Hosea Linge, the son of a famous carver, to resurrect the forgotten craft. You can find him, and his carvings, at Libba, a small village about 22 km before Konos.

The Malanggan carvings were just part of a whole series of ceremonies and rituals which were centred on the north coast, east of Kavieng. The carvings would be displayed during initiation and burial rites. Only one man in a tribal group had the right to carve or display the Malanggans and this was a matter of considerable prestige.

On Masahet Island, a beautiful little isle near Lihir, with a population of less than a thousand, the Catholic mission church has Malanggan carved posts. Panamecho, a village on the west coast, has some old Malanggan carvings. Other places of interest for artefacts on New Ireland are Lamusmus on the west coast and Lihir Island where shell money is still made.

NAMATANAI

A green, quiet little town midway down the coast, Namatanai is only a 15 minute flight from Rabaul. It was an important station in German days and the Namatanai Hotel is on the site of the old German station house. You can find the graves of Dr Emil Stephan, the German administrator, and Mrs Scheringer, wife to another German official from pre-WW I days, in the picturesque old graveyard down the road from the National Works compound on the other side of the airstrip.

Just before you enter the town from Kavieng the road goes through a deep cutting; the old road winds off below it and down on the shore there is a jumble of Japanese tanks and guns which were bulldozed off after the war. From the road you can only see one rusting tank – you have to clamber down the steep cliff face to see the whole pile of them although, unfortunately, the cliff is being used as the town dump and the tanks are disappearing under garbage. It is said their engines still contain oil. About 20 km before Namatanai, there is the mid-section of a Japanese bomber sitting by the roadside.

Places to Stay

The *Namatanai Hotel* (tel 94 3057), PO Box 48, has a pleasant, easygoing atmosphere. It's right down by the waterfront, near the new wharf. There are just four rooms – three with two beds, one with three beds – with fans and private facilities (there's only cold water, but this is no real hardship). Singles/doubles are K30/45. Each room has its own short-wave radio – I even heard an American jazz show. A recent innovation, as in so many hotels around the country, is the video-TV room with movies at night.

Meals are available, breakfasts and lunches at K6, dinner K12. You'll most likely be joined by owner Bernie Gash or members of his family. He's an interesting character who can tell you all manner of stories about Namatanai and its people, past and present. The bar is a good place to come across other locals. There are also some basic, cheaper rooms with shared facilities for K10 in the Gashes' old house.

Alternatively, there's the *Council Accommodation* at K16 a night with shared facilities and no meals. You're better off at the hotel.

Along the waterfront, at the opposite end from the hotel, there's a kai haus with simple meals of fish or chicken on rice for just a kina or so.

Getting There & Away

Talair flies daily from Rabaul for K34. There may be boats from Rabaul, via the Duke of York Islands to the west coast a short distance from Namatanai. See the Kavieng section for information on Highway transport.

THE SOUTH

The southern 'bulge' of the island is still relatively isolated because the roads are not too good. The rugged mountains and heavy rainfall further complicate things. The people in the south are similar to the Tolais of East New Britain, but are less sophisticated than the other New Irelanders who have long been linked by the coast road.

The Marquis de Ray & Cape Breton

The story of the colony of Cape Breton and the Marquis de Ray is one of the most outrageous in the saga of European colonisation in the Pacific. The Marquis had never set foot on New Ireland, yet on the frail basis of a ship's log he contrived to sell hundreds of hectares of land to gullible, would-be settlers at the equivalent of about 40c an acre. He raised no less than $60,000 (an amazing sum for 1879) on the basis of his flimsy prospectus. Unfortunately, many of his colonists paid with their lives as well as their savings.

The Marquis had advertised Cape Breton, near Lambon on Cape St George, as a thriving settlement with fertile soil, perpetual sunshine

and friendly natives. In actual fact there had been no preparation at all and the settlers were dumped into a tangled jungle where the rainfall was so heavy that, even today, there has been virtually no development. And the Reverend George Brown, an early visitor to this part of New Ireland, had found the natives far from friendly.

With only three weeks' supplies and such useful equipment as a mill for an area where grain would never grow, the settlers soon started to die like flies. It's anyone's guess whether malaria or starvation took the larger toll but the Marquis helped things along by sending supply ships from Australia with useful cargoes like cases of note-paper or loads of bricks. Not to mention three more shiploads of naive land-buyers from Europe.

Eventually the pitiful survivors were rescued by Thomas Farrell and his wife Emma, who later became famous as Queen Emma. Much of the equipment abandoned on the beaches of Cape Breton was used to construct her magnificent mansion near Rabaul. Although most of the rescued settlers were sent on to Australia, one 16 year old did eventually become a successful plantation holder – but on New Britain not New Ireland. The grinding stone for the Cape Breton grain mill can still be seen in a park off Mango Avenue in Rabaul and some parts are in Kavieng. The crazy Marquis ended his days in a lunatic asylum in France.

Getting Around

Road Along the north-east coast you can continue in a conventional vehicle from Namatanai through Samo to Danfu and from there to Rei by four-wheel drive. It's possible, with great effort, to walk, canoe and boat right around the southern tip of the island. On the south-west coast the roads are being improved by timber companies and the missing gaps gradually filled in. There's a lot of timber in the south. The road already goes to Pelabong and will extend to Wapi.

Walking On the way south from Namatanai, Samo is where the road used to start getting really rough. After Warangansau Village there is a big hill to Manja and the road is almost deserted after this point. There is a mission at Manja and two

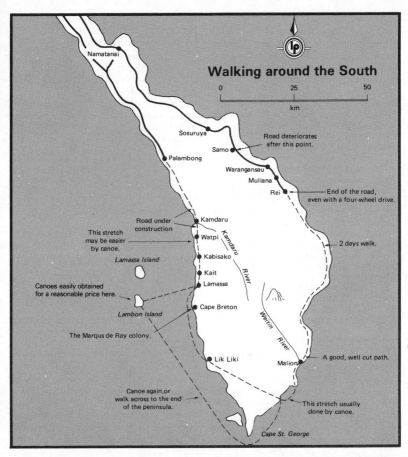

Walking around the South

0   25   50
km

Namatanai

Sosuruya

Samo — Road deteriorates after this point.

Palambong

Warangansau

Muliana

Rei — End of the road, even with a four-wheel drive.

Kamdaru

Road under construction

This stretch may be easier by canoe.

Watpi

Lamassa Island

Kabisako

Kamdaru River

2 days walk.

Kait

Canoes easily obtained for a reasonable price here.

Lamassa

Lambon Island

Cape Breton

The Marqus de Ray colony.

Weirin River

Lik Liki

Malion — A good, well cut path.

Canoe again, or walk across to the end of the peninsula.

This stretch usually done by canoe.

Cape St. George

plantations at Muliana and Manmo, just after Muliana village. After Manja you come to Maritboan Plantation. There is a small plantation near the end of the road.

From the end of the road in Rei it takes about two days to Srar Village – ask the way from the villagers. From Srar to Maliom is fairly easy – a good, well cut path. After Maliom the paths get difficult and some sections of the coast can only be negotiated by canoe. Canoes are reasonable to hire and easily obtained. There is a path

across the southern part of the peninsula or else, if you are lucky enough to pick up an outboard motor, you can go around to Lambon by the cape.

Cape St George is worth seeing, if you can fix it up. Canoes from Lambon to Lamassa are easy to find and there is a path from there all the way to Palambong – although it is better to get a canoe from Kabisalao to Watpi. The road is meant to go from Palambong to Watpi, but the timber companies have been slow.

NEW HANOVER

The island of New Hanover (or Lavongai) is the second largest island in the province, a mountainous, isolated island with productive copra plantations on the volcanic soils of its coastline.

The people of New Hanover are best known for their brave attempt to buy the US President, Lyndon Johnson. When the first House of Assembly elections in PNG were held, the New Hanover voters decided, quite reasonably, that if this was democracy and they could vote for whoever they liked they might as well vote for Lyndon Johnson.

New Hanover went 'all the way with LBJ', but when the American President showed no sign of taking up the island's cause the islanders decided to take more direct action. They refused to pay their taxes and instead put the money into a fund to 'buy' him. They raised quite a large sum but even this example of Texas-style capitalism failed to bring the man to New Hanover.

Eventually the Johnson cult died out and the events were all but forgotten. Until someone on the island started selling Johnson outboard motors. Well, you can imagine . . . .

EASTERN ISLANDS

There are four island groups strung off the north-east coast of New Ireland – Tabar, Lihir, Tanga and Feni. They are only 30 to 50 km offshore and clearly visible from the coast. There are a number of airstrips on the islands, serviced by Talair, and it is also possible to get out to them by local shipping services. In particular there are ships running fairly frequently from Konos to Tabar. Tabar is thought to be the original home of the Malanggan carvings and ceremonies.

The islands are all quite beautiful and their inhabitants are great canoeists. Gold has been found on Lihir Island and mining has begun; by the end of the decade it will be a massive operation. The only problem is that the ore is in the centre of a collapsed volcano caldera and the deeper they drill the hotter it gets. Gold has also been discovered on the Tabar Islands.

There is no organised accommodation on any of these islands so they are very much places for adventurous travellers with open-ended schedules.

ST MATTHIAS GROUP

The islands of Mussau, Emirau and Tench are some distance north-west of New Ireland; they put up a determined resistance to the European invasion. Tench was the last 'uncontrolled' part of the New Ireland region.

During the war there was an American base at Emirau with a larger force than the entire present day population of the group. The people build fine, large canoes without outriggers, which can carry 30 or more people. Tench is also famous for woven mats. These islands and New Hanover make up the sub-province of Lamet – the name comes from the first letters of LAvongai (New Hanover), Mussau, Emirau and Tench.

New Britain

Area 39,807 square km
Population 255,000

The island of New Britain, the largest of PNG's offshore islands, offers a strange contrast between its two provinces. East New Britain (ENB) ends in the Gazelle Peninsula, where there has been lengthy contact with Europeans and the people are economically and culturally sophisticated. Due to the high fertility of the volcanic soil they are also among the most affluent people in the country, despite the high population density.

In complete contrast, the other end of the island, West New Britain (WNB), is comparatively sparsely populated, little developed and did not come into serious contact with Europeans until the 1960s.

For most visitors, New Britain will mean Rabaul – the beautiful harbour city on the Gazelle Peninsula with its dramatic, sometimes too dramatic, cluster of volcanoes.

HISTORY
East New Britain's history has been far from a placid one and it has had a long period of contact with Europeans, if not the longest of any area in PNG. Human settlement was well established many thousands of years before the golden age of European discovery. It is now believed that people began to settle the islands of the Pacific around 10,000 years ago, and that New Britain was settled by that time (based on carbon dating a hearth in a cave near Kandrian in WNB).

Lapita pottery, a distinctive prehistoric pottery with pitted and incised patterns found throughout the Pacific, has also been discovered. Shards dating to 4000 BC have been found on Eloave Island in the St Matthias group, New Ireland, and other finds (of varying antiquity) have been made on New Britain, Manus, New

Ireland, the North Solomons, Vanuatu, New Caledonia and Fiji. Pottery found on Watom Island, to the north of Rabaul has been dated at 600-500 BC.

The Tolai people, now the major ethnic group in ENB, originally came from New Ireland. They took the Gazelle Peninsular from the Baining, Sulka and Taulil people a few centuries before the Europeans arrived. Although the Tolai have a distinct language, they share many customs and physical characteristics with the New Irelanders. The Tolai were a warlike people and there were frequent inter-clan battles.

Early explorers from Europe spent much more time around the northern islands than they did around the mainland. William Dampier, the swashbuckling English pirate-adventurer-explorer, was the first to land in the area. He arrived here early in the year 1700 and named the island New Britain when he sailed around the east coast of New Britain and New Ireland. Although he proved New Britain was an island, separated from the New Guinea mainland by Dampier Strait, it was not until 1767 that Phillip Carteret discovered Dampier's St George's Bay was really St George's Channel when he sailed through it, proving New Ireland was actually a separate island.

A hundred years passed with only occasional contact although many whalers and other sailors passed through St

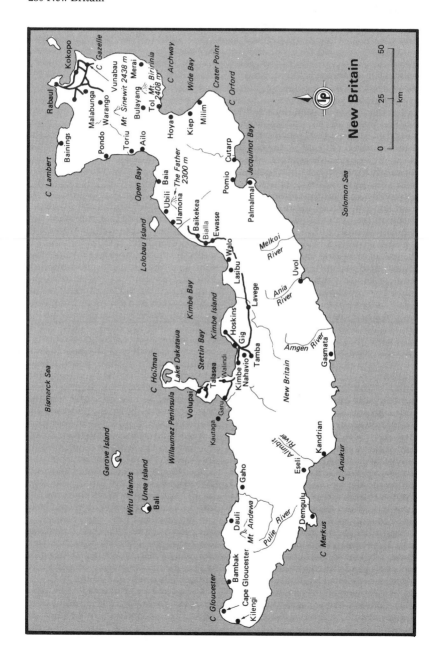

New Britain

George's Channel and sometimes paused to water or provision their boats. Then, in the 1870s, traders started to arrive, often in search of copra. In 1875 the legendary Methodist missionary Dr George Brown showed up and with six Fijians set up the first mission station in the Duke of York Islands, which are in St George's Channel.

Brown could hardly be faulted for lack of energy; apart from working flat out on converting the heathen he also found time to be a keen amateur vulcanologist, a linguist, a scientist, an anthropologist and managed a fair bit of local exploring. While his reception was not the best and only one of his original Fijian assistants survived the first turbulent years, Brown more than merely survived, and left as a respected, even loved, man.

In 1878 a Mrs Emma Forsyth arrived from Samoa, started a trading business at Mioko in the Duke of York Islands and took the first steps towards her remarkable fame and fortune (see the separate section). In 1882 Captain Simpson sailed in on HMS *Blanche*, named the harbour where the town of Rabaul now stands after himself, and the bay after his ship. Two years later the Germans, thoroughly beaten by malaria and the climate on the north New Guinea coast, moved their HQ to Kokopo on New Britain, naming it Herbertshohe.

In 1910 the Germans moved round the bay to Rabaul's present site – the name means mangrove in the local dialect, for the town site was in the middle of a mangrove swamp. The Germans did not have long to enjoy what soon became a very beautiful town: when WW I arrived, Australia invaded New Britain in order to take the German radio station at Bita Paka. The first six Australians to die in the war lost their lives in this action, along with one German and 30 PNG soldiers. A larger contingent of Australians also died when their submarine mysteriously disappeared off the coast during the attack.

For the rest of the war, things carried on much as before. Since Australia was in no position to take over the efficiently run and highly profitable German copra plantations the Germans were allowed to keep on operating under close military supervision. At the end of the war however, the unfortunate planters all had their plantations expropriated and were shipped back to Germany. They were compensated, as part of the war reparations agreement, in German marks, which soon became totally worthless in the bout of hyper-inflation suffered by Germany in the early '20s. One doubly unfortunate individual made his way back to New Britain, started again from scratch and once more built up a thriving plantation. Unfortunately, he neglected to take out Australian citizenship and in WW II his property was expropriated again.

Between the wars, Rabaul continued on its busy and profitable way as the capital of Australian New Guinea, until nature decided to shake it up a little. ENB is the most volcanically active area of the country and nowhere is this more evident than in Rabaul. Blanche Bay, Rabaul's beautiful harbour, is simply the flooded crater of an enormous volcano that is over three km wide. The cataclysmic eruption that formed what is now the harbour took place eons ago, but the Rabaul area has had many more recent upheavals – as the string of volcano cones around the rim of the super-crater indicates.

Sputterings and earthquakes are an everyday occurrence in ENB and it takes more than a little shake to upset the citizens of Rabaul. In 1971 a major quake was followed by a tidal wave that temporarily swamped the city centre, but the last disastrous upheaval took place in 1937. There was plenty of warning: minor quakes became increasingly frequent and sea water boiled and dead fish floated to the surface around Vulcan, a low lying island in the harbour that had appeared after an 1878 eruption. When Vulcan suddenly erupted, 500 Tolais who had assembled on the island for a festival were killed. Eruptions continued all night; 27 hours later when they finally ceased, the low, flat island was a massive mountain joined to the mainland.

The harbour was coated in yellow pumice stone and everything was covered in a film of ash and dust, brought down by a violent thunderstorm that accompanied the eruptions. But that was not all: Matupit started to fume and then erupted for three days. Months later, when an $80,000 cleanup had restored the town, Matupit continued to rumble and cough. The frangipani earned its special place in Rabaul after the eruption for it was the first flower to bloom through the layers of dust and ash.

Government minds soon turned to thoughts of transferring the New Guinea capital to a safer site. The mainland had barely been touched when Australia took over German New Guinea, but now it was much more widely explored and the gold rush in Wau and Bulolo had prompted development. Accordingly, the decision was taken to transfer the HQ to Lae. The move had barely commenced when WW II arrived in Rabaul. Its impact was even more dramatic than the volcanoes'.

After the Japanese attack on Pearl Harbor it was obvious that Rabaul would soon be in danger; women and children were evacuated by the end of December 1941, but there were still about 400 Australian civilians in the town when a huge bombing raid on 22 January heralded the coming invasion. The following day a small contingent of Australian troops was completely crushed by a Japanese assault. Those who managed to escape found themselves cut off in the jungle and isolated from the New Guinea mainland where, in any case, the Japanese had already captured Lae and Salamaua. In an amazing feat of endurance, patrol officers based in New Britain (including the legendary J K McCarthy who retells the operation in his book *Patrol Into Yesterday*) shepherded the surviving

troops along the inhospitable, roadless coast to the southern tip of the island where a flotilla of private boats undertook a mini Dunkirk and rescued 400 of the 700 men who had survived.

The civilians left behind in Rabaul were not so fortunate – not a single one was ever heard from again. It was later established that they were loaded onto a prison ship, the *Montevideo Maru*, and drowned when the ship was torpedoed by an American submarine off the Philippines while it was on its way to Japan.

The Japanese intended to use Rabaul as a major supply base for their steady march south, but the tables were soon turned. With their defeat at Guadalcanal in the Solomons, at Milne Bay and Buna on the New Guinea mainland, and with their naval power shattered in the Battle of the Coral Sea, they were soon on the defensive and Rabaul was made into an impregnable fortress. They dug 500 km of tunnels into the hills, a honeycomb of interconnecting passages used for storage, hospitals, anti-aircraft guns, bunkers, gun emplacements and barracks.

At the peak of the war 97,000 Japanese troops and thousands of POWs were stationed on the Gazelle Peninsula. They had even imported 800 Japanese and Korean prostitutes. The harbour was laced with mines and the roads were camouflaged with trees. And the Allies never came.

MacArthur had learnt the lesson of Guadalcanal and Buna where the bitter fighting had led to enormous casualties on both sides. Never again did the Japanese and Allied forces meet head-on; bases like Rabaul were simply by-passed. The Japanese air force was unable to compete effectively with Allied air power and over 20,000 tons of bombs rained down upon the Peninsula keeping the remaining Japanese forces underground and impotent. When the war ended they were still there, trapped in a bastion that may well have been invulnerable, but was never put to the test.

Rabaul was utterly flattened. Photographs taken just after the Japanese surrender show Mango Avenue, the main street in Rabaul, marked only by occasional heaps of bricks. Over 40 ships lay at the bottom of the harbour, and it took two years just to transfer all the troops back to Japan.

Rabaul soon bounced back, although the evidence of the war is still readily seen. The hills are riddled with tunnels (although many are sealed up for safety's sake), remnants of barges, aircraft, guns, cranes and other military equipment litter the area and the harbour bottom is carpeted with sunken shipping. The transfer of the capital of New Guinea from Rabaul to Lae did not have the negative impact that had been feared, partly because after the war Papua and New Guinea were administered as one territory from Port Moresby.

The Tolai people have a relatively high level of education and economic wellbeing, but their bounteous peninsula is heavily populated so there are considerable land pressures. These problems are compounded by the large percentage of land that was bought from the Tolais by the Germans and is still owned by Europeans.

After the war, as concepts of self government developed, land become a major issue and discontent rose to a fever pitch. Many Tolais wanted all land bought from them in the German days, when they were considerably less sophisticated in their dealings with the west, to be returned. A political organisation, known as the Mataungan Association, sprang up with the aim of subverting the Australian-managed local councils and self government programmes. The Tolais wanted self government, but on their own terms; they successfully boycotted the first pre-independence election and then demanded their own Mataungan leaders be given power. The problem has not gone away, but it is not currently a central issue.

Rabaul's volcanoes have not, however,

been so cooperative. In 1983 Rabaul seemed to be heating up for a repeat of the 1937 eruptions and by early '84 the town was ready for an instant evacuation. At one point women and children were sent away and aircraft were actually standing by. The threatened eruption failed to eventuate, but the situation highlighted, once again, the town's precarious position.

Queen Emma

Queen Emma was one of those larger than life people destined to become legends in their own lifetime. Emma was born in Samoa of an American father and Samoan mother. Her first husband disappeared at sea and in 1878 she teamed up with Thomas Farrell, an Australian trader, and started a trading business at Mioko on the Duke of York Islands. She was an astute businesswoman and she soon realised that a plantation on the rich volcanic soil of the Gazelle Peninsula would be an excellent investment.

With her brother-in-law Richard Parkinson, who conveniently happened to be a botanist, Emma acquired land at Ralum, near Kokopo and became the manager and owner of the first real plantation in New Guinea. When Thomas Farrell died he was succeeded by a steady stream of lovers.

By the time the Germans arrived in New Britain, Emma had extended her little empire to several other plantations, a number of ships and a whole string of trade stores. She made astute use of her American citizenship to avoid possible German takeovers. Emma built a mansion called Gunantambu (you can still see the regal stairway to the front door today) and entertained like royalty. She had her own wharf where she met guests, accompanied by her friends and servants, dressed in the finest clothes Europe could provide, then took them up to the mansion to dine on imported food and champagne.

'Queen Emma' may have been a joke at first, but it was soon a name she had earned. For many years Emma was faithful to her lover Agostino Stalio, who is buried just outside Rabaul, but after his death she married Paul Kolbe. He died in Monte Carlo in 1913 and Emma herself died a few days later. Her empire fell apart soon after she was gone and her fine home was destroyed during the last war.

GEOGRAPHY

New Britain is a long, narrow, mountainous island. It is nearly 600 km from end to end but at its widest point it is only 80 km across. The central mountain range runs from one end of the country to the other. The interior is harsh and rugged, split by gorges and fast-flowing rivers and blanketed in thick rainforest. The highest mountain is The Father (Mt Uluwan) an active volcano rising to nearly 2300 metres. The north-eastern end of the island terminates in the heavily populated, highly fertile and dramatically volcanic Gazelle Peninsula, with the three peaks known as The Mother, North Daughter and South Daughter.

New Britain lies across the direction of the monsoon winds so the rainy season comes at opposite times of the year on the north and south coast. From December to April the mountain barrier brings the heavy rain down on the north coast, while in June to October it is the south coast that has the rain. Rainfall varies widely around the country, at Pomio on the south coast it averages 8500 mm a year (nearly 30 feet of rain!) while in relatively dry Rabaul it is only 3000 mm annually (10 feet of rain a year). Pomio once had over a metre of rain in one week.

The island is divided into two provinces: East New Britain with its capital at Rabaul, and West New Britain with its capital at Kimbe.

PEOPLE

The Tolai people are the the the major ethnic group in ENB and number about 80,000, although it is believed they arrived from New Ireland only a few centuries before the Europeans. Their language is known as Kuanua. The Baining, Sulka and Taulil people, who pre-dated the Tolais' invasion, fled into the mountains.

There are probably four or five thousand Baining people left, and they still perform their spectacular fire dances, costumed in huge, Disney-like masks. If you are lucky enough to be in Rabaul when a fire dance is on, usually at Gaulim, it is an experience not to be missed.

The Mokolkols, a group of nomads who even after WW II continued to make murderous raids on peaceful coastal villages, were far fewer in number. It was not until 1950 that the government finally managed to capture a handful of these people, even though they lived within 100 km of Rabaul! After a spell in the big city, the captives led government officers back to the rest of their clan – there were only 30 in all.

When the first missionaries arrived, the Tolai were still a pretty wild bunch and inter-clan warfare was common. They are a matrilineal society (not to be confused with matriarchal), which means that a child belongs to its mother's clan, not father's. A clan's property is looked after by the senior male, but the land is inherited by one of the man's sister's sons, and his own sons inherit land held by his wife's brother.

Authority was wielded by big men who won their prestige through wealth or military prowess and a powerful, male secret society played an important role in village life, organising ceremonies and maintaining customary laws. Ceremonies featured leaf-draped, anonymous figures topped by masks – the *tabuan* and *dukduk*. A lawbreaker who found a weirdly costumed tabuan at his front door would mend his ways, or else. Today they are rarely seen and if they are, their importance is likely to be largely ceremonial.

Shell money, or *tambu*, retains its cultural significance for the Tolai and is still displayed at traditional ceremonies. Little shells, similar in shape to cowries, that are obtained from WNB, Manus and the North Solomons are strung on lengths of cane and bound together in great rolls called *loloi*.

At one time, Rabaul had a very large Chinese minority, some of whom were descendants of cooks and servants brought in by the German planters.

Over the last couple of editions a fierce debate has raged over whether this illustration depicts a dukduk or a tambuan. We are indebted to Berit Gustafsson for the information that it is a tabuan (note correct spelling). A tabuan has eyes which, if they are painted by an adept, bring a wild and dangerous spirit under human control. The tabuan is the mother of a dukduk, her son. The dukduk is a similar shape but has no eyes; there are several rings around the cone. The dukduk serves male interests, but it is not dangerous. Stay tuned for the next instalment!

Chinatown rose from the ashes of WW II, but many of its inhabitants left after independence. Today, parts of town still have a cosmopolitan atmosphere and bustling energy (especially around the market) although Chinatown is a shadow of its former self. There are also many Papua New Guineans from the less affluent Highlands and Sepik regions, who have been imported to do the boring, unskilled work on the copra plantations that the Tolai are no longer interested in.

East New Britain

Area 19,320 square km
Population 150,000

RABAUL

Lying at the rim of a huge, flooded volcanic caldera, the provincial capital vies with Madang for the title of most beautiful town in PNG – or even the Pacific. It may not have Madang's beautiful waterways and parks, but it does have dramatic volcanoes towering over it on all sides, and beautiful Simpson Harbour. Laid out in grid style, the streets are wide and clean and just about everything is within walking distance.

There is probably more to do and see around Rabaul than any other town in PNG. You can climb volcanoes, inspect war relics and dive over some of the best coral and wrecks in PNG. There is also a better choice of hotels and restaurants than you will find in almost any other town.

Unfortunately, all this is threatened by Matupit Volcano, right at the town's edge, beside the airport. Since a scare in 1984, however, there has been no major activity or threat. The situation is closely monitored, so do not hesitate to visit – the locals are quite blase about the occasional tremor (*guria*). Although business confidence suffered as a result of the 1984 crisis, Rabaul is still a thriving town.

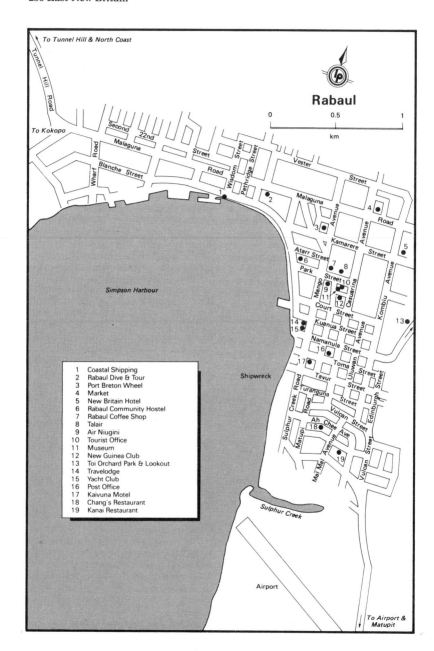

Rabaul

0   0.5   1
km

1   Coastal Shipping
2   Rabaul Dive & Tour
3   Port Breton Wheel
4   Market
5   New Britain Hotel
6   Rabaul Community Hostel
7   Rabaul Coffee Shop
8   Talair
9   Air Niugini
10 Tourist Office
11 Museum
12 New Guinea Club
13 Toi Orchard Park & Lookout
14 Travelodge
15 Yacht Club
16 Post Office
17 Kaivuna Motel
18 Chang's Restaurant
19 Kanai Restaurant

Information

Rabaul is one of the few places in PNG with a tourist office (tel 92 1813), PO Box 385. It's on Park St, east of Mango Avenue, and there's also a notice board at the airport with hotel addresses and information about current events. They have a good supply of pamphlets and maps, and they are helpful and friendly. They also have information on forthcoming cultural events, festivals, sing-sings and the like and may be able to arrange transportation. They're definitely worth visiting; their hours are 8 am to 12 noon and 1 to 4 pm, Monday to Friday.

The town is well serviced with shops, a post office, hire cars – and an excellent market. The major banks have branches and Rabaul is the headquarters for Coastal Shipping and Pacific New Guinea Lines.

Rabaul is also one of the few places outside Moresby where you can get your teeth repaired – try Dr Mills (tel 92 1960) – and the medical services are pretty good.

Things to See

The harbour is magnificent and it still services the rusting tramp freighters which wander along the coastlines of New Britain, New Ireland, the Solomons and among all the islands in between. The market should not be missed, nor the section of bustling Chinese shops nearby.

In the little park, towards the market end of Mango Avenue, by the town and Gazelle area maps, stands the grinding wheel from Port Breton. In 1879 a crazy French Marquis and real estate speculator despatched naive shiploads of would-be colonisers and farmers to Port Breton on New Ireland. The mill stone no doubt gave credence to their hopeless dreams of broad acres of wheat. See the New Ireland chapter.

Across from the Rabaul Community Hostel on the waterfront there's a memorial to the Rabaul prisoners who died on the *Montevideo Maru*.

The Market

The market, or *bung* ('meeting' in Kuanua), is one of the most bustling and colourful in PNG. Like every PNG market it really comes to life on Saturdays. You'll see a wider selection of fruit and vegetables (in larger quantities) than anywhere else in PNG. Scattered amongst the food stalls are bamboo combs, wicker baskets, shells and shell jewellery. It's closed on Sunday.

Museum

A tiny war museum stands opposite the New Guinea Club on the corner of Central Avenue and Clarke St and is open 9 am to 4.30 pm, Monday to Friday, 10 am to 2 pm on Saturdays. Admission is 50t. The museum is housed in Admiral Onishi's war time command bunker.

Outside there's a lightweight Japanese tank, an anti-aircraft gun and a field gun. Inside there's a collection of odds and ends – in two control rooms, Japanese maps can still be seen on the walls. There are also some interesting photos of Allied raids on Japanese ships in the harbour and a photo of Mango Avenue at the end of the war shows just how complete the destruction was. This was the bunker where Admiral Yamamoto spent his last night before being shot down over Bougainville.

Other WW II Relics

There are countless tunnels and caverns in the hillsides around Rabaul. Many of them are now closed, but a knowledgeable local guide can still take you around some amazing complexes. There are nearly 600 km of Japanese-built tunnels around the Gazelle Peninsula.

There is an anti-aircraft gun near the Vulcanology Observatory (one of many) while on the waterfront a scuttled Japanese ship was filled with cement and became a wharf.

The Club

The Club was built just before the war,

gutted during the bombing and subsequently rebuilt to its original plan. It is one of the very few buildings in PNG that survives with any sense of history intact, or any genuinely interesting architectural style. There are some fascinating old photos on the walls, and as you wander around under the high ceilings and slow-moving fans it's easy to be transported to a long gone South Pacific. Not only is it interesting, but it also has cold beer, good food, billiard tables and reasonable accommodation.

German Residency

Nothing remains of the old German residency apart from the stone gateposts and the crumbling staircase. The site offers fine views from a ridge that overlooks Rabaul in one direction and out to the open sea in the other. And those two little cement footpaths from the car park to the two lookout points? Built for Missis Queen's last visit to PNG.

Orchids

The Rabaul Orchid Park overlooks the town from up the hill towards the old German residency. There are many indigenous orchids, including a number of varieties that grow in the branches of frangipani trees. There's also a collection of parrots and New Britain cockatoos, a large and hungry crocodile and a couple of cassowaries.

Things to Do

Underwater ENB is just as spectacular as above water. Rabaul Dive & Tour Services (tel 92 2913), PO Box 1128, behind the Shell Gazelle Autoport on Malaguna Rd, has all the necessary equipment (including snorkelling gear for K3) and can also organise diving courses and tours around the district.

The harbour can be dived all year and boasts 54 WW II wrecks, which are now covered in coral growth. Visibility is often up to 30-40 metres. Snorkelling trips are available for around K12, one tank dive

for K25. The closest beach suitable for snorkelling is Pilapila on the north coast. The Submarine Base is meant to be particularly good for diving, with a spectacular drop-off. See the Beaches & Diving section that follows.

The cheapest and best way to see the region is to head off on the reasonably-priced PMVs. You can't really get lost – when you get to the end of the road, just turn around and come back again! Paivu Tours (tel 92 2916), PO Box 44, has a number of tours around town for K18 per person (minimum of four people) and also has boats for hire.

Climbing one of the volcano cones is hot but rewarding work. If you don't feel up to a trek, however, and you can get together a group of five adults, Pacific Helicopters (tel 92 2198 work, tel 92 1209 home) will drop you off and pick you up from the summit of Mother (the highest peak) for K15 or take you out to Pigeon Island for K35.

Places to Stay – bottom end

The best known Rabaul cheapie is the *Rabaul Community Hostel* (tel 92 2325), PO Box 409, on the corner of Atarr St and Cleland Drive. By PNG standards it's very good value. For K14 singles, K10 students, K20 married couples, you get bed, breakfast, lunch and an evening meal. The food is straightforward and OK, but you must turn up on time if you want to be fed. Breakfast consists of fruit (usually papaya), toast and tea and is served between 6.45 to 7.30 am. Dinner is similarly basic – a generous quantity of meat, potatoes and vegetables plus dessert – and it's served up at 6 pm. Lunch is at 12 noon. The rooms are spartan but reasonably comfortable although there are no fans and they can be hot. Chinese-hotel style, the walls don't reach the floor or ceiling so noise tends to travel.

If you want a bit more luxury, but still at a reasonable price, the *Kanai Guesthouse* (tel 92 1955), PO Box 510, is a comfortable, friendly place. Singles/

doubles are K20/30 with shared kitchen facilities – coffee, tea and milk are supplied. It's more like a converted house than anything else (although it started out as a trade store) so there are only four immaculately clean rooms, with fans. The only disadvantage is that it's a bit of a walk from town on Wee St, but they have a bike you can borrow (highly recommended) and it's not far from the main PMV route between the market and the airport. Moana, the manager, will pick you up from the airport, if you're expected.

The *New Guinea Club* (tel 92 1801, 92 2325), PO Box 40, opposite the War Museum in the middle of town is also good. It's a classic, well-kept, colonial building. To get to the rooms you go through the billiard room which has three beautiful, antique tables. There are 10 rooms at K25/30 for singles/doubles, including breakfast and laundry. Lunch and dinner are also available at reasonable prices and you needn't be a member, or male, although there is some degree of formality. There's a bar, two lounges and satellite TV.

On the corner of Kamarere St and Kombiu Avenue the *New Britain Lodge* (tel 92 2247), PO Box 296, has singles on a shared room basis for K28, doubles for K36. There's nothing flash about the shared bathroom facilities. The downstairs rooms are a bit like cells and although the upstairs rooms are OK, they're not as pleasant as those at the Kanai or the Club.

Places to Stay – top end

The number one hotel in Rabaul is the *Travelodge* (tel 92 2111), PO Box 449, on the corner of Mango Avenue (the main street) and Namanula St. The Travelodge has 40 rooms, all air-con with private facilities. Singles/doubles are K70/90. There is also a pleasant swimming pool and a restaurant. Whether you stay here or not, drop in to look at the photographs of the results of the 1971 tidal wave.

Vying with the Travelodge for number one spot is the *Motel Kaivuna* (tel 92 1766), PO Box 395, only about 100 metres away on the other side of Mango Avenue. There are 32 assorted rooms, all air-con with private facilities. Singles/doubles are K60/70. There is a restaurant, swimming pool and a top floor open-air bar area where counter-style lunches are available. The bar is very pleasant for an evening drink and the food is good.

There is one rather interesting place that more or less bridges the gap between the top-end and bottom-end in Rabaul; or rather out of Rabaul. The *Kulau Lodge* (tel 92 2115), PO Box 359, is a few km out, across Tunnel Hill on the North Coast Rd. It's best known as a popular eating spot (see Places to Eat) but it also has five separate units, built like local Kunai huts, with all mod-cons and in a very pleasant garden setting by the waterfront. Singles/doubles are K48/58. They often put on dances or discos on weekends. It would be worth trying if you wanted some isolation and don't mind catching a PMV (13 km, K1) or have a car available. An impressive complex, including a marina, a dive/fishing shop and a conference centre (including 20 new units) is planned.

Places to Eat

Rabaul has a good range of restaurants. If Chinese is your style then head to Ah Chee Avenue in Rabaul's now depleted Chinatown. The atmosphere has been dampened by the departure of many Chinese, but *Changs* will take you straight back to the late 1940s like a time machine. The manager plays an excellent collection of swing and jazz records. Together with the classic decor, nothing appears to have changed since the Yanks left. The food is also good and it's quite reasonably priced – K5 is about average for a main dish. This is definitely one of the most enjoyable, evocative restaurants in PNG.

Right in the middle of town the *Rabaul Coffee Shop* is a pleasantly relaxed and quite reasonably priced restaurant.

Sandwiches, soups and snacks are K1.50 to K4 and the dinners are K7 to K9. It's open 9 am to 2 pm and from 6.30 pm until late every day except Sunday.

Hennessey's Bake Shop, also on Mango but near the ANZ Bank, is a cut above the average kai haus. They also have pastries and cakes and a few tables out on the sidewalk.

At lunch time or in the early evening you can get excellent-value meals at the various clubs and out of town guests are always welcome (you may have to sign in). The interesting old New Guinea Club (across from the Museum) has good value counter meals and the Rabaul Yacht Club (on Mango Avenue near the Kaivuna and Travelodge) has lunches, and a barbecue dinner on Fridays and Sundays for around K5.

For a flashy night out, Rabaul residents head across to the *Kulau Lodge*, to dine romantically on the waterside. It's about 13 km out of town and you can count on at least K9 for the main course. Equally popular and somewhat lower priced is the excellent Sunday smorgasbord. There's an enormous variety of delicious food served on the long table in the airy dining and bar area.

The top-end hotels/motels all have their own licensed restaurants serving pretty much the sort of food you'd expect them to serve. Shoestring backpackers will find the food in the Community Hostel is quite adequate, edible and filling. And cheap!

Things to Buy

There are no local artefacts of note around Rabaul although shell necklaces and bracelets are popular in the market place. The carvings you will see are either modernistic or local interpretations of other PNG styles – leaping dolphins, prancing sea horses and some highly painted, vaguely Sepik-style masks figure prominently.

The Travelodge has a shop and outside there's a popular little market where people spread out their wares in the evening. Hidden away in their bags, waiting to be whipped out at the slightest sign of interest, are a Rabaul speciality – wooden salt and pepper shakers in the shape of male genitals.

Getting There & Away

Air The approach to Rabaul's runway is highly spectacular since Matupit Volcano is in a direct line from the end of the runway. Aircraft have to make a sharp turn as they approach. If there is any threat of volcanic disturbances, flights can be booked for days in advance.

Air Niugini has an office at the airport (tel 92 1222), PO Box 120, and on Mango Avenue opposite the Travelodge. Rabaul is on their main island route that links from Manus through to Bougainville (see the New Ireland Getting There & Away section), but it is also linked at least once daily to Port Moresby, via Hoskins (WNB) or Kieta (North Solomons) or Lae. The flight from Moresby takes about two hours and costs K157, Lae K131, Hoskins K66, Kieta K100, Kavieng (New Ireland) K66.

Talair (tel 92 2882), PO Box 503, has an office in town near the Information Office and flights to and from a number of centres around the coast of New Britain. There are also quite a few connections from Rabaul to New Ireland and to the associated St Matthias, Tabar, Lihir and Feni archipelagoes. There are no Talair flights to Bougainville. There are four flights a week to Kavieng (K66) and daily flights, except Sundays, to Namatanai. Some costs are Mapua (Tabar Island) K62, Uvol (WNB) K89, Hoskins (WNB) K66.

Sea Rabaul is one of the most important ports in PNG and ships link regularly with the main ports on WNB, Manus, New Ireland, and Bougainville as well as with many smaller islands and places in between. The most important company to look for is Coastal Shipping (tel 92 1733), PO Box 423, on Sulphur Creek Rd, but

Pacific New Guinea Lines also has some interesting voyages (tel 92 3024), PO Box 1764, and there are smaller operators and local boats to consider as well.

You can see the boats moored along the waterfront and if you want to get off the beaten track, asking around at the wharf is likely to be more fruitful than inquiring at the offices.

Some possibilities:

To/From Lae Coastal Shipping (Coastal) has the MV *Beaumaris* which departs for Lae on Saturday, stopping at Bialla (WNB) and Buluma; there are two cabins for K80 and deck class is K44. The MV *Kimbe Express* departs on Tuesdays and goes via Kimbe, but it only has deck class. Pacific New Guinea Line's (PNGL) MV *Kris* leaves on Tuesday afternoon and goes via Bialla and Kimbe, arriving in Lae on Thursday afternoon – it also costs K44. See the Lae To/From Rabaul section.

To/From New Ireland Coastal's MV *Cosmaris* departs fortnightly on Tuesdays for Kavieng and Manus Island; to Kavieng costs K50/25, cabin/deck. The MV *Tikana* departs every Thursday, but only has deck class. PNGL's MV *Kaum* leaves every Monday afternoon for Kavieng (K25) and every alternate week it goes on to Mussau Island in the St Matthias group.

To/From Bougainville PNGL's MV *Kazi* goes to Buka (K25) and Kieta (K34) every Monday afternoon. Coastal's MV *Atolls Enterprise* does the trip monthly for the same price (continuing on to more remote atolls in the North Solomons Province) and the MV *Huris* runs on the route (covering little ports in between) without a schedule.

Elsewhere Coastal's MV *Glomaris* has an interesting fortnightly trip out around the islands like Lihir (K44/27, cabin/deck) and Simberi, and several ships do voyages around the small WNB ports. Coastal's

MV *Cosmaris* departs fortnightly on Tuesdays for Lorengau (Manus Island via Kavieng) for K80/40, cabin/deck and the MV *Atolls Enterprise* does five day trips around the North Solomons for around K15.

Getting Around

The Gazelle Peninsular has a good network of roads and transport facilities. Lots of PMVs run back and forth with fares starting from around 30t. Some PMV fares are: Matupit 40t, Karavia Japanese tunnel 30t, Queen Emma's Matmat 60t, Kokopo K1, Submarine Base 60t. The main station is the market, but if you start walking in the appropriate direction you'll find one. PMVs run from the main road outside the airport to town for 30t. Some run along behind town to the market.

There are also a few taxis; the fare to the airport should be around K3. Getting a taxi, especially early in the morning, can be a hassle as they are without radios. If you have a flight early in the morning you're best to catch a PMV; the big hotels have courtesy buses, as does the Kanai guesthouse. During the day, taxis can usually be found parked along the waterfront park with the drivers fast asleep.

There are plenty of car rental places – Avis (tel 92 1131), Budget (tel 92 2311), Blue Star (tel 92 2063) in the Travelodge, Mall and Brown's (tel 92 1453) on Casuarina Avenue. Hitching around Rabaul is relatively easy.

AROUND RABAUL

Three roads lead out of Rabaul, connecting to the excellent bitumen road network around the Gazelle Peninsula. The roads are another legacy of the German days when they were laid out to connect their productive plantations. One road leads out south-east by the airstrip (and the city dump) to Matupit Island from where you can get canoes across to Matupit Volcano.

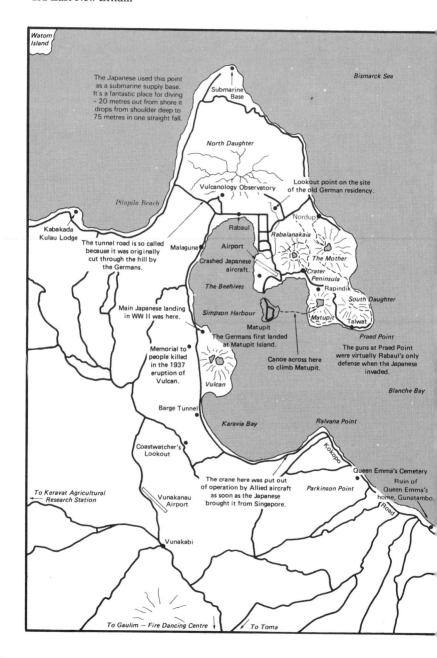

Watom Island

Bismarck Sea

The Japanese used this point as a submarine supply base. It's a fantastic place for diving – 20 metres out from shore it drops from shoulder deep to 75 metres in one straight fall.

Submarine Base

North Daughter

Lookout point on the site of the old German residency.

Vulcanology Observatory

Nordup

Pilapila Beach

Rabalanakaia

Rabaul

Kabakada Kulau Lodge

The tunnel road is so called because it was originally cut through the hill by the Germans.

Malaguna

Airport

The Mother

Crashed Japanese aircraft.

Crater Peninsula

The Beehives

Rapindik

South Daughter

Main Japanese landing in WW II was here.

Simpson Harbour

Matupit

Talwat

Matupit

Praed Point

The Germans first landed at Matupit Island.

The guns at Praed Point were virtually Rabaul's only defense when the Japanese invaded.

Memorial to people killed in the 1937 eruption of Vulcan.

Canoe across here to climb Matupit.

Blanche Bay

Vulcan

Barge Tunnel

Karavia Bay

Ralvana Point

Kokopo

Coastwatcher's Lookout

Queen Emma's Cemetery

To Keravat Agricultural Research Station

Parkinson Point

Ruin of Queen Emma's home, Gunatambo.

Vunakanau Airport

The crane here was put out of operation by Allied aircraft as soon as the Japanese brought it from Singapore.

Road

Vunakabi

To Gaulim – Fire Dancing Centre

To Toma

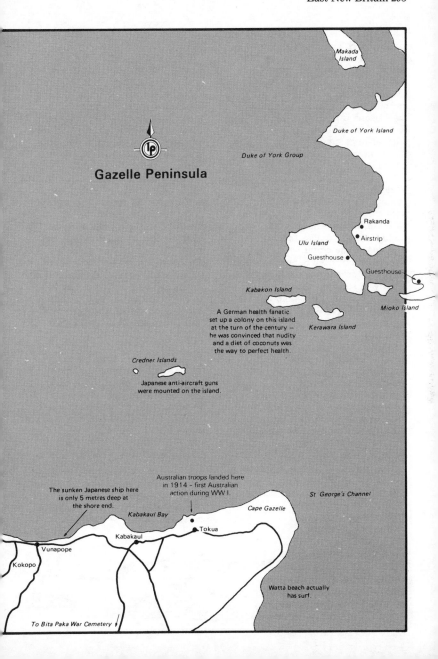

Makada
Island

Duke of York Island

Duke of York Group

Gazelle Peninsula

● Rakanda
● Airstrip

Ulu Island
Guesthouse ●

Guesthouse ●

Kabakon Island

A German health fanatic
set up a colony on this island
at the turn of the century –
he was convinced that nudity
and a diet of coconuts was
the way to perfect health.

Mioko Island

Kerawara Island

Credner Islands

Japanese anti-aircraft guns
were mounted on the island.

Australian troops landed here
in 1914 - first Australian
action during WW I.

The sunken Japanese ship here
is only 5 metres deep at
the shore end.

St George's Channel

Cape Gazelle

Kabakaul Bay

● Tokua

Kabakaul ●

Vunapope ●

Kokopo

Watta beach actually
has surf.

To Bita Paka War Cemetery ↓

The road to the north coast exits Rabaul via Tunnel Hill – during the German days it actually did go through the hill in a tunnel, but it was later opened out to a cutting. The third road continues to skirt the coast round Blanche Bay to Kokopo and beyond. Other roads turn inland from the Kokopo Road, including the Burma Road which climbs up and over the original huge crater rim on its way to Coastwatcher's Lookout and further inland.

Matupit

Despite the threatened eruption, people were still climbing Matupit, even at the height of the scare in early '84. There's a standard and a non-standard way of climbing to the crater of Matupit – the volcano that deluged Rabaul with dust in 1937. Whichever route you take, try to do it early in the day when it's cooler and possibly clearer. First take a PMV to Matupit Village, which is just a little beyond the airport, it's a 25t ride from Rabaul.

Matupit is an island, but only barely, since a bridge connects it with the mainland. A marker on the beach at Matupit commemorates the landing of the first three missionaries in 1882. As soon as you hop off the PMV you'll be pounced on by someone willing to paddle you across to the base of the cone. It costs a kina or two each way to scoot across Matupit Harbour in an outrigger canoe,

but make sure you negotiate the price first.

You're dropped off on the beach from where a clear path runs up to the crater, or more correctly craters, since Matupit has a number of them. A km or so along the beach there's a small Japanese freighter at snorkelling depth. From the beach it's less than a half hour's steady (and hot and sweaty) climb to the crater rim. There's a firmly anchored rope leading down to the bottom of the crater should you want to inspect Matupit from within. It's still mildly active with foul, sulphur-smelling smoke billowing out at various places.

You can follow the craters' rim around in either direction although you can't do a complete circuit since there's a great gash in the rim around the back. It's worth clambering around clockwise towards the highest point, for although Matupit is not the highest cone around the harbour the view from up there is very fine indeed. It's one of those places where you wish you had a camera that could take 360° pictures.

When you've finished looking around you can stroll back down to your canoe or try the alternate descent by following the crater rim right round to the back of the cone and beating your way down through the bush to the coconut plantations and on to the Praed Point road where you can grab a PMV. The path is much steeper and less clearly defined than on the harbour side route. I got down by going

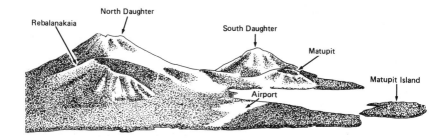

North Daughter · Rebalanakaia · South Daughter · Matupit · Matupit Island · Airport

round anticlockwise then slithering down a steep trail – hard work. I wouldn't recommend trying to ascend that way, although a PMV driver could probably point out a path that skirts the bottom of the volcano.

There is also said to be a volcano beside Matupit, under water in the harbour. Rumours pronounce that the sea floor has risen a metre.

Hot Springs

Not far from the airport, right at the beach, are some hot springs, but they're too hot for bathing – it's really boiling water. To get there turn left past the airport. Follow the road to the end of the sealed part and turn right. A footpath leads down to the beach and the springs. The village here is Rapindik and the beach is known as Bubbly Beach. The red colour of the beach is due to the iron which precipitates from the boiling water.

From the village you can climb the steep path up the side of Mt Rabalanakaia, but since the path is not very clear you should ask directions from the people at Rapindik. From the crater rim you can climb down to the floor of the crater and see gas vents and sulphur deposits.

Aircraft Wreckage

Beside the Rabaul runway there's quite a mass of Japanese aircraft wreckage scattered amongst the palm trees. Just past where the road curves off from beside the strip towards Matupit Village, a dirt road runs off to the right. You're unlikely to have to guide yourself as the local kids have a thriving business showing visitors to the remains. Careful you don't end up with too many guides – even at 10t a time they soon mount up!

There are two main chunks of wreckage. First you'll come to the fuselage midsection and part of the wings of a bomber, then a little further along the much more complete wreckage of a Betty Bomber – the tail section lies upside down behind it. The rising sun is still clearly visible underneath the wing. Various bits of engines, nacelles and undercarriage lie scattered around. As well as lots of Japanese aircraft wreckage the plantation also has lots of mosquitoes so come prepared or get bitten.

Praed Point

If you turn left off the Matupit road, just after passing the airport, a dirt road will take you through coconut plantations, passing between Matupit and South Daughter, through Talwat Village to Praed Point. There are a couple of coastal guns at Praed Point – when the Japanese invaded they were virtually the only defense Rabaul had, but they weren't used. They're of six inch and four inch calibre and the smaller one still traverses. Around here there are a number of Japanese-built gun covers, occupied today by bats, and a few wartime concrete blockhouses. Fish traps extend out into the water. On the other side of the road, as you skirt round Matupit, there is a small, peaceful, Japanese war memorial. PMVs along this road are quite frequent.

Vulcanology Observatory

The road to the Vulcanology Observatory, on the slopes of North Daughter, turns off the Tunnel Hill road and climbs up to the top of the old crater rim, overlooking Rabaul. It is the main vulcanological station in PNG and there's a good view. There are tunnel entrances off the road.

Vulcan

When Vulcan erupted so disastrously in 1937 there was a small cargo ship passing through the narrow channel between the island of Vulcan and the mainland. Today this ship is high and dry and 70 metres from the sea, since Vulcan heaved itself out of the water and is now joined to the mainland. It juts out over a small river and its tanks are still full of oil.

Keravat

Beyond the Kulau Lodge on the north

coast road, Keravat is a major lowland agricultural experimental station where research is carried out on coconuts, oil palms, cocoa, coffee and fruit trees. There is also a forestry department.

The Beehives

The cluster of rocky peaks rising out of the centre of Simpson Harbour are said to be the hard core of the original old volcano. You can visit them by boat and there is some good diving and swimming. When Captain Blanche first visited Rabaul in 1882 these islands were much larger, the bigger one had a village of 200 people. They now have no inhabitants.

Barges

A few km out of Rabaul, on the Kokopo road, a sign points towards the Japanese barge tunnel. A long passage cut into the hill houses a number of Japanese barges used, some say, to carry supplies around the coast at night. Others say they were just held in readiness for emergency use and were never actually operated. Either way they would have been winched down to the sea on a long track as the tunnel is a considerable height above sea level.

There's a 50t admission charge (it can vary) to the tunnel which is said to contain five barges, lined up nose to tail. Without a light it fades into darkness beyond the second barge and the back three are totally invisible. The first one is badly rusted and the second is little better, but the back three are said to be in reasonable condition. Parallel tunnels were used to house supplies and as offices.

A little further around the bay is the wreckage of a huge crane which the Japanese towed here from Singapore. It was bombed as soon as it arrived and was never actually used. Also nearby, along the road towards Kokopo, there are seven more large Japanese tunnels used for storing patrol boats.

Queen Emma Relics

Very few traces of Queen Emma remain in the Rabaul area. Her stately residence, Gunantambu near Kokopo, was destroyed during the war – all you can find today is the impressive staircase which led from the Kokopo waterfront up to the house. The view she must have enjoyed is still magnificent; it's near the Ralum Club.

Her cemetery is a couple of km back towards Rabaul and is signposted. It overlooks the Rabaul-Kokopo road. All that remains of Queen Emma's grave is a cement slab with a hole in the centre – her ashes were stolen a few years after she died. The gravestone of her brother, and of her lover, Agostino Stalio, are in much better shape; the latter with a romantic inscription:

Oh for the touch of a vanished hand and the sound of a voice which is still

About 1½ km north is her brother-in-law, Richard Parkinson's, cemetery, which is even more overgrown. It's called Kuradui after his plantation, but only the tombstone of Otto Parkinson, a suicide in the early 1900s, remains standing. Richard Parkinson is nowhere near as well known as his flamboyant sister-in-law, but he wrote some of the earliest works on New Guinea island anthropology and natural history, a book titled *Thirty Years in the South Seas* and was an enthusiastic botanist who planted many trees in the Rabaul-Kokopo area. His matmat, the local word for cemetery, is near Parkinson Point.

Malmaluan Lookout

Malmaluan Lookout, formerly known as Coastwatcher's Lookout, is just off the Vuruga road, which turns away from the coast a couple of km out of Rabaul towards Kokopo. It offers one of the best views in the area – you look out over Vulcan, the harbour and to the volcanoes beyond Matupit Island. It's well worth the 50t PMV ride – bring your camera.

Beaches & Diving

There is no good place for swimming in the harbour, but a fair bit of diving is done. Ten of the 54 Japanese shipwrecks from WW II are accessible although some of them are quite deep. Many of them went down during one raid on 2 November, 1943. Also in the harbour are a couple of plane wrecks and reef walls. Right in Rabaul, at the end of Turanguna St, just beyond the swimming pool, there's a modern wreck – a small fishing craft which foundered only about 20 metres from shore. It's the home for many colourful, small fish and you can snorkel right through the main holds.

The best places for swimming are on the north coast or further round Blanche Bay. Pilapila, just across Tunnel Hill, is a popular beach spot and close to town. Watom Island is an extinct volcano cone and site of one of the earliest settlements in New Britain. Archaeological finds here have been dated to 600 to 500 BC.

The island is also a good place for walking or snorkelling; it can be reached from Kulau Lodge or Nonga Hospital. Some of the best beaches are round the corner from Cape Gazelle and quite a drive from Rabaul.

Submarine Base is an incredible place for scuba diving – the coral shelves gently away from the beach until there's a vertical reef wall that drops about 75 metres. Swimming over the incredible drop feels like leaping off a skyscraper, but not falling. The Japanese used to provision submarines here during the war.

At Takubar, just beyond Vunapope, there is a Japanese ship which sank right up against the shore – at one end it reaches to about five metres from the surface while at the other end it goes down very deep. There are several places in town where you can rent scuba diving gear or have air bottles refilled. Rabaul Dive & Tour Services (tel 92 2913), Box 1128, behind the Shell Gazelle Autoport on Malaguna Rd, has all the necessary equipment (including snorkelling gear for K3) and can also organise diving courses and tours around the district. They'll give you advice on where to dive.

Vunapope

Just beyond the town of Kokopo, Vunapope is the Catholic Mission centre and one of the largest mission establishments in PNG. Vunapope is pronounced as if it ended in a 'y' and means 'place of the Catholics'. The Catholics arrived in New Britain in 1881, only a few years after the pioneering Methodists, and at first established themselves at Nodup, on the north coast across from Rabaul. They soon moved round to Vunapope near Queen Emma's plantations.

Kabakaul

At Kabakaul, beyond Vunapope and just beyond the turn off to Bita Paka, there's the Ulaveo Museum in an old desiccated coconut factory in the Ulaveo Plantation. It's open daily from 8.30 am to 5 pm and admission is 50t. The museum has an interesting collection of war relics and stone statues but it is now in bad shape and is not worth a special visit.

Bita Paka

Bita Paka War Cemetery is several km inland, the turnoff is a little beyond Vunapope. It contains the graves of over 1000 Allied war dead, including many Indians who came to the Rabaul area as POWs captured in Singapore. There are also memorials to the six Australian soldiers killed in the capture of the German WW I radio station at Bita Paka, to the crew of the Australian submarine that disappeared off the New Britain coast in the same operation, and to the civilians who went down with the *Montevideo Maru*.

A small German cemetery has the graves of men from the first German expedition in the area and from German colonial times. It's near Kokopo town centre – ask about it there.

DUKE OF YORK ISLANDS

The Duke of York group is about 30 km east of Rabaul, approximately midway between New Britain and New Ireland. Duke of York Island is the largest in the group, but there are also a cluster of smaller islands. This was the site for the first mission station in the area, the place where Queen Emma started her remarkable career, and it is also blessed with some beautiful beaches and scenery. There are a couple of places to stay, and transport is easy to find.

Port Hunter, at the northern tip of the main island, was the landing point for the Reverend Brown in 1875 and the site of his first mission. You can still see the crumbling chimney of his house, overlooking the entrance to Port Hunter's circular bay. Near the beach is the cemetery where most of his assistants ended up.

Mioko, where Emma and Thomas Farrell established their first trading station, is a small island off the other end of Duke of York Island. Mioko Harbour is a large stretch of sheltered water between Mioko and Duke of York.

Kabakon, closest of the group to Rabaul, has a rather curious history – a German health fanatic named Engelhardt established a nudist colony here in 1903. He was soon dubbed Mr Kulau (Mr Coconut) by the locals for not only did he consider nudism was the path to perfect health but he supplemented it with a diet of nothing but coconuts. At one time he had 30 or more followers on the island, but coconuts must get boring, even with nude bodies added, and he died alone just before WW I.

Between Rabaul and the Duke of York Group are the two Credner Islands, commonly known as 'the Pigeons'. Small Pigeon is uninhabited and is a popular excursion for snorkelling or picnics.

Contact the Information Office in Rabaul for current information.

Places to Stay

On Mioko Island, off the south end of Duke of York Island, two small tourist huts have been set up – they cost K3 per person per night. There are some cooking facilities, two trade stores and the local people may offer you some fresh produce. However it's best to take everything you need. You can explore all over the island in a couple of hours – the kids will show you some caves and anything else they think you'll find interesting. Boat trips to the reef for fishing can easily be arranged. It's not hard to spend a couple of pleasant days here.

There is also a guesthouse on Ulu Island, which is run by the United Church. Ring 92 1528 and check they have room.

Getting There & Away

It's relatively easy to get to the Duke of York Islands by plane or small ships from Rabaul. Copra boats ply between Rabaul and Mioko, Monday to Friday, leaving the Rabaul wharf between 1 and 3 pm. The trip to Mioko costs K2.50 one-way and takes about 2½ hours. Rabaul Shipping has copra boats that go at 9 am and return in the afternoon for K6 return.

West New Britain

Area 20,487 square km
Population 105,000

Surprisingly, considering the high level of development and many places of interest in ENB, the rest of the island is relatively untouched and little developed. The places to see are mainly around the Williamez Peninsula where the roads are concentrated. The rest of the island – away from the Gazelle and Williamez Peninsulas, plus the stretch of coast around Stettin Bay – is largely virgin rainforest.

There are two particularly interesting accommodation options: the first is the

up-market Walindi Plantation, near
Kimbe, and the shoestring Kautaga
Guest Haus, which is on an island on the
east side of the Williamez Peninsular. See
the Talasea & the Williamez Peninsular
section.

KIMBE

About 40 km from Talasea and the same
distance from Hoskins, Kimbe is the
provincial HQ and a major centre for oil
palm production. Oil palms are three times
more efficient in the production of oil than
coconuts but require a much larger
investment for processing. The projects in
WNB have been a resounding success and
have led to further developments in other
provinces of PNG, notably Milne Bay and
Northern. There's a hospital, post office,
shopping centre, PNGBC bank, and a
daily market. Contact the Culture/
Tourism Office (tel 93 5057), Division of
Commerce, PO Box 427, Kimbe, for
further information on the province.

Kimbe Cultural Centre

Converted from an old plantation house,
the Cultural Centre houses a museum,
artefact shop and art and craft workshop.

Places to Stay

The *Palm Lodge Hotel* (tel 93 5001),
PO Box 32, is adjacent the beach, a short
walk from town. There are 35 rooms with
singles K40 (fan), doubles at K55 (air-con)
and the facilities include satellite TV, a
swimming pool and a restaurant. They'll
pick you up free from the airport, and
they'll also arrange tours.

There's also a club in Kimbe. It may be
possible to stay at the United Church or
camp at the police station.

Getting There & Away

A number of Coastal's and PNGL's ships
call in at Kimbe on their way to and from
Lae and Rabaul – see those sections. The
main airport is at Hoskins. The coastal
road runs from Talasea through Kimbe to
Hoskins where you will find the main

airport in WNB. Talasea-Kimbe or Kimbe-
Hoskins by PMV will cost about K3.

HOSKINS

This small town is a major logging and oil
palm production centre. The oil palm
project is between Hoskins and Kimbe at
Mosa and the company estate is surrounded
by smaller plots worked by migrants from
all over the country. Palm oil is used in the
manufacture of soap and margarine.
There are a number of extinct volcanoes in
the area surrounding Hoskins, and a short
distance inland, at Koimumu, there's an
active geyser field.

Places to Stay

The *Hoskins Hotel* (tel 93 5113), c/o Post
Office, Hoskins, has 15 fan-cooled rooms
and a licensed restaurant. Singles/
doubles are K37/45 including breakfast;
lunch is K5, dinner K9. There is, of course,
also the Hoskins Club.

Getting There & Away

This is the main airport for WNB and both
Talair and Air Niugini flights pass
through; there's at least one flight to the
mainland each day. Fares: Rabaul K66,
Lae K93. Talair also has flights through to
the south coast and around the island.

TALASEA & THE WILLIAMEZ PENINSULA

The pretty little town of Talasea looks
across the bay with its many islands from
Williamez Peninsula. The peninsula is an
active volcanic region, there are even
bubbling mud holes in Talasea. Lake
Dakataua, at the end of the projection,
was formed in a colossal eruption in
1884.

On Pangula Island, across from Talasea,
there is a whole collection of thermal
performers (geysers and fumaroles) in the
Valley of Wabua. The name means 'Valley
of Hot Water' and is only a short walk from
the shops. In the hills behind Talasea are
the wrecks of two US bombers, one of
them a B-24 Liberator, both in reasonable
condition.

Talasea is a centre for the manufacture of shell money. Obsidian, volcanic glass, from here is believed to have been traded from about 3000 BC until recent times. It went from New Britain to New Ireland, Manus and the Admiralty Islands or even further afield, and was used in knives, spears and arrows.

Places to Stay

The *Walindi Plantation* (tel 93 5441), PO Box 4, Kimbe, is between Kimbe and Talasea on the east side of the peninsular. The plantation itself is a large, privately-owned oil palm plantation, right on the shores of Kimbe Bay, and there is a group of attractive and comfortable thatched bungalows. Kimbe Bay is fringed by volcanic mountains, some of which are still active.

Apart from the superb natural surroundings, which are literally stunningly beautiful, the main attraction is the diving, which has many people raving about clear water, volcanic caves draped in staghorn coral and reef drop-offs. Fishing trips and day tours are also organised. All meals and accommodation comes to K45 per day, and a return transfer to Hoskins costs K25. Two dives per day cost another K45.

The *Kautaga Guest Haus* is on a small island off the west side of the peninsular. It's a one hour drive to Garu (there are PMVs from Kimbe) and you then catch a village boat. You can make radio contact from Kimbe through the tourist office. There are five rooms at K5 per person, per night, and everything except food is provided (including cooking utensils and mosquito nets). Make sure you take snorkelling gear, and bear in mind there is no refrigeration. The people of Kou and Poi built the guesthouse from local materials.

AROUND WNB

Mt Langila, on Cape Gloucester at the south-western end of the island, is still active and hiccups and rumbles every few months. Tribes inland from Talasea used to bind their babies' heads to make them narrow and elongated. Other tribes near Kandrian used Malay-style blowguns to hunt birds and fruit bats. The wooden 'darts' are shot through a long bamboo tube.

There's a guesthouse at Bialla: the *Bialla Guest House* that you can contact through the tourist office in Kimbe (tel 93 5057), PO Box 427, Kimbe. There are five rooms for K35/40.

Pomio has been noted for its beliefs, similar to the cargo cult, that the land would be turned into some sort of earthly paradise. The Kimbe islanders, off the Williamez Peninsula, are expert sailors and canoe builders who live on the islands but tend gardens on the mainland.

The Witu Islands, west of the Williamez Peninsula, are about 80 km off the coast and are of volcanic origin. Unea has a peak 738 metres high while Garov, the largest island, has a beautiful bay formed when the sea broke into its extinct crater. During the first 10 years of this century a smallpox epidemic virtually wiped out the people on these fertile and quite heavily populated islands.

North Solomons

Area 10,620 square km
Population 145,000 (Buka 20,000)

The islands that comprise the North Solomons (Buka, Bougainville and a scattering of smaller atolls) are more closely related to the neighbouring, independent Solomon Islands than they are to much of PNG – just as the name suggests. The major island, Bougainville, is green, rugged and little developed, yet it provides a very considerable portion of PNG's gross national product from the massive open-cut copper mine at Panguna. Ok Tedi has taken some of the limelight from the Bougainville mine, but it is still vitally important.

HISTORY
It is not known from where, or when the first settlers arrived on Bougainville. It is possible that that the present dark-skinned Melanesians who inhabit the island first settled as long as 10,000 years ago.

Bougainville acquired its very French name from the explorer Louis Antoine de Bougainville who sailed up the east coast in 1768. Near the narrow passage which separates Bougainville from Buka he came across natives paddling long, artistically carved canoes. They greeted him with cries of 'Buka, Buka' which Bougainville promptly named their island. Actually, *buka* simply means 'who' or 'what' – a very reasonable question to ask! Of course Bougainville was not the first European to drop by; Torres passed by in 1606.

A hundred years later, Catholic missionaries attempted to set up a station at Kieta. They were driven away on their first attempt, but they were more successful the second time around. Bougainville and Buka were considered part of the Solomons group, which was a British possession, until 1898, when they were traded to Germany. The Germans added them to their New Guinea colony and set up copra plantations along the coast, and in return the British had their ascendancy over Vavau in Tonga and the other islands in the Solomons confirmed. Australia seized the North Solomons, along with the rest of New Guinea, at the start of WW I. The Bougainvilleans, however, had a reputation for being 'difficult' and although the island was thoroughly explored by the Australian administration, by the start of WW II the only development was still on the coast.

In mid-1942 the Japanese arrived, swiftly defeated the Australians, and held most of the island until the end of the war. Buka in the north became an important air base, Shortland Island (part of the Solomons) was a major naval base and Buin, at the southern tip of Bougainville, was an equally important base for ground troops.

Australian coastwatchers scored some notable successes on Bougainville, particularly during the battle for Guadalcanal. Jack Read, a district officer, and Paul Mason, a plantation owner, retreated into the jungle after the Japanese occupation. Read watched over Buka Passage, near his former station, while Mason set himself up near Buin in the south. Bomber aircraft from Rabaul and bound for Guadalcanal passed over Buka and Buin and the fighters

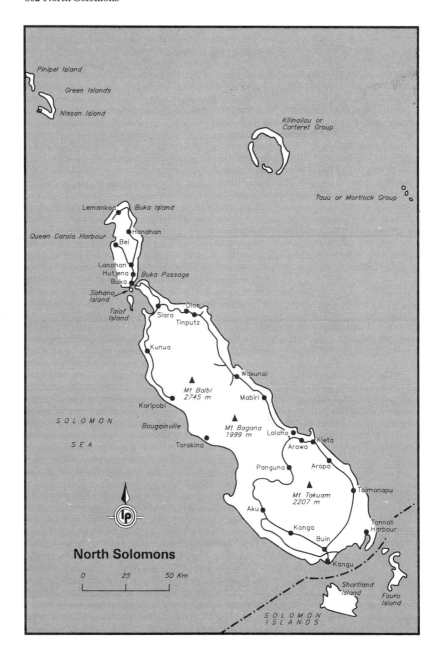

Pinipel Island

Green Islands

Nissan Island

Kilinailau or
Carteret Group

Tauu or Mortlock Group

Lemankoa Buka Island

Hanahan

Queen Carola Harbour

Bei

Lonohan

Hutjena

Buka Buka Passage

Sohano
Island

Taiof
Island

Dios

Siara

Tinputz

Kunua

Wakunai

Mt Balbi
2745 m

Mabiri

Koripobi

SOLOMON

Bougainville

Mt Bagana
1999 m

Loloho

Kieta

Torokina

Arawa

Panguna

Aropa

SEA

Toimonapu

Mt Takuam
2207 m

Aku

Tonnoli
Harbour

Konga

Buin

Kangu

North Solomons

0   25   50 Km

Shortland
Island

Fauro
Island

SOLOMON
ISLANDS

were based right at Buka, allowing the coastwatchers to give the Allied forces a two hour warning of an impending air strikes. This knowledge gave the Allies a tremendous advantage in what many regard as a crucial battle – a turning point in the Pacific war. Miraculously, Paul Mason and Jack Read both survived, despite determined efforts by the Japanese to track them down.

In November 1943, American troops captured the west coast port of Torokina and, in 1944, Australian forces started to fight their way south towards Buin. Fortunately, the war ended before they came into direct confrontation with the main Japanese force. Nevertheless, the cost of the war in Bougainville was staggering. Of 80,000 Japanese troops only 23,000 were finally taken prisoner: 20,000 are thought to have been killed in action and the remaining 37,000 died in the jungles of disease and starvation.

After the war Bougainville returned to normal – a mixture of quiet, subsistence farming and fishing villages and a few plantations. The district HQ was transferred from Kieta to Sohano in Buka Passage but found its way back to Kieta in 1960. Then, in 1964, a major copper discovery at Panguna revolutionised Bougainville. Over K400 million was invested in the development of the mine and its ancillary operations. A new town, roads, a power station and a port were all constructed from scratch. And thousands of workers from around PNG and the world descended, bringing with them a cash economy and all its attendant vices. The district HQ is now at Arawa, the main dormitory town for the mine.

In the lead up to independence, Bougainville was a strong part of the push for an independent grouping of the Bismarck Archipelago islands. That plan quickly faded, but around independence time strong Bougainville secessionist movements sprang up and for a time it seemed like they just might succeed. Their 'difficult' reputation notwithstanding,

the Bougainvilleans have now taken their place in PNG although it is probably no coincidence that the North Solomons Province was the first to have its own local provincial government.

GEOGRAPHY
Bougainville is about 200 km long and 60 to 100 km wide and covered in wild, generally impenetrable jungle. There are two major mountain ranges – in the south the Crown Prince Range and in the north the higher Emperor Range. The highest mountain is Mt Balbi at 2745 metres; Balbi is an active volcano, like its smaller and more spirited cousin Mt Bagana, and is visible from both coasts. The coastal areas are extremely fertile and most of the population is concentrated along them.

Buka, in the north, is separated from Bougainville by a channel only 300 metres wide and a km long. Tidal currents rush through the passage at up to eight knots. In the south Buka is hilly, reaching 400 metres at its highest point. Buka is generally low-lying, apart from this southern hill region, and very wet – annual rainfall is over 600 cms (about 20 feet). There are many coral islands off its south and west coast.

PEOPLE
The people of Bougainville and Buka are often collectively referred to as Bukas and the early German colonisers favoured them due to their energy and abilities. The Bougainville people are instantly recognisable anywhere in PNG due to their extremely dark skins, said to be the blackest in the world. There are 19 different languages on Bougainville.

The Bougainvilleans' relative affluence has, like the Tolai of East New Britain, led to a reluctance to perform the dull work on copra plantations and copra-labourers are imported from other parts of the country. Many people, however, still live in bush-material villages and depend on shifting agriculture for their food.

The impact of the mine has not been

entirely positive. Apart from the problems that come with a cash economy (the destruction of the traditional subsistence/barter economy, and alcohol abuse being perhaps the most obvious) the influx of wealthy, white mine workers has also had an influence.

Although most Buka people are friendly, they are much more reserved and even suspicious than is apparent in most of the other peoples of PNG. The Bougainvilleans are proud of their traditions and culture and, despite the strong influence of the church, are determined to retain them. Always ask permission before entering a village and then ask to see the head man. The juxtaposition of the large expat community and this beautiful island and its people sometimes creates some interesting scenes – like truck loads of village people howling with laughter as they watch Australian surfers falling off some surprisingly good waves.

Fishing
People on the islands north-west of Buka Passage still occasionally fish by the unique kite and spider web method. A woven palm leaf kite is towed behind a canoe and a lure, made of a wad of spider webs, is skillfully bounced along the surface of the sea. Garfish, leaping at the lure, get their teeth entangled in the web and are then hauled in.

Arts
Apart from intricately woven Buka baskets, there are few artefacts still made on Bougainville, although prior to the arrival of the missions, many elaborate carvings were kept in men's houses.

Buka baskets are made from jungle vine. The variation in colour is made by scraping the skin off the vine. They're amongst the most skillfully made baskets in the Pacific, but with prices up towards K20 they're strictly tourist items and are rarely used for food holders as they were originally intended.

KIETA & ARAWA
Kieta is now virtually a satellite to nearby Arawa, and both are dominated by the mine's workers and associated service industries. Kieta is still a quiet little place; jungle-clad hills run down to a rim of beautiful beaches and a harbour, which is sheltered by Pok Pok Island. Its geographically constrained, although attractive, location led to the decision to build a new centre at Arawa on the site of a coconut plantation.

There's a hotel and a few shops and offices in Kieta, but the main commercial centre is Arawa. Arawa was originally just a dormitory town for the mine, but it has now outgrown its older, more attractive neighbour. It's flat and laid out on a grid, with a large government complex, a reasonable shopping centre with airline offices, banks and a public library, a hospital and some schools.

Orientation
Coming north from the airport you first go through Toniva, a suburb of Kieta, then Kieta, which is now virtually a suburb of Arawa, and then 10 km east (over the Kieta Peninsula) Arawa, the main town.

Four km north-west of Arawa is Loloho on Arawa Bay. This is the port to which the copper concentrate is piped down from Panguna, the site of the power station and home to many of the mine workers who live in a village of small prefabricated structures. There's an attractive and popular beach. The mine itself is high in the mountains, often shrouded in cloud and rain, about a 28 km drive south-west from Arawa.

Information
The provincial government has a Division of Communication, Culture and Tourism (tel 97 1195), PO Box 20, Arawa, and they open an office at the airport for Air Niugini's incoming flights. Joseph Mokuma, the Tourism Officer, is very helpful. Air Niugini has offices in Arawa and Panguna (tel 95 1866), PO Box 1038, Arawa; Talair

Top: Simpson Harbour, Rabaul, is ringed with volcanoes; active Matupit is the small, grey, harmless-looking one (ML)
Bottom: Panguna Mine, Bougainville, North Solomons (TW)

Top: Village on Kiriwina Island, Trobriand Islands (RE)
Left: Trobriand children (ML)
Right: Chief's yam house, Sinaketa Village, Kiriwina Island (ML)

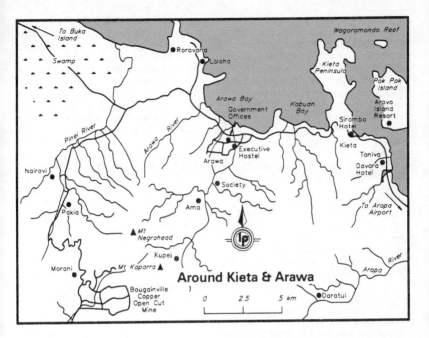

Around Kieta & Arawa

is in Arawa (tel 95 1097), PO Box 374, Arawa.

The supermarket in Arawa is one of the best-stocked in the country. Tauvita Enterprises has a good book shop in the main Arawa shopping centre. Arawa also has a high quality medical clinic with dental facilities (tel 95 2522).

There are vegetable markets at Arawa (Wednesday, Friday and Saturday) and Toniva (every day except Thursday and Sunday) – they open very early and are often packed up by 7 am. There's a fish market in Kieta near the police station.

Things to Do

An expedition to the mine at Panguna is well worthwhile, even if you're not fanatically interested in holes, trucks and rocks. For a start, the scale of the operation is incredible and, secondly, there are excellent views on the way. See the separate section following.

At the end of the harbour road, just before the yacht club, there's the North Solomons Cultural Centre (tel 95 6174) with an interesting collection of historical photos and artefacts, arrows and spears, some basketwork, statuettes and a canoe. It's open weekdays from 8 am to 4 pm.

There's a butterfly farm in an attractive valley alongside the Kerei River. A butterfly farm is not a collection of cages and sad captives but an attractive bush garden with flowering trees and shrubs. Butterflies are attracted to the area and the farmer simply wanders out with a net to collect the huge iridescent creatures. Coming from Kieta, turn left of the Kieta-Arawa road, just over the Kerei River, then drive up a good gravel road for less than a km until you come to a small car park on your left. The 'farmer' lives in the small group of bush-material houses across a gully and will charge K1 for the privilege of wandering around, and K1.50 for photos.

There is clearly great potential for divers in the area. Dive Bougainville (tel 95 2595), PO Box 661, Arawa, has all the necessary equipment and they open a shop at Loloho Beach on weekends. They can be contacted through Tauvita Enterprise's bookshop in Arawa. They're happy to see snorkellers, will hire gear for K4, and, if there's a minimum of four people, will organise a reasonably-priced boat trip. There's good snorkelling at Pok Pok Island.

Surf! Yes, you can hang seven at Bougainville. I saw half a dozen surfers catching reasonable three footers at a righthand point break just off the airport road on the eastern side of the island a few km from Toniva. Once you get out a bit with a boat, beyond the lee of the islands and reefs, there's apparently good surf, including at a place called Shark Alley. Interesting name!

Places to Stay

Bougainville is a disaster area for cheap accommodation. If you're travelling on a shoestring and don't know someone who works at the mine, plan on passing through quickly. There are two hotels in Kieta – both expensive and catering to the Panguna mine people who can presumably afford it. There's also a slightly cheaper resort hotel on beautiful Pok Pok Island, just offshore. The only option in Arawa is, despite all odds, good value.

The *Davara Hotel* (tel 95 6175), PO Box 241, Kieta, is five km out of Kieta towards the airport, at Toniva. It has an attractive site, right on the beach, looking out to an island-dotted sea, although the hotel also has a decent-sized swimming pool. If you had the necessary riches, this would be a very pleasant base for exploring the island, eating good food (the restaurant is excellent) and generally taking it easy. There's a suitably relaxed atmosphere and the staff are friendly. The rooms have everything you would expect (air-con, TVs, etc), but you'll have to pay K65/75 for the privilege. The restaurant has an

excellent eat-as-much-as-you-can seafood smorgasbord on Fridays for K16. They have windsurfers and will also organise half-day sightseeing trips for K20 and boat trips to nearby islands, by arrangement.

The *Siromba Hotel*, formerly the Kieta Hotel, (tel 95 6277), PO Box 228, Kieta, is right in Kieta, but this is hardly a huge advantage since there's very little reason to be so close and you're further from the water. There are 27 rooms, all air-con, self-contained, etc, etc, with a nightly cost of K70/80 for singles/doubles. They also have family triples for K85, so if you were travelling in a group you may be able to do a deal. There's a bar, video TV lounge and restaurant with less than exciting food. You can get some reasonably-priced snacks, like sandwiches for K1.30, and a proper lunch for K8 or so. Most dinner main courses weigh in around K10.

The *Arovo Island Resort* (tel 95 1855), PO Box 44, Kieta, is on a hilly, 10 hectare island off the tip of the Kieta Peninsula. Pok Pok Island, as it is called, is just a 10 minute ferry ride from the Kieta Yacht Club. The ferry runs a regular timetable and will make special crossings for guests – ring in advance. They'll also arrange to pick you up from the airport. Daily costs are K55/65 for singles/doubles, K10 for each additional person. The popular restaurant provides counter lunches and also has reasonably priced food in the evenings – seafood comes from the waters around the island. The resort has a tennis court and the snorkelling is superb.

In Arawa, the *Executive Hostel* (tel 95 1946), PO Box 1341, Arawa, is the one bright light for budget travellers. Unfortunately, it's also used to provide accommodation for members of the provincial parliament when it is sitting, so it's essential to phone or write ahead. It's on Roranu St, which runs along the western side of the hospital, and it's a clean, quite attractive, modern, two-storey building. Singles/doubles are K20/25, there are shared facilities and you can get meals for around K7.

That's it.

Places to Eat

The hotels are the main options, apart from the usual uninspiring kai shops. You will probably be able to get something reasonable to eat at the *Kieta Club*, next door to the Siromba Hotel; it's open every night and visitors are welcome. The *Yacht Club* is also a possibility, especially at the weekend. The *Yum Cha Restaurant* is in the Nafig Club (tel 95 2010) on Chebu St, in Arawa. There's often some sort of entertainment in the club. The *Arawa Country Club* (tel 95 2552) also has meals and visitors can be signed in.

Things to Buy

There's an artefacts shop, on Kuvira Crescent behind Arawa Motors. The collection is quite small and expensive, but the quality is good. There are bows and arrows, shell jewellery and, of course, Buka baskets. It's open 8 am to 12 noon and 1 to 4 pm on weekdays and from 9 am to 12 noon on Saturdays.

Getting There & Away

Air It's 26 km from the airport at Aropa to Kieta and there is no regular bus service – if you haven't arranged to be met, you have to wait for one of the infrequent PMVs running up from the south, or get a ride with another passenger or one of the hotel minibuses. Air Niugini, Talair, Budget and Avis have desks at the airport, and there's also a tourist office, which is staffed for incoming Air Niugini flights.

Kieta is linked to Rabaul, Kavieng, Manus and the north coast by the Air Niugini flight that does this loop. See the Kavieng section in the New Ireland chapter for a complete schedule.

This is also an exit and entry point to the Solomons. Air Niugini flies to Honiara on Tuesdays and Fridays (K111) and Bougair (tel 95 1593), PO Box 986, Arawa, flies to Munda three times a week for K33. See the Getting There chapter.

Bougair also has an extensive network of flights around the North Solomons including to the neighbouring islands.

Sea There are occasional ships from Moresby, but the main connection is the weekly link with Rabaul. There are canoe links with the Solomon Islands from the south – see the Getting There chapter. Coastal Shipping's (tel 92 1733), PO Box 423, Rabaul, MV *Atolls Enterprise* services the scattered islands north and east of Bougainville, including the Mortlocks and Carterets. The local agent is Bougainville Transport (tel 95 6276), PO Box 104, Kieta. Apparently they do different circuits, each trip lasting about five days and costing about K15.

Road The road networks on Bougainville and Buka are rather sketchy. From Kieta the road runs south via Aropa and the airport, down the eastern side of the island to Buin. The eastern road is good all the way, but the west coast road fords some serious rivers and requires four-wheel drive. See the Buin section.

The east coast road runs right up to Buka Passage, but it too requires four-wheel drive. See the Buka section. PMVs run south to Buin for about K5, but there are only private vehicles north to Buka – expect to pay around K14, if you can find someone to take you.

To/From Port Moresby Air Niugini have at least a daily flight connection with Port Moresby for K189. Flight time is one hour, 45 minutes. There are occasional ships from Kieta to Port Moresby.

To/From Rabaul Air Niugini flies from Rabaul to Kieta on Tuesday, Friday and Sunday and in the other direction on Monday, Wednesday and Saturday. The fare is K100 and the flight takes one hour, 20 minutes. The Pacific New Guinea Line's MV *Kazi* does a weekly voyage to Rabaul (K34) via Buka (K25) and Coastal Shipping's MV *Atolls Enterprise* does the trip monthly for the same price. The MV *Huris* runs on the route (covering little ports in between) without a schedule.

Getting Around

There are no taxis, but there are regular PMVs between Toniva and Panguna. See the previous section for airport transport.

The distance from Aropa (the airport) to Toniva is about 10 km and a PMV (they're rare) will cost about 60t; from Toniva to Kieta is five km which will cost about 20t; from Kieta to Arawa is 10 km which will cost about 60t. A PMV from Arawa to Panguna costs K2.

Budget (tel 95 6382), PO Box 146, Kieta, and Avis rent cars and both companies have desks at the airport. Avis also has an office at the Davara Hotel (tel 95 6175).

BOUGAINVILLE COPPER – PANGUNA

High in the centre of Bougainville is one of the world's largest man-made holes – Bougainville Copper's gigantic open-cut mine at Panguna.

A geological expedition discovered copper reserves at Panguna in 1964 and by 1967 the size of the deposit was known to be large enough to justify cutting an access road from Kobuna. Progress from that point was rapid: in 1969 construction of the mining project started, advance sales of copper were made, the temporary road was upgraded and port facilities were constructed. At the peak period for construction, before the mine started commercial operation in 1972, 10,000 people were employed.

Today, 4000 people work for Bougainville Copper and approximately one in five are expats. Most of the workers live in or near Arawa and Panguna. The mine is one of the mainstays of PNG's economy and has contributed K815 million in dividends (the government has a 20% share holding) and taxes, and since 1972 has provided 46% of the country's total export earnings. Copper prices over the last decade have been notoriously fickle, however, and at the end of 1982, after prices had plunged, the state's annual revenue fell to less than K2 million, although this has since recovered. Fortunately, the giant Ok Tedi

mine and recent gold and oil discoveries will reduce the country's dependence. Nobody seems to know quite how long the mine will last, but various dates from 1993 to 2000 are bandied around.

The rush by companies to explore Bougainville in the wake of the Panguna discovery created widespread Bougainvillean discontent. Land is of primary importance to Bougainvilleans and the threat to traditional land owners was regarded with great seriousness. As a result, a moratorium prohibiting further exploration was put in place. The company is now applying pressure on the government to lift this ban, in the hope that further deposits will be found and the company's huge investment in infrastructure might continue to be productive. There seems, interestingly, to be quite a reluctance on the part of the authorities to do so. After all, in Bougainvillean eyes who will benefit from a new mine? Bougainville Copper? The PNG Government? PNG? Or Bougainvilleans?

The mine is quite a breathtaking sight, dwarfing the gigantic mechanical shovels that tear great hunks from the ground and load colossal trucks – each with a capacity of 155 tonnes! Each day about 200,000 tonnes of rock are mined, producing a yearly total of 600,000 tonnes of dry concentrate. The copper comprises less than 1% of the original ore and as the mine is dug deeper the concentration of copper is gradually falling.

The crude ore is first crushed then fed to the ball mills where it is ground with progressively smaller steel balls. It is then passed on to the separator where it is chemically treated until the concentrate is about 30% copper. Lastly, it's pumped as a liquid slurry down a 25 km pipeline to the coast. There it is dried out and loaded onto ships. Japan takes about 50% of the annual production with Germany and Spain as the second and third biggest customers.

Although the percentage of gold and silver in the ore is extremely small – less than a gram per tonne for gold, about two gm per tonne for silver – they make up a considerable part of the mine's earnings.

Getting There & Around

The mine runs free, two hour, guided tours at 10 am and 2 pm; the visitors' office is in the main office complex (tel 97 2800) and you would be wise to let them know you're coming. If you do contact the PR people you might be able to get a lift on one of the company buses that bring workers up from Arawa, or you could get a PMV for K2. The tourist office might also be able to help, and if all else fails there's enough traffic to make hitching feasible. The road is paved all the way.

It's a worthwhile expedition and the views from the road on the way are excellent – you look out over the coast and also see Mt Bagana, an impressive active volcano, in the distance. You climb to over 1000 metres, out of the humid coastal air, into the mountains, which are noticeably cooler and often wetter. Bring a pullover and a rain jacket. You can get a cheap lunch in the company canteen from 11.30 am to 1 pm. It's opposite the large post office and you'll also find Air Niugini, a bank and a well-stocked supermarket.

BUIN

In the south of the island, Buin is extremely wet during the November to April wet season. It is here that the finely made Buka baskets are woven – not, as the name might suggest, at Buka Island in the north. During the war Buin was the site of a very large Japanese army base and the area is packed with rusting relics of the war.

The extensive Japanese fortifications came to nothing because the Australians landed north of Torokina and moved south, instead of making the frontal attack the Japanese had expected. You can see much wreckage at Lamuai and on the Kahili Plantation which you can walk to from Buin.

During the 1975 secessionist movement the police force was kicked out of Buin, but it has now returned. The Buin people produce copra and are fairly well off.

There's a district office, a couple of trade stores, a PNGBC bank, and an interesting, bustling market, with many people coming from the Shortland Islands in the Solomons to sell fish. Saturday is the best day.

Wally Sito owns the trade store on the corner, knows the area well and also runs the Buin Guest House. He may be able to arrange a guide to help you find some of the war relics in the area.

Place to Stay

The *Buin Guest House* (tel 96 1049), PO Box 216, Buin, is a converted house near the government offices. Bearing in mind it is a monopoly catering to visiting public servants it's not too surprising that the cost is K50 per night including meals.

Getting There & Away

There's a good unsealed road from Aropa south to Buin and there are PMVs. It's an attractive, interesting drive. Although they are fairly infrequent they only cost K5 and take about three hours. Apparently there have been problems with over charging on this route – you may have to stand up for your rights. You can complete a circuit and come back through Panguna if you have your own transport, but the road fords several fast-flowing rivers, which would be pretty tough going after rain. There are no longer any regular flights. See the Getting There chapter for notes on the route through to the Shortland Islands.

AROUND BUIN

Apart from the formidable base the Japanese developed, there were plans for resettling a huge number of civilian Japanese in the area – at a place called Little Tokyo. There are plans afoot to develop some village guesthouses in the area, including at the beautiful Tonnoli

Harbour, and for establishing a picnic area on Kangu Beach. Talk to the Tourist Office in Moresby, or write to the Tourist Office in Arawa to get the latest info.

If you take the road straight through Buin, you come to an intersection; turn right to head back to Arawa through Siwai and Panguna, left to Malabita Village or straight ahead for Kangu Beach. If you head for Kangu Beach, keep driving for 10-15 minutes until you spot a small overgrown bunker on the right and a track just past it. This goes through to an open area with a couple of pill boxes and a gun pointing forlornly out to sea. The beach is a long stretch of sand, with islands hovering on the horizon. If you don't turn off to Kangu Beach, you come to the little cove where the open boats from the Shortland Islands pull in and past that you come to a collapsed bridge and an attractive village. Local PMVs run up to the market in Buin. The area is crying out for a reasonably-priced lodge.

Admiral Yamamoto's Aircraft Wreck

The most historically interesting wreck in the area is the aircraft of Admiral Isoroku Yamamoto – the man who planned the attack on Pearl Harbor. On 18 April 1943 he left Rabaul in a Betty Bomber, accompanied by a protective group of Zeroes. He did not realise that the Japanese naval code had been broken by the Americans and that US fighters would be waiting for him near Buin. As his aircraft approached the south of Bougainville the US P-38s pounced, shooting down Yamamoto's aircraft and scoring an enormous psychological victory over the Japanese.

The wreckage of Yamamoto's Betty still lies in the jungle, only a few km off the Panguna-Buin road. It is well signposted, near the village of of Aku, 24 km before Buin, and a path has been cut through the jungle from the road. It's a one hour walk. Unfortunately, there's a bitter feud between the landowners, who tried unsuccessfully to sell a wing to Japan, and

the government, who stopped them. As a result, access to the plane is either completely blocked, or it costs about K20 per person, depending on the mood of the local big man. It's called cutting off your nose to spite your face. Check with the Tourist Office about the current situation.

In 1968, only 400 metres from the Buin-Kangu Hill road, an American Corsair fighter was discovered, where it had crashed in November '43, its pilot still in the cockpit. Just down the beach from the hill itself is a Catholic mission whose small plantation contains three more bombers. There are countless other similar wrecks scattered around the country – some of much more recent arrival.

NORTH TO BUKA

There's a rough road running up the east coast of Bougainville from Kieta to Kokopau on the Buka Passage. Not all of the rivers are bridged so this is a four-wheel drive adventure. On the way you can stop at Wakunai where spears and other traditional weapons can be bought at the Wakunai Marketing Coop. From Wakunai you can make a three day trip to climb Mt Balbi, 2743 metres, the highest mountain on Bougainville. From the summit of this extinct volcano you can see Mt Bagana (1999 metres) the most active volcano in PNG.

BUKA PASSAGE

The narrow channel that separates Bougainville from Buka is steeped in history and legends and packed with beautiful islands. It's also thick with fish just waiting to be hauled out. Sohano Island, in the centre of the passage, was the district HQ from just after the war until 1960. There is a guesthouse on the island today and a free government ferry. Nearby Tchibo Rock features in many colourful local legends.

Saposa is a popular picnic spot and an old meeting ground on the island is marked by traditional carved posts.

Various war relics, including the wreckage of a Japanese fighter in the mangrove swamps, can be seen around Sohano. The current flows through the Buka Passage extremely swiftly and the pontoon that crosses the passage charges K6 per vehicle. There is a market at Buka Passage on Wednesday, Friday and Saturday and a number of Chinese trade stores.

Place to Stay
The *Buka Luman Guest House* (tel 96 6057), PO Box 251, Buka Passage, on Sohano Island used to be the District Commissioner's residence. There are 10 rooms and all meals are included in the overnight tariff of K40 per person. There is a licensed restaurant. It's on Sohano Island in the passage, reached by the free ferry.

BUKA
A crushed coral road runs up the east coast of Buka Island, connecting the copra plantations. Construction of the road caused some local strife between the local council and the locally organised Hahalis Welfare Society, centred around Hanahan. Both of them insisted that road construction was their prerogative and members of the society refused to pay the head tax. Even more colourful was their Hahalis baby farm in the '60s which had a certain flavour of organised prostitution about it. Read John Ryan's *The Hot Land* for the full story.

Hutjena, in the south-east, is the main town and site for the Buka airstrip. Queen Carola Harbour, on the west coast, is the main port on Buka.

Place to Stay
The *Buka Lodge* (tel 96 6057), PO Box 251, Buka, is in the town of Buka and has four comfortable rooms for K35-40.

Getting There & Away
There are no PMVs along the rough east coast road from Kieta, but you might be able to get a ride for around K14 with a private vehicle. Bougair has two flights per day Monday to Friday, and Talair flies from Rabaul on Tuesdays and Saturdays. Pacific New Guinea Line's MV *Kazi* calls in on its weekly Rabaul-Kieta schedule and so does Coastal Shipping's MV *Atolls Enterprise*.

OUTER ISLANDS
There are a scattering of islands far away from Bougainville and Buka which, nevertheless, come under North Solomons jurisdiction. Some are as easily accessible from New Ireland as from the North Solomons.

Nuguria (Fead) Group
The 50-odd islands in the group have a total area of only five square km and a population of not many over 200 Polynesians. They are about 200 km east of New Ireland and a similar distance north of Buka.

Nukumanu (Tasman) Islands
Nukumanu is the largest island in the group with an area of less than three square km. They lie about 400 km north-east of Bougainville and much closer to the extensive Ontong Java Atoll in the Solomon Islands. The population is about 300 Polynesians.

Kilinailau (Carteret) Group
Only 70 km north-east of Buka they comprise six islands on a 16 km circular atoll. The population of about 900 are Buka people who appear to have supplanted earlier Polynesian inhabitants.

Tau (Mortlock) Group
About 195 km north-east of Bougainville the ring-shaped reef has about 20 islands, virtually mid-way on a line drawn from the Carteret to the Tasman Islands. The population of around 600 is predominantly Polynesian.

Green Islands
The Green Islands lie approximately 70 km

north-west of Buka. Nissan and Pinipel Island, a little further north, are the only islands in the group which are inhabited. Total population is about 3200.

Nissan is a large elliptical island and smaller islands lie within its curve. The textbook-perfect atoll was totally evacuated of its local population during WW II and a large American airbase was operated there. After the war vast quantities of supplies were dumped and thousands of drums of fuel were sold at only 3c a gallon. There was no shortage of war surplus material in New Guinea.

Getting There & Away

Bougair have flights to a number of these islands. From Buka to Nissan costs about K64, Kieta to Nissan K80. The MV *Atolls Enterprise* makes regular voyages from Kieta. See the Kieta section.

Milne Bay

Area 20,254 square km
Population 145,000

At the eastern end of PNG, the Owen Stanley Range plunges into the sea and a scatter of islands dots the ocean for hundreds of km further out. This is the start of the Pacific proper – tiny atolls, coral reefs, volcanic islands, swaying palms and white beaches. Yet, there is one big difference to the better known areas of the Pacific – there are virtually no tourists. The Trobriand Islands are the only place in Milne Bay to have developed a tourist industry, but in a busy week there may only be 20 visitors!

HISTORY

The islands of the Milne Bay Province were well known to early Pacific explorers and many of the islands still bear their names. The Louisiade Archipelago, for example, was named after Louis Vaez de Torres, who sailed through them way back in 1606. In 1793 Bruny D'Entrecasteaux donated his cumbersome name to the island group further north and west.

In 1873, Captain John Moresby discovered the deep inlet which he named Milne Bay after Alexander Milne, the Lord of the Admiralty. Moresby had earlier landed on Samarai Island and named it Dinner Island after his most recent meal; it must have been a memorable one. He also paused long enough to run up the flag and claim the whole area for Queen Victoria. The good Queen, however, was not too keen on finding further places where the sun never set and his claim was repudiated.

Even before Moresby came on his empire-building expedition, there had been attempts at permanent European settlements; a mission was set up on Woodlark Island way back in 1847 but the islanders were extremely unenthusiastic

about Christianity and the missionaries who survived their lack of enthusiasm soon departed. After Moresby's visit, traders and other missionaries followed and a thriving trade developed in pearl shells and beche-de-mer, the large sea slugs which are a Chinese delicacy. The Milne Bay area also suffered from 'blackbirding', the forcible collection of 'voluntary' labour for Queensland sugar plantations.

In 1888, gold was discovered on Misima Island, the miners flooded in and, as in other parts of PNG, soon died like flies from the effects of disease, malnutrition and unfriendly natives. A later find on Woodlark Island eventually produced nearly $1½ million in gold at a time when the price was much lower than it is today. With all this passing trade, plus a major missionary station, the island of Samarai established itself as the major port and outpost in the region, a position it was to hold until after WW II.

Soon after the war spread to the Pacific, the Milne Bay area served as the stage for the turning point in the conflict between Japanese and Allied forces. In the Battle of the Coral Sea, the Japanese rush south was abruptly halted. Although this is regarded as a classic naval battle, the Japanese and American warships did not once come within 300 km of each other; the fighting was entirely conducted by aircraft. Some of the most violent

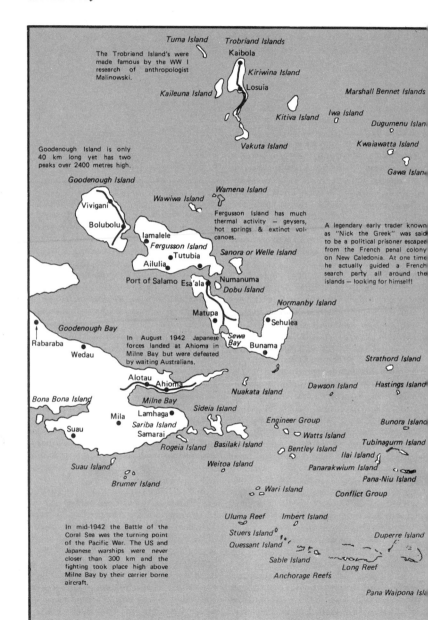

Tuma Island

Trobriand Islands

Kaibola

The Trobriand Island's were made famous by the WW I research of anthropologist Malinowski.

Kiriwina Island

Losuia

Marshall Bennet Islands

Kaileuna Island

Kitiva Island

Iwa Island

Dugumenu Islan

Kwaiawatta Island

Vakuta Island

Goodenough Island is only 40 km long yet has two peaks over 2400 metres high.

Gawa Islan

Goodenough Island

Wamena Island

Wawiwa Island

Vivigani

Fergusson Island has much thermal activity — geysers, hot springs & extinct volcanoes.

Bolubolu

A legendary early trader known as "Nick the Greek" was said to be a political prisoner escapee from the French penal colony on New Caledonia. At one time he actually guided a French search party all around the islands — looking for himself!

Iamalele

Fergusson Island

Sanora or Welle Island

Tutubia

Ailulia

Port of Salamo   Esa'ala

Numanuma

Dobu Island

Matupa

Normanby Island

Sehulea

Goodenough Bay

Rabaraba

In August 1942 Japanese forces landed at Ahioma in Milne Bay but were defeated by waiting Australians.

Sewa Bay

Bunama

Strathord Island

Wedau

Alotau

Ahioma

Nuakata Island

Dawson Island

Hastings Island

Bona Bona Island

Milne Bay

Lamhaga

Sideia Island

Engineer Group

Bunora Island

Mila

Sariba Island

Watts Island

Suau

Samarai

Tubinagurm Island

Rogeia Island   Basilaki Island

Bentley Island

Ilai Island

Panarakwium Island

Suau Island

Weitoa Island

Pana-Niu Island

Brumer Island

Wari Island

Conflict Group

In mid-1942 the Battle of the Coral Sea was the turning point of the Pacific War. The US and Japanese warships were never closer than 300 km and the fighting took place high above Milne Bay by their carrier borne aircraft.

Uluma Reef   Imbert Island

Stuers Island

Duperre Island

Quessant Island

Sable Island

Long Reef

Anchorage Reefs

Pana Waipona Isla

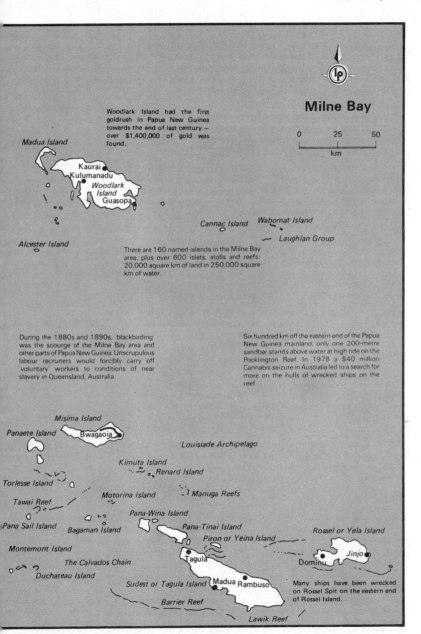

Milne Bay

```
0        25        50
        km
```

Woodlark Island had the first goldrush in Papua New Guinea towards the end of last century — over $1,400,000 of gold was found.

Madua Island

Kaurai
Kulumanadu
Woodlark Island
Guasopa

Cannac Island   Wabomat Island
— Laughlan Group

Alcester Island

There are 160 named islands in the Milne Bay area, plus over 600 islets, atolls and reefs: 20,000 square km of land in 250,000 square km of water.

During the 1880s and 1890s, 'blackbirding' was the scourge of the Milne Bay area and other parts of Papua New Guinea. Unscrupulous labour recruiters would forcibly carry off 'voluntary' workers to conditions of near slavery in Queensland, Australia.

Six hundred km off the eastern end of the Papua New Guinea mainland, only one 200-metre sandbar stands above water at high tide on the Pocklington Reef. In 1978 a $40 million Cannabis seizure in Australia led to a search for more on the hulls of wrecked ships on the reef.

Misima Island
Panaete Island Bwagaoia
Louisiade Archipelago
Kimuta Island
·. ⁀ ⸗ Renard Island
Torlesse Island
Motorina Island ⸗ Manuga Reefs
Tawai Reef
Pana Sail Island Pana-Wina Island
Bagaman Island Pana-Tinai Island
Piron or Yeina Island *Rossel or Yela Island*
Montemont Island
The Calvados Chain Tagula Dominu Jinjo
Duchateau Island
Sudest or Tagula Island Madua Rambuso
Barrier Reef
Lawik Reef

Many ships have been wrecked on Rossel Spit on the eastern end of Rossel Island.

dogfights took place high above Misima Island in the Louisiades. American losses were severe, but the Japanese fleet was crippled and never again played an effective role in the Pacific.

Despite this setback, the Japanese remained determined to capture PNG and in July '42 they landed at Buna and Gona in the Northern Province and pressed south down the Kokoda Trail towards Moresby. In August they made a second landing in Milne Bay, in an attempt to take the eastern end of the island. Again, as in the Coral Sea conflict, the Allies had advance warning and a strong Australian force was waiting for them. In addition, they landed at Ahioma, too far round the bay, and had to slog through terrible swamps to meet the Australians and attempt to take the airstrip. This blunder contributed to their total defeat, the first time in the war that a Japanese amphibious assault had been repelled. Active fighting did not again encroach on the Milne Bay area, but Milne Bay itself became a huge naval base that hundreds of thousands of servicemen passed through.

GEOGRAPHY
The mainland section of the province is extremely mountainous, for the eastern end of the Owen Stanley Range marches almost to the end of the island before plunging straight into the sea.

It is the islands, however, that are of greatest interest in Milne Bay and there are plenty of them – 160 named islands plus more than 600 islets and atolls and untold numbers of reefs waiting to trap the unwary sailor.

The islands are enormously varied, from tiny dots barely breaking the surface of the sea to larger islands such as Fergusson and Goodenough in the D'Entrecasteaux Group. The highest mountain on Goodenough rises to over 2400 metres and there are so many other lesser peaks that, for its size, this is one of the most mountainous places on earth. By

contrast, the Trobriand Islands are virtually entirely flat.

The Milne Bay Islands are divided into seven main groups – Trobriands, Woodlark, Laughlan, Louisiade Archipelago, the Conflict Group, the Samarai Group and the D'Entrecasteaux Group.

CLIMATE
The weather in Milne Bay is very unpredictable – rainstorms can be sudden, unexpected and heavy, while high winds can quickly make the sea very rough. November to January generally has the best and most consistent weather while March to June can usually be counted on to be less windy.

ALOTAU
The district headquarters was transferred from Samarai Island to Alotau on the mainland in 1968, principally because access to Samarai is only possible by sea and the island was already crowded to its limits. Any further expansion had to be on the mainland.

The town is spectacularly sited on the edge of Milne Bay. There's not actually a great deal to do there, you can't look at the view all day and there's not really anything else. It is, for most travellers, just the starting point for a trip to the islands, and it's the only spot to stock up on food and money.

Across Milne Bay from Alotau is Discovery Bay, where Captain Moresby spent several days during his 1873 visit. The mysterious 'moonstones' in the hills behind this bay are, as yet, an unsolved archaeological riddle. Fishing around Alotau is very good.

Orientation
Alotau's airport is at Gurney, 15 km from town, surrounded by a massive, new oil palm development. The commercial centre is laid out on a grid, with everything within a five minute walk, basically around a single block. Most housing, including the lodge and hostel, is

a steep climb up the hill behind. The views are stunning. The bustling port is a short walk to the east of town.

Information

There's a Milne Bay Tourist Bureau (tel 61 1114), PO Box 337, in the provincial government's offices, and although they're not really set up to deal with the public, it would be worth visiting if you want up-to-date information about some of the island guesthouses or want to make radio contact with them.

All the major banks are represented and the shopping is reasonable – you'll see the market on your right as you drive in from the airport.

Harbour

The harbour is a colourful, vibrant part of town, with boats from all over the province. You can easily entertain yourself for hours just watching the comings and goings – the fisherman in the bay, and the brightly-painted island boats loading and unloading, all against the backdrop of mountains falling sheer into blue Milne Bay.

This would be a good place to start if you had the time and the temperament for an unstructured, island-hopping expedition – the longer you sit and watch the more tempted you will be.

Things to Do

Rob Van de Loos runs *Milne Bay Marine Charters* (tel 61 1167), PO Box 176, from the service station on the airport road, a 10 minute walk from town. He has a purpose-built, 11 metre dive boat that can accommodate seven people at K72.50 each per day, food and dives included. The diving, so I'm told, is great.

Places to Stay

The 25 room *Masurina Lodge* (tel 61 1212), PO Box 5, has some air-con rooms and fan-cooled rooms across the street in four cottages with shared facilities and a refrigerator. Singles/doubles are K60/82 with fan, K77/99 with air-con, with a 10% discount for cash. Although it ain't cheap, it is clean, comfortable and friendly. The prices include three good, large meals whether you eat them or not, so be there.

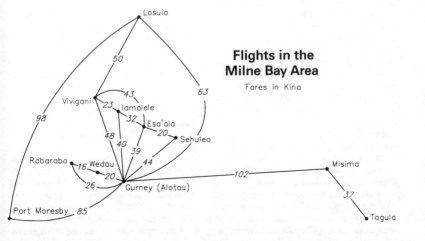

Flights in the Milne Bay Area

Fares in Kina

On Friday night they put on an outdoor barbecue buffet for K5. The lodge is also the local watering hole and is a popular spot to down a few after work. It's up the hill behind town on the second street on the right after the hospital. They'll pick you up from the airport (quite a boon) if they know you're coming.

Further up the hill, the *Government Hostel* has plain but decent accommodation and board for around K25. Contact the Tourist Bureau to check they're not full of visiting Members of the Provincial Parliament. Keep walking up from the hospital until you pass a water tank on your left; the Hostel is on the next street to the right. Walk backwards up the hill or you'll miss the view!

Places to Eat

The *Masuarina Lodge* is your best bet in the evenings; let them know you're coming.

There's an unnamed coffee shop at the end of the arcade opposite the pedestrian steps that make a shortcut up the hill towards the hospital, which has interesting sandwiches, fresh fruit juices, real coffee and other luxuries.

Bobby's, on the other corner of the main block, is a better than average food bar, with tables and chairs.

Things to Buy

There's a well-signposted handicrafts shop next door to the provincial government offices. It has a good range of artefacts, including a lot of stuff from the Trobriands that is, predictably, cheaper on the island. It's worth a look.

Getting There & Away

Air The airport is at Gurney, 15 km from town and getting to and from it is a bit of a problem. There are taxis, but these are expensive and will cost at least K10. The alternative is to cadge a lift, stay at the Masuarina (they'll pick you up), or make some arrangement with the airline company staff. The Talair people are

happy to give you a lift to or from town, and I imagine the Air Niugini people will do the same.

There are Air Niugini connections from Port Moresby to Gurney every day except Friday for K85, but Talair is the most useful carrier for this region. Both companies have offices in town: Air Niugini (tel 61 1100), PO Box 3, Talair (tel 61 1333), PO Box 73.

Talair has a daily flight to Gurney (K85) and direct flights from Moresby to Losuia (Trobriands) on Tuesdays, Wednesdays, Thursdays and Saturdays. There are flights from Gurney to Losuia (K63) on Tuesdays, Wednesdays and Saturdays. They also fly to many of the other islands and airports, including Misima Island (K102), Fergusson Island (K40) and Goodenough Island (K48). On Wednesdays and Saturdays they have an interesting flight that goes to Cape Vogel (K37), Tufi (fjord land in Northern Province, K70), Popondetta (K102) and Lae (K134).

Milne Bay Air (tel 61 1393), PO Box 39, has a couple of charter planes. This may sound expensive, but if you have a group it's not unreasonable: their nine-seater costs K450 per hour, their four-seater, K250.

Sea The ideal way to explore Milne Bay is by sea. Unfortunately there's no regular shipping from other provinces, although it would be worth asking around in Moresby. On the north coast, Lutheran Shipping generally only operates as far east as Lae and Coastal Shipping operates further north.

This is not to say there are no boats, it's just that they're small and unscheduled and you have to be patient waiting for one to come by. Most are heavy, wooden fishing boats with central diesel engines. They're noisy, smelly and they roll a lot. On some regular routes, like Alotau/Samarai, there are standard fares, in this case K5. There are also regular boats to Esa-ala on Normanby for around K15.

Apart from hanging around the harbours

in Alotau and Samarai (Samarai is still the major port for the province), there are a couple of other strategies if you want to get around the islands: the Catholic Bishop would know of mission boats; the supermarkets will know about trading boats; and the Provincial Government's Shipping Coordinator will know about government boats, which do take passengers.

If you can split the costs, and have a fair bit of money to start with, contact Milne Bay Marine Charters (see the Things to Do section). Apart from organising skin diving trips, they also just charter. The MV *Sharee* will cost about K220 per day, including fuel and crew.

One traveller's suggestions for exploring Milne Bay:

Spend a month going around Milne Bay, you don't have to be a millionaire with a yacht to enjoy the islands, coral, fish and villages. Work boats can be hired in Milne Bay and you can go anywhere in a 24-foot work boat with a Yanmar diesel engine. With captain and crew on an extended charter they might cost K80-130 a day. There are hundreds in the province. Masurina Trading or the Tourist Bureau in Alotau could help arrange a charter. Boats are the PMVs of the province but if you cannot afford to charter one, just travel on them and pay the normal fare. Start by going from Alotau to Samarai, then on from there. A month can be spent in island hopping with no trouble. Just have plenty of time.

Or another suggestion:

If you want to go further afield in Milne Bay it is possible to charter a government boat at K300-400 for 24 hours and cruise out as far as the Engineer Islands where you can spend your time snorkelling, diving, fishing or just lying on the deserted beach of an equally deserted atoll, cracking open coconuts. All facilities apart from the boat and crew are provided by you. If you get a group of, say, a dozen together, then you can have a weekend in paradise for only about K50 per person. Keep your eyes and ears open for other charters too.

Tours The ship *Melanesian Explorer*, operated by Melanesian Tours in Madang,

runs tours between Madang and Alotau via the Trobriands twice a month. The tours take seven nights and six days and there are plenty of opportunities for swimming and diving along the way. The ship also spends two weeks of each month operating to and from Madang up the Sepik. For details and schedule information contact Melanesian Tourist Services (tel 82 2766), PO Box 707, Madang.

The other organised way to visit these off the beaten track islands is with Pacific Expeditions (tel 25 7803), PO Box 132, Port Moresby. Their Solomon Seas Expedition explores the Louisiade Archipelago by outrigger canoes, staying in villages.

SAMARAI

The tiny island of Samarai, only 24 hectares in area, was long the provincial HQ and is still a commercial centre and port, despite losing its governmental role to Alotau. Samarai is only five km from the mainland and fairly easily reached by launch from Alotau – which is some distance around the coast on Milne Bay. Although Samarai definitely has seen better days it's a very pretty place in a very beautiful area.

The island lies on China Strait, so named by Captain Moresby because he considered it would be the most direct route from the east coast of Australia to China. It was one of the most attractive settlements in the Pacific and despite being totally burnt out in 1942 by Japanese air raids it is still an interesting little place. A road encircles the island but you can stroll right round it in 20 minutes!

There is a monument to Christopher Robinson, the acting administrator who committed suicide in 1904 (see Western & Gulf section) in Samarai. The inscription notes that he was an 'Able governor, upright man, honest judge. His aim was to make New Guinea a safe country for white men'!

Places to Stay

The *Kinanale Guest House* (tel 62 1239, after hours 62 1337), PO Box 88, can arrange trips to nearby islands and is the main accommodation centre on Samarai. It's a small place, run by a family. Rates are K30/50 singles/doubles, with another K20 per person if you want all your meals. Breakfast or lunch costs K4, dinner K12. They also have pleasant, self-catering flats for K35 per day, K200 per week. There's a 10% discount for cash.

It may also be possible to stay at the *Catholic Church Hostel* (tel 62 1336) and other people on the island may rent basic rooms for K10 a night.

Getting There & Away

There are no regularly scheduled boats between Alotau and Samarai. Many local boats of all sizes, shapes and speeds ply back and forth – finding out about them means going to the dock area and persistently asking around. It can be a pain because nobody really seems to know anything although there are probably boats every day.

If you don't want to stay in Alotau, arrive early in the morning as most boats to Samarai leave before noon. The local cargo boats are slow, taking about four or five hours, but this varies depending on currents and weather conditions. Count on about K10 round trip. If you can get a speedboat all the better – they take about 1½ hours but cost at least twice as much. The guesthouse on Samarai may be able to arrange a boat for you, but plan it before you arrive in Alotau.

There are also regular shipping services from Port Moresby, which is 400 km to the west, but they very rarely take passengers.

Pleasure yachts commonly clear PNG customs at Samarai, so it could be a good spot to pick up a ride, particularly between May and October when the south-westerlies are blowing.

AROUND SAMARAI

There are a number of nearby islands you can conveniently visit from Samarai. The Kwato Mission is on a small island only 20 minutes out by boat. It was one of the earliest mission establishments in Papua and functions as a busy boat building centre. It may be possible to stay in a village.

At tiny Pearl Island, squeezed between the mainland and Sariba Island, there was a pearl farm. It is possible to rent a house that belongs to Ian Pool, who now lives in Samarai – contact the Tourist Bureau.

Deka Deka, another tiny islet, is a popular beach and picnic spot as is nearby Logea Island. The small cluster of the Wari Islands, 45 km from Samarai, is another boat building centre and the people there are also fine potters.

CAPE VOGEL

Although I didn't see it myself, the Tourist Bureau recommended a village guesthouse at Bogaboga Village. It sounds good – first-hand reports will be gratefully accepted. Its a half hour flight from Alotau with Talair (K37) on Wednesdays and Saturdays (MAF also fly there) followed by a canoe trip across a river. Apparently, the attractions include bush trails, waterfalls, good snorkelling (including gear for hire) and artefacts for sale. Take your own food although there is a trade store. Contact the Tourist Bureau for more information.

D'ENTRECASTEAUX ISLANDS

The three comparatively large islands of the D'Entrecasteaux Group are separated from the north coast of the mainland only by a narrow strait. They are extremely mountainous and flying on the spectacular Talair flight between Alotau and Kiriwina in the Trobriands, you pass directly over them.

Goodenough Island

The most north-westerly of the group, Goodenough is amazingly mountainous with a high central range that has two peaks topping 2400 metres. Quite something for an island only about 40 km long from end to end. There are fertile coastal plains flanking the mountain range and a road runs around the north-east coast through Vivigani, site of the major airstrip in the group. There's only an open shelter here – 'one of the less exciting places to spend 12 hours waiting for a plane that didn't show up', reported one visitor.

Bolubolu is the main station on the island, about 10 km south of the airstrip at Vivigani. In the centre of the island there is a large stone, covered in mysterious black and white paintings, which is said to have power over the yam crops.

Fergusson Island
Fergusson is the central island in the group and the largest in size. Although it is mountainous, it pales in comparison to nearby Goodenough. The highest mountain here is only 2073 metres with two other lower ranges from which flow the island's many rivers and streams. Fergusson's large population is mainly concentrated along the south coast. Fergusson is notable for its active thermal region – hot springs, bubbling mud pools, spouting geysers and extinct volcanoes. Thermal springs can be found at Deidei and at Iamalele on the west coast. There is a Methodist mission at Salamo on the south coast.

Normanby Island
Separated from Fergusson by the narrow and spectacular Dobu Passage, the highest mountain on Normanby reaches a mere 1158 metres. There are a number of mission stations dotted around the island; Esa-ala is the district HQ at the entrance to the Dobu Passage. In the passage is tiny, fertile Dobu Island where the Methodists established their first Milne Bay area mission; the mountains rise sheer on both sides of the strait.

In the middle of the south-west coast is Sewa Bay, used by Allied warships during WW II and a port of call for small inter-island ships today. There are strange,

unexplained rock carvings around the bay.

Places to Stay There's a guesthouse at Esa-ala, converted from a government house, which costs K20 per day including meals. Contact the Milne Bay Tourist Bureau for details and bookings.

Getting There & Away You can fly to Esa-ala from Gurney with Talair (K39) on Mondays, Thursdays and Saturdays. There are also regular boats from Alotau and Samarai for around K15.

Amphlett Islands
The tiny Amphlett Islands are scattered to the north of the main D'Entrecasteaux Group. The people here are part of the Kula Ring trading cycle and they make some extremely fine and very fragile pottery.

TROBRIAND ISLANDS
The Trobriand Islands lie to the north of the D'Entrecasteaux Group and are the most accessible and interesting islands in the Milne Bay area. They take their name from Denis de Trobriand, an officer on D'Entrecasteaux's expedition.

The Trobriands are low-lying coral islands, in complete contrast to their southern neighbours. The largest of the group is Kiriwina, and the site for the HQ, Losuia.

The Trobriands were made famous after WW I by the work of Polish anthropologist Bronislaw Malinowski. Apparently, at the start of the war he was offered a choice of internment in Australia or banishment to the remote Trobriands. He sensibly chose the latter and his studies of the islanders, their intricate trading rituals, their yam cults and, to many people most interesting of all, their sexual practices, led to his classic series of books – *Argonauts of the Western Pacific*, *Coral Gardens and their Magic* and *The Sexual Life of Savages*.

The Trobriand islanders have strong

Polynesian characteristics and, unlike people in most other parts of PNG, they have a social system that is dominated by hereditary chieftains who continue to wield a tremendous amount of power and influence. The whole society is hierarchical, with strict distinctions between hereditary classes. It is a matrilineal society (not matriarchal) meaning inheritances are passed through the female side of a family. The chief's sons belong to his wife's clan and he is superseded by one of his oldest sister's sons.

The soil of the Trobriands is very fertile and great care is lavished on the gardens, particularly the yam gardens which have great practical and cultural importance.

The villages are all laid out in a similar pattern – which you can see most clearly from the air as you fly in or out of Kiriwina. The village yam houses form an inner ring, surrounded by sleeping houses, and the whole lot is encircled by a ring of trees and vegetation.

Some Interesting Things to Say

Malinowski, in his all encompassing studies, even makes a detailed foray into the Trobriands language. True to form it has a wide variety of sexual terminology including different ways of referring to male and female genitals depending on whether they're yours, your partners, or somebody else's. Just so you have your sexual terminology lined up before you get there, remember that it is:

Female	Male
my wiga	my kwiga
your wim	your kwim
her wila	his kwila

Since wila is pronounced 'Wheeler', my surname, to say the least, has a rather unfortunate translation. Once they had got over the sheer amazement that anybody could be so dumb as to call himself Wheeler (or *wila*) the girls at the Kiriwina Lodge took great pleasure in calling me *wila* as frequently as possible.

There's plenty of other fun to be had with the local language. If you'd like something nice to whisper in your girl friend's ear try, *yoku tage kuwoli nunum, kwunpisiga* or when things get a bit heavier try *wim, kasesam!* Or for female readers, should you want to belittle some male just shout out *kaykukupi kwim.* (I've always had this urge to write an R-rated travel guide.) You can further enhance your questionable stock of Trobriand phrases at festivals during the yam harvesting season when islanders sing songs of amazing vulgarity known as *mweki mweki.*

Some Less Interesting Things to Say

good morning	*bwena kau kwau*
good afternoon	*bwena la lai*
good night	*bwena bogie*
very good	*sena bwena*
very bad	*sena gaga*
yes/no	*eh/gala*
you/me	*yokwa/yegu*
how much is that (price?)	*aveka besa?*
food	*kaula*
what is your name?	*yokwa amiyagam?*
go away	*kula*
I am going to sleep	*ye bala masisi*

Orientation

Most of the island is flat, although there is a rim of hills (uplifted coral reefs) which run down the eastern side. The central plain is intensely cultivated, to the extent that there are no decent trees left and it is hot and flat. This is where you will find the airport. The roads are reasonable, although unsealed. North of the airport is Kaibola, south is the Kiriwina Hotel and Losuia. The bay on the western side of the island is a huge expanse of very shallow water – so shallow that the canoes are punted along with poles. The eastern beaches are backed by beautiful rainforest and although they all have reefs they look out onto the open sea.

Information

There are very few facilities on Kiriwina. Losuia, the main town, has a wharf, a high school, a police station, a couple of government offices, one small trade store and that is it. The Kiriwina Hotel also has an adjoining trade store, and handles bookings for Talair. There is no bank, so

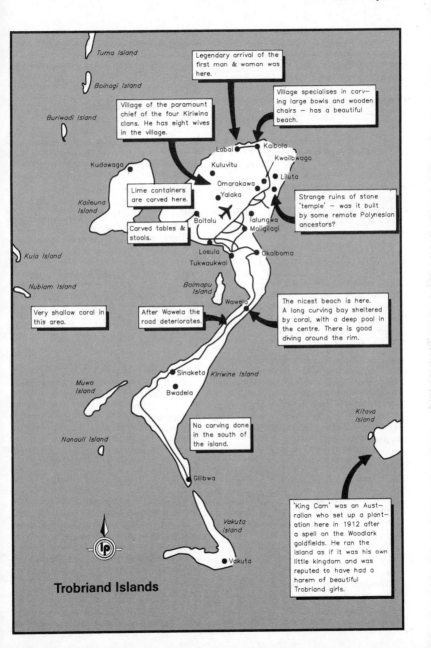

Legendary arrival of the first man & woman was here.

Village specialises in carving large bowls and wooden chairs — has a beautiful beach.

Village of the paramount chief of the four Kiriwina clans. He has eight wives in the village.

Lime containers are carved here.

Carved tables & stools.

Strange ruins of stone 'temple' — was it built by some remote Polynesian ancestors?

Very shallow coral in this area.

After Wawela the road deteriorates.

The nicest beach is here. A long curving bay sheltered by coral, with a deep pool in the centre. There is good diving around the rim.

No carving done in the south of the island.

'King Cam' was an Australian who set up a plantation here in 1912 after a spell on the Woodlark goldfields. He ran the island as if it was his own little kingdom and was reputed to have had a harem of beautiful Trobriand girls.

Trobriand Islands

Tuma island · Boinagi Island · Buriwadi Island · Kudawaga · Kaileuna Island · Kuia Island · Nubiam Island · Labai · Kaibola · Kwailbwaga · Kuluvitu · Liluta · Omarakawa · Yalaka · Boitalu · Ialungwa · Moligilagi · Losula · Tukwaukwdi · Okaiboma · Baimapu Island · Wawela · Muwo Island · Sinaketa · Kiriwine Island · Bwadela · Nanauli Island · Kitava Island · Gilibwa · Vakuta Island · Vakuta you must bring all the cash you will need with you. If you plan to stay in the villages, make sure you bring small denominations. Both the Kiriwina Hotel and the Kaibola Beach accept Amex and Diners Club.

Places to Stay – bottom end

The only alternative for shoestringers is to stay in the villages, but this is not as easy as it sounds. The people are proud and fairly aloof, and they certainly know the value of a kina. They are adept at separating you from your money, and although outright theft is unusual you must keep a close eye on your gear and make sure you establish the price of *everything* in advance with the village head man. Nothing is free.

Apart from the islanders' expertise as traders (see the section on the Kula Ring) and the notion of reciprocal generosity, this attitude might partially be explained by the way the islands have, over the years, been poked and prodded by tribes of naive, insensitive anthropologists. I heard one apocryphal story about a young anthropologist who was welcomed into a village, only to find himself making large financial contributions to feasts, ceremonies and this and that. No doubt he acquiesced in an attempt to ingratiate himself with the people. He lived happily until the day came when he ran out of money, and on that very day the tearful scientist was told to pack his bags!

Beware of the local sense of humour; practical jokes with the *dim dim* (foreigner) as the butt are greatly enjoyed. Teasing aside, the men are OK, if aloof, and the women friendly and courteous. Communication is difficult as Pidgin is not common. School kids usually know some English.

You will need to be fairly fit to cope with the rigours of village life, because although it may look like paradise, it is in reality pretty tough. There is a fair degree of overcrowding, hygiene leaves something to be desired, and the food is uninspiring. Taro, the basis of the villagers' subsistence

diet, is like a stringy version of the potato. You must treat your water unless you are sure it has been boiled.

Having painted the bad side, I must add that people do stay in the villages, and for most it is a fantastic experience. Certainly you must be prepared to pay for what you use (hardly a shocking concept for good capitalist tourists), but you are also likely to meet friendly, interesting people and gain an insight (however limited) into an extraordinary culture.

North of Losuia it is possible to stay in some villages for between K5 and K10 a night; you must make the arrangements with the head man. Make sure you know what you're paying for, or you'll have endless small additions made to the bill. Two villages not far from the airport that have been suggested are Ialungwa and Omarakana. It's also possible to stay in villages south of Losuia although a chief in the area has apparently asked for a ridiculously high fee (K30 a night) and you must accept or leave. Not all are as unreasonable. Again, make sure you set prices in advance.

Places to Stay – top end

Unfortunately there are only two organised places to stay. One is extremely expensive and the other is badly positioned. If tourism is to be encouraged, and there are, admittedly, cultural arguments against this, the island is in dire need of reasonably priced, informal lodges, near villages and good beaches.

The legendary *Kiriwina Lodge* (tel 61 1333), PO Box 2, Losuia, or contact Talair in Alotau, is the island's oldest hostelry. It's no Hilton, however, and if you're expecting a romantic Pacific hostelry with happy, uninhibited, flower-bedecked people, forget it.

It's the island's only boozer, so the bar is a good place to meet people, although it can be fairly drunken. The complete absence of women reminded me unpleasantly of the bad old days in Australia, when bars were segregated. I don't know whether this is due to a management decision or community sanctions, but it certainly was not the case in the past. The hotel once had quite a reputation for breezy, friendly informality, and more. Although there may well have been some exaggeration to the stories, they certainly bear no relation to the present. If you frequent the bar, you will meet whoever else happens to be visiting the island, and some of the local people.

The lodge is on the coast, about a km from Losuia, the main town. It is on the lagoon side of the island and a small section of garden runs down to the water, which is, unfortunately, shallow, swampy and no good for swimming. There are some villages close by but, perhaps due to their proximity to the tourist hotel, they aren't particularly friendly. Sitting on the balcony, drink in hand, watching the beautiful outrigger canoes being poled across the bay and chatting to local people and expats as they come and go is pleasant enough, up to a point. If you want to do any snorkelling, or see anything, however, you'll have to organise transport.

The lodge has 18 rooms and they're straightforward, without air-con, which is no problem since the Trobriands seem to be generally cool and breezy. Daily costs are K45/60 for singles/doubles. Meals are available, though they aren't very good – breakfast and lunch K5, dinner K8.50, sandwiches K3. The lodge has vehicles you can hire from 60t to K1 a km. This can get expensive as it's 20 km to Wawela. There are plans for some beach-side lodges at Wawela, which is a beautiful beach.

The expensive alternative was still under construction when I visited – this seems to have been a slow process – but if early indications are fulfilled, the *Kaibola Beach*, PO Box 15, Losuia, at the northern tip of the island will be excellent. The site is quite magical with shady trees crowding up to a curve of sand, a small offshore island and a village nearby. Accommodation will be in individual, bush-material *bwalas* with electricity, fans and balconies. A dining room, lounge, bar and shop will be housed in a separate building. Janice Huntley, the manager, intends to organise canoe trips, village visits, walks, snorkelling (take your own gear) and scuba diving.

The tariff includes a pick-up from the airport and all meals and activities except diving, but it's not cheap: singles/doubles/triples with private facilities are K105/140/190, singles/doubles without private facilities are K65/120.

Things to Buy

By far the best known artefacts in the Milne Bay area, although not the only ones, are the Trobriand carvings. Like other parts of PNG, certain villages tend to specialise in certain styles and types of carvings. In general, Trobriand carvings are more finely finished and have a more modern appearance than other PNG carvings. Curiously, it is only in the north of Kiriwina that the people carve.

There are a variety of different artefacts, ranging from bowls to walking sticks. The bowls – popular for use as salad or fruit bowls – often have decorative rims or flat surrounds carved like fish or turtles, with shells for eyes. Prices range from K5 for a small one up to K20 or even more for large ones, and the prices rise the further you are from the Trobriands.

Carved statues are usually delicate and elongated with curiously convoluted figures – a woman with a tree kangaroo perched on her head and a crocodile balanced on its tail behind her, for example. Intricately carved walking sticks, which are particularly well finished, are very popular. There are also some squat little carvings – particularly of coupling pigs. Occasionally there are some finely carved erotic scenes, but these are rarely seen. Some of these carvings are made from ebony, which is now very rare and comes only from Woodlark Island.

Stools are also made – solid circular

ones with carved figures holding up the seats. They cost from about K30 in the Trobriands but are rather heavy for carrying away. Three-legged tables are also popular. Lime spatulas and carved gourds for with betel (*buai*), and wooden chains are other items you may see. Traditionally some of the best carving went into the magnificent canoe prows, particularly those used for the Kula Ring trading ceremonies. This *Massim* style of carving can also be seen on important yam house frontages.

Other than carvings, you can get shells and shell money (*bagi*) although the latter is likely to be very expensive. The shell money is made on Rossel Island; it's meticulously ground shell discs with a diameter of about five mm strung like a necklace. If it's genuine, it will cost about K1 a centimetre – beware of plastic imitations. Leaf money (*doba*) is also still used as negotiable currency; it's a bundle of banana leaves with each leaf incised with patterns. The colourful grass skirts are also used as currency (they're worth K3-5) and make interesting buys.

You may be offered stone axe heads, but you should be wary of buying. Many of these implements are extremely old and there are controls on their export. If you do take these out of the country you may well be destroying important archaeological evidence.

The Trobriand Islanders are astute business people, so you should avoid rushing into any purchases. For a start, prices are definitely flexible and until you can judge quality you are at the vendor's mercy. There are always people hanging around the Kiriwina Lodge and the airport (when there are flights) so take your time and don't be bluffed. If you catch a salesman's eye you can come under quite a deal of pressure – be firm, good humoured and polite. It's worth visiting Bill Rudd, next door to the Kiriwina Lodge, as he has a good collection of artefacts (some for sale) and he's very knowledgeable.

Getting There & Away

Talair flies direct to the Trobes from Moresby on Tuesday, Wednesday, Thursday and Saturday for K98, and from Gurney (Alotau) on Tuesday, Wednesday and Saturday for K63.

Getting Around

You can organise tours and transportation using the Kiriwina Lodge's transport. This costs from 60t to K1 per km and can get expensive unless you can share costs – the cost of running a vehicle is very high. From Kiriwina to Wawela is around 20 km, to Kaibola is around 30 km. Insist on being taken to where you want to go and stopping where you want to stop or you'll just end up visiting the driver's friends and village. Half and full day tours with packed lunch and beer are also available.

There are some PMVs which run infrequently, but cheaply – from 50t to K1 will get you to most places from the airport. Almost all private vehicles operate as de facto PMVs. Otherwise, you'll have to walk, and this can get very hot. Make sure you carry water and have a decent hat.

Around the Island

Going north from Losuia is 'inland' to the locals. This area has most of the island's roads and villages and consequently visitors, too. Omarakana, about half-way between Losuia and Kaibola, is where the island's Paramount Chief resides. You'll know you're there by the large, intricate, painted yam house not far from the road. The Paramount Chief presides over the island's oral traditions and magic and strictly maintains his political and economic power. He oversees the important yam festival and kula ritual.

Caves used for swimming and fresh water are found at Tumwalau, Kalopa, Lupwaneta, Neguya, Bobu, Sikau, Kaulausi and Bwaga. Large coral megaliths still exist and, together with designs on some ancient pottery, have linked the Trobes to possible early Polynesian migrations.

At Kaibola Village there's a school and Kaibola Beach lodge. There's excellent swimming and snorkelling at this picture-postcard beach. In the village you can see traditional boats, fishing gear, shark-calling tools and other items. Ask one of the kids who works at or hangs around the lodge to take you to nearby Luebila Village, past the neat gardens of yams, taro, bananas and tapioca.

About 1½ hours' walk from Kaibola is Kalopa Cave near Matawa Village. There are several deep limestone caves housing burial antiquities and skeletal remains. Stories are told of Dokanikani, a giant whose bones are said to be buried with those of his victims in one of the caves. Also along the beach at Kaibola look for the little glow worms at night, clinging to the rocks along the shore.

The trip to Kaibola from Losuia takes about 30 minutes and covers nearly 30 km along the narrow, coral road. The children must often do this long, hot walk because the bus frequently breaks down. At Moligilagi near the east coast bring snorkel, mask and fins to explore the underwater caves. Be careful of logs; an underwater light is a good idea.

South of Losuia the road is even less frequently used and the population smaller. At Wawela there is an excellent, curving sand beach edging a cool, deep, protected lagoon. On a falling tide beware of the channel out to sea from the bay, the current can be very strong. Local kids will sell you various shells for 20 to 50t. Bring your own supplies; there is no store. The Kiriwina bus runs trips down here, and there are plans for a beach-side lodge. Further along, the road squeezes through thick jungle. Look for the enormous vines draped over some of the trees and birds such as parrots.

At Sinaketa there are a couple of traditional kula canoes on the beach.

Local Customs

Yams Yams are far more than a staple food in the Trobriands – they're also a ritual, a sign of prestige, an indicator of expertise and a tie between villages and clans. The quality and size of the yams you grow is a matter of considerable importance. Many hours can be spent on discussions of your ability as a yam cultivator and to be known as a *Tokwaibagula*, a 'good gardener', is a mark of high ability and prestige.

The yam cult reaches its high point at the harvest time – usually July or August. The yams are first dug up in the gardens and before transport back to the village they must be displayed, studied and admired in the gardens. At the appropriate time the yams are carried by the men back to the village with the women guarding the procession.

In the villages the yams are again displayed, in circular piles, before the next stage takes place – the filling of the yam houses. Again there are extended rituals to be observed. Each man has a yam house for each of his wives and it is his brother-in-law's responsibility (in other words his wife's clan's obligation) to fill his yam house. The chief's yam house is always the first to be filled. So yams are not merely a food –

Yam House

they're also part of a complicated annual ritual and an important and ongoing connection between villages.

Sex Malinowski's weighty tomes on the Trobriand Islanders customs led to Kiriwina being dubbed with the misleading title: the 'Island of Love'. It is not surprising that such a label was applied by inhibited Europeans when they first met Trobriand women, with their free and easy manners, their good looks and short grass dresses, but it led to the inaccurate idea that the Trobriands were some sort of sexual paradise.

The sexual customs are different (some might even say, better) than in many other places, but they are not without complicated social strictures and normal human jealousies. Nevertheless, the place must be a Christian missionary's nightmare because there are fewer restrictions than usual.

From puberty onwards, teenagers are encouraged to have as many sexual partners as they choose – without guilt – until marriage, when they settle down with the partner who is chosen as suitable and compatible. Males leave home when they reach puberty and move into the village *bukumatula* or bachelor house. Here they are free to bring their partners back at any time, although preference is usually given to places with a little more privacy! Even

married couples, subject to mutual agreement, are allowed to have a fling or two when the celebrations for the yam harvest are in full swing.

It is said that despite all this activity few children are born to women without permanent partners. Perhaps there are herbal contraceptives, although there are plenty of kids in all the Trobriand villages. The people do not believe there is a connection between intercourse and pregnancy – a child's spirit, which floats through the air or on top of the sea, chooses to enter a woman, often through her head. So much for the significance attached by Christians to the virgin birth!

All this apparent freedom has absolutely no impact on visitors. Freedom of choice is the basis of Trobriand life, so why would any islander choose some ugly, pale, *dim dim* (foreigner) who can't speak like a civilised human, doesn't understand the most basic laws and will probably be gone tomorrow?

Kula Ring Despite modern technology, the trading of the Kula Ring has still not completely died out although the sea voyages in outrigger canoes are unlikely to be as lengthy as in 'the time before'. This traditional, ritual, exchange of goods served to bind islands together in much the same way that yams formed a link between villages and clans. Two

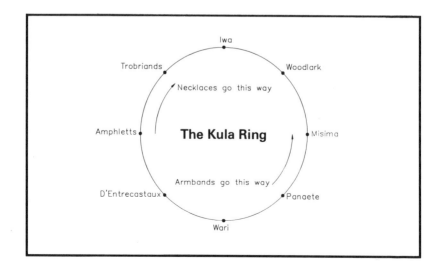

articles are traded in the ring – bagi, the red shell money necklaces, and *mwala* decorated armlets made from cone shells.

The ring extends right around Milne Bay, including the Trobriands, Woodlark, Misima, the D'Entrecasteaux Group and around Samarai. The exchange between islands on the 'ring' is purely ritual, since the goods rarely go out of the ring and are always eventually traded on to the next island in the circuit. Eventually they get right back to their starting point, although this can take many years. The ring goods go in opposite directions – shell necklaces are traded clockwise, armlets counter-clockwise.

Today, traders on the ring sometimes make their voyages on board modern ships but elaborately decorated canoes are still used and villagers from every island still offer hospitality to their 'ring partners' from the next island on the circuit. At the same time as the ritual exchanges are made, other more mundane items are traded – pottery, food, baskets – but not with your 'ring partner'.

Cricket A much more modern custom, but just as colourful, is the unique sport known as 'Trobriands Cricket'. Supposedly introduced by missionaries as a way of taking the Trobriand islanders' minds off less healthy activities it's developed a style of its own, quite unlike anything the MCC ever had in mind. The mere fact that the Trobriands Cricket rule book contains absolutely no mention of how many players make up a team goes some way to explaining how it works. If there's a game scheduled while you're on the island, don't miss it!

WOODLARK ISLAND

The people of Woodlark Island are Melanesians similar to the people on the eastern end of the mainland. Their island is a continuous series of hills and valleys and is highly populated. Woodlark was the site for the biggest gold rush in the country until the later discovery of gold at Edie Creek near Wau. A form of 'greenstone', similar although inferior to the greenstone or jade of New Zealand, was also found here and made into axes and ceremonial stones.

Today the people are renowned for their beautiful wood carvings made of mottled ebony. Since there is less demand for their work than that of the more frequently visited Trobriands, due to their isolation, the carvings tend to be extremely well crafted. Kulumadau is the main centre although there is now an airstrip at Guasopa. Woodlark is east of the Trobriands and north of the Louisiade Islands. It takes its name from the Sydney ship *Woodlark* which passed by in 1836 although the local name is Murua.

The Laughlan Group is a handful of tiny islands and islets 64 km east of Woodlark.

LOUISIADE ARCHIPELAGO

The Louisiade Archipelago received its name after Louis Torre's 1606 visit, but it was probably known to Chinese and Malay sailors much earlier as there are distinct traces of Asian heritage in the racial mixture. The name was originally applied to the whole string of islands including the group now known as the D'Entrecasteaux.

Sudest or Tagula Island

Largest island in the archipelago, Sudest had a small gold rush at about the same time as Woodlark. It consists of a similar series of valleys and hills, highest of which is Mt Rattlesnake at 915 metres.

Rossel Island

Most westerly of the islands – if you discount uninhabited Pocklington Reef – Rossel's rugged coastline ends at Rossel Spit which has had more than its fair share of shipwrecks. An airstrip was built here in 1980.

Misima

Mountainous Misima Island is the most important in the group with the district HQ at Bwagaoia. Mt Oiatau at 1037 metres is the highest peak on the island. Misima too had a gold rush, although this took place between the wars, much later than on the other islands of Milne Bay. A major new mine is now being developed.

During the brief span when Papua was a

British colony rather than an Australian one, the people of Misima were thought of as the most dangerous and difficult in the country. Today Misima has about half of the total population of the archipelago.

Places to Stay The *Misima Guest House* in Bwagaoia is usually fully booked, because of the new mine, so you must make reservations well in advance through the Milne Bay Tourist Bureau. There are 12 twin rooms for K25 per person; breakfasts and lunches cost K5 and dinner is K8.

Calvados Chain & Conflict Group

The long chain of islets and reefs between Sudest and the mainland make navigation through the Milne Bay area an exacting and often dangerous operation. None of the islands are of any great size. To the west they terminate with the three islands of the Engineer Group.

Index

MAPS

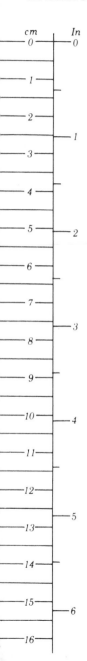

Temperature

To convert °C to °F multipy by 1.8 and add 32

To convert °F to °C subtract 32 and multipy by ·55

Length, Distance & Area

	multipy by
inches to centimetres	2.54
centimetres to inches	0.39
feet to metres	0.30
metres to feet	3.28
yards to metres	0.91
metres to yards	1.09
miles to kilometres	1.61
kilometres to miles	0.62
acres to hectares	0.40
hectares to acres	2.47

Weight

	multipy by
ounces to grams	28.35
grams to ounces	0.035
pounds to kilograms	0.45
kilograms to pounds	2.21
British tons to kilograms	1016
US tons to kilograms	907

A British ton is 2240 lbs, a US ton is 2000 lbs

Volume

	multipy by
Imperial gallons to litres	4.55
litres to imperial gallons	0.22
US gallons to litres	3.79
litres to US gallons	0.26

5 imperial gallons equals 6 US gallons
a litre is slightly more than a US quart, slightly less
than a British one

Lonely Planet

Lonely Planet published its first book in 1973. Tony and Maureen Wheeler had made a lengthy overland trip from England to Australia and, in response to numerous 'how do you do it?' questions, Tony wrote and they published *Across Asia on the Cheap*. It became an instant local best-seller and inspired thoughts of a second travel guide. A year and a half in South-East Asia resulted in their second book, *South-East Asia on a Shoestring*, which they put together in a backstreet Chinese hotel in Singapore in 1975. The 'yellow book', as it quickly became known, soon became *the* guide to the region and has gone through five editions, always with its familiar yellow cover.

Soon other writers started to come to them with ideas for similar books – books that went off the beaten track and took an adventurous approach to travel, books that 'assumed you knew how to get your luggage off the carousel,' as one reviewer described them. Lonely Planet grew from a kitchen table operation to a spare room and then to its own office. It also started to develop an international reputation as the Lonely Planet logo began to appear in more and more countries. In 1982 *India – a travel survival kit* won the Thomas Cook award for the best guidebook of the year.

These days there are over 60 Lonely Planet titles. Nearly 30 people work at our office in Melbourne, Australia and another half dozen at our US office in Oakland, California.

At first Lonely Planet specialised exclusively in the Asia region but these days we are also developing major ranges of guidebooks to the Pacific region, to South America and to Africa. The list of walking guides is growing and Lonely Planet is producing a unique series of phrasebooks to 'unusual' languages. The emphasis continues to be on travel for travellers and Tony and Maureen still manage to fit in a number of trips each year and play a very active part in the writing and updating of Lonely Planet's guides.

Keeping guidebooks up to date is a constant battle which requires an ear to the ground and lots of walking, but technology also plays its part. All Lonely Planet guidebooks are now stored and updated on computer, and some authors even take lap-top computers into the field. Lonely Planet is also using computers to draw maps and eventually many of the maps will be stored on disk.

The people at Lonely Planet strongly feel that travellers can make a positive contribution to the countries they visit both by better appreciation of cultures and by the money they spend. In addition the company tries to make a direct contribution to the countries and regions it covers. Since 1986 a percentage of the income from each book has gone to aid groups and associations. This has included donations to famine relief in Africa, to aid projects in India, to agricultural projects in Nicaragua and other Central American countries and to Greenpeace's efforts to halt French nuclear testing in the Pacific. In 1987 $30,000 was donated by Lonely Planet to these projects.

Lonely Planet Distributors

Australia & Papua New Guinea Lonely Planet Publications, PO Box 88, South Yarra, Victoria 3141.
Canada Raincoast Books, 112 East 3rd Avenue, Vancouver, British Columbia V5T 1C8.
Denmark, Finland & Norway Scanvik Books aps, Store Kongensgade 59 A, DK-1264 Copenhagen K.
Hong Kong The Book Society, GPO Box 7804.
India & Nepal UBS Distributors, 5 Ansari Rd, New Delhi – 110002
Israel Geographical Tours Ltd, 8 Tverya St, Tel Aviv 63144.
Japan Intercontinental Marketing Corp, IPO Box 5056, Tokyo 100-31.
Netherlands Nilsson & Lamm bv, Postbus 195, Pampuslaan 212, 1380 AD Weesp.
Singapore & Malaysia MPH Distributors, 601 Sims Drive, #03-21, Singapore 1438.
Spain Altair, Balmes 69, 08007 Barcelona.
Sweden Esselte Kartcentrum AB, Vasagatan 16, S-111 20 Stockholm.
Thailand Chalermnit, 108 Sukhumvit 53, Bangkok 10110.
UK Roger Lascelles, 47 York Rd, Brentford, Middlesex, TW8 0QP
USA Lonely Planet Publications, PO Box 2001A, Berkeley, CA 94702.
West Germany Buchvertrieb Gerda Schettler, Postfach 64, D3415 Hattorf a H.
All Other Countries refer to Australia address.

Lonely Planet Guides to the Region

South-East Asia on a Shoestring
For over 10 years this has been known as the 'yellow bible' to travellers in South-East Asia. The fifth edition has updated information on Brunei, Burma, Hong Kong, Indonesia, Macau, Malaysia, PNG, the Philippines, Singapore, and Thailand.

Indonesia – a travel survival kit
This comprehensive guidebook covers the entire Indonesian archipelago. Some of the most remarkable sights and sounds in Asia can be found amongst these countless islands and this book has all the facts.

Australia – a travel survival kit
Australia is Lonely Planet's home territory, and this book has the insider information to help you see it all – from the eerie emptiness of the red centre to the rainforests and golden beaches of the east coast.

Micronesia – a travel survival kit
Amongst these 2100 islands are beaches, lagoons and reefs that will dazzle the most jaded traveller. This guide is packed with all you need to know about island hopping across the north Pacific.

Solomon Islands – a travel survival kit
The Solomon Islands are the Pacific's best kept secret. If you want to discover remote tropical islands, jungle-covered volcanoes and traditional Melanesian villages, this book will show you how.

Indonesia phrasebook
A little Indonesian is easy to learn, and your efforts will be appreciated. Lonely Planet's phrasebooks are pocket-sized and designed to give a stock of phrases and vocabulary covering all aspects of life on the road, and provide guides to pronunciation and basic grammar.

Papua New Guinea phrasebook
Pidgin is the lingua franca for Papua New Guinea, and is also spoken (with minor variations) in the Solomon islands, Vanuatu and parts of Irian Jaya.

Also available are _travel survival kits_ to New Zealand, Tahiti, Fiji, Rarotonga & the Cook Islands, and guides to Bushwalking in Australia and Tramping in New Zealand.

Lonely Planet Guidebooks

Lonely Planet guidebooks cover virtually every accessible part of Asia as well as Australia, the Pacific, Central and South America, Africa, the Middle East and parts of North America. There are four main series: 'travel survival kits', covering a single country for a range of budgets; 'shoestring' guides with compact information for low-budget travel in a major region; trekking guides; and 'phrasebooks'.

Australia & the Pacific
Australia
Papua New Guinea
Bushwalking in Papua New Guinea
Papua New Guinea phrasebook
New Zealand
Tramping in New Zealand
Rarotonga & the Cook Islands
Tahiti & French Polynesia
Fiji
Micronesia

South-East Asia
South-East Asia on a shoestring
Malaysia, Singapore & Brunei
Indonesia
Bali & Lombok
Indonesia phrasebook
Burma
Burmese phrasebook
Thailand
Thai phrasebook
Philippines
Pilipino phrasebook

North-East Asia
North-East Asia on a shoestring
China
China phrasebook
Tibet
Tibet phrasebook
Japan
Korea
Korean phrasebook
Hong Kong, Macau & Canton
Taiwan

West Asia
West Asia on a shoestring
Turkey

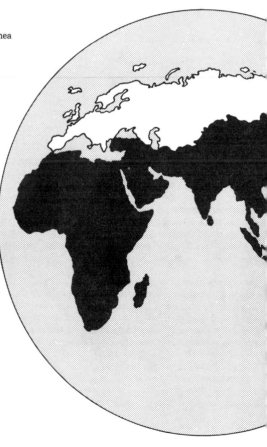

Mail Order

Lonely Planet guidebooks are distributed worldwide and are sold by good bookshops everywhere. They are also available by mail order from Lonely Planet, so if you have difficulty finding a title please write to us. US and Canadian residents should write to Embarcadero West, 112 Linden St, Oakland CA 94607, USA and residents of other countries to PO Box 88, South Yarra, Victoria 3141, Australia.

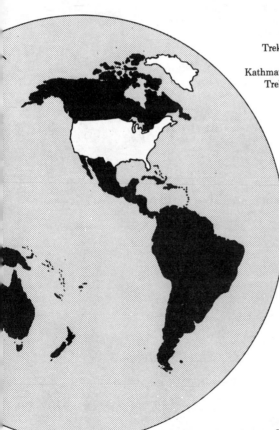

Indian Subcontinent
India
Hindi/Urdu phrasebook
Kashmir, Ladakh & Zanskar
Trekking in the Indian Himalaya
Pakistan
Kathmandu & the Kingdom of Nepal
Trekking in the Nepal Himalaya
Nepal phrasebook
Sri Lanka
Sri Lanka phrasebook
Bangladesh

Africa
Africa on a shoestring
East Africa
Swahili phrasebook
West Africa

Middle East
Egypt & the Sudan
Jordan & Syria
Yemen

North America
Canada
Alaska

Mexico
Mexico
Baja California

South America
South America on a shoestring
Ecuador & the Galapagos Islands
Chile & Easter Island
Peru

Lonely Planet Update

We collect an enormous amount of information here at Lonely Planet. Apart from our research there's a steady stream of travellers' letters full of the latest news. For over 5 years much of this information went into a quarterly newsletter (and helped to update the guidebooks). The new paperback *Update* includes this up-to-date news and aims to supplement the information available in our guidebooks. There will be four editions a year (Feb, May, Aug and Nov) available either by subscription or through bookshops. Subscribe now and you'll save nearly 25% off the retail price.

Each edition has extracts from the most interesting letters we have received, covering such diverse topics as:
- how to take a boat trip on the Yalu River
- living in a typical Thai village
- getting a Nepalese trekking permit

Subscription Details
All subscriptions cover four editions and include postage. Prices quoted are subject to change.
USA & Canada – One year's subscription is US$12; a single copy is US$3.95. Please send your order to Lonely Planet's California office.
Other Countries – One year's subscription is Australian $15; a single copy is A$4.95. Please pay in Australian $, or the US$ or £ Sterling equivalent. Please send your order form to Lonely Planet's Australian office.

Order Form

Please send me

☐ One year's subscription – starting next edition.   ☐ One copy of the next edition.

Name (please print) ....

Address (please print) ....

....

....

Tick One

☐ Payment enclosed (payable to Lonely Planet Publications)

Charge my   ☐ Visa   ☐ Bankcard   ☐ MasterCard   for the amount of $ ....

Card No .... Expiry Date ....

Cardholder's Name (print) ....

Signature .... Date...

US & Canadian residents
Lonely Planet, Embarcadero West, 112 Linden St,
Oakland, CA 94607, USA
Other countries
Lonely Planet, PO Box 88, South Yarra, Victoria 3141, Australia